60 Years of EU-Korea Relations, 1963-2023: Looking Back, Looking Forward

Edited by Kim Sihong, Lee Moosung, Nicola Casarini and Eric J. Ballbach

Co-funded by the European Union

"The European Commission support for the production of this Publication does not constitute an endorsement of the contents which reflects the views only of the authors, and the Commission cannot be held responsible for any use which may be made of the information contained therein."

First Published December 29, 2023

Published by HANKUK UNIVERSITY OF FOREIGN STUDIES KNOWLEDGE CONTENTS & PRESS
107, Imun-ro, Dongdaemun-gu, Seoul 02450, Korea
Tel.) 82-2-2173-2497 Fax.) 82-2-2173-3363
E-mail) press@hufs.ac.kr
Online) http://press.hufs.ac.kr

ISBN 979-11-7199-073-3 [93340]
Price 36,000 Won

Preface

This book commemorates the 60th anniversary of the bilateral relations between the Republic of Korea and the European Union (EU), offering reflections on the past and insights into the future. Since establishing official diplomatic relations in 1963, there were few substantial exchanges between the two sides in the early period. However, the unification of Eastern and Western Europe in the 1990s, coupled with the deepening of globalization, laid the foundation for a strong partnership.

This period coincided with Korea's efforts to diversify its international relations after the successful hosting of the Seoul Olympics. Recognizing the significance of Asia, the EU articulated its "Towards a New Asia Strategy" in 1994, culminating in a Framework Agreement for Trade and Cooperation with the Republic of Korea in 1996.

As the 21st century unfolded, the multilateral trade order faced obstacles under the Doha Development Agenda at the WTO, prompting a shift towards bilateral trade agreements. After two and half years of negotiations, the EU and Korea signed the Free Trade Agreement (FTA), fostering rapid development in bilateral relations. Currently, both parties hold the Strategic Partnership through the revision of the existing Framework Agreement.

The 50th anniversary in 2013 marked a milestone where both parties affirmed each other as like-minded partners. In 2014, the Crisis Management Agreement was reached, solidifying the relationship as Korea became the first Asian country to sign major political, economic, and security agreements. And the Korea-EU Summit in Seoul on May 22nd, 2023, reasserted regional and global cooperation, consolidating the strategic partnership.

In the current landscape marked by changes in globalization, geopolitical tensions, and shifts in global supply chains, both the EU and Korea uphold free trade as natural partners with shared values. They also advocate for a rules-based international order, human rights, and a market economy.

Looking ahead, we anticipate further strengthening of bilateral relations, with a particular focus on promising areas such as green partnership, digital collaboration, and joint efforts in health and research and development.

This publication of the 60th-anniversary book is made possible by the generous support of the EU and the Ministry of Foreign Affairs of the Republic of Korea. I extend my heartfelt gratitude to the contributors from both Korea and Europe who played a crucial role in the success of this book project.

Kim Sihong
(Professor and Jean Monnet Chair,
Graduate School of International and Area Studies, Hankuk University of Foreign Studies)

Foreword 1

RYU JEONGHYUN
AMBASSADOR OF THE REPUBLIC OF KOREA TO THE KINGDOM OF BELGIUM AND THE EUROPEAN UNION AND PERMANENT MISSION TO THE NATO

The year 2023 marks the 60th anniversary of the diplomatic relations between the Republic of Korea and the European Union. In this meaningful year, Korea and the EU held the Korea-EU Summit in May, not only commemorating the six-decade journey but also charted a course for the next 60 years. In a world characterized by dynamic shifts and challenges, Korea and the EU pledged to deepen and expand our partnership particularly in the futures-oriented areas such as green, health and digital.

"60 Years of Korea-EU Relations, 1963-2023: Looking Back, Looking Forward," stands as a comprehensive volume curated by distinguished scholars and experts from Korea and Europe. As we stand at the crossroads of our diplomatic ties, this volume offers readers a retrospective lens through meticulously researched chapters, traversing the various dimensions of the Korea-EU partnership.

From the early years explored by Kim Sihong to contemporary issues discussed by experts such as Eric J. Ballbach, Mason Richey, and Lee Moosung, the book delves into diplomatic, political, and security interactions between Korea and the EU. Nicola Casarini and Bernhard Seliger provide insights into the EU's role on the Korean Peninsula and EU-DPRK Relations, respectively, addressing one of the world's most challenging diplomatic arenas.

Kang Yoo-duk examines economic and trade relations, Ahn Sangwook explores the transformation of the global supply chain, and Chung Saewon dissects the challenges and opportunities in cyber security and data partnership. Educational and cultural cooperation are illuminated by Kim Bongchul and Yoon Sungwon.

Chapters such as Reciprocal Perceptions on Korea and the EU by Han Jeonghun, R&D and Technology Cooperation by Tomasz Wierzbowski, and The Future of EU-Korea Relations by Michael Reiterer weave together the threads of the past, present, and future.

As we navigate through these pages, the aim is to capture the essence of this enduring partnership and illuminate the path forward. Now we're living in the inter-twined world, where the impacts of regional issues can be felt all across the world. Security and peace of Europe is inseparable from that of the Indo-Pacific. Recent geopolitical crises in Ukraine, the DPRK's nuclear and missile program, and the Israel-Palestine conflict have underscored the need for robust collaboration among like-minded partners to address these complex challenges.

The ROK-EU Summit in Seoul in 2023 May stands as a testament to the robustness of our relationship, with a commitment to addressing common global challenges arising from geopolitical crisis. Recognizing the inseparable prosperity and security of Europe and the Indo-Pacific, I would like to highlight that Korea and the EU should strive together to further promote rules-based order worldwide. In conclusion, these short remarks express the anticipation for a brighter future for Korea and the EU, built on the foundation of a steadfast and forward-looking partnership for the freedom, peace and prosperity of the region.

Foreword 2

MARÍA CASTILLO FERNÁNDEZ
EU AMBASSADOR TO THE REPUBLIC OF KOREA

2023 is a special year for the EU and the Republic of Korea as we are celebrating the 60th anniversary of the establishment of diplomatic relations in 1963.

Looking back, the EU-Korea relations have greatly expanded over the past six decades, along with far-reaching changes and advances in our societies, economies, scientific fields of study and digital technologies. Both sides have grown into strategic partners sharing universal values, promoting peace, prosperity and security, but also addressing important global challenges such as climate change and a global pandemic.

The European Community developed into a unique economic and political union, the EU, which is today also a major global provider of security, development and environmental protection. South Korea has transformed into the fourth largest economy in Asia and, an aspiring global pivotal state more engaged in the Asia-Pacific and global challenges.

The ROK was the first country in Asia with whom the EU concluded three key agreements, an encompassing Framework Agreement, an ambitious Free Trade Agreement, and a Framework Participation Agreement in crisis management operations. The EU-ROK relationship is deep and encompasses around 40 regular dialogues covering economic, political, security and cultural cooperation.

Looking forward, and as reaffirmed by our respective leaders during the 10th EU-ROK Summit, the EU-ROK partnership is grounded in common interests and the shared values of democracy, human rights, the rule of law, effective multilateralism, open, free and fair trade, and the rules-based international order.

Through the recently launched EU-Korea digital and green partnerships, we will deepen cooperation on various digital and data protection issues and on industrial competitiveness, and on transitioning towards a net-zero economy by 2050. We will expand cooperation in sectors such as climate change, energy and environment, education, health, transport and Research and Innovation, in a future-oriented and mutually beneficial way, including in the framework of our respective Indo-Pacific strategies and the EU's Global Gateway.

Reflecting on this journey and broadening the breadth of the EU-ROK relations is a shared endeavor, which benefits from a regular dialogue between the academic, economic and scientific world and policy makers on the complex interplay of geopolitical and socio-economic factors. It is in this spirit, that I believe this publication by distinguished Korean and European scholars will provide interesting lenses to analyse and inspire the EU-Korea Strategic Partnership.

TABLE OF CONTENTS

Six Decades of Korea-EU Relations, 1963-2023

KIM SIHONG

Introduction

Korea and the European Union (EU) have maintained close relations since the establishment of diplomatic relations in July 1963. During the Cold War before 1989, both Korea and the EU were members of the U.S.-centered free world and maintained joint support in the East-West confrontation, and bilateral relations were mainly focused on economic and trade developments.[1] Since the establishment of the European Union in 1993, as the movement for European integration has expanded and developed into the field of Common Foreign and Security Policy (CFSP), the importance of cooperation in the diplomatic and security fields has also increased, including the establishment of a channel for political dialogue between the ROK and the EU.

Bilateral relations between the ROK and the EU entered a new phase after 2005. On the one hand, the Doha Agenda under the World Trade Organization has stalled, and multilateral trade relations have become a manifestation of the crisis, and the major countries turned to bilateral free trade agreements. Negotiations of U.S.-Korea Free Trade Agreement began earlier than those of the Korea-EU Free Trade Agreement, but it came into effect on July 1, 2011. On the other hand, while the 1996 Framework Agreement focused on trade and cooperation, negotiations to upgrade the Agreement were held at the same time as the negotiations for the Free Trade Agreement, with the mutual recognition that bilateral relations are showing signs of rapid development, and the conclusion was reached in 2010. As a result, the two parties concluded major agreements in the economic and political fields, establishing a so-called strategic partnership.[2]

In 2014, the two sides reached an Agreement on crisis management, enabling close cooperation in the field of security, and South Korea was able to work closely together in the fields of political affairs, economy, and security. It has emerged as a significant actor as it was the first country to sign major agreements with the European Union in the above three fields. It is also significant that more than 40 bilateral committees and dialogues have been put into operation up to now to enhance the breadth and quality of cooperation based on the new Framework Agreement, and the EU-ROK relationship that advocates free trade is more important than ever in today's reality where the liberal trade order is under threat.

Korea-EU 60 years

In order to look back upon the 60 years of ROK-EU relations, it may be possible to take a thematic and period-by-time approach. Here, we will try to summarize the development process by examining the important issues and issues of bilateral relations that occurred during each period.[3] The division can be divided into 1963 to 1992 as the dawn, 1993 to 2002 as the beginning of institutionalization, 2003 to 2012 as the 40th anniversary and the beginning of the period when we began to examine the meaning of full-fledged bilateral relations, 2013 when we commemorated the 50th anniversary, and the period after 2013, when we can assess the future prospects by examining the significance of the 60th anniversary.

The Advent of Bilateral Relations, 1963-1992

The context behind the establishment of diplomatic relations between Korea and the then European Economic Community (EEC) on July 24, 1963, was not very clear. On the South Korean side, it is said that the Economic Planning Board (EPB) took the initiative rather than the Ministry of Foreign Affairs,[4] and from a European perspective, the establishment of diplomatic relations with South Korea was part of a series of diplomatic relations established with the former colonies as newly independent countries after the war. In July 1963, the European Economic Community established diplomatic relations with the 18 former colonial countries in Africa, and with Japan in 1959. The situation in South Korea was such that the regime of Rhee Seung-man was toppled by the April 19 student movement and attempted a year-long parliamentary cabinet system, and the economic and social situation deteriorated to the point of emergency rule through a military coup d'état on May 16, 1961. At the time, South Korea was the poorest country in the world in terms of per capita gross domestic product, even below that of North Korea.[5]

During the transition to democracy after the military revolution in 1962, South Korea established diplomatic relations with a series of newly born countries. Among European countries, at that time, West Germany is remembered as the country that helped Korea's struggling economy. Park Chung-hee government, which was elected in December 1963, planned a tour of Europe, which was originally scheduled to visit France, West Germany, and Egypt, but only visited West Germany due to financial burden. The President Park met guest workers from Korea, mostly coal miners and nurses. In fact, much of their salaries were sent to South Korea in the form of remittances, and they are considered to have contributed significantly to the Korean economy, which was in desperate need of foreign currency at the time.

Europe was a role model for Korea, the poorest country, and it also provided a lot of implications for the early economic development initiatives. For example, a study on Italy's state-owned holding company was examined as part of a strategy to promote rapid growth in Korea.[6]

France and Italy have strengthened relations with Korea in areas such as fisheries, power generation, and patents, and Korea has established diplomatic relations with European countries such as Belgium, Greece, the Netherlands, Portugal, Iceland, Switzerland, Luxembourg, Austria, the Vatican, and Malta in the first half of the 1960s. Therefore, the establishment of diplomatic relations with the European Economic Community is understood as part of the new government's foreign policy to gain international recognition, and at the same time, it can be seen as the beginning of bilateral relations in terms of economy and trade. However, the European Economic Community at the time focused more on internal economic integration than on external relations, so it is presumed that it would have been difficult for Korea and the Economic Community at that time to pursue broad diplomatic relations. Initially, the Korean Ambassador to Switzerland was in charge of relations with the European Economic Community, and in November 1969, the Permanent Mission to the EEC was established.

The 1970s are remembered as a time of détente. After 1969, under the influence of German Chancellor Willy Brandt's Ostpolitik policy, the North-South dialogue continued, which eventually led to the North-South Joint Communiqué on July 4, 1972. This period also created an opportunity for Europe to establish itself as a market for Korea's export-led growth policy. Bilateral relations in the 1980s did not show any tangible changes, but Europe is understood to have focused on internal activities with the adoption of the Single European Act (SEA), which marked an important milestone in European integration. Nonetheless, intermittently, Korean prime ministers and ministers visited Europe to engage in dialogue with the European Community, and in October 1986, a European trade mission to Korea was sent. In terms of the institutional development of bilateral relations, in February 1989 the Korean Delegation to the EC was separated into an independent mission, and in January 1990 the EC Mission was established in Seoul.

Establishment of the European Union and Institutionalization of Bilateral Relations, 1993-2002

On November 9, 1989, when the Berlin Wall, a symbol of the Cold War, fell, Western Europe and the world entered a new era. The reunification of Germany with the fall of the Wall was a revolutionary change that reshaped the political horizon of Europe. The European Community, which had been committed to economic integration and the expansion of membership, now attempted to experiment with expanding the scope of management beyond the economy.

In the case of South Korea, the resumption of political democratization, including the democratic election of the president in 1987, and the successful hosting of the 1988 Seoul Olympic Games manifested the miracle of the country from being the poorest country in the world that experienced the 6.25 fratricidal war to becoming an advanced industrial country in a short period of time. Now that international travel rates have become more relevant, and import restrictions have been lifted, Korea has entered an era of material abundance in which European goods are imported in large numbers. Besides, Korea had to diversify its trade by breaking away from the trade relations centered on the United States and Japan during the Cold War, and it made various efforts to open up as a strategy to actively respond to the wave of globalization that had swept across the world. Eastern European countries, which were experiencing system transformation from real socialism to the end of the Cold War, were diverted into the best investment destinations for Korean capital, and active trade relations were also activated in terms of market diversification.

The situation in Europe was even more dramatic, and it marked a quantum shift in the speed and quality of integration. The member states of the European Community seized this moment and reached an agreement to expand their efforts centered on economic integration to include political, diplomatic, and socio-cultural spheres. With the Maastricht Treaty in 1993, the European Community has expanded into the European Union, and the beginning of collective efforts in the field of diplomacy and security provides an opportunity for the EU to reconsider its foreign policy stance and to develop a renewed interest in Asia in particular.

Towards a New Asia Strategy of 1994 was a document that represented a change in interests and a shift in the way Europe looked at Asia in a new way. In the document, Europe considered so far Asia as a former colony and confessed that it did not treat Asia as an equal partner. Europe has focused its postwar foreign policy on transatlantic relations with the United States, and its bilateral relations with Asia in the fields of trade and politics have not risen significantly. However, the rise of Japan, the Four Dragons, and China led to the realization that the region could no longer be considered as a secondary object. In fact, it has even expressed a sense of crisis that Europe could be left behind from the center of the world if it failed to redefine its relations with East Asia in preparation for the coming 21st century.

Based on the New Asia Strategy, the European Union signed a series of cooperation agreements with individual countries, and Korea also jumped on the bandwagon and reached the agreement on the Framework Agreement on Trade and Cooperation on October 28, 1996. Three days before the agreement was signed, South Korea became the second Asian country to join the Organization for Economic Development and Cooperation (OECD) after Japan. The agreement entered into force in 2001 and has become thereafter a document defining the relationship between Korea and the European Union.[7] However, the emphasis on trade in the title of the document confirms that Korea has not yet been the subject of diplomatic relations that encompass both politics and other areas compared to major countries such as Japan and China. Nonetheless, the two parties agreed to cooperate in the political field and institutionalize dialogue channels. The Joint Declaration on the Political Dialogue was adopted, laying the basic framework for ROK-EU relations.[8] In September 1998, the Permanent Mission to the European Union and the Embassy of Korea to Belgium were reunited and continue to this day.

The EU's new Asia strategy raises the need for regional cooperation not only in bilateral dimension but also in multilateral aspects. In 1996, Europe and Asia launched a new summit forum called the Asia Europe Meeting (ASEM). The first meeting was held in Bangkok, Thailand, and was noted as a meaningful forum for the leaders of Europe and Asia to share issues of mutual interest through various multilateral and bilateral meetings. The conference took the form of a biennial and alternating between the European and Asian continents, emphasizing the flexibility of not having a permanent secretariat. However, the Asia Europe Foundation (ASEF) was established in Singapore under ASEM to coordinate various events between the two continents in the fields of education, culture, religion and youth.

In 2001, the European Commission published a document entitled Europe and Asia: A Strategic Framework for Enhanced Partnerships which set the stage for a commitment to the relationship between the two regions in the 21st century. In this document, Europe tried to promote peace and security at the regional and global levels. The goals include continuing to strengthen trade and investment relations with Asia, promoting economic development by identifying the causes of poverty in underdeveloped countries, promoting human rights and democracy and the rule of law and good governance, enhancing cooperation with Asian countries at the global level by identifying the threats and opportunities of globalization, and finally making efforts to raise awareness between Europe and Asia.

40th Anniversary and Establishment of Strategic Partnerships, 2003-2012

Entering the 21st century, the two parties were in different circumstances. In the case of Korea, the foreign exchange crisis in 1997 destroyed the myth of growth overnight. It entered a new century with a gradual recovery through the efforts of many years, but it was also a time when signs of polarization began to appear due to the opening of the market and the failure of a large number of economic actors. As the flow of world trade was focused on multilateralism, Korea was also participating in the Doha Agenda under the World Trade Organization and seeing an opportunity.

In the case of Europe, the euro, a single currency, was finally in the process of a new historical experiment in which it was accepted in the market. The European economy was in relatively good shape, and it was enjoying a period of peace where no security threat was felt. After the end of the Cold War, countries in Eastern and Central Europe went through a period of preparation to join the European Union, and in 2004, ten countries became members as a group. This confidence led to an attempt to draft a constitution for the European Union, but was opposed and resulted in a more relaxed form of the Lisbon Reform Treaty in 2009.

In 2003, on the occasion of the 40th anniversary of EU-ROK relations, the two countries held a meeting of experts in Brussels to reflect on the past and look forward to the future. In Korea, the Korea Institute for International Economic Policy (KIEP) and in Europe, the European Institute for Asian Studies (EIAS) participated in the event, which provided an opportunity to examine the past, present, and future of bilateral relations. Discussions on the North Korean nuclear issue with the Korea Peninsula Energy Development Organization (KEDO) were also included, but there has not yet been an in-depth discussion on issues such as global dimension, so it has not yet reached the level of comprehensive diplomatic relations including political affairs.

At the time, the European Union had prepared a European Security Strategy (ESS), which gave the impression that the EU was enjoying an era of peace that did not take into account external threats.[9] In this strategy, which advocated effective multilateralism, Europe expressed confidence in spreading its successful experience of regionalism around the world, and in reality, there was no security threat from Russia in Europe at the time, and the prevailing atmosphere was optimistic about prosperity and peace coexisting, with a large number of real socialist countries on the verge of joining the EU.[10]

By 2005, the Doha Agenda had effectively ceased, forcing major industrialized nations to shift their trade focus from multilateralism toward bilateral relations. From Europe's point of view, a new trade strategy report titled Global Europe in 2006 proposed a new policy direction to promote a bilateral free trade agreement and attempted a trade agreement with South Korea.

From South Korea's point of view, the stagnation of the WTO has made it difficult for South Korea to maintain a passive attitude as an economy heavily dependent on foreign trade, and it is making efforts to overcome difficulties through active bilateral agreements. Following the Korea-US FTA, the trade agreement with the European Union led to an ambitious strategy to become an FTA hub in East Asia.

The free trade agreement between Korea and the European Union has historical significance in that it was signed between industrialized countries. Until then, the EU has avoided FTAs with industrial countries, but the agreement with Korea was intended to set a new standard and serve as a role model or template in negotiations with other countries, as a comprehensive and all-encompassing attempt. Negotiations on the comprehensive and high-level EU-Korea FTA agreement, which began in May 2007, were provisionally signed in Brussels on October 15, 2009, and entered into force on July 1, 2011.

In 2007, the EU proposed to the Korean government to revise the Framework Agreement in order to further strengthen bilateral relations and enhance complementarity. Negotiations began in June 2008 and have been held six times. After formal text negotiations and three informal meetings, the agreement was initialed in London on October 14, 2009, by the two negotiating representatives, Kim Eun-jung, Director-General of the European Affairs Directorate General of the Foreign Ministry of Korea, and Alan Seatter, Director of North America and East Asia of the European Commission's Directorate General of External Affairs.

From the EU's point of view, there are five reasons why the existing framework agreement should be revised. First, the agreement was prepared a decade ago and is outdated in many respects. Second, when the FTA comes into effect, both Korea and the EU need to look at various issues from a more fundamental perspective. Third, in areas where bilateral relations are dynamic, existing framework agreements are insufficient, such as climate change, environment, energy security, education, culture, health, transportation, and information society, which need to be expanded and reinforced. Fourth, agreements between the Republic of Korea and the EU as global partnerships should include shared values and mutual implementation on issues of international nature, including human rights, non-proliferation of weapons of mass destruction (WMD), the fight against terrorism, migration, and cooperation at the level of the International Criminal Court. Lastly, existing agreements need to be improved, as they do not mention the dimension of political cooperation on core values at the region and globally.[11]

The revision of the Framework Agreement is in line with the signing of the Free Trade Agreement and is an important change that seeks to elevate the bilateral relationship into a strategic partnership. The revised agreement contains a wide range of contents, and at the time, there were opinions that the Ministry of Foreign Affairs could establish the status of the European Union as a separate directorate general and establish its status as the fifth power regarding the Korean Peninsula in a situation where the importance of the European Union was increasing.

Whereas the 1996 agreement was biased towards trade, the newly revised framework agreement has been expanded and strengthened to include political, economic, social, cultural, scientific, and technological issues, as well as new global ones such as climate change,

WMD, and immigration. Also, while the 1996 agreement was about 20 pages long, the new agreement is 64 pages.

The revised agreement further strengthened cooperation in the economic field, while greatly expanding and strengthening the areas of cooperation in the fields of political affairs, internal affairs, and the judiciary. Expansion and strengthening of existing areas of cooperation include Economic Policy Dialogue, Business Sector, Taxation, Tariffs, Competition, Information Society, Science and Technology, Transportation, Consumer Protection, Health, Employment, and Social Issues, Environment and Natural Resources, Climate Change, Agriculture, Rural Development and Forestry, Fisheries and Oceans, and Development Assistance.

On the other hand, the newly established areas of cooperation include political affairs (strengthening political dialogue, non-proliferation of weapons of mass destruction, international crimes, terrorism, etc.), internal affairs and justice (legal cooperation, personal information protection, immigration, cybercrime, law enforcement, etc.), media, education, tourism, civil society, administrative cooperation, and statistics.

The amended agreement sets forth a new direction and vision for the development of EU-ROK relations. It can be evaluated as providing a legal and institutional basis for Korea and the EU to strengthen cooperation at the regional and global levels as equal partners, to promote balanced development in various fields such as politics and economics as the two pillars of Korea-EU relations along with the Korea-EU FTA, and to establish a strategic partnership between Korea and the EU.[12]

During the negotiation process of the revised agreement, there were considerable differences of opinion on the conflict resolution process, but the two sides were able to conclude the negotiations with mutual respect as equal partners. In the past, the EU has used the approach of revoking part or all of the agreements in the event of a problem in the establishment of relations with former colonial or developing countries, especially if human rights and democracy, which the EU values are threatened. However, in the negotiation process with Korea, the EU acknowledged equal partnership, and in some areas, Korea is said to have taken initiatives, presenting new aspects.

The formal signing of the agreement was hoped for by the EU Foreign Ministers' Meeting in December 2009, but it was only possible at the Brussels summit in 2010 due to the three-month time required for translation work. Through this, it was possible to expect an upgrade from the operation of the Joint Steering Committee of the Deputy Minister to the level of Vice Minister or Minister.

The EU-ROK strategic partnership was formally proposed by Commission President Barroso at the Korea-France summit on the sidelines of the ASEM summit in Beijing, China, in October 2008.[13] At the EU-ROK summit held in Seoul on May 23, 2009, the two sides agreed to build a strategic partnership based on the EU-Korea FTA and the revised EU-Korea Framework Agreement. Later, with the entry into force of the above two agreements, the strategic partnership was officially launched in 2010.

The Framework Agreement provides an institutional basis for cooperation in various fields such as political affairs, economy, society and culture, and internal affairs, and on the other hand, it contributes to the promotion of trade and investment relations through FTAs. It is understood that the Korea-EU FTA is governed by the higher norms of the Framework Agreement, and it is mentioned that all aspects of the new agreement are covered by the FTA. It is understood that Korea's intention in this attempt was based on the recognition that, first, it would utilize the EU's New East Asia Policy in a way that would serve Korea's national interests; second, the EU would induce China to become a responsible partner of the international community; and third, it recognized the need for the EU's influence on issues of the Korean Peninsula.[14]

It is based on the idea that the EU can develop into a strategic partner comparable to the four powers surrounding the Korean peninsula and can contribute to resolving the North Korean issue to a certain extent. Thus, the EU can be used as a practical cooperation partner for the Korean government's realization of Global Korea, and it is expected to provide models in the fields of social welfare, internal affairs, judiciary, and education, and to strengthen cooperation in cutting-edge science and renewable energy technologies.

50th Anniversary and Maturity of Bilateral Relations, 2013-2022

In 2013, the Republic of Korea and the European Union celebrated the 50th anniversary of the establishment of diplomatic relations. The significance of the half-century was something special, and various events were held throughout the year to commemorate it in Seoul and Brussels. The slogan of the 50th anniversary was "Forward Together," and following the establishment of strategic partnerships, bilateral committees in more than thirty sectors have matured dramatically in terms of the quantity and quality of relations.

The 7th EU-ROK summit created an opportunity to bring this atmosphere to a new height. At the same meeting held in Brussels on November 8, 2013, the "Joint Declaration on the 50th Anniversary of the Establishment of Diplomatic Relations" marked a close partnership at the quasi-alliance level. On the occasion of the 50th anniversary, regular dialogue on issues of mutual interest as well as supporting organizations have been established, such as the EU-Korea Research and Innovation Center and the Korean Cultural Center in Brussels, the adoption of the Joint Declaration on Educational Cooperation, and the establishment of the Cultural Cooperation Committee and the Korea-EU Forum.[15]

On July 11, 2013, the Korean Society of Contemporary European Studies (KSCES), in collaboration with the European Union Institute for Security Studies (EUISS), held an international conference in Brussels to commemorate the 50th anniversary of bilateral relations. What is remarkable is that in comparison with the 40th anniversary meeting in 2003, topics in the fields of politics, foreign affairs, and security took center stage. While the 40th anniversary seminar dealt on trade and included some North Korea issues, the 50th anniversary meeting focused on security issues, which had not been discussed much in the past in light of the establishment of a strategic partnership, and in particular, non-traditional security topics such as cyber, environment, energy, and maritime were the main themes. It is also significant that the meeting took a typical 1.5-track format, with the Managing Director of the Asia-Pacific of the European External Action Office (EEAS) and the Korean Ambassador to the European Union participating. The ROK delegation's visit to NATO headquarters also provided a valuable opportunity to explore new trends on security issues.

In 2014, both Korea and the EU signed a Crisis Management Agreement (FPA, Framework Participation Agreement on Crisis Management), which had special relevance. South Korea had the intention of conducting Middle Power Diplomacy while advocating a global Korea, and the EU intended to build a justification by inviting its strategic partners to participate in its security operations in its neighbors. As a result of these mutually shared interests, Korea has gained the status of the first partner of the European Union to upgrade the Framework Agreement on Political Affairs and to conclude a Free Trade Agreement in the fields of economy and trade, as well as a Crisis Management Agreement in the field of security. During the ratification process, there were some disagreements from the opposition parties at the time, but it was later ratified, and in the spring of 2017, the ROK Navy's Cheonghae Unit was dispatched from the port of Busan to participate in Operation EU NAVFOR Atalanta, the European Union's anti-piracy operation off the coast of Somalia, and successfully returned home.

At the 8th EU-ROK Summit held in Seoul on September 15, 2015, the main agenda was to enhance security cooperation, strengthen economic and trade cooperation, and consolidate cooperation on global issues such as climate change, development cooperation, and counterterrorism cooperation. It seems to be a pity that the president of the European Commission did not attend the meeting due to scheduling reasons, but it could not help but get rid of the impression that Korea's position in East Asia compared to China and Japan was not sufficiently considered.

In 2018, on the seventh anniversary of the implementation of the Korea-EU FTA, various evaluations were conducted, and the two sides agreed on a partial revision of the agreement and are in the process of discussion. While European countries' exports to South Korea have increased since the entry into force of the free trade agreement, the entry of Korean products into Europe has not met expectations, which has led to criticism in the domestic media, but since 2017, the balance has been renewed. In 2020, both Korea and the EU commemorated a decade of strategic partnership, and in 2021, ten years of Korea-EU FTA.

60th Anniversary of Korea-EU Relations

In 2023, Korea and the EU commemorated the 60th anniversary of their bilateral relations. Both parties are strategic partners, and with the Free Trade Agreement and Framework Participation Agreement on Crisis Management, they enjoy robust institutional relationships. More recently, due to the drastic change in international order in which strategic competition is prevalent, both Korea and the EU should engage more in cooperation in data partnerships, climate action, science, and technological areas.

The recent summit clearly demonstrates the current state of affairs. In fact, the 10th ROK-EU summit, held in Seoul on May 22, is significant in many aspects. Examining the outcome of the talks and the Joint Statement, it is evident that efforts have been made to reinterpret bilateral relations and conform to the changing international order.

The main findings of the 10th summit are as follows: first of all, it is significant that it is the first summit since the Pandemic and after the formation of new leadership both in Europe and South Korea. Since 2010, the two parties have undergone a process of rapid institutional development, establishing strategic partnerships and signing Framework Agreement upgrades, Free Trade Agreement, and Crisis Management Agreement.

The summit was, in fact, a step forward in the strategic partnership.[16] Various partnerships have been newly established, demonstrating that they recognize each other as needed while addressing global issues in the turbulent international order. In particular, it can be assessed that an equal partnership has become possible in the sense that the demand for cooperation in strategic areas in which both sides have strengths and winning edges has been expressed.

According to the summit's Joint Statement, the two sides are putting forward a global agenda and revealing close cooperation.[17] The Indo-Pacific strategies of the Republic of Korea and the European Union include cooperation at the level of the EU's Global Gateway. This is something that has not been seen in past summits and is accepted as an acknowledgment of South Korea's international status.

In contrast to past statements that only mentioned the Korean peninsula issue or North Korea's nuclear program, the EU welcomes the ROK's statement of position on Ukraine crisis and expresses its expectations for the ROK's role by calling for more expanded support. It also expresses concern about human rights in North Korea, citing joint efforts. Both parties emphasized the importance of maintaining peace and stability in the Taiwan Strait. It reaffirms the importance of a free, open, and rules-based Indo-Pacific (FOIP) region, emphasizing its need to be grounded in inclusiveness, the rule of law, and fundamental freedoms in the region.

The new partnership could be summarized in several points. First of all, in order to materialize the EU-Korea Digital Partnership agreed upon in 2022, both parties begin negotiations to reach a binding agreement in the field of digital trade. The partnership includes cooperation on semiconductors, next-generation mobile networks, quantum and high-performance computing, artificial intelligence, and online and digital platform regulation. The annual Digital Consultative Meeting will review progress and explore ways to expand cooperation, including cooperation with relevant international organizations.

Furthermore, the Joint Statement announced the launch of the EU-Korea Green Partnership, highlighting the existential threat posed by the triple global crises of climate change, biodiversity loss, and pollution, and the need to accelerate the transition to a carbon-neutral, nature-friendly, circular, and resource-efficient economy. Regarding the health care sector, which has emerged since the Pandemic, the ROK-EU has launched an administrative agreement on emergency preparedness and response in the field of medical response measures. Through this, they pledged to promote the development of cooperation for the effective management of transboundary health problems.

Korea and the EU also welcomed the commencement of negotiations on Korea's accession to the European Union's research and development program, Horizon Europe, and pledged to strengthen exchanges in the fields of science and innovation through cooperation and investment in research and development, as well as increased researcher mobility. Until now, Korea has been in a passive position of responding to proposals from European universities and research institutes in order to participate in the program, but if it is confirmed as an associate member, it will be able to form an independent research team and submit proposals.

A commemorative seminar was held in Brussels on May 2, co-organized by SNU EU Centre and Louvain Centre for Global Governance with the support of the Korean Embassy in Brussels. The topic was Korea-EU 60: A New Era Together. This event was also taken in the format of 1.5 Track Diplomacy in that the Secretary General of EEAS and Korean Ambassador to the EU, together with some members of the Korean Parliament participated. Political, economic, and educational sessions are composed reflecting changing international waters such as the emergence of the Indo-Pacific.

Meanwhile, the year 2023, in which the Pandemic has been overcome, is marked by signs of a new international order in many aspects. The outbreak of a full-scale war in Europe after World War II raises existential questions for Europeans about security issues. These changes, led by the revival of geopolitics, have made the era of globalization operating as a single production system in the past few decades a thing of the past. Recent terms such as friendshoring and nearshoring are ones that assume exclusive solidarity with like-minded countries or strategic allies. Many countries around the world are expanding their armaments, and authoritarian regimes are being held up as an alternative model, leading to conflicts and tensions.

The significance of the above changes in the international order for Europe and the European Union is considered to be extraordinary. The post-war order has been dominated on the one hand by Atlanticism, and Europe has been able to enjoy a special position in the process. This is because the alliance between the United States and Europe has enjoyed seventy years of prosperity in terms of security, the collective defense system of NATO and the economic system of capitalism. However, the US Asia Pivot policy caused a certain degree of embarrassment to Europeans, and during the Trump administration, it was severely hurt by a series of policies that virtually rejected Europe outright. President Trump's removal of the White House climate change website on his first day in office has already become legendary, and his consistent refusal to engage in close dialogue with Europe has led to the need for Europe's own diplomatic strategy.[18]

The concept of so-called strategic autonomy was born out of this background. In other words, NATO's collective security and defense system has not yet weakened, but the perception that Europe must be responsible for its own destiny has gradually gained voice.[19] The war in Ukraine has dealt a decisive blow to this trend. In terms of security, the European Union has also proposed new policies such as the Strategic Compass in 2022, an ambitious strategy to strengthen Europe's defense capabilities by 2030, conscious of the war that has arrived on the continent. In fact, the era of peace on the continent is now coming to an end, and it is being accepted as a more active response to the conflicts and tensions that are to come.

In the case of South Korea, it recently presented its vision of becoming a global pivotal state and proposed an Indo-Pacific Strategy and a National Security Strategy by expanding its diplomatic horizon beyond the Korean peninsula. In doing so, it is enhancing South Korea's status as a responsible global actor and pursuing a more proactive diplomacy.

In today's situation, where security and the economy are closely linked, economic security is a policy issue that both Europe and South Korea regard. South Korea places economic security at the core of its national agenda, and the European Union has also expressed its importance on economic security through various opportunities. This is unfolding in the context of a new approach and response to China. However, it is clear that the emphasis here is not on de-coupling with China, but more on de-risking, which means not excluding China in various multilateral venues. While close cooperation between countries with similar positions is important for the stable supply of strategic materials and key raw materials, trade with China cannot be overlooked in economic fields.

In regional and global diplomacy, the European Union's Indo-Pacific strategy is increasing its profile in Asian countries. Thus, it is understood as an expression of the expectation that Europe can play a role in containing China on issues such as the South China Sea regarding freedom of navigation. The common endeavor between Korea and the EU in third countries is considered to be a promising field. This should be in the context of the systematic management of the Global South, which has been growing in power in recent years.[20] This is because if both parties' Indo-Pacific strategies or Europe's Global Gateway and South Korea's development cooperation program meet, synergy can be demonstrated.[21] The emphasis on qualitative infrastructure and issues with China's Belt and Road Initiative is expected to increase the likelihood of cooperation. In addition, the United States and Europe are working closely together in this area, so cooperation with like-minded countries will be attainable.

Conclusion

Based on the six decades of the EU-Korea relations, we have examined the historical overview of the bilateral relations. Certainly, current international reality is causing us to witness the emergence of division and conflict under the name of the Second Cold War, as well as geopolitics and geoeconomics, after the past 30 years of globalization and relative prosperity.[22] In the past, South Korea has been a fast learner who has been boosting its economy through free trade. However, with the advent of strategic competition between the United States and China, Russia's invasion of Ukraine, and the Pandemic, it is facing new challenges such as a stable supply chain of key strategic materials.

In particular, developing countries, known as the Global South, are expressing skepticism over the international order led solely by the United States and Europe in response to these new challenges. Hence, armed with pragmatism, the position of Korea is that whether it is the United States or China, it can cooperate if it is in their interest. In addition, the revival of BRICS causes increasing the number of countries in the Global South that sympathize with this system. In the case of Brazil, it is insisting on settling international trade in currencies other than U.S. dollars, and China and Russia are agreeing with it, thereby supporting the thesis of multipolarity in international relations.[23]

Korea is advocating value diplomacy based on solidarity with countries with similar positions based on triangular cooperation between the United States and Japan. More recently, South Korea has shown flexibility by adding pragmatic diplomacy, and it is important to note that South Korea's Indo-Pacific strategy is not limited to regional diplomacy. From a geopolitical point of view, it is being accepted as a global and grand strategy that virtually only excludes West Africa. This trend is also expressed in the National Security Strategy in 2023 and is expected to guide South Korea's diplomacy in the coming years.

The Republic of Korea and the European Union have continued to strengthen their ties through bilateral institutional development. The bilateral relations of the past 60 years are positively evaluated in that they have reached an agreement to actively apply the changes of the international community in recent years. The remaining task is the refinement of foreign policy. And it has to start from the concept of strategic culture. This is because diplomacy is no longer limited to solely diplomats, and effective results can be achieved when the understanding and practice of relevant expert groups and ordinary citizens are combined in the policy-making process and its implementation. This can be applied to public diplomacy as well, and it is likely that it will have to be reflected in the formulation and implementation of foreign policy in the future.

Endnote

1. Kim Sihong, Development and Prospect for Korea-EU Relations, *Journal of Contemporary European Studies*, Vol.27, No. 3, 2009, p. 3.
2. Choi Jinwoo, Establishment of EU's Strategic Partnership and Korea-EU Relations, *Journal of Contemporary European Studies*, Vol.28, No. 3, 2010, p. 57.
3. Kim Sihong (Ed.), *Korea-European Union Relations*, Seoul: Huine, 2019, pp. 22-23.
4. Ahn Byungeok et al., *Understanding and Prospect of the EU*, Seoul: Nopighipi, 2014, p. 246.
5. Kim Sihong, Korea's Strategy towards the EU: From a Strategic Partner to a Privileged Partner, in Hungdah Su (Ed.), *Asian Countries' Strategies towards the EU in an inter-regionalist Context*, Taipei: National Taiwan Univ Press, 2015, pp. 56-57.
6. Korea Development Bank Research Department, *State Holding Company in Italy, IRI-ENI,* Seoul: KDB, 1969.
7. The main contents of the EU-Korea Framework Agreement are as follows: granting the most favored nation treatment; trade cooperation, including improving market access conditions, promoting fair competition in economic activities, and consultation on opening up procurement markets; ensuring the effective protection of intellectual, industrial and commercial property rights; promoting cooperation in the field of technical regulations, standards and conformity assessment; proper consultation in the process of imposing anti-dumping, countervailing duties; promoting economic and industrial cooperation, scientific and technological cooperation, environmental conservation and energy cooperation; cooperation in the field of culture and information to enhance mutual understanding; cooperation in development assistance in third countries, etc.; Establishment of a joint committee to implement the agreement and seek ways to expand cooperation.
8. The EU-ROK Joint Political Declaration includes the establishment of the EU-ROK Troika Foreign Ministers' Talks on an annual basis, the holding of high-level briefings on major diplomatic and domestic issues, and the promotion of exchanges between the National Assembly and the European Parliament.
9. Javier Solana, *A Secure Europe in a Better World. European Security Strategy,* Brussels: European Commission, 2003.
10. Kim Sihong, NAPCI and Trilateral Cooperation: Prospects for South Korea-EU Relations, in Nicola Casarini (Ed.), *Promoting Security Cooperation and Trust Building in Northeast Asia: The Role of the EU,* Rome: Edizioni Nuova Cultura, 2017, pp. 36-37.
11. Ahn Sangwook, Revision of Korea-EU Framework Agreement and Bilateral Relations, *EU Brief,* Vol. 1, No. 6, Yonsei-SERI EU Centre, 2009, p. 8.
12. Kim Eunjung, Effectuation of Lisbon Treaty and the Establishment of Korea-EU Strategic Partnership, *Diplomacy,* No. 92, p. 36.
13. There are 11 countries with which the EU has a strategic partnership. United States, Russia, China, South Korea, Japan, India, Canada, Brazil, Mexico, South Africa and ASEAN, and South Korea became the EU's tenth strategic partner in 2010.
14. Kim Eunjung, Ibid, p. 37.
15. MOFA Korea Western Europe Division, *Facts about the EU*, Seoul: MOFA, 2020, pp. 81-82.
16. Kim Sihong, Results of 10th Korea-EU Summit and Prospects for Future Cooperation, *Journal of European Union Studies*, 2023, No. 67, pp. 295-296.
17. European Commission, *Joint Statement EU-ROK Summit 2023*, Brussels: European Commission, 2023.
18. Kim Sihong, Sino-US Rivalry and a Decade of Korea-EU Strategic Partnership, *Journal of Contemporary Europe-*

an Studies, 2020, Vol. 38, No. 3, p. 12.

19. Kim Sihong, The EU's External Policy: Multipolarity, Strategic Autonomy and Indo-Pacific Strategy, *Journal of European Union Studies*, 2021, No. 59, p. 222.
20. Aude Darnai el al. A new world order: What, why and how? Global South Experts Turn the Tables, Stimson, 2023.
21. Kim Sihong and Michael Reiterer (Eds), *Connecting Europe and Asia: Security, Economy and Mobility*, Seoul: Huine, 2023, p. 12.
22. Olaf Scholz, The Global Zeitenwende: How to Avoid a New Cold War in a Multipolar Era, *Foreign Affairs*, 2023.
23. Filippo Fasulo et al., The World is Changing: Who Will Set the Rules?, *ISPI Focus and Fact Checking*, 2023.

The 2010 Framework Agreement and its Impacts on Managing Political Relations between the ROK and the EU

ERIC J. BALLBACH

Introduction

The EU-ROK Framework Agreement (FA),[1] which was signed on May 10, 2010 and entered into force on June 1, 2014, is the central institutional agreement managing political relations between Brussels and Seoul. While political cooperation between Seoul and Brussels has long been treated as a less urgent issue than the economic relationship, the introduction of the FA, together with the Framework Participation Agreement and the upgrade of relations to a strategic partnership, has brought the political pillar of EU-South Korea relations to the fore.[2] Against this background, this chapter analyzes the 2010 agreement and discusses how it has influenced the development of political relations between the EU and the ROK in different issue-areas.[3] It is shown that the FA has significantly enhanced political cooperation between the EU and the ROK on a wide range of topics. Yet, although the agreement foresees several types of action, it remains vague regarding their actual implementation. Moreover, the actual level of cooperation in the different sectors varies significantly.

The 2010 Framework Agreement: An Overview

The FA, which was signed in 2010 and entered into force in 2014, provides a legal basis for cooperation between the EU and the ROK on a range of issues and subject areas in which the two sides want to cooperate more closely. While "[m]any of them fall under the canvas of economic relations, (…) [underscoring] that this is an agreement laying the foundations of the EU-ROK relationship more broadly, (…) most areas covered by the Framework Agreement are political in nature."[4] Hence, the FA "provides the overarching framework for the political pillar of the EU-ROK relationship."[5]

The Predecessor: The 1996 Framework Agreement for Trade and Cooperation

In contrast to other significant economic actors in the Asian region such as India, Pakistan, ASEAN, and Japan, until the mid-1990s, the EU had not concluded any economic, let alone political agreements or arrangements with the ROK. Yet, plans to formalize the relationship between the two partners were already hinted at in the 1994 Communication.

As such, the 1996 Framework Agreement for Trade and Cooperation (FATC) between the European Community and its Member States, on the one hand, and the Republic of Korea, on the other hand, on October 28, 1996, was the first tangible step to strengthen relations between Seoul and Brussels.[6] This instrument is described as a 'third generation' cooperation agreement, meaning that it promotes broad cooperation on a range of topics.[7] The Agreement contains provisions aimed at fostering the growth of two-way trade and investment, and encouraging cooperation initiatives in justice and home affairs, science and technology and culture. Moreover, specific articles of the FATC mandate cooperation on a wide range of policy issues, including drugs and money laundering, energy, environmental matters, development assistance and culture, information and communication.[8] Notably, through the attached Political Declaration, the FA aims to intensify the political dialogue between the two sides. Article 3 of the FATC provides that:

> "a regular political dialogue, based on shared values and aspirations, shall be established (…) [which] shall take place in accordance with the procedures agreed in the Joint Declaration between the European Union and the Republic of Korea on this subject."[9]

Given the lack of substantive obligations, arguably the most important aspect of the 1996 FATC was the creation of an "institutional machinery to oversee the implementation of the Agreement and the development of stronger ties."[10] Most notably, a Joint Committee composed of representatives of the EU and Korea was established under Article 19 of the Agreement, which, among others, was charged with ensuring that the Agreement operates properly and making recommendations for promoting further expansion in trade and cooperation between the two parties. The institutional framework established with the FATC was a crucial step in increasing mutual trust and understanding necessary to further develop their relations in a more substantive manner. Hence, after the 1996 Framework Agreement entered into force, the parties agreed on several other sectoral agreements designed to further cooperation in specific areas. For instance, in 1997 the two sides concluded an Agreement on Cooperation and Mutual Administrative Assistance in Customs Matters, in 2006 an Agreement on Scientific and Technological Cooperation, and in 2009 the parties concluded the Agreement concerning Cooperation on Anti-Competitive Activities.

Yet, as both the ROK (in 2003) and the EU (through the Global Europe Communication in 2006) announced renewed trade strategies that heavily focused on launching Free Trade Agreements (FTAs), and with bilateral relations moving beyond mere economic cooperation, the FATC soon was in need of being updated.

Contents of the 2010 Framework Agreement

Negotiations for the EU-ROK Framework Agreement began in June 2008, and it was signed in 2010 before entering into force in 2014. The FA was intended to create a permanent institutional and legal framework for relations between the EU and the ROK, updating and replacing the 1996 FATC once it entered into force in 2014.[11] With economic cooperation now being primarily dealt with through the institutional framework provided by the FTA, the 2010 FA "addresses a much broader range of political, economic, social, and cultural issues" compared to the 1996 FATC.[12]

〈Figure 1〉 Cooperation areas as proposed by the Framework Agreement

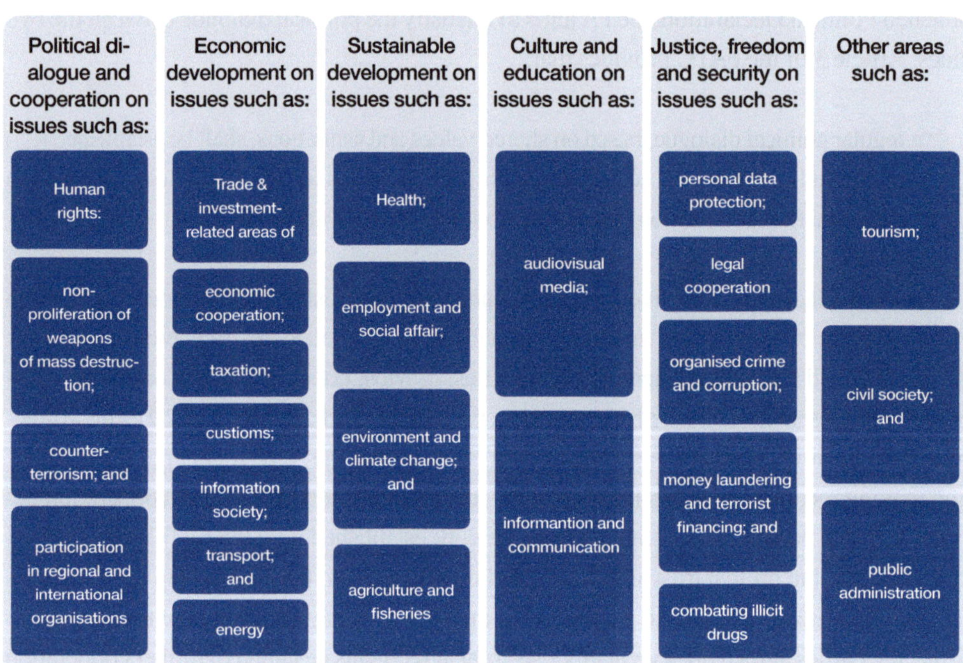

Source: Author

The central aims of the FA are to intensify political dialogue between the ROK and the EU and to further boost their economic relations.[13]

While the FA sets a basic framework for future cooperation between the ROK and the EU, the actual development of closer ties depends on tangible actions being taken on the basis of the FA. As such, the FA foresees several types of actions such as:[14]

- conducting regular political dialogues;
- developing joint projects to implement a future vision for strengthening their partnership;
- promoting collective efforts in relevant regional and international fora and organizations to respond to global issues;
- raising the roles and profiles of both Parties in each other's regions, through various means including cultural exchanges, the use of information technology, and education;
- promoting people-to-people contacts and understanding.

Generally speaking, the Agreement does not specify the form of cooperation, and it leaves it to the discretion of the parties to design an appropriate framework in which to cooperate, which meets their needs at any point in time.[15] As such, the Joint Committee provides the institutional mechanism through which cooperation and consultations are managed, although it does not have an exclusive role, and the parties may choose to cooperate through other avenues such as summit meetings at leaders' level, consultations at ministerial level, senior officials' level exchanges or specific sectoral dialogues on issues of common interest.[16]

The Joint Committee

Article 44 of the FA calls for the establishment of a Joint Committee consisting of representatives from both sides "to facilitate the implementation and to further the general aims of this Agreement as well as to maintain overall coherence in the relations and to ensure the proper functioning of any other agreement between the Parties."[17] It is thus tasked with ensuring that the agreement functions effectively.

It took until 2016 until the two sides agreed on the adoption of the rules of procedure of the Joint Committee and the establishment of specialized working groups as well as their terms of reference.

〈Table 1〉 Joint Committee Meetings

Joint Committee Meeting	Date	Place
1st Joint Committee Meeting	May 2001	Seoul
2nd Joint Committee Meeting	July 2003	Brussels
3rd Joint Committee Meeting	July 2004	Seoul
4th Joint Committee Meeting	July 2005	Brussels
5th Joint Committee Meeting	June 2006	Seoul
6th Joint Committee Meeting	June 2007	Brussels
7th Joint Committee Meeting	February 2009	Seoul
8th Joint Committee Meeting	March 2010	Brussels
9th Joint Committee Meeting	2011	Seoul
10th Joint Committee Meeting	September 2012	Brussels
11th Joint Committee Meeting	September 13, 2013	Seoul
12th Joint Committee Meeting	November 26, 2014	Brussels
13th Joint Committee Meeting	June 2016	Seoul
14th Joint Committee Meeting	December 2017	Brussels
15th Joint Committee Meeting	December 13, 2018	Seoul
16th Joint Committee Meeting	January 2020	Brussels
17th Joint Committee Meeting	February 2021	Online
18th Joint Committee Meeting	June 2022	Seoul
19th Joint Committee Meeting	March 2023	Brussels

Source: Author

Impact of the Framework Agreement

As noted above, the FA proposes cooperation on a wide range of sectors and topics, foreseeing several types of action. As it remains vague regarding their actual implementation, this chapter analyzes the development of EU-ROK relations in five particular actions foreseen by the FA.[18]

Cooperation, Coordination, and Dialogue

While the FA does not stipulate the scale and frequency of cooperation, it does suggest that there are some areas within the Agreement that should be subject to a regular process of consultation. Among others, the Agreement expressly requires the parties to establish "a regular political dialogue, based on shared values and aspirations (…) in accordance with procedures to be agreed between [Korea] and the [EU]."[19] While not providing details about how such dialogues should be structured, it does stipulate that this political dialogue should explicitly address the topics of democracy and human rights, international peace and security, arms control and other “major international issues of common interest.”[20] Regarding its implementation, the Agreement only states that the dialogue will take place through a variety of channels, including summit meetings at leaders’ level, consultations at ministerial level and briefings at senior officials’ level, among others. There is no denying the impact of the FA on the political dialogue between the EU and the ROK. After the FA was enacted, both because of necessity and demand from both sides, dialogues on specific subject matters were arranged and the pillar of political dialogue has grown considerably and has begun to operate through multiple channels, including the EU-South Korea Summit, political dialogues, joint committees, trade committees, ad-hoc meetings, and the EU-Korean Parliamentarians’ Council.[21]

As is the case for all bilateral relationships, the coming together of two heads of government (the presidents of the Council and the Commission in the case of the EU) constitutes the most senior form of political exchange between the EU and the ROK. The entry into force of the 1996 Framework Agreement in 2001 was also quickly followed by the establishment of high-level summits between the parties, which took place four times before the Framework Agreement was agreed on in 2010.[22]

〈Table 2〉 Summit Meetings

Summit	Date	Place
1st ROK-EU Summit	2002	Copenhagen
2nd ROK-EU Summit	2004	Hanoi
3rd ROK-EU Summit	2006	Helsinki
4th ROK-EU Summit	2009	Seoul
5th ROK-EU Summit	2010	Brussels
6th ROK-EU Summit	2012	Seoul
7th ROK-EU Summit	2010	Brussels
8th ROK-EU Summit	2015	Seoul
9th ROK-EU Summit	2018	Brussels
10th ROK-EU Summit	2023	Seoul

Source: Author

While the first four summit meetings took place on the sidelines of the Europe-Asia Meeting, in 2010, the first stand-alone EU–Korea summit was held during which the strategic partnership was formally launched. This indicated a change in emphasis, whereby Korea was no longer treated as a strand of the EU's Asia strategy, but, rather, as a priority partner.[23] The closer political cooperation enabled by the FA is clearly reflected in the Joint Statements adopted at the summit meetings. For instance, the Joint Statement adopted at the May 2023 summit meeting in Seoul both reflects a significant deepening of bilateral ties between Korea and the EU and presents an implementation plan for parts of the agenda. Most notably, the EU and the ROK agreed to establish a strategic dialogue at the foreign ministerial level to enhance their cooperation on global peace and security, expanding cooperation under the ROK-EU Digital Partnership and Green Partnership, launching a Health Emergency Preparedness and Response system, calling for cooperation between the EU's Coordinated Maritime Presence (CMP) in the Pacific with Korea's Navy, continuing cyber policy consultation, and promising cooperation on the regulation of AI, among other policy areas. The EU offers Korea association with its €95 billion research and innovation program, Horizon Europe, as well as people-to-people participation in its Erasmus+ student exchange program.

Below the summit level, other high-level political meetings between the EU and the ROK encompass the EU-ROK Foreign Ministers' Meeting (FMM) and the "High-Level Political Dialogue" (HLPD). While the former is thus far held irregularly, the latter is a pivotal bilateral consultative mechanism on political affairs in place since 2011. The HLPD aims to "exchange views on bilateral issues in the political sector, regional situations and multilateral cooperation measures."[24] The HLPD is held on the Vice Foreign Minister level on the side of the ROK and the Deputy Secretary-General of the EEAS on the EU-side. It aims to strengthen political dialogue and thus the overall strategic partnership. The HLPD is held irregularly with meetings having thus far been conducted in November 2011 in Seoul (1st meeting), in October 2012 in Brussels (2nd meeting), in July 2013 (3rd meeting), 2015 (4th meeting), 2019 (5th meeting), 2020 (6th meeting), and 2021 (7th meeting).

While the above-mentioned dialogues usually cover a broad range of topics, the EU and the ROK also hold a range of political dialogues covering specific topics:

〈Table 3〉 Political Dialogues between the ROK and the EU

Dialogue	Est.	Frequency
Non-proliferation, disarmament, and arms control	2005	Not annual
Policy consultation on development cooperation	2008	Not annual
Middle East and North Africa	2012	Annual
Cyber Policy Consultations	2014	Annual
Informal Consultations on the DPRK	2011	Not annual
Security and Defense Issues	2015	Not annual

Dialogue	Est.	Frequency
Working Group on Counter-Terrorism	2018	Not annual
Working Group on Energy, Environment and Climate	2018	Annual
Transport Dialogue	2022	NA

Other formats of political dialogue include the Policy Planners Consultations, the Consultations on Asian Regional Affairs, and the Consultations on Human Rights, none of them annual. The dialogues, as stipulated by article 3 of the Framework Agreement, are an important building block of the EU-ROK relationship. The above-listed political dialogues and consultations on specific topics enable exchanges between EU and ROK representatives and policymakers on a regular basis.

Joint projects

A second form of action foreseen under the Framework Agreement is the development of 'joint projects.' Again, the FA does not stipulate a particular form which such projects may take, stating that they may be conducted across a number of different issues governed by the Agreement. One area explicitly mentioned in the FA is development assistance. At the sixth EU–Korea summit in 2012, the parties agreed to coordinate their engagement in in-country assistance, and it is possible that the parties may design joint development assistance projects in a particular country, in order to make the most effective and efficient use of their development aid. Another area where joint projects may be undertaken according to the FA is in relation to energy, where the Agreements mention the "conduct of joint studies and research."[25] Joint scientific and technical projects are also encouraged under the 2007 Agreement on the Scientific and Technological Cooperation between the European Community and the ROK and the two sides have subsequently established a Joint Science and Technology Cooperation Committee. Indeed, science and technology may be a particularly profitable area for the development of joint projects, given the range of expertise of both parties in this regard. As pointed out by Chung and Lee, as of 2017, "South Korea has participated in 29 collaborative projects with the EU, 13 Marie Skłodowska-Curie actions, and one European Research Council grant under Horizon 2020."[26] Moreover, the ROK and the EU have launched a joint research project on climate change, the Korea-EU ETS Project (KETS).

Cooperation in regional and international fora

A third type of action under the Framework Agreement is the promotion of collective efforts in relevant regional and international fora and organizations. In other words, the Framework Agreement and its institutions may be used as a coordinating process, prior to negotiations on issues of common concern. For instance, Article 24 of the FA states that in order to deal with upcoming challenges, they are committed to taking measures to mitigate greenhouse gases and to coordinating their policies within the UNFCCC. In line with the priority areas of the 2023 Green Partnership, the EU and the ROK have agreed to promote climate action on the international stage, in multilateral and plurilateral fora, notably as major donors of climate finance and as facilitators of a just transition in third countries. The two sides agreed to cooperate in multilateral fora, with a view to ensuring mutual supportiveness for international trade and environmental policies. Also, they agreed to cooperate to support developing countries and emerging economies with their implementation of climate and environment policies. Both sides also affirmed their willingness to work together bilaterally and in international fora including the Conferences of the Parties (COP) under the UNFCCC and the CBD, as well as the G20 and the OECD. Moreover, South Korea has participated as an invited country at the G-7 meetings in 2021 and 2023 and the NATO summits in 2022 and 2023.

The negotiation of additional agreements

The Framework Agreement also explicitly provides for the possibility for the parties to adopt additional "specific agreements in any area of cooperation falling within its scope."[27] Such agreements are one way in which the parties can develop a more detailed legal framework for their mutual relations, reflecting the dynamic nature of the relationship. There are already a number of specific agreements which the parties have concluded, including the 2010 Free Trade Agreement, the 2009 Competition Agreement, the 2007 Science and Technology Agreement and the 1997 Customs Agreement. All of these agreements form part of the common institutional framework established by the Framework Agreement, and they should be implemented in a coherent and coordinated manner.

Some other areas in which specific agreements may be useful are highlighted in the Framework Agreement itself, for example, in relation to the regulation of shipping agency activities or illegal migration. Moreover, specific agreements may be negotiated in other areas, where a need is subsequently identified by the parties. Indeed, the ability to conclude additional agreements means that the legal framework for EU-Korea relations will remain dynamic, and the partners will be able to respond to new and emerging challenges, as time goes on.

Against this background it is notable that the EU and the ROK have agreed on a number of sector-specific partnerships, i.e., a digital partnership, a green partnership and a (yet to be established) security partnership.[28] As stated in the Joint Statement released after the 2023 EU-ROK summit meeting, both sides agree that these new partnerships between the EU and the ROK will further strengthen the bilateral Framework Agreement signed in 2010.

Increasing Security Cooperation

Since the enactment of the FA and the upgrading of bilateral relations to a strategic partnership, security cooperation between the EU and the ROK has successively increased. In fact, the inclusion of international peace and security is one of the most notable developments in the FA, especially when compared to the 1996 FATC. Security cooperation is mentioned frequently in the preamble to the 2010 FA and it is addressed in several substantive articles.

The FA comprises a broad scope of security threats, including terrorism, serious crimes of international concern, the proliferation of weapons of mass destruction and their means of delivery, climate change, energy and resources insecurity, poverty, and financial crisis. To respond to such threats, the Agreement calls for cooperation in sectors of mutual interest, notably promoting democratic principles and respect for human rights, countering the proliferation of weapons of mass destruction, combating illicit trade in small arms and light weapons, taking measures against the most serious crimes of concern to the international community; combating terrorism; cooperation in regional and international organizations.[29] Overall, the security areas included in the FA are those on which both the EU and Korea have common interests for cooperation, even though the level of interests may not be equal for the two parties in all areas. Also, the degree of policy specification in the given areas may not be the same for them, either. The mutual interests of the two, however, can be found in the fact that the standard clauses are modified for deeper and stronger cooperation in the Framework Agreement. Also, the inclusion of non-traditional security issues – for example, cybercrime, money laundering and organized crime – indicates that the two parties have a willingness for comprehensive security cooperation.[30]

Indeed, with both sides seeking to diversify their foreign relations in the context of the continuing US-China conflict and amid tension over Russia's invasion of Ukraine and North Korea's nuclear threats, security cooperation between the EU and the ROK has substantially progressed since the Agreement was adopted. As summarized by Casarini, the EU and South Korea have fostered bilateral security cooperation particularly in four areas, i.e., nuclear non proliferation and disarmament, cybersecurity, space policy and technology, and preventive diplomacy and crisis management.[31]

For instance, the EU and its member states play an active role in countering Pyongyang's weapons programs and other malfeasance, often in close consultation with the international community and South Korean counterparts. Mostly visibly, perhaps, the EU vigorously enforces both standard international and enhanced voluntary sanctions against NK as a part of the effort – led by SK, Japan, and the US – to curb that country's WMD (especially nuclear) and missile development.[32]

In 2018, the EU adopted a specific conclusion on Enhancing Security Cooperation in and with Asia.[33] The resulting ESIWA project aims at enhancing security engagement in and with Asia by supporting tailor-made cooperation with six pilot countries (India, Indonesia, Japan, the Republic of Korea, Singapore, and Vietnam) in such areas as counter-terrorism/prevention of violent extremism (CT/PVE), cybersecurity, maritime security, hybrid threats, and crisis management. As noted above, at the 2023 summit, the leaders of the ROK and the EU jointly decided to start a military dialogue with the aim of developing a security partnership, amid tension over Russia's invasion of Ukraine and North Korea's nuclear threats. In that respect, the two sides also agreed to establish a strategic dialogue at the foreign ministerial level to enhance their cooperation on global peace and security. In light of contemporary global shifts, South Korea and the EU also seek to reinforce cooperation on economic security, including early warning systems to detect and address potential supply chain disruptions in key industries, such as semiconductor chips. Considering the many areas in which the two sides can and already did boost security links and their similar views and approaches to the Sino-American rivalry, Seoul and its European partners are poised to further boost security cooperation, not least as both sides have adopted their respective Indo-Pacific strategies in 2021 and 2022, respectively.

Limitations of the Framework Agreement

The FA provides a framework for (1) expanding and developing relations between Korea and the EU, (2) upgrading from general cooperation to strategic partnerships and (3) strengthening cooperation on major international issues. According to Chae, South Korea has long focused primarily on (1), while the EU has focused primarily on (2) and (3).[34] However, in light of the intensifying US-China conflict and Russia's war against Ukraine, and the subsequent strengthening endeavors of both the ROK and the EU to diversify their foreign relations, this mismatch seems void. However, it is yet unclear what implications a change in government in Seoul would have.

Managing Future Relations in Light of Limited Resources

The war in Ukraine has triggered a rapid reassessment of defense and security policies across Europe, including significant increases in defense spending in most EU member states as well as comprehensive military and financial support provided by the EU to Ukraine. While these developments did not lead to a decline in EU involvement in the Indo-Pacific, as was feared by quite a number of observers, it is crucial to understand that resources are limited when planning future EU-ROK cooperation. Even before Russia's war against Ukraine, some observers already criticized the scope of cooperation covered by the FA as "too wide", therefore raising hard-to-accept "controversial or political and social issues" lacking consensus.[35] While one might argue that the increasing US-China conflict as well as Russia's war against Ukraine have removed many of the boundaries and limitations that have thus far hindered deeper security cooperation between the EU and the ROK, especially with the recent expansion of bilateral relations the question of capacity limits must be discussed openly between the two sides. Against this background, the two sides should establish a regular review mechanism which evaluates the different dialogues. As priorities may shift and some issue-areas may be discussed in the context of more than one dialogue channel, a regular review in terms of the achievement of central objectives, duplicity and practicality could be helpful to streamline the respective debates and that making cooperation more resource-efficient.

Managing Expectations

Relations between the EU and South Korea have changed noticeably since the Framework Agreement was adopted. As shown, this change in particular found expression in the dramatic expansion of dialogue channels between Brussels and Seoul as well as in the increase of cooperation in the security sector. There is no doubt that the EU's changed role has also led to specific expectations on the part of regional partners such as the Republic of Korea. Yet, especially in light of Russia's war of aggression against Ukraine, which will continue to constrain the EU's financial capabilities and resources, the twin objectives of deeper EU engagement in the Indo-Pacific on the one hand and continued comprehensive support for Ukraine on the other may conflict.

Conclusions

Political relations between the EU and the ROK have come a long way since the FA was adopted in 2010. Both quantitatively and qualitatively, i.e., both in terms of depth and level of institutionalization, but also in terms of topics and issues addressed, the two sides have significantly strengthened their relationship over the past decade. With the enactment of the FA, the political pillar of EU-South Korea relations has begun to operate through multiple channels, including the EU-South Korea Summit, political dialogues, joint committees, and, more recently, partnership agreements. In addition to formal bilateral relations, ad hoc meetings have brought together experts from both parties, covering policy agendas that include North Korea, cybersecurity, development, and human rights.[36]

With geopolitical realities shifting and both sides looking for reliable partners beyond their mere vicinity, the ROK and the EU are poised to further boost political and even security cooperation – with the latter having long been a rather neglected aspect of their relationship.

At the same time, the ever-widening relationship between the EU and the ROK will likely raise expectations that could be difficult to manage as both sides have to operate with limited resources.

Endnote

1. Official Journal of the European Union, Framework Agreement between the European Union and its Member States, on the one part, and the Republic of Korea, on the other part, https://eur-lex.europa.eu/legal-content/EN/TXT/PDF/?uri=CELEX:22013A0123(01) (accessed 09 September 2023).
2. Bridges, Brian, The European Union and the Korean Conundrum, in: Balme, Richard and Bridges, Brian (eds.), Europe-Asia Relations, Palgrave Macmillan, London 2008.
3. Aside from the Framework Agreement itself, this study analyzes official documents (such as the EU-ROK summit Joint Statements, statements from the Joint Committee, meeting documents, and press statements) based on a qualitative content analysis.
4. Pacheco-Pardo, Ramon, Desmaele, Linda and Ernst, Maximilian, EU-ROK Relations: Putting the Strategic Partnership to Work, KF-VUB Korea Chair Report, 15 October 2018, https://www.korea-chair.eu/eu-rok-relations-putting-the-strategic-partnership-to-work/ (accessed 02 September 2023).
5. Pacheco-Pardo, Ramon, Desmaele, Linda and Ernst, Maximilian, EU-ROK Relations: Putting the Strategic Partnership to Work, KF-VUB Korea Chair Report, 15 October 2018, https://www.korea-chair.eu/eu-rok-relations-putting-the-strategic-partnership-to-work/ (accessed 02 September 2023).
6. Official Journal of the European Union, Framework Agreement between the European Union and its Member States, on the one part, and the Republic of Korea, on the other part, https://eur-lex.europa.eu/legal-content/EN/TXT/PDF/?uri=CELEX:22013A0123(01)
7. Harrison, James, An Introduction to the Legal Framework for EU-Korea Relations, in: Ibid. (ed.), European Union and South Korea: The Legal Framework for Strengthening Trade, Economic and Political Relations, Edinburgh University Press, 2013, Kindle-Version (p. 3).
8. Harrison, James, An Introduction to the Legal Framework for EU-Korea Relations, in: Ibid. (ed.), European Union and South Korea: The Legal Framework for Strengthening Trade, Economic and Political Relations, Edinburgh University Press, 2013, Kindle-Version (p.11).
9. Harrison, James, Overview of the EU-Korea Framework Agreement, in: Ibid. (ed.), European Union and South Korea: The Legal Framework for Strengthening Trade, Economic and Political Relations, Edinburgh University Press, 2013, Kindle-Version (p. 149).
10. Harrison, James, An Introduction to the Legal Framework for EU-Korea Relations, in: Ibid. (ed.): European Union and South Korea: The Legal Framework for Strengthening Trade, Economic and Political Relations, Edinburgh University Press, 2013, Kindle-Version (p. 3),
11. Framework Agreement, Article 43.
12. Harrison, James, Overview of the EU-Korea Framework Agreement, in: Ibid. (ed.), European Union and South Korea: The Legal Framework for Strengthening Trade, Economic and Political Relations, Edinburgh University Press, 2013, Kindle-Version (p.150).
13. Framework Agreement, Title I, Article 2.
14. Framework Agreement, Title I, Article 2.
15. Harrison, James, Overview of the EU-Korea Framework Agreement, in: Ibid. (ed.), European Union and South Korea: The Legal Framework for Strengthening Trade, Economic and Political Relations, Edinburgh University Press, 2013, Kindle-Version (p. 153).
16. Framework Agreement, Title II, Article 3.
17. Article 44 (2) of the Framework Agreement holds: "The Joint Committee shall: (a) ensure that this Agreement operates properly; (b) monitor the development of the comprehensive relationship between the Parties; (c) request,

as appropriate, information from committees or other bodies established under other agreements falling under the common institutional framework and consider any reports submitted by them; (d) exchange opinions and make suggestions on any issue of common interest, including future actions and the resources available to carry them out; (e) set priorities in relation to the aims of this Agreement; (f) seek appropriate methods of forestalling problems which might arise in areas covered by this Agreement; (g) resolve any dispute arising in the application or interpretation of this Agreement by consensus in accordance with Article 45(3); (h) examine all the information presented by a Party regarding non-execution of the obligations and hold consultations with the other Party to seek a solution acceptable to both Parties in accordance with Article 45(3)."

18. Wolfgang Pape, EU-Korea Relations to Promote Regulatory Cooperation in Economic Policies, in Particular Industrial Development Policies, in: EU-Korea Relations in a Changing World, 2013, 278.
19. Official Journal of the European Union, Framework Agreement between the European Union and its Member States, on the one part, and the Republic of Korea, on the other part, https://eur-lex.europa.eu/legal-content/EN/TXT/PDF/?uri=CELEX:22013A0123(01).
20. Official Journal of the European Union, Framework Agreement between the European Union and its Member States, on the one part, and the Republic of Korea, on the other part, https://eur-lex.europa.eu/legal-content/EN/TXT/PDF/?uri=CELEX:22013A0123(01).
21. Ministry of Foreign Affairs Republic of Korea 2018.
22. The summit meetings have to be distinguished from the "leaders' meetings", usually informal meetings at the level of heads of state or government held in physical or online (video conference) format. The last leaders' meeting between the EU and the ROK was held online in June 2020 and brought together the President of the European Council, Charles Michel, the President of the European Commission, Ursula von der Leyen, and the President of the ROK, Moon Jae-in. See: European Council, Republic of Korea-EU leaders' video conference meeting, 30 June 2020, https://www.consilium.europa.eu/en/meetings/international-summit/2020/06/30/.
23. As noted above, this coincided with the conclusion of two other agreements, which, today, form the main pillars of the legal framework for EU–Korea relations, namely the Free Trade Agreement and a new Framework Agreement.
24. Republic of Korea, Ministry of Foreign Affairs, ROK and the EU to Hold the 2nd High-level Political Dialogue, Press Release, 9 October 2012, https://www.mofa.go.kr/eng/brd/m_5676/view.do?seq=311772&srchFr=&amp%3BsrchTo=&amp%3BsrchWord=Committee&amp%3BsrchTp=&amp%3Bmulti_itm_seq=0&amp%3Bitm_seq_1=0&amp%3Bitm_seq_2=0&amp%3Bcompany_cd=&amp%3Bcompany_nm=&page=531&titleNm=.
25. Framework Agreement, Title IV, Article 17.
26. Chung Sae Won and Lee Jae-Seung, Building the pillars of the EU-South Korea strategic partnership, Asia Europe Journal (2019), 17: 327-340 [334].
27. Framework Agreement, Title IX, Article 43.
28. The EU-ROK digital partnership was launched in November 2022, in which both parties agree to cooperate on semiconductors, next generation mobile networks, quantum and high-performance computing, cybersecurity, Artificial Intelligence, and platforms, data and skills. The partnership is carried out through the establishment of a "Digital Partnership Council," a ministerial-level dialogue format which meets annually to set the priorities for the coming year and share best practices, helping to create common goals. On May 22, 2023, the EU and the ROK established a Green Partnership, which focuses on several priority areas, including strengthening efforts on combating climate change, increasing cooperation on environmental issues, supporting a clean and fair energy transition, and working with third countries to facilitate their green transition, among others. At the May 2023 summit, the leaders of the ROK and the EU also jointly decided to work towards the establishment of a security partnership. In that respect, the two sides also agreed to establish a strategic dialogue at the foreign ministerial level to enhance their cooperation on global peace and security.
29. Jun Hae-Won, Cooperation in the Field of International Peace and Security: A Newcomer to the Legal Framework for EU–Korea Relations, in: Harrison, James, European Union and South Korea: The Legal Framework for Strengthening Trade, Economic and Political Relations, Edinburgh University Press, 2013, Kindle-Version (p. 178)
30. Jun Hae-Won, Cooperation in the Field of International Peace and Security: A Newcomer to the Legal Framework for EU–Korea Relations, in: Harrison, James, European Union and South Korea: The Legal Framework for Strengthening Trade, Economic and Political Relations, Edinburgh University Press, 2013, Kindle-Version (p.

187).

31. Casarini, Nicola, The EU's Growing Security Cooperation With South Korea, The Diplomat, 25 March 2021, https://thediplomat.com/2021/03/the-eus-growing-security-cooperation-with-south-korea/ (accessed 12 September 2023).

32. See: Ballbach, Eric J., Moving Beyond Targeted Sanctions: The Sanctions Regime of the European Union against North Korea, SWP Research Paper 4 (February 2022), German Institute forInternational and Security Affairs, https://www.swp-berlin.org/publications/products/research_papers/2022RP04_SanctionsEUNorthKorea_Web.pdf.

33. Council of the European Union, Enhanced EU Security Cooperation in and with Asia, Council Conclusions, 28 May 2018, https://www.consilium.europa.eu/media/35456/st09265-re01-en18.pdf.

34. Chae Hyungbok, Legal issues in the Korea-EU relationship, in: Casarini, Nicola, Fiori, Antonio, Kim Nam-Kook, Lee Jae-Seung, Pacheco Pardo, Ramon (eds.), The Routledge Handbook of Europe–Korea Relations, 2022: 290-306 (293).

35. Chae Hyungbok, Legal issues in the Korea-EU relationship, in: Casarini, Nicola, Fiori, Antonio, Kim Nam-Kook, Lee Jae-Seung, Pacheco Pardo, Ramon (eds.), The Routledge Handbook of Europe–Korea Relations, 2022: 290-306 (295).

36. Ministry of Foreign Affairs Republic of Korea 2018.

EU-ROK Security Relations
Historical Challenges, Contemporary Progress, and Future Outlook

MASON RICHEY

Introduction

2023 marks sixty years of diplomatic relations between the European Union (EU) and the Republic of Korea (ROK). Over those sixty years, the EU-ROK relationship has flourished into a strategic partnership on the back of major growth in the two polities' economic exchange, political cooperation, mutual cultural influence, and security cooperation.

An EU-ROK Free Trade Agreement has permitted total bilateral exchange of goods, services, and commodities to rise to more than 130bnUSD annually, covering major sectors such as vehicles, machinery, chemicals, agriculture, critical industrial and high-tech products, finance, transportation, and information services.[1] On the diplomatic and political fronts, as of 2023 EU-ROK leader-level meetings and ministerial visits have never been more frequent or more substantive, addressing cooperation in areas ranging from the war in Ukraine to climate change to cybersecurity to aid/development assistance to scientific exchange to international trade. In 2023 alone, important EU-ROK leader-level summits have taken place on the sidelines of the G7 and at a stand-alone in Seoul, while ministerial-level meeting throughput in Seoul and Brussels has increased rapidly after disruption caused by the COVID-19 pandemic.[2] And this is in addition to relations between the ROK and EU member states, which have featured ministerial- and leader-level meetings at the G7, the G20, the NATO summit, and other multilateral fora.[3] EU-ROK mutual influence in the culture, sport, and education/scientific arenas is also extensive. The ROK and the EU are major sources of globally prominent audio-visual content and sporting events (Olympic Games, football, etc.), as well as university student and faculty exchange.[4]

The areas of EU-ROK cooperation mentioned above are all well known. This chapter, however, aims to bring descriptive and analytical focus to an often underappreciated dimension of the EU-ROK strategic partnership: the development and extent of meaningful security cooperation. While it is still the case that the ROK's critical military alliance partner remains the US, several developments in the international system have opened up possibilities for a greater security role for the EU in the Indo-Asia-Pacific and broader ROK choice in security partners. For one, increasing multipolarity of the international system—following Cold War bipolarity and immediate post-Cold War US unipolar hegemony—has opened previously foreclosed opportunities for inter-regional security cooperation. Beyond that, there has been a rise in the demand for global governance and public goods production—due to climate change, cybersecurity risks, the growth of the importance of space, etc.—even as multilateral institutions (notably the United Nations) have become increasingly incapable of meeting that demand. Consequently, new forms of inter-state, "minilateral," regional, and inter-regional cooperation have emerged to attempt to fill the gap. Lastly, the breakdown in the rules-based international order means the emergence of new threats requiring creative security cooperation for responding to these threats, not only in terms of new patterns of behavior between and among traditional security partners, but also new configurations of states for whom security cooperation is, historically speaking, not the norm.[5] All three of the above factors have helped make it the case that the EU and the ROK have seen their security cooperation grow.

In presenting and assessing the development of EU-ROK security relations, this chapter proceeds in the following way. Following this section I Introduction, section II provides the context—both within Europe and the ROK, as well as in terms of the international arena—by which EU-ROK security relations have taken shape. Section II covers the state of play of EU-ROK security relations, with a focus on discussing the ongoing lines of effort of EU-ROK security cooperation, as well as the areas in which the two polities have struggled to make progress despite the need to do so. Finally, section IV concludes with a look at the prospects for EU-ROK security cooperation going forward.

Dynamic Context

EU-ROK security relations take place in a dynamic context of both international system and domestic political developments that condition the scope and depth of their cooperation. To begin with, EU-ROK security relations are subject to the vicissitudes of the prevailing contemporary, multipolar geopolitics: the Indo-Pacific's emergence as the most vital region worldwide; regional and global power competition between the US and China; Russian revisionism; the path dependence of the US's bilateral alliance network in the Indo-Pacific; and emerging global governance issues such as climate change, public health, and cybersecurity. The counterpart to these international system issues is the shifting domestic political factors that are specific to each polity.

These realities—both international and domestic—support selected cooperative behavior between the EU and the ROK, while making other lines of effort more difficult. And some of these realities do both. To start with the incentives for more cooperation, Asian middle-power states, like the ROK, have not only become partners capable of shaping changes to the international system through collaboration with extra-regional actors, but they have also become desirable partners for like-minded polities, such as the EU, which want more influence in the Indo-Asia-Pacific and more support from Indo-Asia-Pacific states for challenges both global and regional. Meanwhile, as Indo-Asia-Pacific states have developed into growth engines, the EU and its member states have been compelled to follow the US in its "pivot" to Asia. Expressions of this include growing EU trade agreements with Indo-Asia-Pacific states as well as more comprehensive EU strategic partnerships, notably including security components.

The EU Global Strategy, Indo-Pacific Strategy, and Strategic Compass describe areas for Europe's role in East Asia, especially in domains such as weapons nonproliferation, trade, international rule of law, climate change and green growth, provision of maritime security and access to global maritime commons, and digital cooperation.[6] The EU considers the ROK to be an important partner in these areas. For its part, the 2023 ROK National Security Strategy mirrors many of these concerns, and singles out the EU and its member states for cooperation in these domains, with a special emphasis on economic security cooperation and building like-minded diplomatic coalitions to deal with crises.[7]

Second, as for disincentives to EU-ROK security cooperation, assorted economic and domestic political factors are impediments: terrorism, economic malaise, time and resource-intensive (im)migration management, post-Brexit effects, and political extremism (especially Euroscepticism) sometimes lead the EU and its member states to inward-focused preoccupations. Meanwhile domestic political scandal, weak GDP growth, the nuclear and conventional threat from the Democratic People's Republic of Korea (DPRK), and politico-economic aimlessness following three decades of democratic and capitalist development can make it challenging for the ROK to muster the political will to act far beyond Northeast Asia.

Thirdly, some aspects of international affairs have no clear-cut effect on EU-ROK security cooperation, variously both incentivizing and disincentivizing it. Perhaps the most acute examples are Russian revisionism—most notably aggression in Ukraine—and instability in Europe's southeastern flank and Mediterranean neighborhood. On the one hand, the Russia-Ukraine war has been a burden on both time and resources within the EU, compelling it to focus foreign, security and defense policies and materials on areas of geographic proximity. The same thing is true for the various wars in the Middle East, as well as the migration flows crossing the Mediterranean. On the other hand, Russia's violation of Ukrainian sovereignty has been so sustained and brazen that it has made it (a) relatively easy for Europe to galvanize support from like-minded states (such as the ROK, Japan, Australia, and New Zealand) interested in supporting the rules-based international order, and (b) important for states with significant defense-industrial bases (such as the ROK) to contribute arms (even if indirectly) to support Ukraine militarily. This type of effort—such as the ROK backfilling lethal arms to Poland, which had directly transferred arms to Ukraine—has required security and defense cooperation between the EU (and its member states) and the ROK.

Another state of affairs with a variable influence on EU-ROK security cooperation is US-China rivalry in the Indo-Pacific, which has differential effects—often in tension with each other—on Europe's relations with several East Asia states, including the ROK. Seen from one perspective, the US and China are involved in high-stakes, destabilizing geostrategic rivalry in a number of hard security areas—in the South China Sea, the DPRK, Taiwan, anti-access/area-denial (A2/AD) in the western Pacific, etc.—that largely exclude involvement from the EU, which lacks the regional military capabilities to participate in these conflicts, even if it wanted to. Nonetheless, from a different perspective, the competition between the global superpower and the aspiring regional hegemon causes many Indo-Pacific states to hedge by deepening partnerships with polities outside the US-China dyad. In this regard, the EU is a natural choice for a state like the ROK, which shares interests and values and has a long-standing history of cooperation in the diplomatic and economic spheres.

Finally, the US-led alliance system in East Asia, and in particular the alliance with the ROK, casts a significant shadow of path dependency. US-ROK security and defense cooperation is historically quite exclusive (as many military alliances are), and to the extent that this remains the case it impedes other polities from increasing engagement with the ROK in the security and defense sector. Numerous reasons make it the case that Seoul is reticent to diversify partners, when it is an issue of strategic security: (a) as defense cooperation with the US requires equipment (especially technological) interoperability between ROK and US military forces, this increases the costs/risks and potential downsides of ROK procurement from non-US military suppliers; (b) diplomatically, Seoul is cautious to avoid the impression of lowering the importance of relations with Washington, a risk-averse mentality that limits the ROK's ability to collaborate with other partners in core security and defense areas; (c) finally, like all middle powers, Seoul is constrained by limits on its bandwidth to work with partners, and this translates into the need to prioritize the full maintenance of its defense and security alliance commitments to the US, which in turn means that increasing cooperation with non-US partners is a challenge to the ROK's political, military, and economic resources.

Nonetheless, in light of a threat landscape that includes global and cross-regional challenges—Chinese revisionism, Russian aggression, and North Korean nuclear proliferation—the US has begun to prioritize the transformation of the bilateral Indo-Pacific alliance system into a networked model of "minilateral" configurations. The most well-known are trilateral and quadrilateral groupings such as AUKUS and the Quad, but the US re-conceptualization of its alliances includes space for the EU and its member states (as well as NATO) to play a greater security role both in the Indo-Pacific, including with East Asian partners such as the ROK.

EU-ROK Security Relations

EU-ROK security cooperation is based on a strategic partnership anchored in shared values and common interests, both of which have grown significantly as the ROK has transitioned into a mature democracy, global economic powerhouse, and major regional security and defense actor (and indeed with a burgeoning global security and defense profile).[8] The foundation of the EU-ROK strategic partnership is the Framework Agreement (2010) setting out the contours of Brussels-Seoul political dialogue and cooperation. The Framework Agreement is complemented by a 2011 Korea-EU Free Trade Agreement, which was the EU's first comprehensive "next generation" FTA with an Indo-Pacific state. The security component of the EU-ROK strategic partnership is outlined in the Framework Participation Agreement (2014) that enables ROK participation in Common Security and Defense Policy (CSDP) missions and operations. The ROK was the first of the EU's strategic partners to sign each of the three agreements on political, trade, and security cooperation, and Seoul remains the only East Asian state to participate in EU-led crisis-management operations on the foundation of a formal agreement covering guidelines on financing, deployment conditions, chain of command, etc.

Mechanisms for institutional cooperation—as found with the documents fleshing out the EU-ROK strategic partnership—are useful and necessary building blocks for security relations, but are insufficient and need to be accompanied by shared threat perceptions. Shared threat perceptions are important for the sustainability of security cooperation between the EU and the ROK, as they provide some protection from the vicissitudes of domestic politics and bureaucratic battles over scarce resources. A 2021 study by Richey and Christiansen—based on interviews with elites both in Europe and the ROK—showed that the EU and the ROK shared a perception of direct, significant threat in three security areas: climate change and energy security, cybersecurity, and economic security.[9] Unsurprisingly, these were also areas in which the EU and the ROK cooperate closely. A fourth security area—nonproliferation of weapons of mass destruction—also features significant EU-ROK cooperation, despite differing threat perceptions. In the 2021 study by Richey and Christiansen, ROK respondents reported a high threat level (due to the proximity to the DPRK), while the European respondents reported a low threat perception. Notwithstanding that difference, the existence of significant cooperation with the ROK on nonproliferation was hypothesized to arise from the fact that nonproliferation is anchored in international law, which the EU and its member states work to uphold regardless of direct threat level. In the case of EU-ROK relations, this means collaborating on a number of areas—policy dialogue, sanctions enforcement, diplomatic coordination—to impose costs on the DPRK's nuclear and missile programs.

Also as concerns shared threat perceptions, it is worth noting that the 2021 Richey and Christiansen study is based on a data set that stops prior to the 2022 Russian full-scale invasion of Ukraine. It is thus reasonable to assume—and anecdotal evidence supports this conclusion—that the EU threat perception on military security has shifted upwards (towards the level the ROK already had, given the proximity of the DPRK) and now tracks a closer level of military cooperation with the ROK.[10]

The EU-ROK crisis management agreement has been employed in carrying out joint missions as a part of EUNAVFOR Operation Atalanta, an EU-led effort to deter and combat piracy in the area extending from the Gulf of Aden into the western Indian Ocean.[11] Anti-/counter-piracy is a natural issue for which the EU and the ROK can cooperate: both Seoul and Brussels have similar regional free trade interests (notably the massive throughput of commercial and commodity cargo), are dedicated to maintaining international law (piracy is *hostis humani generis*), and in this case can rely on a UN-mandate as a legal and normative support for their cooperation.

Since 2010 Operation Atalanta has been a major success, nearly eradicating piracy—of cargo, ship equipment and technology, and kidnapped commercial sailors—along the critical shipping routes leading out of and into the Gulf of Aden. The maritime region has seen pirate attacks drop from approximately 170 per year in the early 2010s to less than 5 by 2019, with current attacks essentially at 0.[12] The ROK has worked hand-in-hand with the EU and its member states in this effort for more than a decade, deploying its ROKS Chungmugong destroyer (a part of the Cheonghae anti-/counter-piracy unit) under the aegis of the EU-ROK crisis management agreement.[13] Over that time period, ROK warships faced 20+ armed pirate aggressions while protecting 20,000+ ship passages and holding a perfect record in preventing attacks on World Food Programme vessels transporting humanitarian aid to Somalia.[14] In addition to the EU dimension of coordination and planning, ROK participation in Operation Atalanta has meant that ROK navy warships have sailed with frigates and corvettes of Italy, Denmark, Germany, France, and other EU member states (including the UK, when it was still a part of the EU). This has, in turn, supported an increase in the number of

European states—e.g., Germany, France, and the UK—sending naval assets for port calls with the ROK.[15]

In addition to the CSDP mission EUNAVFOR Operation Atalanta, EU-ROK security cooperation takes place in numerous other domains, as the Framework Agreement identifies areas of collaboration between the two signatories, including provisions on nonproliferation of weapons of mass destruction (WMD), cyberthreats, money laundering and illicit trafficking, and promotion of human rights and the international legal order in general. Burgeoning EU-ROK cooperation on cybersecurity and cyberthreats is especially notable, with an annual Vice-Ministerial-level meeting (ongoing since 2013, with a hiatus for COVID) serving to support institutionalization of the EU-ROK Cyber Dialogue.[16] EU-ROK cyber cooperation is also housed within the EU's ESIWA (Enhancing Security In and With Asia) program, which includes the ROK as a partner, as well as the EU-ROK Digital Partnership.[17] The latter was launched in November 2022, and, beyond covering elements of cybersecurity dialogue and best-practices exchange, the EU-ROK Digital Partnership also addresses digital standards and coordination in areas at the intersection of technology and economic security, such as a common vision for 6G, semiconductor research, high-performance computing (e.g., quantum computing), and artificial intelligence.

Of course the US and China are the major players in the security and defense space of East Asia, and consequently Europe is a secondary actor, yet both the EU and its member states make other meaningful contributions to the integrity of the East Asian and Indo-Pacific order. In the first place, Europe has a huge economic footprint (both in terms of value and geographically) in East Asia, and this is accompanied by a security interest in maintaining the norms, rules, and principles of the current international/regional regime. Accordingly the EU and its member states actively support the international/regional system in terms of international law in variegated areas: nonproliferation, human rights, maritime security, counter-terrorism, sea-lines-of-communication, sanctions, and territorial and maritime dispute resolution. These actions contribute indirectly to ROK national security by promoting a stable, predictable environment within which it can operate between pressure from China and the demands of alliance obligations to the US. For its part, the ROK has a similar profile on the above-listed areas, and is an important EU and member state regional partner in forming diplomatic coalitions to protect the rules (to the extent possible) for the above-listed areas.[18]

Regarding the DPRK dossier, the EU and its member states have an unheralded but important function in pushing back against Pyongyang's nuclear and missile programs, as well as other behavior that contravenes international law or menaces the stability of the international system. In fact, the EU's security role on the Korean peninsula vis-à-vis the DPRK goes back to the mid–1990s–early 2000s, when the EU supported the Korean Peninsula Energy Development Organization (KEDO), which, pursuant to the 1994 Agreed Framework, was intended to finance the development of civilian energy projects in the DPRK in return for Pyongyang's cessation and eventual dismantlement of its nuclear weapons program.[19] The EU supported KEDO financially, including EU contributions of 15–20mn USD annually from 1997–2002.[20] Although the EU did not have a strong public voice in crafting the provisions of the denuclearization aspiration that was the foundation for KEDO, the EU nonetheless coordinated closely with the ROK and the US in evaluating and assessing the results of the deal. Ultimately the Agreed Framework fell apart in 2003 and KEDO—along with the EU—ceased occupying a significant place in hard security on the Korean peninsula. The follow-on Six Party Talks included the DPRK, the ROK, China, the US, Japan, and Russia in discussions about how to stop and roll back Pyongyang's nuclear weapons program. The EU was not offered a place in the talks, in significant part because the main actors—including the ROK—did not believe that the EU was a meaningful regional hard security actor.

Nonetheless, in the sphere of DPRK nuclear nonproliferation efforts, the EU remains engaged on three fronts in which cooperation with the ROK is crucial. First, and perhaps most visible, the EU and the ROK coordinate closely on diplomatic messaging (including at the UN, G20, etc.) that names-and-shames the DPRK for its illegal nuclear and missile proliferation activities.[21] Although this obviously falls far short of concrete compellent action, it does force Pyongyang to play diplomatic defense at the UN and regional fora, and serves to remind other states of their obligations to uphold sanctions against the DPRK. Second, and perhaps most important, the EU seriously enforces (to the best of its ability) compliance with international and augmented voluntary sanctions against Pyongyang in order to restrict its financing of and access to external inputs for the development of nuclear and missile programs.[22] This effort—both at the EU and member state level—is done in close consultation with the ROK, as well as with the US and Japan. The EU's own sanctions—in addition to those implemented on the basis of UN Security Council resolutions—have slowly but surely grown since 2016 to cover an important range of commodities, education and research exchange (especially in science), and professional training.[23] Companies in the EU are banned from investing in DPRK industries tied to conventional weapons, including metallurgy, chemicals, mining and refining, aviation, and information technology. Meanwhile several EU member states—Germany, France, Denmark, Italy, Spain, inter alia—are active in the Proliferation Security Initiative (PSI), which also includes the ROK.[24] This informal grouping of states cooperates to build capacity for maritime proliferation interdiction, contribute naval forces for interdiction missions, set standards and rules for PSI efforts, and supply experts in international law and international security for the PSI.[25]

Third, and perhaps somewhat underappreciated, the EU has had a role to play in human security provision—humanitarian aid and human rights protection—on the Korean peninsula, often in cooperation with the ROK. During the 1990s the EU—in coordination with the

ROK—donated 100+mnUSD in aid to the DPRK. On the human rights front, the EU (along with Japan) has, for eighteen consecutive years, co-sponsored UN General Assembly resolutions aiming at Pyongyang's human rights abuses, and the process leading up to this has often featured input and consultation from the ROK (although this was not the case during the ROK presidency of Moon Jae-in, who de-prioritized the issue in order to push forward peace dialogue with the DPRK).[26] In some years—including a re-start in 2022, following a four-year hiatus under Moon Jae-in—the ROK has co-sponsored the resolutions.[27]

The EU's efforts on the DPRK human rights front are increasingly seen as connected to the hard security situation on the Korean peninsula as well, which makes cooperation with the ROK even more important. First, the Kim Jong Un regime—in its current form—requires systematic civil, political, and human rights abuses to remain in power domestically, and the regime's continued existence—in its current bellicose form—is inherently an external-facing security risk (WMD development, destabilizing foreign relations, etc. Thus human rights abuses are linked to North Korean security threats by virtue of sustaining the Kim regime. Second, in order to provide resources for weapons development and the maintenance of a bellicose garrison state, the Kim regime's repressive apparatus supports systems of resource (food, medicine, mobility, housing, etc.) allocation that drive the mass population to acutely critical need. Third, in some cases, the North Korean population's human rights are directly violated through forced labor that serves as an input for weapons production.

Finally, a range of areas of EU-ROK security cooperation have either emerged recently or taken on increasingly more dramatic importance. The latter of these descriptions pertains to the environment and climate change, where the EU and the ROK have substantially augmented their cooperation. The most critical cooperative mechanism in this regard is the EU-ROK Green Partnership, which was signed in 2023 and identifies numerous areas for greater collaboration and exchange: achieving climate change goals through cooperation on carbon pricing, methane emissions, and climate finance; biodiversity loss, plastic reduction, and implementation of the Kunming-Montreal Global Biodiversity Framework; clean and fair energy transition (fossil fuel reduction, low-carbon hydrogen, batteries, and green mobility), carbon capture and storage; inter alia.[28]

This deepening EU-ROK cooperation on a human/soft security issue is complemented by growing coordination between Seoul and Brussels (and the EU capitals) on how to support Ukraine in its pushback against Russian aggression. In the first place, the ROK has become a useful supplier of arms into the European military market.[29] The biggest headlines followed a multi-billion-dollar deal to supply Poland with K2 tanks, K9 howitzers, fighter aircraft, and other weapons that can backfill supply that Warsaw drew down as a result of exporting arms to Ukraine. Finland has also purchased K9 howitzers in part to address added defense needs in light of Russian regional revisionism, and other EU member states are in play as purchasers as well, notably Romania and the Baltic states. However, these arms sales are not just opportunistic, taking advantage of strained US and European defense industry limitations; rather, they also mark the fact that the ROK has taken a clear stance—whether it be through President Yoon's visit to Kyiv, or at the UN and other multilateral fora, as well as bilaterally with the EU and member states—condemning Russian aggression against Ukraine and opting to support Ukraine (even if only indirectly[30] with lethal arms) by making it easier for Kyiv's EU partners to transfer arms because they can access re-supply via the ROK.

It is worth noting in this regard that the ROK and the EU are increasingly clear that threats to international order are no longer confined to regions or theaters, such as Europe or East Asia, but rather have a cross-regional character. The ROK's presence in European security issues—like Ukraine—requires working with EU partners, as well as with NATO insofar as the ROK has stepped up its global partnership with NATO through the advent of the Asia-Pacific Four grouping (ROK, Japan, New Zealand, Australia). Conversely, the EU sees converging cross-regional security threats and opportunities, and thus welcomes a greater ROK presence in Europe at the same time that Brussels and the EU capitals are trying to grow their presence in the Indo-Asia-Pacific, with the ROK as a privileged strategic partner.

Conclusion

The EU (and its member states) and the ROK have succeeded in launching and sustaining meaningful, sustainable security relations, with cooperation leading to a positive sum scenario in which both European and Indo-Asia-Pacific security are better off as a result of this cooperation. For the future, however, numerous challenges facing Europe and the ROK may diminish the overall power that both sides can bring to the table, in turn hampering their ability to provide support for each other's security issues in light of non-conventional threats, non-state actor malfeasance, or potential destabilizing state revisionism by China, Russia, or the DPRK.

For the ROK, the major short-term difficulty is still the DPRK, as Pyongyang's nuclear and conventional capabilities, posture, and hostile rhetoric complicate Seoul's capacity to aspire to grow its application of scarce capabilities to crisis management outside its near abroad. In the long term, one of the ROK's trickiest challenges is domestic, as politico-economic corruption and scandal indicate shortcomings in the ROK's foundational institutions. In addition, the country is hurtling toward a serious demographic crunch while also trying to adapt its economy to the imperatives of the new, creativity-driven globalization.

For the EU and its member states, there are numerous difficulties in augmenting (or even sustaining) its current contribution to East Asian security and order, and by extension to the security on an around the Korean peninsula. One difficulty is that Europe has complex, incoherent relations with China, which is variously considered a partner (on climate change), a competitor (in economics/trade), and a rival (in regards to a vision of the international order). As a result Europe has been cautious about using its sizeable economic strength to pressure Beijing into better, less destabilizing actions in East Asia, or to convince it to take a harder line toward the DPRK. The EU has adopted a more geopolitical stance, but business interests are still important in directing EU-China relations. Ultimately, the EU and its member states stand confronted with the same challenge as always: they have the diplomatic and economic strength to potentially to intervene—with strategic partners like the ROK—in selected Indo-Asia-Pacific security affairs, but the political will to do so is inconsistent, notably with respect to Beijing.

Notwithstanding that caveat, there remain opportunities for Europe to make contributions to security and order in East Asia in general and to the ROK in particular. As hinted at in concluding the above section, transatlantic security cooperation in and with Asia could mark a sea change in regional security. Brussels and Washington would potentially succeed in stabilizing security threats by linking Atlantic and Pacific security networks and building out patterns of collaboration between NATO and the AP4 countries. There is also a possibility (and perhaps even a necessity) for creating better space and cybersecurity cooperation between Europe and East Asian states such as the ROK (and Japan). Finally, although Pyongyang is a hard target, the EU could contribute to the slowing of Kim Jong-un's nuclear and missile programs by imposing sanctions ("secondary" sanctions) on more banks and financial institutions that play a role in connecting the DPRK's foreign exchange activities to its illegal weapons programs.

Endnote

1. European Commission (DG Trade). South Korea. European Commission. https://policy.trade.ec.europa.eu/eu-trade-relationships-country-and-region/countries-and-regions/south-korea_en; Eurostat. 2020. South Korea-EU trade in goods statistics. Eurostat. https://ec.europa.eu/eurostat/statistics-explained/index.php?title=South_Korea-EU_-_international_trade_in_goods_statistics&oldid=497225#EU-South_Korea_trade_by_type_of_goods
2. Sara Kim. 2023. "G7 summit, bilateral meetings highlight Yoon's diplomatic super week." *Korea Joongang Daily*. May 15. https://koreajoongangdaily.joins.com/2023/05/15/national/diplomacy/Korea-Yoon-Suk-Yeol-diplomacy/20230515175758177.html; Lee Haye-ah. 2023. "Full text of joint statement adopted at S Korea-European Union summit." Yonhap. May 22. https://en.yna.co.kr/view/AEN20230522008300315
3. Lee 2023, May 22; Lee Haye-ah. 2023. "Yoon to embark on trip to Indonesia, India to attend ASEAN, G20 summits." *Yonhap*. September 5. https://en.yna.co.kr/view/AEN20230905000900315
4. European Union External Action Service. 2021. "The European Union and the Republic of Korea." European Union External Action Service. https://www.eeas.europa.eu/south-korea/european-union-and-republic-korea_en?s=179#6356
5. Mason Richey and Leif-Eric Easley. 2022. "Russia Attacks and the International Order Strikes Back." *Journal of International Peacekeeping* 25/2: 195-203.
6. European Union External Action Service. 2016. A Global Strategy for the European Union's Foreign and Security Policy. European Union External Action Service. https://www.eeas.europa.eu/eeas/global-strategy-european-unions-foreign-and-security-policy_en; European Union External Action Service. 2021. EU Indo-Pacific Strategy. European Union External Action Service. https://www.eeas.europa.eu/eeas/eu-indo-pacific-strategy_en; European Union External Action Service. 2022. A Strategic Compass for Security and Defence. European Union External Action Service. https://www.eeas.europa.eu/sites/default/files/documents/strategic_compass_en3_web.pdf
7. Office of the President of the Republic of Korea. 2023. National Security Strategy: Global Pivotal State for Freedom, Peace, and Prosperity. file:///C:/Users/hufs/Downloads/230607_%EC%9C%A4%EC%84%9D%EC%97%B4%20%EC%A0%95%EB%B6%80%EC%9D%98%20%EA%B5%AD%EA%B0%80%EC%95%88%EB%B3%B4%EC%A0%84%EB%9E%B5(%EC%98%81%EB%AC%B8).pdf
8. European Union External Action Service. 2020. EU-Republic of Korea Strategic Partnership. European Union External Action Service. EU-Republic of Korea Strategic Partnership | EEAS (europa.eu)
9. Mason Richey and Thomas Christiansen. 2021. "Security Cooperation between the EU and South Korea." In *The European Union's Security Relations with Asian Partners* (Thomas Christiansen et al eds.). Springer Verlag.
10. Ibid.
11. European Union External Action Service. EU Naval Force Operation Atalanta. European Union External Action Service. https://eunavfor.eu/
12. Ibid.
13. NAVCENT Public Affairs (US Naval Forces Central Command). 2023. "Ships Supporting Two Multinational Anti-Piracy Task Forces Train Together in Gulf of Aden." Defense Visual Information Distribution Service. May 17. https://www.dvidshub.net/news/445173/ships-supporting-two-multinational-anti-piracy-task-forces-train-together-gulf-aden
14. Qatar News Agency. 2020. "South Korea to Send Naval Destroyer to Combat Piracy in Gulf of Aden." Qatar News Agency. June 1. https://www.qna.org.qa/en/News-Area/News/2019-08/13/south-korea-to-send-naval-destroyer-to-combat-piracy-in-gulf-of-aden

15. The Korea Herald. 2021. "British submarine arrives in Busan ahead of aircraft carrier's port call." *The Korea Herald.* August 21. https://www.koreaherald.com/view.php?ud=20210812000702; *Korea Times.* 2021. "German frigate Bayern visits Busan." Korea Times. December 2. https://www.koreatimes.co.kr/www/nation/2022/05/120_319889.html?tw; Michael Lee. 2023. "French minister meets with president, stress commitment to Indo-Pacific security." *The Korea Joongang Daily.* April 16. https://v.daum.net/v/HcNBtB5Jia

16. European Union External Action Service. 6th Annual EU-Republic of Korea Cyber Dialogue. European Union External Action Service; European Commission. 2023. Speech by Commissioner Breton on cybersecurity at the High-Level Conference on Cybersecurity in the Republic of Korea. European Union External Action Service. https://ec.europa.eu/commission/presscorner/detail/en/SPEECH_23_3661

17. European Union External Action Service. 2019. Enhancing Security Cooperation In and With Asia. European Union External Action Service. https://www.eeas.europa.eu/sites/default/files/factsheet_eu_asia_security_july_2019.pdf; European Union External Action Service. 2023. EU and Republic of Korea Digital Partnership: strengthening our economic resilience. European Union External Action Service. https://ec.europa.eu/commission/presscorner/detail/en/ip_23_3607

18. European Union External Action Service. 2021. Republic of Korea: Consultations on security and defense. European Union External Action Service. https://www.eeas.europa.eu/eeas/republic-korea-consultations-security-and-defence_en

19. European Commission. 1997. European Union joins North Korean nuclear security body. European Commission. https://cordis.europa.eu/article/id/9049-european-union-joins-north-korean-nuclear-security-body; NTI. 2009. KEDO: Korea Peninsula Development Organization. Nuclear Threat Initiative. https://www.nti.org/education-center/treaties-and-regimes/korean-peninsula-energy-development-organization-kedo/

20. Ibid. Ibid.

21. European Union External Action Service. 2023. Republic of Korea: 19th Joint Committee with the European Union takes place in Brussels. European Union External Action Service. March 10. https://www.eeas.europa.eu/eeas/republic-korea-19th-joint-committee-european-union-takes-place-brussels_en

22. European Council. 2023. EU restrictive measures against North Korea. https://www.consilium.europa.eu/en/policies/sanctions/history-north-korea/

23. Numerous DPRK individuals and entities are also sanctioned (with travel bans and asset freezes).

24. PSI (Proliferation Security Initiative). PSI. https://www.psi-online.info/

25. Ibid.

26. Yonhap News Agency. 2022. "UN General Assembly passes N. Korean human rights resolution for 18th consecutive year." *Yonhap News Agency.* Dec. 16. https://en.yna.co.kr/view/AEN20221216001100325;

27. Yonhap New Agency. 2023. "S. Korea seeks formal consultation with US, EU on NK human rights." *Yonhap News Agency.* January 15. https://en.yna.co.kr/view/AEN20230115001200325

28. European Commission. 2023. European Green Deal: EU and Republic of Korea launch Green Partnership to deepen cooperation on climate action, clean energy and environmental protection. European Commission. May 22. https://ec.europa.eu/commission/presscorner/detail/en/ip_23_2816

29. Jens Kastner. 2022. "South Korean arms find interest in Europe amid Ukraine war." *Nikkei Asia.* September 9. https://asia.nikkei.com/Business/Business-Spotlight/South-Korean-arms-find-interest-in-Europe-amid-Ukraine-war; Joyce Lee and Josh Smith. 2023. "Insight: inside South Korea's race to become one of the world's biggest arms dealers." *Reuters.* May 29. https://www.reuters.com/business/aerospace-defense/inside-south-koreas-race-become-one-worlds-biggest-arms-dealers-2023-05-29/

30. The ROK has supplied Ukraine with billions of dollars in direct non-lethal aid.

The EU-Korean Strategic partnership[1]

LEE MOOSUNG

Introduction

When the US-China rivalry began to surface, the EU and Korea could not remain isolated from these new geostrategic dynamics. Given their political, economic, and military interests closely related to the positions and responses of these regional and global hegemonic powers, they are also forced to decide how to cope with it both individually and collectively. Against this backdrop, this paper argues that there is a leeway to overcome or at least circumvent the current dilemma. Given the normative nature of the EU's foreign policy and its corresponding methodology, and its political power inducing South Korea's support as a like-minded partner, the paper contends that the EU-Korean strategic partnership could be another example of self-fulfilling prophecy, as it would provide a social space where both parties may not be bounded by the US-China rivalry, but by their collectively shared ideas, values, and norms, even when they are prompted to present their own strategies towards the Indo-Pacific. The contention of the paper will thus be testified by examining the normative nature of the EU, the underpinning frameworks of the EU-Korea strategic partnership, and the individual strategies of these partners towards the Indo-Pacific.

With territorial disputes revolving around the South China Sea straining China's relations with its adjacent countries,[2] and when some of the parties in conflict increasingly rely on the US to ensure their territorial integrity, the US-China rivalry began to surface. Such a strategic competition now leads to speculation about whether a new Cold War is in the offing. Such a concern is not groundless, but rather based on empirical reality, not least when some of the regional countries are increasingly facing a new, but difficult, question of whose side they have to take.

The frontlines of the US-China rivalry are now being extended, and the EU and Korea cannot remain isolated from these new geostrategic dynamics.[3] They appear to be entrapped in this dilemmatic situation, when they also find it increasingly difficult to make their strategic and normative choices. Given their political, economic, and military interests closely related to the positions and responses of these regional and global hegemonic powers,[4] they are also forced to decide how to cope with it both individually and collectively.

Despite such a growing concern and its geopolitical implications due to the intensifying US-China competition, this paper argues that there is leeway to overcome or at least circumvent the current dilemma. Given the normative nature of the EU's foreign policy and its corresponding methodology, and its political power inducing South Korea's support as a like-minded partner, the paper contends that the EU-Korean strategic partnership could be another example of self-fulfilling prophecy. Providing a social space where both parties may not be bounded by the US-China rivalry, but by their collectively shared ideas, values, and norms, the strategic partnership is also likely to follow the same trajectory as it used to, even against the backdrop of the Indo-Pacific that has emerged as a new context intensifying the US-China rivalry, and presenting new kinds of challenges.

To achieve this objective, we will first discuss how to examine the political and policy implications of the normative power Europe discourse for the future development of the strategic partnership, positing it as a foreign policy instrument reflexively representing its self.[5] In addition, both strategic and normative considerations of Korea will also be scrutinized, asking whether it would remain as a like-minded partner, meeting the original normative objectives of the strategic partnership, or whether it would deviate from its hitherto trajectory. It is through these discussions that we envisage the future trajectory of the EU-Korea partnership, explore whether it will be a new test bed to reiterate the EU's strategic partnership with Korea as different not only in its focus and the methods, and, last but not least, discuss its political implications when it is compared with an alliance or similar sort of partnership but bounded by state-centricity.

The next section, Section Two, examines the theoretical framework, specifically introducing some of the extant debates concerning the normative power Europe discourse, and then the ways the strategic partnership would help consolidate its self-identity. Section Three unpacks the basic frameworks underpinning the EU-Korea strategic partnership, discussing how they make their political, economic and security cooperation feasible. Section Four delves into the development of geostrategic environment, when the Indo-Pacific emerges as a new focal point of geostrategic competition, and thus presents new tasks and challenges both the parties also have to cope with. The last section summaries the findings of the paper with some further implications.

The EU, its self, and the strategic partnership

Realists assert that the identity of (state) agent is dependent on material interests, and exogenous to the system affecting its behavior.[6] Yet constructivists interpreting their relationship suggest a different epistemological position. As opposed to the realist assumption, they would instead argue that interests are dependent on identities, and that identities, as distinct phenomena, are core in explaining action, assuming that they are either a motivation phenomenon or a cognitive and structural one.[7]

The assumption that the identity of actors is endogenous to social interaction also helps make sense of the EU's idiosyncratic identity formation process. Of a wealth of studies attempting to define the EU, the first is to conceptualize the EU as a civilian power. The civilian power conception was first suggested to highlight the civilian nature of the Community in both its internal governance and external relations. The reliance more on diplomacy, economic, and political incentives than on military forces was believed to have made the EC a different power.[8] Yet despite such an initial effort to its conceptualization, Bull, among others, questioned its civilian power identity, pointing to the return to power politics of the 1980s, and the corresponding limitation of the Community being agentic in international affairs. He thus argued that the Community would be at best an aggregation of states, that its scope of power and influence would at most be dependent on the lowest common denominator of bargaining among the member states, and that its actorness, be it civilian or else, is likely to be undermined over time.[9]

As opposed to the account of Bull, and also in comparison with the civilian power concept of Duchêne, Manners characterized the EU as a normative power. Asking whether or not the EU has the ability to conceptualize what is normal in world politics, he has fueled the discussion on the normative power Europe discourse. One of his points is that its hybrid polity that incorporates both supranational and international forms of governance has enabled the EU to overcome the statist ontology in world politics, make itself a novel kind of actor, and prescribe world politics away from the bounded expectations of state-centricity.[10]

When the concept of normative power Europe was first proposed, the main concern and focus was how to unearth its ontological aspect: it was not its performative power as an agent. Yet there soon followed ensuing debates that went beyond the hitherto discourse concerning the political effects of normative power EU. Diez, for example, revisited the discourse of a normative power EU. Highlighting its tendency to turn third parties into significant 'others', he paid particular attention to its self-reflexive attempt to essentialize its present self and its past other, whose history was largely marked by conflictive inter-state relations.[11]

As long as states are the only and most important unitary actors in international politics, inter-state conflicts are inevitable, and the EU is also a victim of such an international system.

To transcend the conflictive nature of international relations, the way the EU is structured and governed is an inevitable consequence. And that is why its basis norms, such as promoting human rights, respecting the rules of law, and practicing a functioning market economic system and liberal democracy, have also been embodied, for example, as Copenhagen criteria: they have in effect helped make its own members continuously aware of the significance of the historical and political legacy, and also oblige new members to accommodate them as preconditions for their EU membership.

The discussion on the performative aspect of the EU as a normative power has been further refined by an argument more specifically stressing its ethical traits. According to this view, by virtue of the principles of living by example, by duty of its actions in being reasonable, and by consequence of its impact on doing least harm, the EU is also able to maintain its biographical narrative as a normative power, and some of the substantive principles that constitute its self-identity should thus be practiced both coherently and consistently.[12]

As the identity of the EU is constructed, not given, so is the strategic partnership as a context in which its identity is represented and consolidated. This is largely because the EU-Korean strategic partnership is posited to institutionally help the Union and Korea project and enforce formally or informally the values they share.[13] If so, it seems necessary to investigate the EU's normative identity formation process in light of the contextual effects to be created by the strategic partnership as a next step.

There are two ways to discuss the self-identification process. One is based on the neorealist penchant for systemic theory, the other is the holistic one that adopts a more encompassing perspective incorporating domestic and international phenomena.[14] Notwithstanding such a difference, the focus of the paper lies in the systemic perspective, positing the strategic partnership as a social space where we can discuss the constitutive role of social interaction and the political meanings attached. That is, when the partnership creates an institutional structure constituting states as legitimate actors, their foreign policy practices are constructed in a way conducive to the reproduction of such structures and vice versa. If there exists such a co-constitutive process that is reducible to actors acting in line with self-identity, the ensuing question is how the partnership acts in a holistic way as a structure, and how the role to be played in building identity would have its own relevancy.

As Michalski and Pan rightly argue, the roles to be played within a particular context are indicative of the way actors assert their international identities, while enhancing their status and prestige as global actors.[15] It is this assumption that enables us to incorporate the contextual effects resulting from the US-China rivalry in the parameters of discussion, and analyze its likely impact on the EU-Korean strategic partnership in the Indo-Pacific. The examination of such a re-configured strategic environment may well demonstrate how their social interactions develop, befitting their normative identity, as well as whether and how the original objectives of the strategic partnership would be met or challenged.

Keeping these theoretical implications in mind, we will from now on turn to the question of how the EU-Korean strategic partnership in which the EU's self-identity as a different kind of actor is also tested is to be reflexively represented. This reflexive representation undoubtedly helps figure out the differences in terms of the ways the strategic partnership would cope with the current context of US-China rivalry, the degree of inclusiveness when both the EU and Korea set their agendas, and the normative nature of the methodology employed for its implementation.

To achieve this objective, three areas have to be focused on. The first is the economic cooperation embedded in the free trade agreement context. The second is the political cooperation. How their political cooperation evolves is thus subject to further investigation, when traditional and untraditional forms of security are important political agendas. Last but not least, security cooperation, albeit seldom, but along with the two above mentioned fields, is to be explored, with a particular emphasis on the extent and the scope of their security cooperation.

The basic frameworks of the EU-Korea strategic partnership

The bilateral relationship between the EU and Korea was upgraded to a strategic partnership in 2009. Its formal announcement in October 2010 made the strategic partnership the main framework for the bilateral economic, political, and security cooperation.

Of the diverse forms of cooperation, the economic cooperation seems to be the most remarkable. Despite some controversies as to whether the FTA is an integral part of the partnership, it is hard to deny that the FTA has underpinned the EU-Korea economic relationship, a sort of end result of the EU taking a more aggressive attitude towards outsiders by the adoption of the Global Europe communication in 2006.[16] Agreed in 2010, coming into force in 2011, the FTA between the EU and Korea has undoubtedly laid the institutional ground for mutually-reinforcing cooperation.

Tackling strategic trade barriers in East Asia based on its FTA with Korea, the EU has made a more aggressive advancement into the local markets. Korea has also benefited a lot. For example, the FTA has made its entry into the EU market easier than before. It has also allowed it to benefit from participating and creating a global level playing field. This is a so-called "Brussels effect" of rule and standard setting.[17] In addition, they both also see some political benefits. The economic cooperation initially started between the EU and Korea also creates a spillover effect, leading to adjacent countries in the region taking a similar step.[18] The Economic Partnership Agreement between the EU and Japan might be a case in point, as the latter appears to have been either forced or encouraged to take a similar footstep, acknowledging it beneficial for its economic prosperity. If such a functional spillover effect first starts among like-minded countries, and then spills over to other countries in competition, if not, in conflict, peaceful co-existence among adjacent countries is not hard to envisage, but creates a new norm that the EU and Korea could also make their own contributions.

There are also some institutional attempts and corresponding actions for bilateral political cooperation. It is largely based on the framework agreement, a successor of the 1986 Framework Agreement for Trade and Cooperation. As a comprehensive legal framework, the agreement adopted in 2006 has laid the groundwork for political cooperation, enabling both parties to address a wide range of issues.[19] They include promoting human rights, free markets, and multilateralism, boosting cooperation in science and technology, education, climate change, and development assistance. And cooperating to address such a wide range of issues of global concerns has also led both the EU and Korea to engage in regional and global issues more proactively.[20] So, in this post-Cold War era where discussions on new attention to address non-traditional security issues are needed, and these activities are accepted as part of world politics, and therefore normal, the active responses from the EU and Korea to these new challenges would make their partnership more normative, as all this should anyway be measured by their ability to conceptualize what is normal in world politics.

The cooperation for crisis management operations is the result of the separate Framework Agreement, but it still allows the EU and Korea to extend their interests beyond the political and economic realms.[21] The Crisis Management Participation Agreement, a legal foundation for the bilateral security cooperation, has also made Korea's cooperation in the EU-led crisis management operations legitimate. Although there is only one example relevant in this context, the bilateral cooperation in fighting against maritime piracy, protecting vessels, and monitoring fishing activities off the coast of Somalia nonetheless, all suggests the potential of their bilateral security cooperation down the road.[22] In addition, the joint military mission involving both the EU and Korean naval forces could also indicate their will and commitment to ensure the hard security of regional and global concerns in a normative way: in fact, their focus has been how to foster the culture of prevention, and this has been well represented in their past efforts to emphasize peace keeping operations, humanitarian operations, and the like.[23]

It is now time for the EU and Korea strategic partnership to have just turned the corner of its 10th anniversary, but there are also some tasks and challenges lying ahead, due to the intensification of the US-China rivalry. Under these circumstances, whether the EU and Korea remain committed to the primary objective of their partnership has important political and normative implications. This, more specifically, would once again summon the questions of whether and to what extent the EU is able to ensure political stability of the region, strengthen its economic interests, and maintain the normative inclination of their strategic partnership. If so, a more specific inquiry of their individual strategy towards the Indo-Pacific seems to be compelling.

Indo-Pacific Strategies

The Indo-Pacific Partnership originated from the "Free and Open Indo-Pacific concept rolled out by the Trump administration in late 2017. It is this concept that has since then developed an overarching logic governing the relationship between the US and its allies, and also prompted them to cooperate to strengthen regional institutions and rule-based international orders. Yet there is as much doubt as to whether the Indo-Pacific strategies are to counter "Chinese disruption and American dysfunction".[24] In addition, if it is also understood as an alternative middle-power coalition aiming to balance a rising China, both the EU and Korea cannot stay aloof, but have been forced to determine their own positions.

The Korean side

As opposed to the previous government which somewhat remained cautious and lukewarm towards the Indo-Pacific, the Yoon government made clear its stand, stepping out of its predecessor's strategic ambiguity. Making the Indo-Pacific one of its foreign policy priorities, the Yoon government has built its national strategy toward the region, with the publication of "Strategy for a Free, Peaceful, and Prosperous Indo-Pacific region."[25] And the three principles of inclusiveness, trust, and reciprocity do well to represent South Korea's commitment.[26]

The strategy paper of Korea being examined, there appears to be three overarching pillars, reflecting all the nine core lines of effort for its Indo-Pacific strategy. The first pillar underscores the commitment of Korea to upholding and diffusing universal values and norms. So, its first emphasis is to realize the vision of a free Indo-Pacific, while helping build regional order based on norms and values. A rules-based approach being a precondition for the stability and prosperity of the Indo-Pacific region, Korea also finds it imperative to stand with international society and curb actions threatening universal norms and values. In addition, as a model democracy, Korea also made it clear that it would remain committed to promoting freedom, democracy, the rule of law, and human rights.

The second pillar is about the methods to enhance regional security. Although Korea's previous government appears to have refrained from either supporting or participating in small-scale and multilateral security cooperation,[27] the Yoon government took a different position. Reflecting the change of its attitude and underscoring its commitment to the security area, Korea's strategic paper selects security issues as one of its key priorities with a particular emphasis on its non-proliferation and counterterrorism efforts. Given the security environment revolving around the Korean peninsula, and Korea's extant effort for non-proliferation anddisarmament, it seems inevitably that it focuses on these issues as part of its efforts to enhance regional security. Moreover, it also maintains that this issue cannot be solved by Korea alone, but requires pan-regional cooperation.

On top of its unambiguous commitment to hard security issues, new security threats have also been mentioned as its key priorities. To enhance its counter-terrorism capacities, measured by its fight against money laundering, terrorist financing, and proliferation financing, as well as its commitment to space security, Korea also elevates its regional cooperation beyond the state level, and makes the dimension of cooperation more inclusive and comprehensive.

Yet the scope of security issues Korea attempts to address has become wider with both traditional and non-traditional security included.[28] For a comprehensive security cooperation, its focus has also been placed on the question of how to cope with a wide range of non-security issues, ranging from maritime security aiming at the protection of sea lanes, counter-piracy, and safety of navigation, to cyber and health security.

In addition, building economic security networks is also one of its top policy priorities, not least when the Indo-Pacific is home to the world's largest and fastiest-growing economies, accounting for about 62 percent of global GDP in 2020.[29] Thus it seeks to contribute to the building of economic networks revolving around the Indo-Pacific by helping ensure stable and resilient supply chain management, as well as free trade and rule-based economic order.

The third pillar is concerned with cooperation on the functional issue. To strengthen cooperation in critical domains of science and technology and close the digital gap, Korea seeks to facilitate regional cooperation in critical domains of science and technology, including semiconductors, artificial intelligence, quantum science, advanced biology, next-generation telecommunications, and space. In addition, Korea also made its commitment to supporting the region's achievement of sustainable development goals, proactively responding to climate change, energy transition, and energy, and also joining regional efforts to ensure better resilience to transnational challenges.

The fourth pillar concentrates on engaging in "contributive diplomacy" through tailored development cooperation partnerships. Commensurate with its economic stature, and strengthening the foundation for realizing peace and prosperity in the Indo-Pacific region, Korea expresses its intention to share the experiences and knowledge accumulated thus far, and help meet the aspirations of the countries in the region to achieve their national development and economic growth. As a method for this object, it also announced that it would help foster the mutual understanding and exchanges, specifically via exchanges between youths, and also through cultural exchange. By doing so, it seeks to make effective and attractive ways to connect youths and cultivate shared historical awareness in the Indo-Pacific region. And public diplomacy initiatives that will particularly focus on the digital and cultural domains where Korea has a competitive edge could be understood in a similar context.

The EU side

Just as South Korea makes its position towards the Indo-Pacific much clearer than before, the EU has also made its own attitude, different from its initial reluctance. Based on the Council Conclusion that guides its Indo-Pacific strategy, the EU aims to make the Indo-Pacific region stable, secure, and prosperous. Promoting democracy, the rule of law, human rights, and international law, it demonstrates its own intention to actively engage in a wide range of issues ranging from development to the health system.[30] In addition, well aware of intense geopolitical competition in the Indo-Pacific, which in turn increases tensions on trade, supply chains, and the like, it also seeks to make its approach and engagement based on a long-term perspective and a rule-based approach.

There are five ways to reinforce the EU's strategic focus, presence, and actions in the region.[31] They are also categorized by three pillars, depending on the themes in focus and methodologies employed. The first pillar concerns which partners to work with. The partnership the EU first seeks to pursue are regional actors in the Indo-Pacific. Of others, the ASEAN-led regional architectures are cited as a core framework for their close partnership, assuming they are conducive to the development of a coherent overall approach and the establishment of its political partnership in the Pacific Ocean. It is such partnerships that will help the EU, as well as its core member states, like France and Germany, to diversify their ties beyond China.[32]

The EU's commitment to supporting the international community's global agenda comes as the next step. It therefore appears legitimate for the EU to promote human rights, sustainable management of natural resources, and ocean governance, while helping reduce disaster risk exacerbated by climate change and prioritizing the health sector, a crucial area for future cooperation.

The second pillar covers the issues to be addressed. First, the main concern of the EU is to advance the economic agenda of global and regional concerns and protect supply chains. There are two specific ways to achieve this objective. One is to promote key EU economic interests, principles, and objectives aiming to ensure a strong, balanced, and inclusive socio-economic recovery and growth, facilitate sound macroeconomic policies, and help institutional capacity building as well as regional integration. The other is to strengthen its strategic trade position and level the playing field in the Indo-Pacific.

In addition, the EU also seeks to play its own role in the area of security and defense. There are three specific ways to achieve this objective. Above all, we can see the explicit intention of the EU to proactively respond to challenges to international security, such as maritime security, malicious cyber activities, disinformation, terrorism, violent extremism, and hybrid threats. On top of this, there is a strong will on the part of the EU to cope with conventional security threats associated with nuclear proliferation, arms race, and the dual use of technological exports. Moreover, it also made it clear that it will help counter acts of piracy and armed robbery as a form of maritime security, while simultaneously assessing the opportunity to establish a so-called Maritime Aeas of interest in the Indo-Pacific.

The third pillar is related to the methods for addressing the issues mentioned above. For this objective, the EU argues that a high quality of connectivity needs to be ensured in order to make sure diverse dimensions of connectivity, such as digital, transport, energy, and human, that they also have to be consistent with international norms and standards, and that their connectivity priorities and actions are also pursued in a level-playing field. Last but not least, there is an EU attempt to enhance cooperation in higher education, science, and technology with like-minded partners by making digital governance through more ambitious global standards and regulatory approaches which include artificial intelligence, in line with international law, including EU values and principles on privacy, data protection, and security with the support of open trade and cross-border data flows. All this is going to pave the way for the advancement of the collaboration in the fields of research, innovation, and digitalization.

Conclusion

The mutual interests of the EU and Korea in the Indo-Pacific will surely create a window of new opportunity to strengthen their strategic partnership. Instead of being bound by the U.S.-China rivalry, they are highly likely to develop their future partnership, making it more inclusive and normative in terms of issues to be addressed and methods employed. In addition, what makes such a scenario a possibility is largely because of their commitment embodied in their strategic paper that they will practice some of the new basic principles of global politics such as a rule-base international order, the role of multilateralism and democracy in their approach towards the region.[33]

Under these circumstances, it has been found that they will focus on areas, which are considered new policy priorities in this post-Cold War era. That is why they have, and will also, focus on trade issues, connecting them with the concept of economic security. Instead of solely focusing on their self-interests, they made it clear that they would act in such a way as to meet and consolidate a liberal international order. Their cooperation in the area of non-traditional agendas is also likely to make the normative feature of their partnership further reinforced. Their growing interests and likely cooperation in green transition, digital governance and partnerships, and connectivity are some of its glaring examples. Last but not least, their previous cooperation of counter-piracy exercises off the coast of Somalia is a good example in envisaging how Korea and the EU would act, if they faceed similar kinds of security threats near the waters of the Indo-Pacific. This is how both the EU, and its member states, such as France, Germany, and the Netherlands, will react, if they are confronted with similar challenges.[34] If so, there is no reason for Korea to follow suit, as it is its staunch ally as shown by its participation in the EU's crisis management operations.

While both the EU and Korea will surely cooperate in a variety of areas, with their normative commitment in mind, this does not necessarily mean that they will also remain immune to the spectre of power politics. Given their close economic and political relations both with the US and China, and given that they are also not free from their geostrategic influence, they also have to come up with their own ways of coping with this transformational geostrategic environment. How to strike a balance between material interests and normative commitment and how to strike a diplomatic balance when they purse certain policies (if this would unexpectedly affect their relations with either of these superpowers) thus remain as lingering questions to be carefully approached.

Despite such a concern, however, the future development of the EU-Korea strategic partnership is not very different from the way it used to be. This is not groundless at all, not least when we take into account the normative identity of the EU and the like-minded commitment from Korea, which has indeed underpinned the overall governance of their strategic partnership. If so, the initial suggestion of whether the future trajectory of the EU-Korea strategic partnership would meet its normative objectives even amid the intensifying US-China rivalry would not shoot wide of the mark.

References

Ballbach, Eric J., "South Korea's Evolving Indo-Pacific StrategyOpportunities and challenges for cooperation with the EU". SWP Research Paper. No. 2/2023, pp. 1-37.

Bull, Hedley. "Civilian Power Europe: A Contradiction in Terms?". Journal of Common Market Studies. Vol. 21. No. 2 (1982), pp. 149-170.

Buzan, Barry, Ole Wæver, and Jaap De Wilde (1998). Security: A new framework for analysis. Lynne Rienner Publishers.

Casarini, Nicola. "Rising to the Challenge: Europe's Security Policy in East Asia amid US-China Rivalry". The International Spectator. Vol. 55. No. 1 (2020). pp 78-92.

Diez, Thomas. "Constructing the Self and Changing Others: Reconsidering Normative Power Europe'". Millennium. Vol. 33. No. 3 (2005). Pp. 613-636.

Duchêne, François. "Europe's Role in World Peace". Mayne, Richard (ed.). Europe Tomorrow: Sixteen Europeans Look Ahead. London: Fontana, 1972, pp. 32-47.

Council of the European Union. "EU Strategy for cooperation in the Indo-Pacific". Council Conclusion (16 April 2021).

European Commission. "Global Europe: Competing in the World: A Contribution to the EU's Growth and Jobs Strategy". COM (2006) 567 final, European Commission, accessed May 1, 2023, https://eur-lex.europa.eu/LexUriServ/LexUriServ.do?uri=COM:2006:0567:FIN:en:PDF.

European Union. "FRAMEWORK AGREEMENT for Trade and Cooperation between the European Community and its Member States, on the one hand, and the Republic of Korea, on the other hand". Official Journal of the European Communities 44 English edition (March 30 2001).

European Union. "AGREEMENT between the European Union and the Republic of Korea establishing a framework for the participation of the Republic of Korea in European Union crisis management operations". Official journal of the European Union 57, English edition (June 5 2014).

Jun, Hae-won. "ROK and EU Crisis Management Operations as Global Security Partners (Politics / Security)". JPI Policy Forum 218 (June 2018), pp. 4-5.

Holslag, Jonathan "The Elusive Axis: Assessing the EU–China Strategic Partnership", Journal of Common Market Studies, Vol. 49, No. 2 (2011), pp. 293-313.

Kim, Jiye and Raswant, Arpit. "Australian perspective on engaging with South Korea in the Indo-Pacific". Asian Politics & Policy. (2022). vol. 15, No. 1, pp. 48-62.

Kim, Nam-Kook, and Jae-Seung Lee. "Conclusion: Future challenges in Korea-the EU relations." Fiori, Antonio, Casarini, Nicola, Pacheco, Pardo, Ramon, Kim, Nam-Kook and Lee, Jae-Seung (eds.). The Routledge Handbook of Europe–Korea Relations. Routledge, 2021, pp. 438-441.

Lee, Moosung. "The strategic partnership between the EU and Korea." Fiori, Antonio, Casarini, Nicola, Pacheco, Pardo, Ramon, Kim, Nam-Kook and Lee, Jae-Seung (eds.). The Routledge Handbook of Europe–Korea Relations. Routledge, 2021, pp. 233-242.

Medcalf, Roy. Contest for the Indo-Pacific: Why China Won't Map the Future. Melbourne: La Trobe University Press, 2020.

Manners, Ian. "Normative power Europe: a contradiction in terms?." Journal of common market studies. Vol. 40. No. 2 (2002), pp. 235-258.

Manners, Ian. "The normative ethics of the European Union". International affairs. Vol. 84, No. 1 (2008), pp. 45-60.

Michalski, Anna, and Zhongqi Pan. "Role dynamics in a structured relationship: the EU–China strategic partnership". Journal of Common Market Studies. Vol. 55. No. 3 (2017), pp. 11-627.

Mohan, Garima. "A European Strategy for the Indo-Pacific". The Washington Quarterly. Vol. 43. No. 4 (2020), pp. 171-185

Office of the President, Republic of Korea. "Strategy for a Free, Peaceful, and Prosperous Indo-Pacific Region" (28 December 2022)

https://www.president.go.kr/newsroom/ briefing/HC81lhZw.

Pardo, Ramon Pacheco Pardo, Linde Desmaele and Maximilian Ernst. "EU-ROK relations: Putting the Strategic Partnership to Work". KF-VUF Korea Chair Report.

Pardo, Ramon Pacheco. "South Korea's Indo-Pacific Strat-egy: The European Dimension". (Brussels School of Governance, 24 January 2023), https://csds.vub.be/south-koreas-indo-pacific-strategy-the-european-dimension.

Price, Richard, and Christian Reus-Smit. "Dangerous liaisons? Critical international theory and constructivism". European journal of international relations. Vol. 4. No. 3 (1998), pp. 267-269.

Reiterer, Michael. "The 10th anniversary of the EU-Korea Strategic partnership." VUB-KF Chair, Policy Brief. 2020/09.

Shambaugh, David. "U.S.-China Rivalry in Southeast Asia: Power Shift or Competitive Coexistence?". International Security. Vol. 42. No. 4 (Spring 2018), pp. 85-127.

Smith, Michael, and Huaixian Xie. "The European Union and China: The Logics of 'Strategic Partnership'". Journal of Contemporary European Research. Vol. 6. No. 4 (2010), pp. 432-448.

Wendt, Alexander (1994) "Collective Identity Formation and the International State", American Political Science Review, Vol. 88, No. 2,

Endnote

1. This paper is a revised and updated version of Moosung Lee (2023) "The EU-Korean Strategic partnership and the Indo-Pacific strategies", EU 연구, vol. 67, pp. 89-112.
2. David Shambaugh, "U.S.-China Rivalry in Southeast Asia: Power Shift or Competitive Coexistence?", *International Security*, Vol. 42, No. 4 (Spring 2018), pp. 85-127.
3. Nicola Casarini, "Rising to the Challenge: Europe's Security Policy in East Asia amid US-China Rivalry", *The International Spectator*, Vol. 55, No.1 (2020): pp. 78-92.
4. Nam-Kook Kim and Jae-Seung Lee, "Conclusion: Future challenges in Korea-the EU relations", Antonio Fiori, Nicola Casarini, Ramon Pacheco Pardo, Nam-Kook Kim, and Jae-Seung Lee (eds), *The Routledge Handbook of Europe–Korea Relations* (Routledge, 2021), pp. 438-441.
5. For further discussion about the normative nature of the EU-Korea strategic partnership, see Moosung Lee (2021). "The strategic partnership between the EU and Korea", Antonio Fiori, Nicola Casarini, Ramon Pacheco Pardo, Nam-Kook Kim, and Jae-Seung Lee (eds), *The Routledge Handbook of Europe–Korea Relations* (Routledge, 2021), pp. 233-242.
6. For the relationship between the material interest and self-identity, see Kenneth N Waltz, Kenneth, *Theory of international politics* (New York: Random House, 1979).
7. Alexander Went, "Collective Identity Formation and the International State", American Political Science Review, Vol. 88, No. 2 (1994), p. 385.
8. François Duchêne, (1972) 'Europe's Role in World Peace', in Richard Mayne (ed.) Europe Tomorrow: Sixteen Europeans Look Ahead (London: Fontana, 1972), pp. 32-47.
9. Hedley Bull, "Civilian Power Europe: A Contradiction in Terms?", *Journal of Common Market Studies*, Vol. 21, No. 2 (1982), pp. 149-170.
10. Ian Manners, Ian, "Normative power Europe: a contradiction in terms?", *Journal of common market studies*, Vol. 40, No. 2 (2002), pp. 235-258.
11. Thomas Diez, "Constructing the Self and Changing Others: Reconsidering Normative Power Europe'", *Millennium,* Vol. 33, No. 3 (2005), pp. 613-636.
12. Ian Manners, "The normative ethics of the European Union", *International affairs,* Vol. 84, No. 1 (2008), pp. 45-60.
13. Michael Smith and Xie Huaixian, "The European Union and China: The Logics of 'Strategic Partnership'", *Journal of Contemporary European Research,* Vol. 6, No. 4 (2010), p. 435.
14. For further discussion, see Richard Price and Christian Reus-Smit, "Dangerous liaisons? Critical international theory and constructivism", European journal of international relations, Vol. 4, No. 3 (1998), pp. 267-269.
15. Anna Michalski and Zhongqi Pan, "Role dynamics in a structured relationship: the EU–China strategic partnership", *Journal of Common Market Studies,* Vol. 55, No. 3 (2017), p. 612.
16. European Commission, "Global Europe: Competing in the World: A Contribution to the EU's Growth and Jobs Strategy," COM (2006) 567 final, European Commission, accessed May 1, 2020, https://eur-lex.europa.eu/LexUriServ/LexUriServ.do?uri=COM:2006:0567:FIN:en:PDF. (accessed June 20 2023)
17. Michael Reiterer, "The 10th anniversary of the EU-Korea Strategic partnership." *VUB-KF Chair, Policy Brief* 2020/09 (2020), p. 10
18. Lee, Moosung, *op. cit.,* p. 236.
19. European Union, "FRAMEWORK AGREEMENT for Trade and Cooperation between the European Community

and its Member States, on the one hand, and the Republic of Korea, on the other hand," *Official Journal of the European Communities* 44 English edition (March 30 2001), p. 46

20. Jonathan Holslag, "The Elusive Axis: Assessing the EU–China Strategic Partnership", *Journal of Common Market Studies*, Vol 49, No. 2 (2011) p. 295.
21. European Union, "AGREEMENT between the European Union and the Republic of Korea establishing a framework for the participation of the Republic of Korea in European Union crisis management operations", *Official journal of the European Union* 57, English edition (June 5 2014), p. 3
22. Ramon Pacheco Pardo, Linde Desmaele and Maximilian Ernst, "EU-ROK relations: Putting the Strategic Partnership to Work", *KF-VUF Korea Chair Report*, p. 5.
23. Hae-won Jun, "ROK and EU Crisis Management Operations as Global Security Partners (Politics / Security)", *JPI Policy Forum* 218 (June 2018), pp. 4-5.
24. Rory Medcalf, *Contest for the Indo-Pacific: Why China Won't Map the Future* (Melbourne: La Trobe University Press, 2020).
25. Office of the President, Republic of Korea, "Strategy for a Free, Peaceful, and Prosperous Indo-Pacific Region" (28 December 2022), https://www.president.go.kr/newsroom/ briefing/HC81lhZw (accessed May 1 2023).
26. Ibid., pp. 23-41
27. Jiye Kim and Arpit Raswant, "Australian perspective on engaging with South Korea in the Indo-Pacific", *Asian Politics & Policy*, vol. 15 (2022), p. 56.
28. For more discussion, see Barry Buzan, Ole Wæver and Jaap De Wilde, *Security: A new framework for analysis.* (Lynne Rienner Publishers, 1998).
29. Garima Mohan, "A European strategy for the Indo-Pacific", *The Washington Quarterly*, vol. 43, no. 4 (2020), p. 174.
30. Council of the European Union, "EU Strategy for cooperation in the Indo-Pacific", Council Conclusion (16 April 2021). (accessed June 1 2023)
31. *Ibid.*, pp. 3-10.
32. Garima Mohan, *op. cit.*, p. 171
33. Eric J. Ballbach, "South Korea's Evolving Indo-Pacific Strategy Opportunities and challenges for cooperation with the EU", *SWP Research Paper*, No. 2/2023, (2023) pp. 1-37.
34. Ramon Pacheco Pardo, "South Korea's Indo-Pacific Strategy: The European Dimension," (Brussels School of Governance, 24 January 2023), https://csds.vub.be/south-koreas-indo-pacific-strategy-the-european-dimension (accessed June 20 2023).

EU and the Korean Peninsula

NICOLA CASARINI

Introduction

The European Union (EU) has contributed to peace and security on the Korean Peninsula since the early 1990s, following the end of the Cold War which opened up new possibilities for ROK-EU cooperation. On October 28, 1996, the two sides adopted the EU-Korea Framework Agreement and the 'Joint Declaration on the Political Dialogue,' transforming their relationship into a comprehensive cooperation system encompassing all major policy areas.

The entry into force of the Treaty of Lisbon on December 1, 2009 gave the EU new foreign policy instruments and established the European External Action Service – Europe's diplomatic service. In South Korea, democracy became firmly established with progressive presidents – Kim Dae-jung and Roh Moo-hyun – replaced by Lee Myung-bak, a conservative president committed to increasing South Korea's visibility and influence in the global scene. These developments led the EU and South Korea to upgrade their ties to a strategic partnership in 2010.

A Framework Agreement covering political cooperation entered into force in 2014, allowing the ROK and the EU to establish or reinforce a host of bilateral dialogues on a wide range of issues, in particular in the areas of traditional security threats – such as non-proliferation and disarmament – as well as non-traditional security issues such as cybersecurity,[1] providing the two sides with a legal and more solid foundation upon which to further their cooperation on the Korean Peninsula.[2]

This chapter examines Europe's role in contributing to Korean security, including the promotion of inter-Korean relations and of multilateral dialogue mechanisms to deal with North Korea's nuclear and missile threats, as well as EU support for Seoul's initiatives aimed at peace and security in North East Asia. The first part examines the development of the EU's strategy towards the Korean Peninsula and its distinctiveness compared to the United States, South Korea's most important ally. The second part explores three cases in which the EU and the ROK have sought to cooperate to advance dialogue and trust-building on the Korean Peninsula. They are: (i) the 'Sunshine Policy' in its various versions; (ii) the process of ROK-China-Japan trilateral cooperation; (iii) the Six Party Talks.

It is argued that the EU has proved to be: (i) an independent variable for peace support on the Korean Peninsula, only marginally influenceable by Washington when it comes to supporting trust-building between the South and the North; (ii) an asset for those ROK policymakers – be they progressive or conservative – committed to promoting dialogue and reconciliation with the North and to creating a cooperative environment among North East Asian nations.

EU strategy towards the Korean Peninsula

A distinctive EU strategy towards the Korean Peninsula began to emerge only in the mid-1990s, following recognition that security developments in the region would have an impact on Europe's prosperity. Since the early 1990s, Asian markets have become increasingly important for the Union's global competitiveness and socio-economic welfare position. In 1994, the European Commission issued the document: *Towards a New Asia Strategy*,[3] followed in 2001 by *Europe and Asia: Framework for an Enhanced Partnership*,[4] which argued that the prosperity of Europe may be jeopardized by the deterioration of the security environment in the Asian region and that any instability on the Korean Peninsula would have a bearing on the EU.

The first element of the EU's strategy towards the Korean Peninsula is thus the promotion of Europe's economic interests in the region. For instance, Kim Dae-jung's Sunshine Policy was studied carefully by a select group of EU policymakers in Brussels and other European capitals since Seoul's changing attitude towards the North could have significant implications for the emerging EU's Asia strategy and for advancing Europe's economic interests in an area of the world that had become crucial for Europe's growth prospects. While US economic relations with the DPRK did not change and remained at a very low level, mainly confined to humanitarian aid, the EU seized the opportunity of Kim Dae-jung's engagement policy with the North to boost commercial ties with the ROK and the DPRK. The EU had prepared a package of financial incentives which included targeted investments in some of the areas for cooperation flashed out by Kim's idea of the 'South-North economic community'. South Korea's Sunshine Policy was perceived in Europe as a possibility to foster commercial ties with the two Koreas without, however, having to commit to regional security which was left to the care of the US.[5]

A second element of the EU's strategy towards the Korean Peninsula is support for diplomacy and multilateral security initiatives. This includes an implicit support for the US system of alliances, given Europe's inability to deploy military assets in the region – but also the backing of multilateral initiatives such as the Six Party Talks as well as initiatives developed outside Washington's reach, such as the process of Trilateral Cooperation among South Korea-China-Japan.

Europe's support for multilateral initiatives aimed at addressing Korean security has taken different forms, including political declarations and financial backing. For instance, at the ASEM-3 in Seoul in 2000, both the EU and Asian nations stated their explicit concerns regarding the security situation on the Korean Peninsula, issuing the Seoul Declaration for Peace on the Korean Peninsula in which they supported implementation of the South-North Joint Declaration, including humanitarian issues.

A third element of the EU's strategy has been added in the last few years in the form of upgraded security cooperation with like-minded countries, a stance made clear by Federica Mogherini in her speech at the Shangri-La Dialogue in Singapore on June 1, 2019. Mogherini was at the time the Union's High Representative for Foreign Affairs and Security Policy, and her speech identified Korean security as a top priority for EU security policy in East Asia.

In May 2018, the EU issued the document: *Enhanced EU security cooperation in and with Asia* committing to explore possibilities to deepen security cooperation with its Asian strategic partners in areas such as maritime security, cybersecurity, counter-terrorism, hybrid threats, conflict prevention, and the development of regional cooperative orders.[6] Following up on this, the EEAS and the European Commission launched a pilot project in December 2018 to support tailor-made security cooperation with an initial set of five countries: India, Indonesia, Japan, the Republic of Korea, and Vietnam, with particular focus in four areas: maritime, counter-terrorism, crisis management (peacekeeping/CSDP), and cybersecurity.[7]

EU-US similarities and differences

The EU's strategy towards the Korean Peninsula presents many overlaps, but also significant differences, with that of the US. The first is that the focus of the EU in Northeast Asia is on 'cooperation, not competition' – an approach which contrasts to the US' strategy in the region which is increasingly framed in terms of competition with China. Recent EU policy documents emphasize the term 'cooperation' with all Asian nations – including Beijing –, in stark contrast to the US' National Security Strategy of the Trump and Biden administration which focuses on maintaining American primacy within the 'free and open' Indo Pacific.[8] In this context, the US' framing of the Korean Peninsula is one characterized by two competing camps opposing each other: China-Russia-North Korea versus US-Japan-South Korea – a framing which is in line with the last Strategic Concept of the North Atlantic Treaty Organization (NATO),[9] but not with recent documents on Asia by the EU.[10]

The second substantial difference has to do with Europe's persistent support for diplomatic initiatives aimed at inter-Korean dialogue and trust building, including an unwavering backing for all versions of South Korea's engagement policy with the North since the late 1990s – an approach that the EU has defended and acted upon even when aspects of it cut against the grain of US strategic interests in the region.

The third difference, which is possibly the most consequential one, is related to Europe's support for initiatives aimed at regional cooperation in North East Asia – an approach which contrasts to Washington's preference for bilateral relations and reliance on the US system of alliances. The EU is the international actor that has more consistently lent its backing to the process of trilateral cooperation based on the annual Trilateral Summit of the heads of state and government of China, Japan, and South Korea. The Trilateral Summit was first proposed by Seoul in 2004, as a meeting outside the framework of the ASEAN + 3 (the Association of Southeast Asian Nations plus China, Japan, and South Korea) – itself a by-product of the Asia–Europe Meeting (ASEM) – with the three major economies of North-East Asia having a separate forum to themselves.[11]

There has emerged a pattern when it comes to the EU's approach to the Korean Peninsula. When US-ROK relations worsen, often due to differences regarding North Korea and Washington's criticism of Seoul's efforts at reconciliation with Pyongyang and in promoting cooperative mechanisms with neighboring countries, including China, Europe remains – and even becomes more - active on the Korean peninsula. For instance, it was in the context of deteriorating US-ROK relations at the beginning of the 2000s that the EU would pursue more decisively its policy of full support for Kim Dae-jung's Sunshine Policy, beginning a trend that would characterize ROK-EU relations ever since.

Another example occurred throughout 2018-19, when the Trump administration was asking South Korea to withhold from improving inter-Korean relations until there was a proper US-North Korea negotiation process; and there was no indication that the US wanted to partake in a multilateral regime.[12] Yet, the EU consistently supported Moon's engagement policy with the North and backed the process of ROK-China-Japan trilateral cooperation as a further mechanism to deal with Pyongyang, notwithstanding the fact that the EU had joined the US and the rest of the international community in imposing some of the harshest sanctions against the regime in Pyongyang. In addition to supporting Moon's trust building between the two Koreas and the resumption of the Six-Party Talks, some EU member states such as Sweden offered to host the Talks if the concerned parties agreed.

Europe's activism vis-à-vis Korean security has thus focused on: (i) bolstering initiatives towards reconciliation and trust building between the two Koreas such as the 'Sunshine Policy' in its various versions; (ii) supporting regional dialogue forums such as the process of ROK-China-Japan trilateral cooperation; (iii) backing of regional multilateral mechanisms such as the Six Party Talks.

Europe and the Sunshine Policy

The EU has consistently supported the inter-Korean dialogue and the various versions of the 'Sunshine policy' put forward by South Korea. Following the positive conditions created by the negotiated solution for the first nuclear crisis in the mid-1990s and the launch of the Sunshine Policy, several European countries and the EU started a process of engagement with North Korea and of support for inter-Korean relations and reconciliation. The combination of these two factors – the improved willingness of the EU to play a role in the region and the positive environment surrounding North Korea and inter-Korean relations – led to a phase characterized by a relevant engagement of Europe on the Korean Peninsula.

Before the Sunshine Policy, Europe had already become involved in inter-Korean relations by joining the executive board of the Korean Peninsula Energy Development Organization (KEDO) whose main task was to build two light-water reactor nuclear plants in North Korea in order to alleviate the chronic shortages of energy in the country while keeping under strict control the nuclear development of the country. The EU agreed to donate US$15 million per year, which was later increased to US$20 million. The total contribution of the EU to the organization reached more than US$120 million according to the last annual report published by the organization in 2005.[13] Europe's participation in KEDO fulfilled two important goals: helping stabilize the situation on the Korean Peninsula and stopping nuclear proliferation.

After the election of Kim Dae-Jung and the launch of the Sunshine Policy, the EU would seize the opportunity of Kim's engagement policy with the North to boost commercial ties with both the ROK and the DPRK. This was made possible by the Sunshine Policy's separation of politics and economics, which basically meant fostering economic relations with the North without assimilating them to Pyongyang's good behavior in other areas. Past ROK governments' rigid linkage between politics and economics – meaning that any sort of provocation by the North had deep repercussions in the economic sphere as well – had contributed to a deadlock between the two countries; the Sunshine Policy demonstrated a great degree of flexibility by emphasizing economic interactions – pivotal in creating a more peaceful and collaborative atmosphere – while limiting the government's role primarily to matters of humanitarian and other official assistance.

The Sunshine Policy was based on the so-called 'flexible reciprocity,' or 'give first and take later,' through which the South allowed the North to reciprocate Seoul's measures at some point in the future. This principle would regulate government-to-government economic cooperation, for example in building infrastructures, while humanitarian assistance would not need any negotiation between the two parts.[14] Kim's approach was met with interest in Europe, since the EU had adopted a similar approach when dealing with some accession countries. In the eyes of EU policymakers in Brussels, Kim's 'flexible reciprocity' would allow Europe to promote ties with Pyongyang without those pre-conditions which were traditionally imposed by Washington.

The main examples of this cooperation aimed at creating a 'South-North economic community' were projects like the establishment of the industrial complex in the Kaesong area, the reconnection of the railway Seoul-Sinuiju, or the development of the touristic area at Mount Kumgang. Despite the fact that some of these initiatives were completed by the following administration, they represented a clear effort in the trust-building process between the two countries. While the US was largely absent from these dynamics, the EU had instead prepared a package of financial incentives which included targeted investments in some of the areas for cooperation flashed out by the idea of the 'South-North economic community'.

EU official documents would stress the importance of inter-Korean cooperation and reconciliation, such as the European Commission's memo on the relations with South Korea issued in March 2001, which included a full section on 'Support to the inter-Korean reconciliation process',[15] or the European Commission's report released in 2001, which directly mentioned the Sunshine Policy and the European support for inter-Korean dialogue.[16]

The Sunshine Policy's greatest achievement was possibly represented by the Inter-Korean summit that took place in Pyongyang in mid-June 2000. Beyond its symbolic importance, the summit's meaningfulness was represented by the Joint Declaration, signed by the leaders of the two countries, who agreed to continue cooperating on a wide array of subjects.[17] The Nobel Peace Prize awarded to Kim Dae-jung in December of the same year provided additional backing to Europe's strategy of full support for the Sunshine Policy – a policy that would be continued, under different names and forms, also by ROK conservative administrations.

NAPCI

The EU gave its full backing to the Trust-Building Process on the Korean Peninsula, and the Northeast Asia Peace and Cooperation Initiative (NAPCI) put forward by former South Korean President Park Geun-hye. In the joint declaration in commemoration of the 50th anniversary of diplomatic relations between the European Union and the Republic of Korea, issued on November 8, 2013, it is said that 'The EU supports the ROK's Trust-building Process on the Korean Peninsula and welcomes the Northeast Asia Peace and Cooperation Initiative ... as a way of building dialogue and trust in the region.'[18]

Former ROK President Park Geun-hye unveiled NAPCI in a speech to a dedicated joint session of the US Congress on May 7, 2013. Her proposal called for North-East Asian nations to enhance cooperation, first on 'soft' security issues (such as climate change, terrorism prevention, cyber-technology, and nuclear safety) before expanding the trust-building process to more sensitive areas. NAPCI was an expanded version of Park Geun-hye's 'Korean Peninsula trust process' – or Trustpolitik, as it was commonly referred to. By trying to establish 'mutually binding expectations based on global norms,'[19] Trustpolitik would aim to promote greater exchanges and cooperation between the two Koreas with a view to building confidence and reducing tensions in the area.

While recognizing the distinctive characteristics of North-East Asia, NAPCI took inspiration from Europe's experience. On several occasions, Park Geun-hye made explicit reference to the history of European integration and to Franco -German reconciliation. On March 26, 2014, for instance, at a summit in Berlin, President Park and German Chancellor Angela Merkel discussed the history of Franco–German rapprochement as well as Germany's reunification and their possible relevance, respectively, for Northeast Asia in general and the Korean Peninsula in particular. Two days later, in Dresden, the ROK President gave a speech entitled 'An Initiative for Peaceful Unification on the Korean Peninsula,' in which she proposed to the DPRK that 'we jointly establish an 'inter-Korean exchange and cooperation office' tasked to advance reunification.[20] In the same speech, President Park explicitly linked the trust-building process on the Korean Peninsula to NAPCI with the stated objective to address 'North Korea's security concerns through a multilateral peace and security system in North East Asia.'

The Northeast Asia Peace and Cooperation Initiative had thus two objectives: (1) the easing of tensions between the two Koreas; and (2) the creation of the conditions for a "grand reconciliation" between China, Japan, and South Korea, which might pave the way for a vast free-trade zone among the three powers as a step toward overcoming nationalism and addressing North Korea's nuclear threat. In this plan, the US would maintain the role of an external security balancer while the EU would take the lead in providing diplomatic backing to Park's initiative. However, after South Korea's Constitutional Court ruled to formally end impeached President Park Geun-hye's term in office on March 10, 2017, NAPCI was shelved.

ROK's new President, Moon Jae-in, elected on May 10, 2017, would declare on a number of occasions his commitment to engage North Korea as well as promote regional cooperation and trust building. In this vein, the Moon administration proposed the Northeast Asia Plus Community of Responsibility-sharing, which can be seen as an improvement and reconceptualization of NAPCI. It was based on three components: the Northeast Asia Platform for Peace and Cooperation; the New Northern Policy; and the New Southern Policy.

The Moon's Presidency

Moon Jae-in promised other key foreign policies during his election campaign, including the building of "Permanent Peace in the Korean Peninsula" and the "New Economic Map of Korean Peninsula," an economic vision for a peaceful Korean Peninsula. These initiatives would be pursued under the government's broader strategy of promoting a "Northeast Asia Plus Community for Responsibility-sharing." Under this plan, there are the three following foreign policy axes: (1) strengthening Korea, China, and Japan trilateral cooperation; (2) resuming the Six-Party Talks; (3) building the Northeast Asia Plus Community for Responsibility-sharing by integrating other existing multilateral security cooperation mechanisms. The EU declared various times its support for ROK President Moon Jae-in's initiatives since they were in line with Brussels' long-standing commitment to promote dialogue and reconciliation on the Korean Peninsula. Europe's unwavering support for Moon's initiatives was in stark contrast to the position of US President Donald Trump who made clear his preference for bilateral relations, as well as his distrust for multilateralism and regional cooperation, during his first meeting with Moon on June 30, 2017.[21]

When Moon Jae-in renewed an appeal for an end-of-war declaration in front of the General Assembly of the United Nations in September 2021, the EU welcomed the idea - though recognizing that such an initiative would not have the same strategic consequences for Europe as it would for the US.[22] For the Moon administration, a symbolic and non-legally binding end-of-war declaration would have boosted confidence and been a beneficial and non-threatening means to encourage Pyongyang to return to talks. Washington was skeptical of the Moon administration's proposal, since an end-of-war declaration could move another step toward dismantling the US-headed United Nations Command which in turn could weaken the legitimacy of America's military presence on the peninsula. US National Security Advisor Jake Sullivan declared that Moon's aim to formally end the Korean War before denuclearizing North Korea was inconsistent with Washington's security commitments in the region.

The Biden administration certainly improved relations with the ROK, which had been strained under Trump. Yet, the White House was skeptical of Moon's engagement policy with the North, including Moon's use of the process of ROK-China-Japan trilateral cooperation to reach out to Pyongyang. The European Union, on the other hand, continued to look favorably at the Moon administration's efforts to build trust and cooperation with neighboring nations. The process of ROK-China-Japan trilateral cooperation has traditionally received support from Europe, but a lukewarm response - if not upfront opposition - from Washington.

The EU and Trilateral Cooperation

The Trilateral Cooperation process is the only consultative mechanism which involves the leaders of the three North-East Asian nations and seeks to deal with the question of security on the Korean Peninsula from a purely regional perspective. The first Trilateral Summit took place in Fukuoka (Japan) in December 2008 when the three countries met to discuss regional cooperation, the global economy, disaster relief, and North Korea. In September 2011, the Trilateral Cooperation Secretariat (TCS) was launched: based in Seoul, the TCS is an international organization whose goal is to promote peace and prosperity between China, Japan, and South Korea. Based on equal participation, each government covers one-third of the overall operational budget.

From 2012 to 2015, however, no Trilateral Summit took place due to separate disputes over historical grievances as well as maritime territorial claims. On November 1, 2015, the sixth Trilateral Summit was held in Seoul. From 2015 to 2018 no further summits would take place. Relations between China, Japan, and South Korea have continued to be strained due to a variety of issues, ranging from World War II apologies and the interpretation of history to territorial disputes between the three nations. The 7th Trilateral Summit was held in May 2018 in Tokyo with North Korean nuclear negotiations topping the agenda. The 8th Trilateral Summit took place in December 2019, when the leaders of China, Japan, and ROK met in Chengdu (China) to exchange their views on the current regional situation and the threat posed by North Korea's nuclear and missile programs. Since 2019, there has been no Trilateral Summit, though the process of trilateral cooperation has continued to advance at the level of ministerial meetings and civil society. Since its inception in 2008, the three Northeast Asian nations have established numerous trilateral consultative mechanisms, including almost 40 ministerial meetings and almost 200 cooperative projects.[23]

The US has traditionally given lukewarm support to ROK-China-Japan trilateral process, as Washington continues to rely on its military alliances with Japan and South Korea.[24] This trend has accelerated under US President Joe Biden who has reached out to allies in East

Asia, as demonstrated by the US-Japan-South Korea trilateral meeting held at the margin of the NATO summit in June 2022 and the boosting of their defense cooperation occurred at Camp David in August 2023.[25] The EU, on the other hand, remains the staunchest international supporter of the process of ROK-China-Japan trilateral cooperation, both politically and financially. For instance, the EU Delegation in Seoul would regularly invite young students who participate in the Young Ambassadors Program organized by the Trilateral Cooperation Secretariat to various workshops - funded by the EU - with the aim of promoting mutual understanding and the sense of friendship among future leaders of South Korea, Japan, and China. Alongside support for the process of trilateral cooperation, the EU has also backed the Six Party Talks, notwithstanding the fact that the EU was never part of them.

The EU and the Six Party Talks

The EU and the ROK have time and again sought to relaunch the Six Party Talks. For instance, at the Asia-Europe summit held in Helsinki in September 2006, South Korean President Roh Moo-hyun and the EU issued a Joint Statement urging Pyongyang to rejoin the Six Party Talks, to implement the '9.19 Joint Statement' signed by six parties in 2005 for the denuclearization of the Korean Peninsula and not to carry out ballistic missile tests.[26] In these circumstances, ROK President Roh highlighted the role of the Helsinki Process and of the European Coal and Steel Community (ECSC), which led to respectively the creation of the Conference on Security and Cooperation in Europe (CSCE, later OSCE from 1995) and the EU, as a model for multilateral cooperation in North-East Asia. Seoul was keen on having Brussels jointhe Talks since the EU, as a substantial contributor of aid to North Korea, could play an important political role in the denuclearization of the Korean Peninsula. In the end, however, the EU was kept out of the Talks which eventually turned out to be ineffective and ended in a stalemate.

In June 2017, The Wall Street Journal revealed that the European Union was in discussions with South Korea and China about taking a potential role as a broker for negotiations with North Korea on ending its nuclear program. The discussions reflected concern in Brussels, Seoul, and Beijing that sanctions alone were not persuading Pyongyang to halt its nuclear program and that negotiations were needed to avoid military conflict.[27]

Seoul has recognized various times that the EU could play a role in revitalizing the Talks, since Brussels could bring to the negotiating table its recent experience dealing with the Iran's nuclear dossier. The EU has become actively involved in the multilateral negotiations on the Iranian nuclear program that have led to the Joint Comprehensive Plan of Action – JCPOA, known commonly as the Iran nuclear deal - signed in Vienna by the UN Security

Council P5 (China, France, Russia, the UK, and the US) plus Germany and the European Union - the so-called P5+1 - with the Iranian regime on July 14, 2015. The format of the P5+1 dealing with the Iran nuclear dossier has many similarities to the Six Party Talks. The experience of the Helsinki Final Act signed in 1975, at the height of the Cold War, shows that cooperation is possible even with an enemy armed with nuclear weapons.

The Yoon's Presidency

Whereas former President Moon Jae-in focused on building an inter-Korean peace process, President Yoon Suk-yeol is following in the footsteps of previous conservative administrations in seeking the abolition of North Korea's nuclear weapons program as a prerequisite for all further engagement with the North, making the 'realization of North Korea's complete denuclearization' Yoon's top foreign and security policy priority.[28]

Although Yoon's approach is significantly different from that of his predecessor, some efforts at engaging the North have been made in recent times. For instance, in August 2022, the Unification Minister Kwon Youngs presented the Audacious Initiative, which aimed to achieve complete denuclearization of North Korea through large-scale support for Pyongyang in the economic, military, and political sectors. The North, however, quickly rejected the proposal.

ROK President Yoon is prioritizing ties with the US and Japan, framing the Korean Peninsula as an area characterized by two competing camps opposing each other: China-Russia-North Korea versus US-Japan-South Korea. Following Russia's invasion of Ukraine, the EU has also intensified cooperation with the US in the context of NATO and hardened its position vis-à-vis China and North Korea. In this vein, there has been a coordinated European presence in North-East Asia in the monitoring of UN sanctions on North Korea in recent times.[29]

In 2022, Sweden and Finland, which have traditionally been assets of the EU in making arbitration between the US and North Korea and for advancing the reasons of dialogue with the DPRK due to their neutrality, have applied for joining NATO, following Russia's invasion of Ukraine. Finland became a member in 2023, while Sweden's accession is still in the balance at the time of writing. It remains to be seen, however, whether the EU will lose part if its strategic advantage in brokering US-DPRK dialogue once, after Finland, also Sweden becomes an official member of the North Atlantic Treaty Organization, since their joining has essentially to do with Russia's posture is Europe.

Conclusion

Since the establishment of their relations in 1963, the EU and the ROK have sought to cooperate to bring peace and security to the Korean Peninsula. While Cold War dynamics would limit the scope of their collaboration, the demise of the Soviet Union in 1991 opened up new possibilities. In the last decades, Seoul and Brussels have been able to join forces to contribute to Korean security, for instance by promoting the Six Party Talks. EU-ROK collaboration has also taken the form of Brussels' unwavering support for Seoul's 'Sunshine Policy' in its various versions and of EU's backing for the process of ROK-China-Japan trilateral cooperation.

The geopolitical situation on the Korean Peninsula has worsened in recent years. The election of ROK President Yoon in 2022 has reduced South Korea's engagement with the North and the space that an actor like the EU could play in advancing inter-Korean relations. However, past collaboration between Brussels and Seoul aimed at fostering dialogue and trust-building on the Korean Peninsula is an asset—in terms of experience and expertise acquired by the two sides over the last decades—that can be revamped in the future should ROK policymakers wish to do so.

Over the years, the EU has proved to be an independent variable for peace support on the Korean Peninsula, only marginally influenceable by Washington when it comes to supporting trust-building between the South and the North. Europe has thus become an asset for those ROK policymakers—be they progressive or conservative—committed to promoting dialogue and reconciliation with the North and to creating a cooperative environment among North East Asian nations.

Should the international community have to adapt to a nuclear DPRK, the EU is ideally positioned to spearhead efforts together with South Korea to create a multilateral security organization in North East Asia—something akin to the Organization for Security and Co-operation in Europe (OSCE) —which could serve as a primary instrument for early warning, conflict prevention, and crisis management. Should this happen, it would be the culmination of decades-long EU-ROK cooperation efforts at contributing to peace and security on the Korean Peninsula

Bibliography

Boulet Gertjan, Michael Reiterer, Ramon Pacheco Pardo (eds.), Cybersecurity Policy in the EU and South Korea from Consultation to Action, Basingstoke: Palgrave-Macmillan, 2022.

Casarini Nicola, *EU-Korea Security Relations,* London: Routledge, 2021.

Casarini Nicola, 'Europe's comprehensive approach to Northeast Asia's security', *Monde Chinois* 53(1): 94-102, 2018. https://www.cairn.info/revue-monde-chinois-2018-1-page-94.htm

Cha Victor, *Powerplay: The Origins of the American Alliance System in Asia,* Princeton: Princeton University Press, 2016.

Council of the EU (Foreign Affairs) Conclusions on *Enhanced EU security cooperation in and with Asia,* Brussels, 28 May 2018.

Council of the EU – General Secretariat (Working Paper), *EU security cooperation in and with Asia under the Partnership Instrument,* Brussels, 3 December 2018 (WK 15000/2018 INIT).

European Commission, *Towards a New Asian Strategy – Communication from the Commission to the Council,* Brussels, 13 July 1994.

European Commission, *Europe and Asia: A Strategic Framework for Enhanced Partnerships – Communication from the Commission to the Council,* Brussels, 4 September 2001.

European Commission and European External Action Service, *Connecting Europe & Asia: The EU Strategy,* Brussels, 26 September 2019.

European Commission and European External Action Service, *The EU Strategy for Cooperation in the Indo-Pacific* (JOIN/2021/24), Brussels, 16 September 2021.

European Commission, *EU-Republic of Korea Relations, Brussels,* MEMO/01/111, 30 March 2001.

Fiori Antonio and Marco Milani, 'Europe and Inter-Korean Relations', in Nicola Casarini, Antonio Fiori, Nam-Kook Kim, Jae-Seung Lee, Ramon Pacheco Pardo (eds.), *Routledge Handbook of Europe-Korea Relations,* London: Routledge, 2022.

Joint Declaration in Commemoration of the 50th Anniversary of Diplomatic Relations between the European Union and the Republic of Korea (15875/13), Brussels, 8 November 2013, www.consilium.europa.eu/uedocs/cms_data/docs/pressdata/en/ec/139428.pdf

Korean Peninsula Energy Development Organization, *2005 Annual Report,* New York, 31

Endnote

1. Gertjan Boulet, Michael Reiterer, Ramon Pacheco Pardo (eds.), *Cybersecurity Policy in the EU and South Korea from Consultation to Action*, Basingstoke: Palgrave-Macmillan, 2022.
2. Nicola Casarini, *EU-Korea Security Relations*, London: Routledge, 2021.
3. European Commission, *Towards a New Asian Strategy – Communication from the Commission to the Council*, Brussels, 13 July 1994.
4. European Commission, *Europe and Asia: A Strategic Framework for Enhanced Partnerships – Communication from the Commission to the Council*, Brussels, 4 September 2001.
5. Antonio Fiori and Marco Milani, 'Europe and Inter-Korean Relations', in Nicola Casarini, Antonio Fiori, Nam-Kook Kim, Jae-Seung Lee, Ramon Pacheco Pardo (eds.), *Routledge Handbook of Europe-Korea Relations*, London: Routledge, 2022.
6. Council of the EU (Foreign Affairs) *Conclusions on Enhanced EU security cooperation in and with Asia,* Brussels, 28 May 2018 https://www.consilium.europa.eu/en/press/press-releases/2018/05/28/deepening-eu-security-cooperation-with-asian-partners-council-adopts-conclusions/pdf
7. Council of the EU – *General Secretariat (Working Paper), EU security cooperation in and with Asia under the Partnership Instrument,* Brussels, 3 December 2018 (WK 15000/2018 INIT).
8. Donald Trump, *National security strategy of the United States of America.* Washington, DC: White House, 2017 - https://www.hsdl.org/?abstract&did=806478. See also: Joe Bide, National security strategy of the United States of America. Washington, DC: White House, October 2022 - https://www.whitehouse.gov/wp-content/uploads/2022/10/Biden-Harris-Administrations-National-Security-Strategy-10.2022.pdf
9. *NATO 2022 Strategic Concept,* Brussels, 29 June 2022 - https://www.nato.int/nato_static_fl2014/assets/pdf/2022/6/pdf/290622-strategic-concept.pdf
10. European Commission and European External Action Service, *Connecting Europe & Asia: The EU Strategy,* Brussels, 26 September 2019 - https://www.eeas.europa.eu/eeas/connecting-europe-asia-eu-strategy_en. See also: European Commission and European External Action Service , The EU Strategy for Cooperation in the Indo-Pacific (JOIN/2021/24), Brussels, 16 September 2021, https://eur-lex.europa.eu/legal-content/en/TXT/?uri=celex:-52021JC0024
11. Nicola Casarini, 'Europe's comprehensive approach to Northeast Asia's security', *Monde Chinois* 53(1): 94-102, 2018. https://www.cairn.info/revue-monde-chinois-2018-1-page-94.htm
12. Ramon Pacheco Pardo, *North Korea - US Relations From Kim Jong Il to Kim Jong Un*, London: Routledge, 2021.
13. Korean Peninsula Energy Development Organization, *2005 Annual Report,* New York, 31 December 2005, Appendix 1(B), p.13.
14. Moon Chung-in, *The Sunshine Policy. In Defense of Engagement as a Path to Peace in Korea,* Seoul: Yonsei University Press, 2012.
15. European Commission, EU Republic of Korea Relations, Brussels, MEMO/01/111, 30 March 2001.
16. European Commission, *Europe and Asia,* 2001.
17. South-North *Joint Declaration*, 15 June 2000 - https://peacemaker.un.org/sites/peacemaker.un.org/files/KP%20KR_000615_SouthNorth%20Joint%20Declaration.pdf
18. *Joint Declaration in Commemoration of the 50th Anniversary of Diplomatic Relations between the European Union and the Republic of Korea* (15875/13), Brussels, 8 November 2013, p. 2, www.consilium.europa.eu/uedocs/cms_data/docs/pressdata/en/ec/139428.pdf

19. Park Geun-hye, "A New Kind of Korea," in *Foreign Affairs,* Vol. 90, No. 5 (September/October 2011), p. 14, www.foreignaffairs.com/articles/northeast-asia/2011-09-01/new-kind-korea

20. Park Geun-hye, *An Initiative for Peaceful Unification on the Korean Peninsula,* Dresden, 28 March 2014, www.korea.net/Government/Briefing-Room/Presidential-Speeches/view?articleId=118517

21. The White House, *Remarks by President Trump and President Moon of the Republic of Korea Before Bilateral Meeting,* Washington, 30 June 2017, www.whitehouse.gov/the-press-office/2017/06/30/remarks-president-trump-and-president-moon-republic-korea-bilateral

22. Interview, European External Action Service, Brussels, September 2022.

23. https://www.tcs-asia.org/en/cooperation/dashboard.php

24. Victor Cha, *Powerplay: The Origins of the American Alliance System in Asia,* Princeton: Princeton University Press, 2016.

25. William Gallo, 'US, Japan, South Korea Leaders Voice Concerns About North Korean Aggression', *Voice of America,* 29 June 2022 - https://www.voanews.com/a/japan-south-korea-leaders-meet-on-sidelines-of-nato-summit-/6637746.html

26. 'South Korea, EU Urge Pyongyang to Rejoin 6-Party Nuclear Talks', *Voice of America,* 31 October 2009.

27. Jeremy Page and Laurence Norman, 'EU Discussing Role as Broker on North Korea', *The Wall Street Journal,* 20 June 2017 - https://www.wsj.com/articles/eu-discussing-role-as-broker-on-north-korea-1497991275

28. Sang Hyun Lee, 'What to Expect for US-ROK and Inter-Korean Relations Under Yoon Suk-Yeol', *38North,* 25 March 2022 - https://www.38north.org/2022/03/what-to-expect-for-us-rok-relations-and-inter-korean-relations-under-yoon-suk-yeol/

29. Philip Shetler-Jones, *Europe's Area of Maritime Interest in Northeast Asia,* IAI Papers 22/33, December 2022 - https://www.iai.it/sites/default/files/iaip2233.pdf

Towards a new start in EU-DPRK (North Korea) relations
when, how, and why

BERNHARD SELIGER

Introduction

With the departure of the last European diplomats and aid workers in 2020-2021 in the wake of the Corona pandemic, EU-North Korea relations reached a deep through. Since the start of diplomatic relations in 2002, the simmering nuclear crisis has gradually made more and more forms of normal cooperation impossible: trade relations, cultural relations, and political relations dried up and only a fraction of former humanitarian assistance was given by 2019. The decision of North Korea in 2020 to completely isolate the country due to the Corona pandemic was the last straw: by now, all European embassies are empty and all aid workers have left the country. At the same time, North Korea slipped into a renewed deep hunger crisis making humanitarian aid more necessary than in a long time. Towards the end of 2023, North Korea finally started to reopen. This paper discusses, if and how a restart of as well humanitarian and diplomatic relations is possible and what necessary steps the EU could take to improve the opening.

North Korea, as the adage goes, is the "hermit kingdom", one of the most isolated countries in the world. While this is certainly true, there were and are times, when suddenly the North Korean government springs to external action. The summit diplomacy of 2018 until April 2019 was such a phase, and – to a lesser extent – the diplomatic activities involving China and Russia since September 2023 are an example. However, the meantime, from the closing of the country in January 2023 to today, is a good example of the rigorous isolationism of the government of North Korea, regardless of human and political costs involved.

And even in the times of greater activity and openness, relations are always difficult and never really deep. The European Union (EU) has a policy of critical engagement with the Democratic People's Republic of Korea (DPRK). Its goals are to support a lasting diminution of tensions on the Korean peninsula and in the region, to uphold the international non-proliferation regime, and to improve the situation of human rights in the DPRK (https://www.eeas.europa.eu/eeas/dprk-and-eu_en). Most EU states have diplomatic relations with North Korea, besides Estonia, which did not establish these relations and France, which does not recognize North Korea. For this reason, the EU itself also does not have a formal diplomatic representation in North Korea. In the past, this position was partly filled by the so-called Food Security Office (FSO) established by the EU, though this is manned not by diplomats but staffed by consulting companies, and partly by the EU embassy in Seoul, which in particular in the early to mid-2000s was quite active in exchanges with the North.

Among the older diplomatic relations of North Korea are those within the former socialist bloc, like Poland, Bulgaria, or Romania. While North Korea was never formally part of any structures of this bloc, like the COMECON or the Warsaw Pact, it nevertheless was economically integrated to some extent and had regular exchanges with other socialist countries, while at the same time being active in the so-called bloc-free movement. After the breakdown of the socialist international order in the early 1990s, North Korea withdrew from most international exchanges, re-calling students and technical exchange staff. At that time, North Korea underwent its most serious economic crisis to date, the famine costing between hundred thousands and millions of lives. In 1995, after devastating floods, North Korea, on the brink of a breakdown, asked the international community for aid. Then, the relations with the EU and its network of aid organizations began and actors like Welthungerhilfe (formerly also known as German Agro Action), Concern and others began. Humanitarian aid soon gained a massive scale and for almost ten years up to one-third of the North Korean population depended on food aid. Additionally, the EU was also active in the attempt to provide energy to North Korea in exchange for a freeze of the nuclear program with the so-called KEDO.

Since 1999, support for the sunshine policy has also become an issue. Kim Dae-Jung asked Western European states to establish relations with North Korea. This happened in 2001 and afterwards, there was a very brief phase of optimism regarding an experimental, but very meaningful program of technical and financial aid for North Korea (Frank 2002). Unfortunately, only a year later, in 2002, saw the onset of the "2nd nuclear crisis" with the revelation by North Korea that it had worked secretly as well on uranium enrichment and plutonium-based nuclear weapons. Some European states established embassies in North Korea and some humanitarian activity started; however, the hope for improved economic relations on both sides expressed by politicians and academics alike (Yoon 2001) did not materialize. Indeed, on the whole it was really from the establishment of diplomatic relations to today the history of a constant decline, which will be discussed in the next section (2.). The third section contains general considerations for a return to North Korea. The question of the "how" of the return of diplomatic and humanitarian actors is discussed in section 4, followed by a conclusion (5.).

2002-2022: A review of the decline of EU-North Korea relations, in particular during the time of the pandemic

It is ironic, but the whole period of EU-DPRK relations after their establishment in 2001 can be seen as a long, two-decade decline. In the end, all European embassies in Pyongyang are completely empty and their insides destroyed, and the North Korean embassies in European cities just live with a minimum of diplomats, who are long overdue for return to their country, sometimes serving seven years, but barred from return by the self-imposed isolation of North Korea after COVID. Other actors from NGOs or international organizations also left North Korea at the beginning of the COVID crisis. Very few European actors are still related to North Korea in a more direct way, for example, by carrying out online trainings with North Korean participants, though most still have sporadic e-mail contacts or contacts through the embassies in their home countries.

The history of relations between European countries and North Korea is very different according to country. Largely, there are three groups of countries: first, those of the old socialist bloc (like Poland, the Czech Republic, Romania, and Bulgaria), which still have old ties with North Korea and, in most cases, also an embassy in North Korea. Some countries did rearrange their ties after the transition in 1990, for example, when Czechoslovakia divided into the Czech and Slovak Republic. While these states, to some extent, still maintain old ties, they also adapted their policies (see the Czech case Novotna 2023). Others emerged newly from the former Soviet Union, like the Baltic states, Ukraine, and Belarus, and had to newly form relations with North Korea. Estonia never did so (Elblaus 2021). The Western European states mostly had diplomatic relations only after the start of the sunshine policy of South Korea, when Kim Dae-Jung asked them to establish ties to support an engagement policy with the North. A few countries, like Switzerland, already had relations with North Korea, and many countries after 1995 were engaged in providing humanitarian aid. Germany is a special case, since until 1989 the East German Democratic Republic (GDR) had close ties with the North, then the embassy was closed, with only a caretaker living there, and only in 2001 diplomatic relations were re-started with the unified Germany. Finally, there is the case of Paris, which does not even recognize North Korea as a state (as opposed e.g. to Estonia, which just does not have diplomatic relations with North Korea). Ironically, nevertheless France, and in particular Paris, are well-loved by the North Korean elite (Levi 2023). The diplomatic mission to UNESCO, headquartered in Paris, doubles effectively as an embassy there.

The mid- to end 1990s, a phase called "arduous march" in North Korea due to mass starvation, was the heyday of humanitarian aid to North Korea. With the start of diplomatic relations there was the hope for closer, full-scale cooperation. The EU drafted a technical assistance program, embassies were opened, and cultural and political missions were exchanged. However, soon the "second nuclear crisis", starting with the North Korean admission of a secret uranium enrichment and plutonium program, ended these attempts. Aid was largely confined to the humanitarian sector. The EU only had two programs with North Korea in the mid-2000s under a non-humanitarian focus, as part of the "Asia Invest" initiative. With each nuclear and missile test relations became worse. One reason was that embassies in Europe and students sent by North Korea to Europe often engaged in sourcing for the illegal weapons programs. In some cases that led to a regular tit-for-tat. For example, the Berlin embassy of North Korea and the Pyongyang Embassy of Germany saw various rounds of reduction of diplomatic personnel, mostly due to the fear in Germany that embassy personnel could be used for such illegal activities. Also, the one stable source of income of the North Korean embassy in Berlin, the rental of a part of the large embassy complex in the heart of Berlin as a youth hostel, was closed down after a long legal battle in 2020 (Hotham 2020). Generally the period from 2010, when North Korea aims to create a nuclear arsenal became undeniable, to 2020, when the COVID pandemic broke out, saw an almost complete end to trade with North Korea, as well as an end of the few places in Eastern Europe where North Korean workers were employed, like a shoe manufacturer in the Czech republic of shipyards in Poland. Diplomatic relations were largely toned down. The EU regularly sponsored human rights condemnations of North Korea in the United Nations. And while the EU strongly supported the short phases of engagement, like 2018 to April 2019, they remained overall skeptical. Alexandrova (2019) speaks of the 2010s as a phase of an "abandonment of engagement". Ballbach sees the policy of "critical engagement" by 2019 as a failure (Ballbach 2019) and argues for more targeted sanctions (Ballbach 2022).

The biggest issue of contention was the nuclear and missile development of North Korea. Outlawed by various UN sanctions, it was regularly condemned by the EU. When the EU in 2020 called for the lowering of tensions (Choy 2020a), North Korea warned the EU for meddling in their affairs (Kim/ Hotham 2020) and called the EU absurd (Choy 2020b). Like South Korea and the USA, beside their support for UN sanctions the EU also started to introduce their own sanctions on North Korea. Most of them had no practical effect at all, but they were a kind of virtue signaling. Most of them were directed toward persons or institutions involved in the development of the nuclear and missile programs. When in 2022 new sanctions on twelve people and institutions were decided (Bremer 2022a), North Korea promptly complained about the "hostile policy" of the EU (Bremer 2022b). The condemnation of North Korea´s militaristic policy was not only confined to the EU itself, but also carried into other institutions, for example the 2022 G7 summit (Bremer 2022c). In this case, North Korea coolly replied that it had never recognized EU sanctions at all (Jung 2022). After that, another round of EU sanctions started in December 2022 (Jewell 2022).

Sanctions are, however, a rather weak policy instrument. Not only did they ultimately fail to contain North Korea´s nuclear and missile program—though one might argue that they certainly helped to slow down the program—but also they were and are regularly violated. Increasingly, due to a geo-political environment of a new Cold War with a Chinese-Russian-North Korean bloc versus a stronger Western front, including the strengthened South Korean-Japanese-US alliance, sanctions violations are open. European states therefore took a strong stance against those violations they could policy themselves in their own territory. This included the reselling of the North Korean exports to China in Europe (Fromer 2020a), though the problem of exports to China ultimately ending up in North Korea is much larger (Fromer 2020b). A newly emerging issue from the mid-2010s was cybercrime, but only in the time of pandemic it really became a major issue. In July 2020, the EU sanctioned North Korea for cybercrime for the first time(Choy 2020), a year later, in May 2021, the sanctions were extended (Jung 2021).

Lastly, there is the issue of human rights. With the start of diplomatic relations, the problems of massive human rights violations in North Korea were already well-known. The EU started a human rights dialogue with North Korea, modeled after a similar dialogue program with China, which however after only one session broke down. Several attempts to restart it were later unsuccessful. The condemnation of North Korea´s human rights situation in the United Nations, which is regularly co-sponsored by the EU, is taken as a sign by North Korea that the EU is not interested in a real dialogue, defined as "open ended" on the question if there are any human rights violations in North Korea. Still, for a long time the EU did not put additional pressure on North Korea through sanctions regarding human rights. When the embassies of EU states were still running, this was a measure of safety for embassy personnel, and also came from the desire to leave open a certain window of opportunity for dialogue and cooperation. When finally in March 2021 for the first time the human rights situation was sanctioned by the European Union, this showed that cooperation with North Korea had broken down completely (Jewell 2021, Zwirko 2021). In particular, new reports of the killing of Christians in DPRK led to more condemnations (Bremer 2022d), with the North Korean answer being to call the European Parliament a "gang of liars" (Bremer 2022e). In the past, North Korea had rather frequent contact with the European Parliament. The Delegation of the European Parliament to the Korean Peninsula visited North Korea, and North Korean visitors to Brussels regularly also went to the Parliament. However, the tense relations with the European Parliament showed with the abrupt cancellation of a planned dialogue program of the North Korean embassy in Germany, which is also responsible for relations to the European Union, twice in the time of the pandemic (O´Carroll 2021a and 2021b). A video call with the nead of the Delegation of the European Parliament to the Korean Peninsula, the Austrian Lukas Mandl, did not result in any further exchanges (Kim 2021). In September 2022 there was another attempt to restart diplomatic relations with Brussels (Derr/ Chung 2022), but again it was cancelled after a week of discussions (O´Carroll 2022). One reason for that could be that North Korean diplomats have generally extremely limited discretion in their job and are not able to discuss issues freely with their counterparts in the world, and at the same time, during the pandemic, the guidelines and talking points from Pyongyang were simply lacking. In such a situation, any exchanges might be literally dangerous for North Korean diplomats, once they return to their homeland. In December 2022, the EP again condemned the human rights situation in North Korea (Bremer 2022f). All this will also weigh on the question, if and how relations after COVID can be restarted.

The responsibility of the North Korean embassy in Berlin for European affairs is a rather new development. In former times, when humanitarian aid was also much larger, the embassy dealing with EU affairs was in London. This became a problem after the highly publicized defection of Thae Yong-Ho, vice ambassador, who restarted a career in South Korea as a conservative politician. When Brexit happened, the role of the London embassy for European affairs also became de facto obsolete, and was shifted to Berlin. Reportedly, the North Korean embassy in Berlin was rather reluctant to accept this new burden, since it did not come with additional funding. Since then, relations with the EU are best on standby, the embassy is rather inactive (Fromer-Hotham 2020). In European media, there are regularly stories on North Korea, most of which focus on the military threats, human rights, or the bizarreness of the North Korean regime. Mostly, North Korea tends to greet these articles with silence. A notable exception was when the documentary "The Mole" by the Danish filmmaker Mads Brügger created a stir in international relations, exposing illegal weapons manufacturing, drug manufacturing, and money laundering in North Korea. The movie follows the chef Ulrich Larsen, who for ten years participates in the Korean Friendship Association, an organization to garner support for North Korea throughout the world. Together with the head of that organization, the Spanish citizen Alejandro Cao de Benós, Larsen travelled to North Korea and signed a contract on weapons manufacturing and drug production in the third state (see the website of the movie, https://themolecph.com/). In this case, North Korea reacted promptly, because the revelations were so embarrassing and also potentially dangerous, with the UN showing interest in them. Not surprisingly, North Korea rejected the revelations, all of which are on camera, as fabrications (O`Carroll 2020, Kasulis

– Choy 2020). Also not surprisingly, later China agreed with North Korea, since the material was filmed in an "illegal manner" (O`Carroll 2021c).

When the COVID pandemic broke out in China in late 2019 and became public in January 2020, North Korea took the most radical possible measures to prevent the entry of the virus: declaring it a matter of utmost importance for national security, the country first stopped all air and railway traffic and entry of cars and trucks from China, and then a few days later extended this ban to Russia. Those, who absolutely had to enter the country, had to undergo a mandatory quarantine of 30 days. Effectively, the whole country of 25 million people had been shut down, closed to the outside. This also included trade; only indispensable deliveries of goods, for example medical aid, were let in by special arrangement. Later entry into North Korea was completely forbidden, a ban upheld for almost three years. Foreign diplomats and aid workers left the country in groups, with a highly publicized and ridiculed trip of Russian diplomats by a hand-driven railcart across the railway bridge to Russia in Rason. The European embassies prepared for a "temporary" closure – at that time few foresaw that it would take more than three years to return (O`Carroll 2020b). Some NGOs still worked on new programs, like the NGO Concern of Ireland, which received a new sanctions exemption, while the country was already effectively closed (Zwirko 2020). By early 2021, all Western diplomats and most of those from other countries, as well as all foreign aid workers and UN staff had left the country. Less than 300 foreigners, mostly Chinese and Russians, remained in the country, with 9 ambassadors and 4 charge d´affaires still in place. The largest embassies remained those of Russia and China, and they too saw a gradual decline in their staff. After the outbreak of COVID, North Korea was very keen to get more information on the virus, and in the beginning, it also discussed with its external partners ways to contain the virus. The EU stressed in international discussions that North Korea was eligible for vaccine aid, despite sanctions (Fromer 2020c). However, North Korea repeatedly rejected the proposals for the delivery of vaccines by the international vaccine initiative. The situation even led to a call by the UN Human Rights Council to let vaccines and COVID aid enter the country (Bremer 2022g).

It was not the first time, North Korea took such drastic steps: similar measures were taken when the SARS epidemic arose, and during the outbreak of the Ebola epidemic, North Korea had a similar shutdown maintained for more than half a year. However, the current three-year isolation is unprecedented. In a way, as a measure to reduce the risk of an epidemic outbreak, this made sense in the case of North Korea. North Korea has a very tightly controlled border with only very few entry points, but, the health facilities inside the country often lack even basic equipment for detecting, let alone controlling new epidemics like the new corona virus. This is even a problem in the current quarantine: all North Koreans returning from China have been quarantined near the border. But it is not clear, if really all of them could be tested negatively for the new corona virus. In the past, North Korea has had a number of aid projects, among them with Caritas Internationalis, where PCR (polymerase chain reaction) instruments have been given to the country, but it is not clear, if there are enough reagents to run these. And, in China, the sourcing of necessary equipment like personal protective equipment or disinfectants got more and more difficult. Rumors about cases of the new corona virus were rampant in the country. To make the fight against the corona virus a national priority is therefore understandable. Less clear is, how single measures like a practical house arrest of all foreigners—they were not allowed any more to leave the diplomatic quarters, go shopping, or go to restaurants downtown—could help the fight against the new corona virus. After two years of occasional reports of the outbreak of corona in North Korea, finally in May 2022 the North Korean government admitted an outbreak in Pyongyang. According to subsequent North Korean reports, more than a million people contracted COVID, described as fever, but miraculously after a few days the fever was again under control. While the strict management of people movements indeed might have considerably restricted the outbreak of COVID in the country, the figures did not make sense from the point of view of epidemiology. Since that time, there have been some more reports on temporary restrictions on movement and quarantine in various parts of the country, but not more nationwide alert.

Clearly, shutting down the whole country had severe effects on the economy. Price hikes for daily necessities like cooking oil in border cities to China like Sinuiju occurred. Nevertheless, the effects might be less severe than in almost any other country in the world, given North Korea's extraordinary economic isolation and low degree of dependence on foreign trade. In effect, North Korea has long been the most isolated country measured by the external trade ratio. While this changed from 2000 to 2015, afterwards the sanctions imposed by the UN on practically all exports and many imports led to a renewed phase of disintegration with the world economy (in fact, the Chinese economy, where the overwhelming part of exports went and where up to 95 percent of imports originated). So, the new corona virus shock was less pronounced, and might not at all have been felt in particular by the rural population, which still lives largely in a form of subsistence economy, with very few foreign goods (like, for example, textiles) entering the country. The effect was much bigger for the urban middle classes, and this is important, since their loyalty is necessary for the stability of the regime. Over time, however, again all people felt the effects, with fewer fertilizers coming in, reducing harvests, and even the most basic medicines lacking. While, due to the ongoing closure, there is no exact data on the humanitarian situation, all available anecdotal data points to another facet of near-famine in North Korea. Kim Jong-un himself admitted the "worst-ever" economic situation in 2021 and made reference to another "arduous march".

The European Union, devoid of any information from the ground and regular diplomatic contacts, remained committed to humanitarian relief. In 2021, the EU grated disaster aid amounting to 590000 euros (Kim 2021b). However, due to the closure of the country, the aid could not be delivered. The bleak economic situation improved only very slowly with a careful re-opening in early 2023. While some North Koreans, like university students, have been re-called and allowed back into their country, no regular traffic with foreign countries has been re-established. The mass exodus of foreigners was seen by outside observers as a critical point (Everard 2021). However, it might well be that, to some extent, it led to a very comfortable situation for the North Korean regime, when also the little bit of exchange and monitoring by Western diplomats and international aid workers was suspended. But also, the European Union is less and less inclined to make special time and room for engagement with North Korea, or, in the words of Glyn Ford, shows it a "cold shoulder" (Ford 2023). The current North Korean diplomatic initiative with Russia, which includs the mass delivery of ammunition and weaponry to Russia to further its aggression against Ukraine, certainly will not help to set the mood for a return of diplomats to Pyongyang, after it is feasible again, probably next year. Radical voices recommend to expel North Korean diplomats, to make the life of North Korea even more difficult (Lee 2022). Others think of the re-start by single states, e.g. Poland (Levi 2022). In the next section, general considerations for restarting relations will be discussed.

Restarting humanitarian cooperation and diplomatic relations – some general considerations

The sketch of EU-North Korea history in the last two decades shows a generally declining, disappointing trend: the diplomatic relations, which started with high hopes for an opening up of North Korea and denser economic, political, and cultural contacts, almost immediately came to an abrupt halt with the advent of the second nuclear crisis, and afterwards relations were always in crisis mode. The COVID pandemic forced European diplomats out of the country – why should they return at all, given the dismal relations? There are a number of reasons why relations with North Korea maintain their importance. Much of the policy of the USA, South Korea and also the EU in the last twenty years was built on the implicit belief that North Korea was a failed state showing signs of decay and decline, which could lead to an implosion like in the case of other socialist countries. This was indeed the case in the early 1990s, when the state capacity of North Korea was weakest and also when North Korea´s allies, in particular China, were in a much weaker position than today. However, the collapse did not occur, but policies did not really adjust to this. Sanctions, officially never intended to harm the North Korean economy as such, but just to stop the development of the nuclear and missile programs, were designed to harm the North Korean economy, and often unspoken or outspoken, the hope was attached that North Korea would not survive this. Unfortunately, this view disregarded two facts: first of all, as long as China is there, North Korea has an ally which has no interest in losing the buffer function, and North Korea has vis-à-vis the American troops for China. Also, North Korea is already probably the least integrated economy in the whole world, or one of them at least, and further reduction of trade had only a limited impact on the stability of the country.

For a rational European diplomacy, wishful thinking (that North Korea would collapse) cannot substitute the reality; realpolitik is necessary, and that means that the continued existence of North Korea has to be assumed (while still being prepared for the possibility of a sudden implosion). The isolation policy without China is naïve, and cannot work. This means that European (and generally, Western) policies vis-à-vis North Korea have to include a policy toward China, too. In the current situation of a new Cold War, with new alliances rapidly forming, this is exceedingly difficult, but remains necessary.

A second important consideration is that North Korea is often depicted as a monolithic state with a leader deciding everything, but this is far from the truth. Instances of policy debates can be seen in the state´s media, and there are, depending on organizations in North Korea and also factions, different opinions about cooperation (McEachern 2010). Therefore, policies can and should target different partners for interaction and strategically strengthen desirable partners. For example, cooperation with the Ministry of Land and Environment Protection, which carried out many of the humanitarian projects in North Korea as well as environmental projects, has a relatively great deal of experience dealing with international donors and is genuinely interested in peaceful and fruitful interaction. This is clearly different from other ministries, from the Korean Workers Party or from other entities, not to speak of the North Korean military. A rational North Korean policy therefore has to try to use these differences to strategically strengthen forces more inclined to peaceful interaction with the rest of the world. Among the instruments are study trips, scholarships, cooperation in humanitarian projects, etc.

Last but not least, the German and European example of overcoming division shows that there was a small but slowly growing sphere of a political human exchanges, in particular in family relations, but also, for example, in a part of the academic exchanges, which was successfully separated from politics, military questions, and ideology. This allowed for exchanges far beyond those possible with North Korea (as well for the rest of the world as, in particular, for South Korea). European states and their diplomatic representations can participate in creating such an a-political space, as well through diplomatic representations, e.g. on family reunions, to North Korea, as through cultural policy initiatives.

Given these reasons for interaction with North Korea, naturally, some caveats apply: First of all, interaction should not undermine international sanctions and pressure in the fields of missile and nuclear policy as well as human rights. Principally, this is guaranteed by adhering to sanctions also internationally by the Panel of Experts on sanctions. But governments have to be on alert for deliberate or also sometimes accidental break of sanctions. A recent example from Germany concerns a publicly funded research project between a North Korean physical scientist and a German scientist in the field of laser technology (Deutsche Welle 2022). Interaction with North Korea also has to be transparent. Secret negotiations with North Korea, in particular those involving the transfer of funds, will undermine public trust. This does not mean that everything has to always be said openly; confidential talks are sometimes very important. But there should be in negotiations no short-cuts from established democratic rules. This is an important point, since all relations to North Korea are very special, and rare, and since North Korea almost always tries to circumvent general rules, claiming to be a special case. While this can sometimes be necessary (e.g., requirements for scholarship students in North Korea need to be adapted to the lack of exchanges, e.g. in the field of language certificates), it should not lead to unjustified preferential treatment. In particular, in the early sunshine policy this was a birth defect with later grave consequences.

Dealing with North Korea necessitates that North Korea be treated not only as a target to destabilize, but genuinely as a partner, in particular in humanitarian projects. While there could and should be an ultimate goal to work toward the opening up of North Korea, partnership means to treat projects, project implementing agencies and North Korean personnel honestly and respectfully, as far as project work goes. If not, projects will be seen as foreign incursions and lead to less rather than more trust. But trust is the ultimate currency needed to work toward a more open North Korea. While there might well be actors who are primarily concerned with the destabilization of North Korea, e.g. certain defector groups, this cannot be the attitude and policy of either diplomats or aid workers in North Korea. On the other hand, taking North Koreans seriously as partners does not mean following all their ideological demands: bowing before statues of the leaders, buying and bringing flowers to the notorious Kim Il Sungia – Kim Jong Ilia shows etc. This can be reasonably declined, and will rather foster the status of aid groups.

Finally, discussing the reason to be in North Korea, is has to be recognized that information flows, one very important goal of cooperation, will change North Korea, which is desired. But this is not only true for informal or “subversive” information, but equally so for open, formal information. Information shared with project partners in aid projects, e.g., in the fields of forestry or agriculture, will enhance the controlling power of these partners, also vis-à-vis the bureaucracy. It is a form of empowerment which is in the long run very important to achieve great autonomy for individuals and organizations from the powerful central bureaucracy.

If diplomatic relations with North Korea are desirable, as the above paragraphs show, does this also give enough justification for a representation by embassies and aid offices on the ground? Again, we have a number of political and humanitarian reasons to consider. First, in the field of politics the mere existence of Western embassies and aid offices, and the – albeit limited – freedom of these to move around Pyongyang, and with advance notification and permit the rest of the country – has a restraining influence on North Korea. Being forced to interact with foreigners more frequently is very important in a country which has so few opportunities for peaceful interaction with foreigners. In these interactions, North Korea will also learn more about the various policies and political standpoints of the foreign diplomats. In most other countries such contacts would be negligible or easily substitutable by other forms of communication. But the very isolation of North Korea makes every contact doubly valuable.

This argument can also be reversed: it is important for European countries to know what is going on in North Korea. Even if the possibility of observing politics in North Korea is severely restricted, there are important clues to be gleaned simply from observing the situation in Pyongyang. The food situation, the status of imported goods, propaganda slogans (while most of them today can be found in North Korean official publications, some of the most revealing and important ones cannot), "poko" (administrative orders dealing with new policy issues mostly nowhere to be found in official publications), and the impressions from talks with North Koreans all add up to form a better imagine than one purely achieved by observation from the outside. While every single one of these activities might be seen as negligible, together they can be important. The former German ambassador to Pyongyang, Thomas Schäfer, in his discussion of policy debates in North Korea after the change from Kim Jong-Il to Kim Jong-Un extensively draws on such observations, together with official information (Schäfer 2021).

There is a third, maybe more elusive, but also important political aspect to the European presence in Pyongyang and North Korea. It can serve as a beacon of hope for a change in the North Korean regime. The history of the Cold War shows how important embassies could be for dissidents, but also the normal population, as images of the "otherness" compared to a largely uniform regime. Clearly, this function is, at the moment, very limited. Even in the best of times, European embassies, like all other embassies, were under extreme surveillance, and ordinary citizens could never enter the embassy quarter. But even for young diplomats, e.g. in the Foreign Ministry of North Korea, exchanges and the occasional visit to the embassy could bring some additional experience and maybe hope for more exchanges.

Besides the political reasons to be on the ground, there are also clear humanitarian reasons. Humanitarian projects in North Korea will not happen by purely sending money or aid goods to the country. Monitoring aid is necessary for a multitude of reasons, starting with sanctions compliance, the building of trust for donors, to the monitoring of technical aspects, e.g. in using aid goods in agriculture, or administering drugs and vaccines, etc. While it can well be argued that the current humanitarian crisis in North Korea was avoidable, simply by shifting resources from military development to food imports, this is basically true for humanitarian crises all around the world. If the aim is to help suffering people, then aid should return as soon as possible to North Korea, given the lack of food and medicines. But even then, with the knowledge that returning is rational, necessary, and urgent, it does not yet determine how such a return should be organized: every organization for itself? In tandem with others? Diplomats before aid, or aid before diplomats? Then the next section will discuss the possibility of an organized, coordinated return as the best possible action.

Restarting humanitarian cooperation and diplomatic relations – the case for a big bang solution

North Korea, in dealing with foreign powers, has a long experience of expecting, and often getting, a special deal due to its allegedly special situation. Moreover, it has followed for decades a policy of "divide et impera", trying to squeeze the maximum in concessions out of others by dealing piecemeal with them, and often dealing with them in a way offering special access as a concession and later doing the same to another counterpart. For decades, the policy of equidistance between the Soviet Union and the People´s Republic of China, during the rift between both, allowed North Korea to gracefully accept the courtship of both of them. In dealing with European states, as with embassies in Pyongyang in general, North Korea did not simply lay down universal rules, following for example the Vienna Convention (which was never fully adhered to by North Korea), but rather allowed preferential access and privileges according to the perceived status of the country involved and the potential importance of the country as a partner. During the COVID pandemic, North Korea asked embassies which complained about the rules laid down by North Korea, essentially making diplomats prisoners in their embassies, to accept the rules as they were or to leave the country. It is very questionable, if a simple return to the status quo ante will be possible. Very likely, a concerted approach to the return will increase the bargaining power of diplomats (which is anyway pretty small, given the apparent lack of interest in North Korea).

At the same time, being back as the first is still, to some extent, attractive for foreign diplomats. This is partly related to a sporting sense among the (former) resident embassies, partly a question of personal job descriptions (an ambassador designated for North Korea needs to be there, or he could easily be re-assigned, maybe to a less interesting or prestigious job), and partly a question of documenting the importance of a certain country, even if it is only important in the eyes of North Korea´s leadership. A rush to North Korea to be the first (or among the first) being back could however put countries and NGO at a disadvantage vis-à-vis North Korea, since it would not make them bargain hard for their status in North Korea. A minimum requirement should be the vow to uphold the Vienna Convention (United Nations 2005) – this was already a problem before the COVID pandemic, since some regulations, e.g. on the freedom of traveling in the country (article 26) were not fully implemented. A re-negotiation to achieve the same or better terms than before 2020 might be successful, if it comes not from a single government alone, but as a concerted demand from returning governments and NGOs alike. For the NGO, a larger freedom of movement would be even more important – since they are not diplomats, and at the same time mostly work on humanitarian projects outside of Pyongyang. It might look naïve to expect such a re-negotiation to be successful, given the strained international relations with European countries. But, if all countries would agree and put some potential sanctions on North Korea, too, it might work. These sanctions include first much stricter rules of residence for North Korean diplomats: For example, North Korean diplomats in Germany are free to travel in Berlin and Brandenburg (the surrounding state). Given the size of Brandenburg, this means that control of their movement, in particular, once they leave Berlin, is barely possible. A restriction to Berlin, which is very similar to the restriction that diplomats have to stay in Pyongyang, would be a first countermeasure. Even more, if North Korea would put up unsustainable conditions on a return to Pyongyang, even a complete expulsion of North Koreans from EU countries could be considered. North Korea would not be insensitive to that, partly due to the real interests they still have in relations with these countries and partly also because of the loss of prestige which would accompany such a move. Ironically then, threatening expulsion could make a return to Pyongyang more realistic, and to better terms than before.

However, how could such a move happen in practice? Already in 2023, a number of meetings took place with restricted groups of actors, some of them stakeholders under the UN, some of them governments meeting in a contact group, and some of them assembled by NGOs. These are, however, insufficient to put realistic pressure on North Korea. The best solution would be a large, encompassing stakeholder conference to be brought together, ideally under the auspices of the European Union and in Brussels, though other conveners might also be possible. These could bring together government actors, international organizations and international NGOs, other stakeholders like academics and think tanks involved in the discussion, and individuals with knowledge of North Korea and cooperation with North Korea. South Korea most likely would not be part of it, since South Korean involvement would invariably politicize discussions much more. The stakeholder meeting could then first of all define goals of return vis-à-vis North Korea (a "wish list"). Ideally, it should include France and Estonia, dangling the carrot of recognition in front of North Korea.

One important task of return would also be a new way to finance embassies and aid work in North Korea. Due to international and US sanctions, no banking channel does exist any more to deal with North Korea. In the last ten years, for these reasons, most of the embassy, UN, and NGO business had to be carried out in cash. This situation is widely unpopular and dissatisfying. It is logistically difficult, dangerous, and expensive. It opens up the door for corruption, among the donors, but in particular also among the receivers, a situation not at all desirable from the point of view of donors. A much better way would be the creation of a "good bank", as a single-purpose entity to finance the abovementioned businesses (Seliger 2010). It would, to some extent, follow the ill-fated Instex example. Instex, the Instrument in Support of Trade Exchanges, was a European special-purpose vehicle established in 2019 to facilitate non-USD and non-SWIFT transactions for trade with Iran without breaking US sanctions. It was originally joined by Belgium, Denmark, the Netherlands, Finland, and Sweden. The purpose of Instex transactions was limited to humanitarian activities, like buying medicines or food. However, after only one single successful transaction, in March 2023, the mechanism was ended. The opposition of the US might have been a crucial problem. In the case of a "good bank" for North Korea, preparatory talks with the US would be crucial, too.

Such negotiations would be anyway necessary, since another important issue would be to achieve a better, i.e. more smooth track record of humanitarian activities in North Korea. The advent of the sanctions regime after 2016 meant that suddenly many activities were unduly prolonged, and that some large, state sanctions evaders practically went unpunished, while small NGO, in particular in the US, had problems bringing in necessary documents and evading OFAC restrictions. This created a lot of frustration, which has been partly alleviated by successive reports and action on reports by the Panel of Experts. But still, a speedier clearance under the sanctions system, like a de minimis rule, or group exemptions for certain goods, would be helpful. Given the actual humanitarian crisis in North Korea, it would be great for returning NGO and embassies to offer this as a kind of incentive for North Korea.

Finally, a stakeholder conference should also discuss the relationship between humanitarian relief and longer-term structural change. In the past, discussing structural change, for example, in the field of agriculture, was barely possible due to ideological opposition from North Korea. However, there are methods which can enhance structural change: scholarships, bringing North Korea into international organizations and conventions, instead of isolating them, upscale of activities from model to nationwide, etc. All this should also be discussed, so that a return to North Korea would not simply mean a return to the same working conditions as before 2020, or even worse, but would also bring new approaches for longer-lasting change.

Conclusion – is a big bang solution thinkable?

As we saw, for a number of reasons, a "big bang" solution of a coordinated return of at least all European actors, embassies, and NGOs alike, would be the best solution. However, it seems unfortunately rather unlikely. One reason is that currently the general interest of European governments in returning to North Korea exists, but only as a very sidelined project. The Russian aggression in Ukraine and since October 2023 the Hamas terrorist attacks, widening to a war in the Near East, are far more preoccupying, for absolutely understandable reasons. But these events are not singular: North Korea started to deliver ammunition and most likely weapons to Russia. The Hamas spoke of the day which would come when they would fight side-by-side with North Korea. This shows that in a multilateral, open world order one cannot simply neglect what happens in other world regions. The lack of a convener of a stakeholder conference for North Korea is an important problem. Without such a convener, who devotes material and financial resources to such a conference, it will likely never take place. Smaller formats, as the aforementioned contact group of governments willing to return to North Korea or NGO-led discussions on returning to North Korea are far less able to create the pressure necessary in their own countries and in North Korea to come to favorable terms of return to the country. There is still a small window of opportunity to do so, before a piecemeal return starts, probably early next year.

References

Alexandrova, Iordanka (2019). "The European Union's Policy Toward North Korea: Abandoning Engagement," International Journal of Korean Unification Studies, Vol. 28, No. 1, 2019, pp. 33–62.

Ballbach, Eric (2022). Moving Beyond Targeted Sanctions The Sanctions Regime of the European Union against North Korea, SWP Research Paper no. 4, Berlin: German Institute for International and Security Affairs, Internet file: https://www.swp-berlin.org/publications/products/research_papers/2022RP04_SanctionsEUNorthKorea_Web.pdf. [07.03.2023]

Ballbach, Eric (2019). The end of Critical Engagement: on the failures of the EU's North Korea strategy, ARI 101/2019 - 6/11/2019 - Elcano Royal Institute, Internet file: https://media.realinstitutoelcano.org/wp-content/uploads/2021/11/ari101-2019-ballbach-the-end-of-critical-engagement-on-failures-of-eus-north-korea-strategy.pdf [07.03.2023]

Bremer, Ifang (2022a, 22. April). European Union sanctions 12 people and entities linked to DPRK weapons program. NK News.

https://www.nknews.org/2022/04/european-union-sanctions-12-people-and-entities-linked-to-dprk-weapons-program/ [07.03.2023]

Bremer, Ifang (2022b, 25. April). North Korea accuses EU of 'hostile policy' after new sanctions go into effect. NK News.

https://www.nknews.org/2022/04/north-korea-accuses-eu-of-hostile-policy-after-new-sanctions-go-into-effect/?t=1678148465

Bremer, Ifang (2022c, 30. May). G7 foreign ministers condemn North Korea for 'yet another' ICBM launch. NK News.

https://www.nknews.org/2022/05/g7-foreign-ministers-condemn-north-korea-for-yet-another-icbm-launch/ [07.03.2023]

Bremer, Ifang (2022d, 7. April). Report on North Korea killing Christians galvanizes EU to condemn rights abuses. NK News.

https://www.nknews.org/2022/04/report-on-north-korea-killing-christians-galvanizes-eu-to-condemn-rights-abuses/ [07.03.2023]

Bremer, Ifang (2022e, 20. April). North Korea slams European Parliament as 'gang of liars' after human rights vote. NK News.

https://www.nknews.org/2022/04/north-korea-slams-european-parliament-as-gang-of-liars-after-human-rights-vote/ [07.03.2023]

Bremer, Ifang (2022f, 6. December). European Council renews human rights sanctions on top North Korean officials. NK News.

https://www.nknews.org/2022/12/european-council-renews-human-rights-sanctions-on-top-north-korean-officials/ [07.03.2023]

Bremer, Ifang (2022g, 19. May). UN human rights agency calls on North Korea to open borders to COVID-19 aid. NK News.

https://www.nknews.org/2022/05/un-human-rights-agency-calls-on-north-korea-to-open-borders-to-covid-19-aid/ [07.03.2023]

Chung, Chaewon (2022, 6. June). North Korea takes aim at G7 as it insists it has never recognized UN sanctions. NK News.

https://www.nknews.org/2022/06/north-korea-takes-aim-at-g7-as-it-insists-it-has-never-recognized-un-sanctions/ [07.03.2023]

Choy, Min Chao (2020a, 31. March). European states condemn "provocative" missile testing by North Korea. NK News.

https://www.nknews.org/2020/03/european-states-condemn-provocative-missile-testing-by-north-korea/ [07.03.2023]

Choy, Min Chao (2020b, 17. June). North Korea slams "absurd" European Union calls for deescalation of tensions. NK News.

https://www.nknews.org/2020/06/north-korea-slams-absurd-european-union-calls-for-de-escalation-of-tensions/ [07.03.2023]

Choy, Min Chao (2020c, 22. July). European Union to impose sanctions on North Korean companies due to cyberattacks. NK News.

https://www.nknews.org/2020/07/european-union-to-impose-sanctions-on-north-korean-companies-due-to-cyberattacks/ [07.03.2023]

Derr, Arius & Chung, Yeji (2022, 30. September). North Korea has reached out to EU to arrange meeting next month: Sources. NK News.

https://www.nknews.org/2022/09/north-korea-has-reached-out-to-eu-to-arrange-meeting-next-month-sources/ [07.03.2023]

Deutsche Welle (2022). Despite UN sanctions German Research Institute worked with North Korean scientists, Internet file:

https://www.dw.com/en/despite-un-sanctions-german-research-institute-worked-with-north-korean-scientists/a-63890089 [07.03.2023]

Elblaus, Erko (2021, 7. October). Taekwondo, tourism and trade: Estonia's ties with North Korea. NK News.

https://www.nknews.org/pro/taekwondo-tourism-and-trade-estonias-ties-with-north-korea/ [07.03.2023]

Everard, John (2021, 12. April). North Korea faces uncertain future after mass exodus of UN and foreign NGO staff. NK News.

https://www.nknews.org/pro/north-korea-faces-uncertain-future-after-mass-exodus-of-un-and-foreign-ngo-staff/ [07.03.2023]

Ford, Glyn (2023). "From Coy to Cold Shoulder - The European Union and North Korea," Asia-Pacific Bulletin, Washington, D.C. East-West Center,

https://www.eastwestcenter.org/publications/coy-cold-shoulder-european-union-and-north-korea. [10.10.2023]

Frank, Rüdiger (2002), "EU - North Korean Relations: No Effort Without Reason," International Journal of Korean Unification Studies,Seoul: Korea Institute of National Unification, Vol. 11, no. 2, pp. 87-119.

Fromer, Jacob (2020a, 11. May). Some North Korean exports to China resold in EU and South Korea, data suggests. NK News.

https://www.nknews.org/pro/some-north-korean-exports-to-china-resold-in-eu-and-south-korea-data-suggests/ [07.03.2023]

Fromer, Jacob (2020b, 12. May). Millions of dollars' worth of exports to China likely rerouted to North Korea. NK News.

https://www.nknews.org/pro/millions-of-dollars-worth-of-exports-to-china-likely-rerouted-to-north-korea/ [07.03.2023]

Fromer, Jacob (2020c, 6. April). Countries must "clarify" sanctions won't block COVID-19 aid to North Korea: EU. NK News.

https://www.nknews.org/2020/04/countries-must-clarify-sanctions-wont-block-covid-19-aid-to-north-korea-eu/ [07.03.2023]

Fromer, Jacob & Hotham, Oliver (2020, 9. March). Following Brexit, North Korean embassy in Germany now running relations with EU. NK News.

https://www.nknews.org/2020/03/following-brexit-north-korean-embassy-in-germany-now-running-relations-with-eu/ [07.03.2023]

Hotham, Oliver (2020, 28. Januar). North Korean embassy-linked Berlin hostel must be shut down, German court rules. NK News.

https://www.nknews.org/2020/01/north-korean-embassy-linked-berlin-hostel-must-be-shut-down-german-court-says/

Jewell, Ethan (2022, 13. December). EU targets North Korea nuclear program with new sanctions after missile tests. NK News.

https://www.nknews.org/2022/12/eu-targets-north-korea-nuclear-program-with-new-sanctions-after-missile-tests/ [07.03.2023]

Jewell, Ethan (2021, 8. Dezember). European Council renews human rights sanctions against North Korean officials. NK News.

https://www.nknews.org/2021/12/european-council-renews-human-rights-sanctions-against-north-korean-officials/ [07.03.2023]

Jung, Won-Gi (2021, 19. May). EU extends sanctions to combat cyberattacks from North Korea and others. NK News.

https://www.nknews.org/2021/05/eu-extends-sanctions-to-combat-cyberattacks-from-north-korea-and-others/ [07.03.2023]

Kasulis, Kelly & Choy, Min Chao (2020, 16. Oktober). North Korea slams 'The Mole' documentary as 'nonsense' and demands raw footage. NK News.

https://www.nknews.org/2020/10/north-korea-slams-the-mole-documentary-as-nonsense-and-demands-raw-footage/ [07.03.2023]

Kim, Jeongmin (2021a, 26. October). EU open to video talks with North Korea after diplomats withdraw from meetings. NK News.

\https://www.nknews.org/2021/10/eu-open-to-video-talks-with-north-korea-after-diplomats-withdraw-from-meetings/ [07.03.2023]

Kim, Jeongmin (2021b, 31. March). EU grants almost $590,000 to help North Koreans cope with climate disasters. NK News.

https://www.nknews.org/2021/03/eu-grants-almost-590000-to-help-north-koreans-cope-with-climate-disasters/ [07.03.2023]

Kim, Jeongmin and Hotham, Oliver (2020, 7. March). North Korea warns of "grave response" to EU states' condemnation of missile test. NK News.

https://www.nknews.org/2020/03/north-korea-warns-of-grave-response-to-eu-states-condemnation-of-missile-test/

Kim, Min-hyung and Jinwoo Choi (2020). "What kind of power is the EU? The EU's policies toward North Korea's WMD programs and the debate about the EU's role in the security arena," Asia Europe Journal, Vol. 18, pp. 1-16.

Lee, Sung-Yoon (2022, 25. Oktober). Expel North Korean diplomats to send a message to Kim Jong Un. NK News.

https://www.nknews.org/2022/10/expel-north-korean-diplomats-to-send-a-message-to-kim-jong-un/ [07.03.2023]

Levi, Nicolas (2023, 14. February). How Paris became the favorite European escape of North Korea's elite. NK News.

https://www.nknews.org/2023/02/how-paris-became-the-favorite-european-escape-of-north-koreas-elite/ [07.03.2023]

Levi, Nicolas (2022, 5. September). Why Poland could play a key role in efforts to engage North Korea. NK News.

https://www.nknews.org/pro/why-poland-could-play-a-key-role-in-efforts-to-engage-north-korea/ [07.03.2023]

McEachern, Patrick (2010). Inside the Red Box: North Korea's Post-Totalitarian Politics, Contemporary Asia in the World, New York: Columbia University Press.

Novotna, Tereza (2023, 20. January). How the Czech Republic positions itself between hawks and doves on North Korea. NK News.

https://www.nknews.org/pro/how-the-czech-republic-positions-itself-between-hawks-and-doves-on-north-korea/ [07.03.2023]

O'Carroll, Chad (2022, 12. October). North Korea cancels meeting with EU diplomatic service: Sources. NK News.

https://www.nknews.org/2022/10/north-korea-cancels-meeting-with-eu-diplomatic-service-sources/ [07.03.2023]

O'Carroll, Chad (2021a, 14. October). First North Korean delegation to attend EU-related meetings since pandemic began. NK News.

https://www.nknews.org/2021/10/first-north-korean-delegation-to-attend-eu-related-meetings-since-pandemic-began/ [07.03.2023]

O'Carroll, Chad (2021b, 22. October). North Koreans pull out of EU-related meeting without explanation. NK News.

https://www.nknews.org/2021/10/north-koreans-pull-out-of-eu-related-meetings-without-explanation/ [07.03.2023]

O'Carroll, Chad (2021b, 9. September). China tells UN 'The Mole' isn't a credible source for sanctions investigations. NK News.

https://www.nknews.org/2021/09/china-tells-un-the-mole-isnt-a-credible-source-for-sanctions-investigations/ [07.03.2023]

O'Carroll, Chad (2020a, 15. Oktober). North Korean embassy official calls 'The Mole' documentary a 'total fabrication'. NK News.

https://www.nknews.org/2020/10/north-korean-embassy-official-calls-the-mole-documentary-a-total-fabrication/ [07.03.2023]

O'Carroll, Chad (2020b, 27. February). Some European missions in Pyongyang to temporarily close amid coronavirus fears. NK News.

https://www.nknews.org/pro/some-european-missions-in-pyongyang-to-temporarily-close-amid-coronavirus-fears/ [07.03.2023]

Schäfer, Thomas (2021) From Kim Jong Il to Kim Jong Un: How the Hardliners Prevailed: On the Political History of North Korea (2007 - 2020), self-published without place.

Seliger, Bernhard (2010). Creating a Good Bank for North Korea (and a bad bank within) – Creative Capacity-Building as a Domain for Asian-European Cooperation, Europe – North Korea, Between Humanitarism and Business?, Global Cultural and Economic Research, No. 6, Berlin: LIT, pp. 225-245.

United Nations (2005). Vienna Convention on Diplomatic Relations 1961, Internet file: https://legal.un.org/ilc/texts/instruments/english/conventions/9_1_1961.pdf [07.03.2023]

Yoon, Deok-Ryong (2001). Economic implications of improved DPRK-EU relations, The Journal of East Asian Affairs, Vol. 15, no. 2 (Fall/ Winter 2001), pp. 324-343.

Zwirko, Colin (2021, 22. March). EU hits North Korea with human rights-related sanctions for the first time. NK News.

https://www.nknews.org/2021/03/eu-hits-north-korea-with-human-rights-related-sanctions-for-the-first-time/ [07.03.2023]

Zwirko, Colin (2020, 3. April). Irish NGO granted humanitarian sanctions exemption for North Korea projects. NK News.

https://www.nknews.org/pro/irish-ngo-granted-humanitarian-sanctions-exemption-for-north-korea-projects/ [07.03.2023]

Korea-EU Trade Relations from a Global Supply Chain Perspective

A Review through Global Value Chain Data

KANG YOO-DUK

Introduction

Global supply chains, which have historically been driving forces behind the growth of global trade, are now facing a myriad of challenges. The escalating competition for supremacy between the United States and China has prompted other countries to consider reshaping or bringing their supply chain operations closer to home or reducing their scale to retain control. At the same time, multinational corporations are shifting their focus away from solely chasing economic efficiency in constructing their supply chains, and instead, they are placing greater emphasis on stability. This shift in focus was triggered by the supply disruption caused by the COVID-19 pandemic, which exposed vulnerabilities in supply chains on a global scale. As a result, companies are adopting strategies to diversify their supply chains, increase their inventory levels, and prioritize risk management throughout their supply chain operations. These developments are contributing to a noticeable decline in the once-prevailing positive perceptions of globalization.

This international trend presents significant challenges for Korea, which needs to develop trade policies that reconcile the traditional principles of globalization, marked by an emphasis on economic efficiency, with the growing economic security concerns of major nations. In this context, this study aims to examine the trade relations between Korea and the European Union (EU) through the lens of supply chains. It is worth noting that the EU is Korea's primary export market, and the Korea-EU Free Trade Agreement (FTA) represents Korea's first FTA with a major advanced economy. However, the current landscape differs significantly from the mid-2000s, when the Korea-EU FTA negotiations began. During that era, the global economy enjoyed an unprecedented boom, fostering rapid growth in international trade. Many countries, including Korea, implemented various policies, such as FTAs, to access foreign markets, reflecting the prevailing trend of free trade. Conversely, today, the concept of free trade faces substantial challenges. Particularly, recent discussions on supply chain reorganization have the potential to hinder the growth of international trade, which had previously thrived due to the expansion of the global value chains (GVCs).

The primary objective of this study extends beyond merely examining fluctuations in Korea's exports to the EU following the initiation of the Korea-EU FTA. Since many tariffs are either immediately eliminated or gradually phased out over several years, the impact on trade expansion is fundamentally tied to static factors. On the other hand, shifts in trade that occur several years after the implementation of an FTA are more likely to be influenced by structural factors. These include industrial reconfiguration, changes in trade specialization, and the emergence of new industries. Therefore, assessing dynamic changes in bilateral trade relations solely based on the overall change in trade volume can be misleading. This metric can be influenced by various factors, including economic conditions and exchange rates in the partner country, in addition to tariff adjustments. For that reason, this study seeks to measure the extent to which Korea's exports contribute to the industrial production of European countries through GVCs. Essentially, this study employs a supply chain perspective to scrutinize Korea-EU trade relations. This approach is guided by two critical considerations: First, direct trade (Korea-EU) based exclusively on customs clearance data focuses solely on final goods exports, disregarding indirect exports via third countries using intermediate products under the GVC framework. Secondly, the EU, encompassing 27 diverse countries, exhibits significant income disparities and specialized industrial profiles.[1]

Current Status of Korea-EU Trade Relations

Trends in Korea-EU Trade Relations

Korea has been a notable beneficiary of the rapid expansion of international trade. In 1974, Korea's trade exceeded $10 billion for the first time, achieving this milestone again by surpassing $100 billion just 14 years later in 1988. Subsequently, the country reached the $500 billion mark in 2005 and the monumental $1 trillion milestone in 2011. This remarkable growth was also reflected in Korea's global export share, which increased from a mere 0.27% in 1970 to a substantial 3.01% by 2012. In parallel, Korea's trade openness, measured as a percentage of GDP, surged from 33% to 105% over the same period.[2] This surge in trade has had an increasingly significant impact on economic growth and employment.

Korea's trade with the EU has developed alongside its overall trade growth, reflecting a changing economic configuration in Europe. Trade between Korea and Europe experienced significant growth during the mid-2000s. Between 2001 and 2008, Korea's trade with the EU exhibited an average annual growth rate of 15.2%, surpassing the corresponding growth rates of its trade with the United States and Japan, which stood at 6.8% and 10.9%, respectively, over the same period. Only trade with emerging markets outpaced this rate of growth. The notable upswing in Korea-EU trade during this period can be attributed to the EU's expansion into Central and Eastern Europe and the adoption of the euro, both of which stimulated trade and investment within Europe, thereby fostering robust economic growth.

〈Figure 1〉 Korea's Trade with its Partners

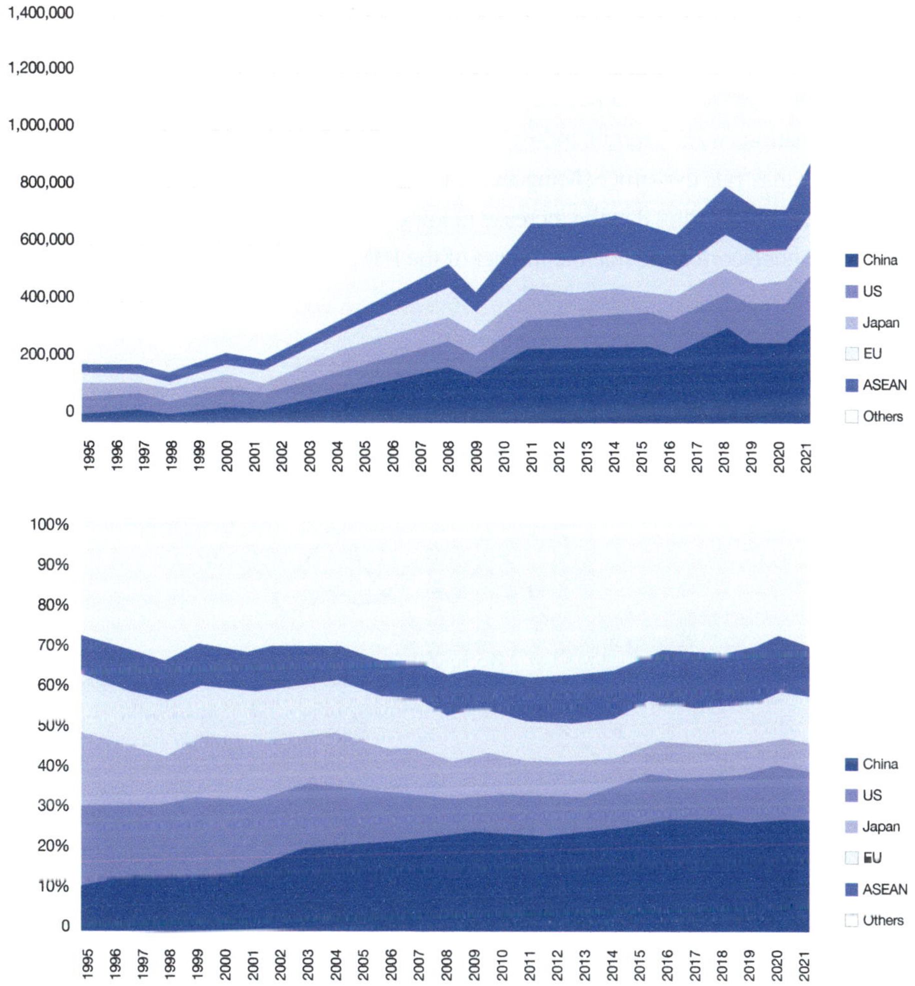

Note: Million US dollars. / Source: Author's elaboration based on the KITA data.

Figure 2 illustrates Korea's exports and imports to the EU over the years. Exports and imports followed a similar trajectory until 2008, but a substantial divergence occurred thereafter. Exports surged notably before the onset of the 2008 global financial crisis but subsequently exhibited fluctuating patterns, remaining in the range of $50 to $60 billion. In 2021, following the post-COVID-19 recovery, exports experienced a significant upswing, reaching $69.6 billion. In contrast, imports maintained a consistent upward trajectory throughout the period. Imports from the EU, which had dipped to $32.2 billion in 2009, soared to $71.7 billion in 2021. The trend of imports growing at a faster pace than exports persisted over an extended period. As a result, Korea's trade balance with the EU gradually eroded, turning into a deficit in 2012 for the first time since 1997, after registering a surplus of $19.3 billion in 2007. Notably, in 2014, the trade deficit reached $10.7 billion. The deterioration of the trade balance coincided with the implementation of the Korea-EU FTA in July 2011, sparking debates over the FTA's performance. Several studies have indicated that the worsening trade balance with the EU was influenced by multifaceted factors, including cyclical elements, demand fluctuations within certain industries (e.g., shipping), offshoring of production facilities, and exchange rate dynamics (Kang and Kim, 2013; Je, 2015; Kang, 2016; Porto, 2018). It is particularly noteworthy that the increase in imports was significantly influenced by tariff elimination, underscoring the notable impact of the FTA on trade dynamics.

〈Figure 2〉 Korea's Trade with the EU

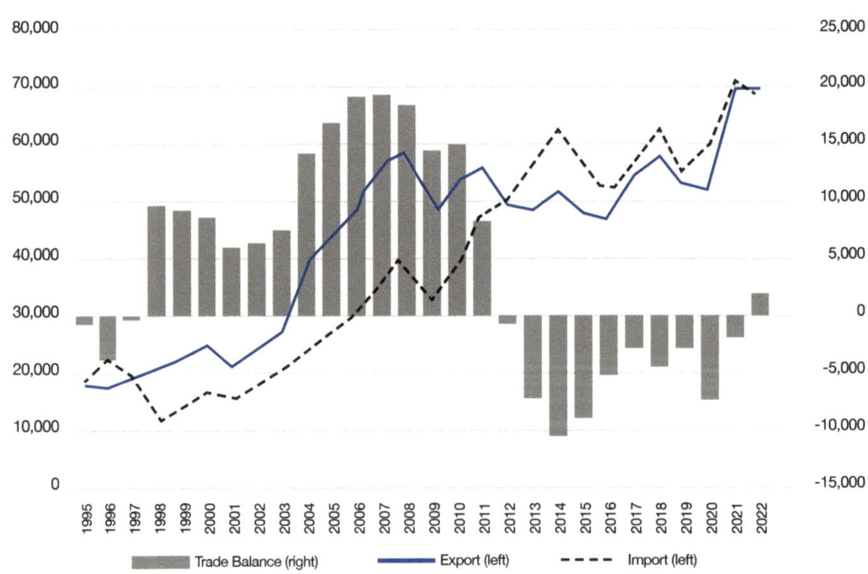

Note: Million US dollars.
Source: Author's elaboration based on the KITA data.

Trade Relations by Country and Product

Trade between Korea and individual countries indeed mirrors the distinctive industrial characteristics of each country, as shown in Figure 3. Korea has consistently recorded a trade deficit with Germany, France, and Italy. While exports and imports were relatively balanced between 2007 and 2008, subsequent years saw a notable surge in imports, resulting in a significant and persistent trade deficit until 2015. The increase in imports can be attributed to the rising inbound shipments of various items, including automobiles and mechanical equipment (Germany), aircraft and parts (France), and high-end consumer goods (France and Italy). Initially, trade with the UK registered a surplus; however, under the Korea-EU FTA, tariffs on North Sea crude oil were removed, and imports of British crude oil surged significantly, resulting in a trade deficit. On the other hand, trade with the four countries in Central and Eastern Europe consistently exhibits a surplus structure, with exports significantly exceeding imports. This surplus results from substantial investments by Korean companies in local production, leading to substantial Korean exports of intermediate goods to the host countries of the investments. While variations exist among these countries, exports experienced rapid growth between 2005 and 2009, illustrating the phenomenon where investments trigger exports. Notably, the exported items predominantly consist of intermediate goods such as automobile parts and electronic/mechanical components. These components are processed in local factories and subsequently re-exported to Western European markets. Thus, the trade relationship between Korea and the EU reflects a sequence from Korea to Western Europe via Central and Eastern Europe.

〈Figure 3〉 Korea's Trade with EU Member Countries (selected)

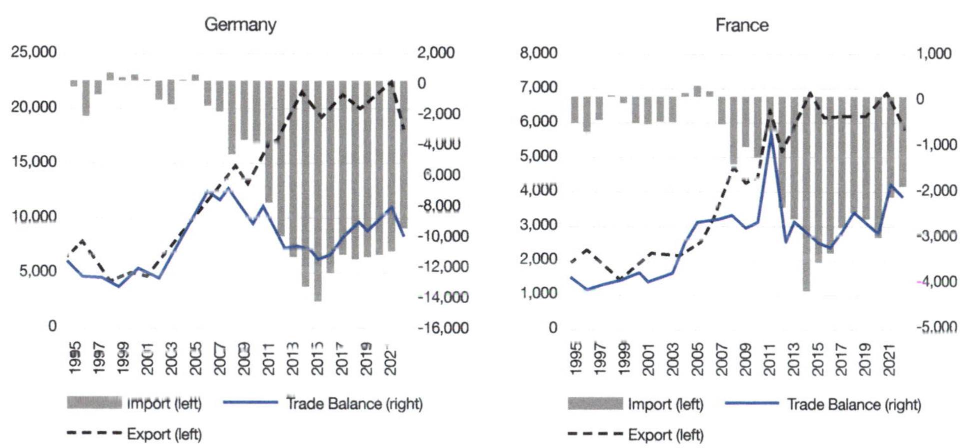

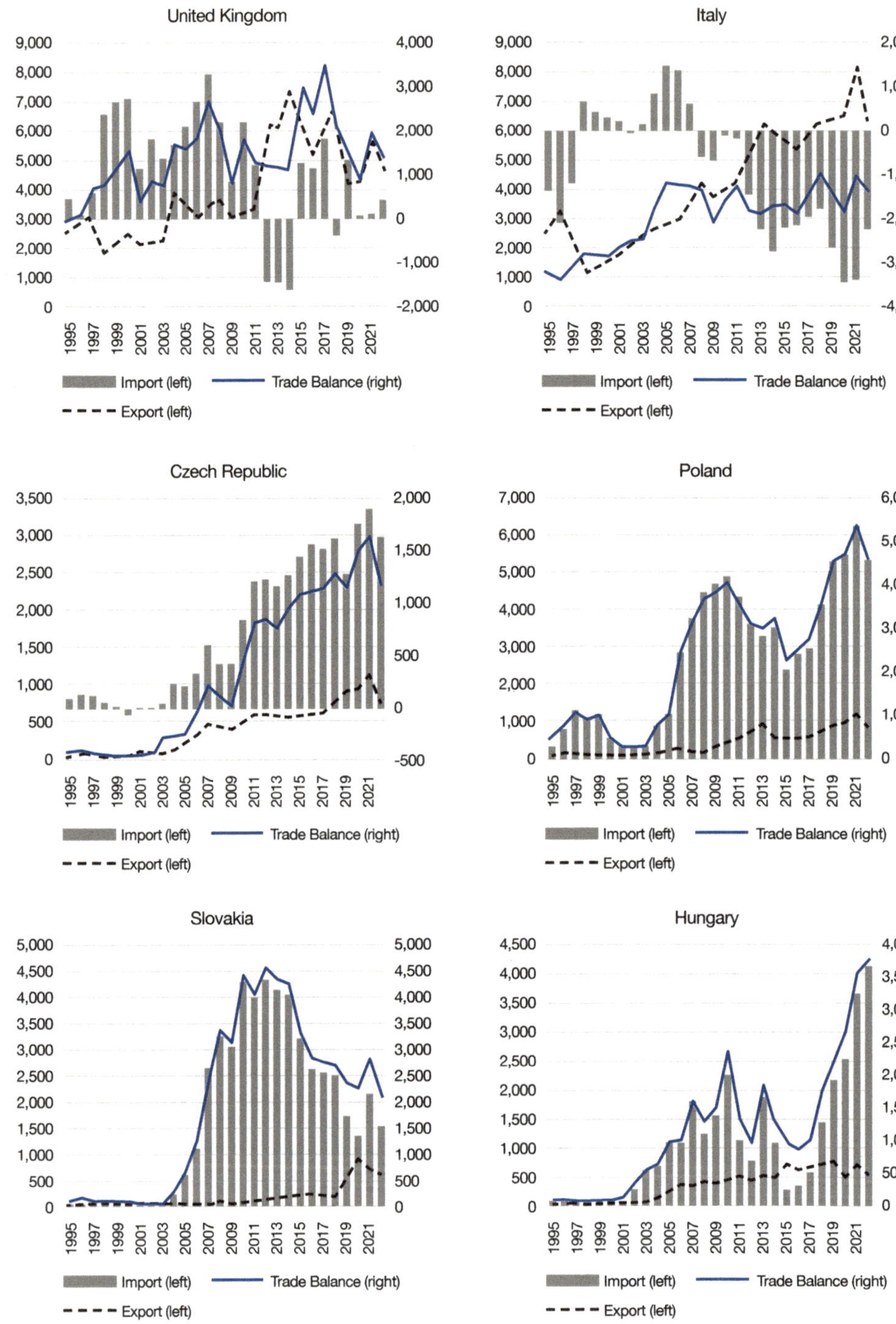

Note: Million US dollars.

Source: Author's elaboration based on the KITA data.

Table 1 offers a summary of the top 20 items that make up the highest proportion of Korea's exports to the EU. In 2011, aligning with the commencement of the Korea-EU FTA, the leading items included 'ships and parts,' followed by 'automobiles' and 'LCDs and sensors.' Notably, ship exports accounted for a substantial 22.7% of total exports during that period. However, as of 2021, major export items remained relatively consistent with those in 2011, but there was a significant shift in their proportions. Notably, the share of ship exports notably decreased from 22.7% to 8.9%, resulting in export values declining by over 50%. One of the most remarkable changes occurred in the category of 'flat panel displays (LCDs) and sensors,' which dropped from $5.47 billion in exports in 2010 to a mere $360 million in 2021, subsequently falling out of the top 20 items. This shift was primarily driven by Korean investments shifting away from LCD production and redirecting their focus toward other items on a substantial scale. Similarly, the proportion of wireless communication devices also contracted, primarily as a result of Korean production facilities relocating overseas. In contrast, the export share of automobiles surged during the period from 2011 to 2021. The three major items (based on MTI 3 units) that experienced rapid export growth were pharmaceuticals, batteries, and machinery (as shown in Figure 4). Pharmaceutical exports exhibited steady growth but witnessed a significant surge during the pandemic. Battery exports expanded notably due to the widespread adoption of electric vehicles and the establishment of local production facilities by domestic companies. Previously, Korea's exports to the EU faced criticism for being highly concentrated in specific sectors such as ships, electronics/wireless communications, and automobiles (Kang and Kim, 2013). However, the proportion of exports in these sectors decreased as exports of new categories surged, thereby reducing the concentration on specific products. An examination of the Herfindahl-Hirschmann index revealed that product concentration decreased between 2011 and 2021.

〈Table 1〉 Korea's top 20 export items to the EU (2011, 2021)

Year 2011					Year 2021				
	MTI	Items	Amount	Share (%)		MTI	Items	Amount	Share (%)
1	746	Ships and parts	12,665	22.7	1	741	Automobile	10,063	14.5
2	741	Automobile	5,737	10.3	2	746	Ships and parts	6,179	8.9
3	836	LCD and sensor	3,886	7.0	3	742	Automotive Parts	4,244	6.1
4	742	Automotive Parts	3,747	6.7	4	214	Synthetic resin	3,514	5.1
5	133	Petroleum products	2,949	5.3	5	226	Pharmaceuticals	3,213	4.6

Year 2011					Year 2021				
	MTI	Items	Amount	Share (%)		MTI	Items	Amount	Share (%)
6	812	Wireless communication device	2,810	5.0	6	613	Steel plate	2,969	4.3
7	831	Semiconductor	2,547	4.6	7	835	Batteries and storage batteries	2,711	3.9
8	613	Steel plate	1,609	2.9	8	831	Semiconductor	2,689	3.9
9	214	Synthetic resin	1,255	2.2	9	228	Fine chemical raw materials	2,681	3.9
10	813	Computer	1,210	2.2	10	812	Wireless communication device	2,389	3.4
11	725	Construction, mining machinery	1,016	1.8	11	813	Computer	2,196	3.2
12	821	Video equipment	972	1.7	12	310	Plastic products	1,550	2.2
13	320	Rubber products	932	1.7	13	725	Construction, mining machinery	1,368	2.0
14	711	Prime movers and pumps	712	1.3	14	711	Prime movers and pumps	1,154	1.7
15	310	Plastic products	630	1.1	15	320	Rubber products	1,056	1.5
16	228	Fine chemical raw materials	537	1.0	16	790	Other machinery	1,027	1.5
17	723	Metal machine tools	471	0.8	17	842	Industrial electrical equipment	893	1.3
18	751	Machine elements	465	0.8	18	814	Electronic application equipment	862	1.2
19	614	Steel pipes and steel wires	419	0.8	19	751	Machine elements	801	1.2
20	715	Optical equipment	417	0.7	20	133	Petroleum products	739	1.1
		Total of 20 items	44,986	80.6			Total of 20 items	52,298	75.2
		Total exports	55,806	100			Total exports	69,576	100

Source: Author's elaboration based on the KITA data.

〈Figure 4〉 Korea's Export to the EU by Product Group

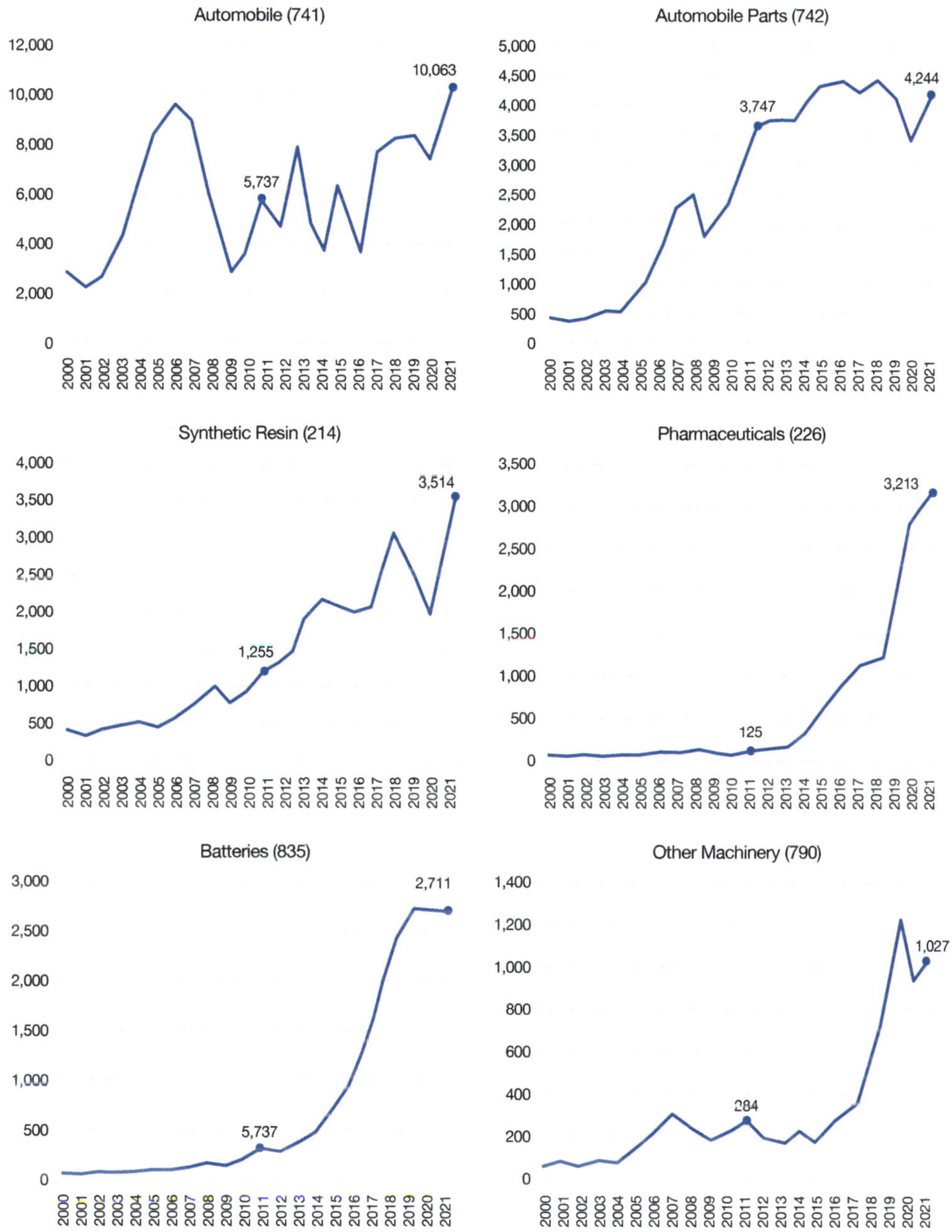

Note: Million US dollars.
Source: Author's elaboration based on the KITA data.

Korea's imports from the EU, categorized by item, are summarized in Table 2. When comparing 2011 and 2022, the top three items remained consistent, but their proportions increased significantly (as illustrated in Figure 5). The share of automobiles in total imports surged notably from 6.6% to 12.2%, marking a 178% increase in terms of value. The proportion of semiconductor manufacturing equipment nearly doubled, with imports from the Netherlands, the largest contributor, more than tripling between 2011 and 2021. It's worth noting that annual import volumes vary widely for these high-value equipment goods. Items exhibiting similar trade statistics characteristics include 'aircraft and parts.' Additionally, pharmaceuticals also recorded a notable increase of 173%. Imports of high-end consumer goods, such as personal items and clothing, displayed steady growth. Consequently, Korea's trade with the EU indicated an inclination toward increased product concentration during the decade following the implementation of the Korea-EU FTA. This shift reversed the previous trend and led to heightened product concentration in both exports and imports. An interesting point to note is the introduction of North Sea Brent oil imports, which were previously absent before 2010 but have now become a significant component of Korea's imports, albeit with annual variations.

〈Table 2〉 Korea's top 20 import items from the EU (2011, 2021)

Year 2011					Year 2021				
	MTI	Items	Amount	Share (%)		MTI	Items	Amount	Share (%)
1	741	Automobile	3,151	6.6	1	741	Automobile	8,750	12.2
2	732	Semiconductor manufacturing equipment	2,627	5.5	2	732	Semiconductor manufacturing equipment	7,429	10.4
3	226	Pharmaceuticals	2,126	4.5	3	226	Pharmaceuticals	5,807	8.1
4	742	Automotive Parts	2,044	4.3	4	511	Personal miscellaneous goods	2,773	3.9
5	711	Prime movers and pumps	1,870	3.9	5	815	Measurement control analyzer	1,946	2.7
6	751	Machine elements	1,653	3.5	6	711	Prime movers and pumps	1,924	2.7
7	815	Measurement control analyzer	1,526	3.2	7	742	Automotive Parts	1,796	2.5
8	747	Aircraft and parts	1,447	3.0	8	831	Semiconductor	1,738	2.4
9	228	Fine chemical raw materials	1,359	2.9	9	133	Petroleum products	1,627	2.3
10	831	Semiconductor	1,251	2.6	10	751	Machine elements	1,492	2.1
11	746	Ships and parts	961	2.0	11	441	Clothes	1,409	2.0
12	511	Personal miscellaneous goods	950	2.0	12	111	Gold silver and platinum	1,307	1.8
13	790	Other machinery	926	2.0	13	228	Fine chemical raw materials	1,300	1.8
14	618	Alloy pig iron and scrap metal	782	1.6	14	15	Food	1,255	1.7
15	721	Textile and chemical machinery	747	1.6	15	131	Crude oil	1,192	1.7
16	133	Petroleum products	739	1.6	16	24	Processed livestock products	1,139	1.6

Year 2011					Year 2021				
	MTI	Items	Amount	Share (%)		MTI	Items	Amount	Share (%)
17	214	Synthetic resin	734	1.5	17	814	Electronic application equipment	1,069	1.5
18	22	Meat	715	1.5	18	842	Industrial electrical equipment	1,062	1.5
19	811	Wired communication equipment	708	1.5	19	22	Meat	996	1.4
20	814	Electronic application equipment	705	1.5	20	229	Other fine chemical products	966	1.3
		Total of 20 items	27,024	57.0			Total of 20 items	47,007	65.5
		Total imports	47,444	100			Total imports	71,740	100

〈Figure 5〉 Korea's Import from the EU by Product Group

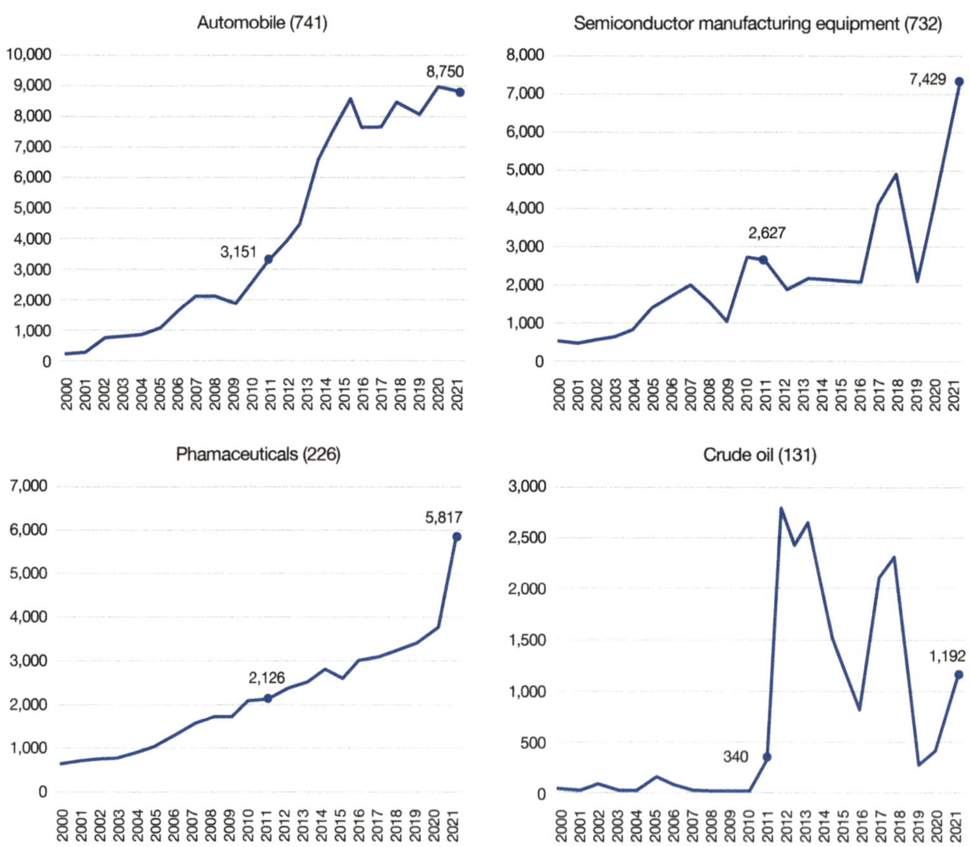

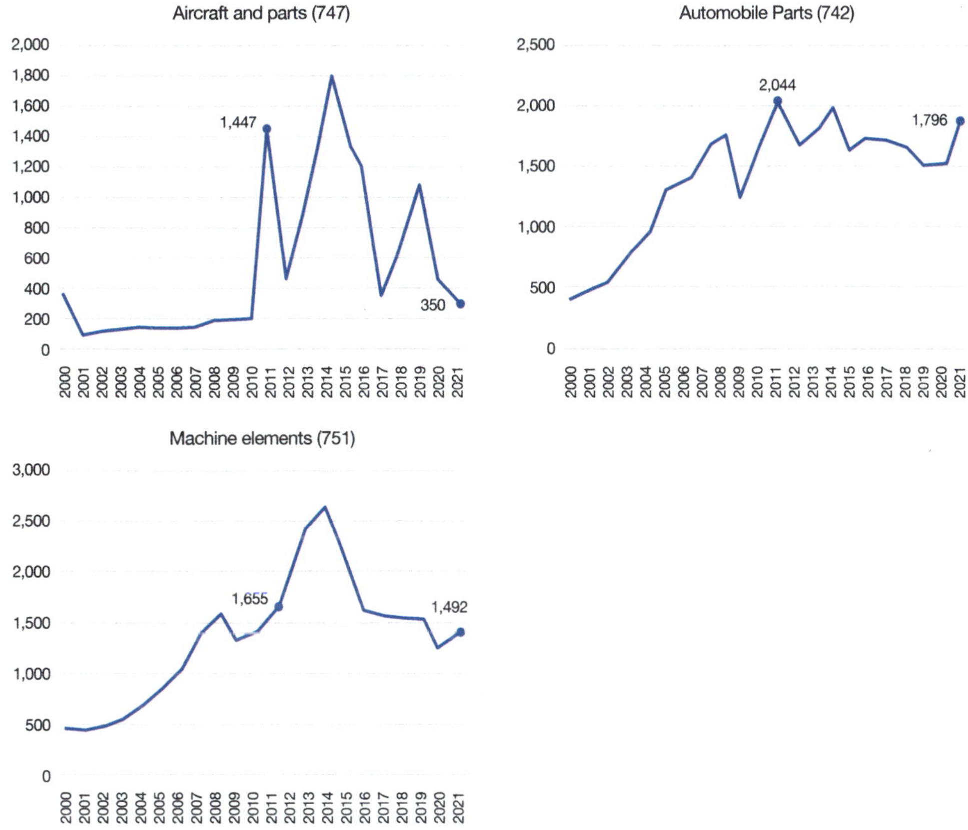

Korea-EU Trade Relations and GVC

Characteristics of Korea-EU Trade Relations and GVC

Since the 1980s, foreign direct investment (FDI) has experienced significant growth, creating connections between production bases in investing countries and host nations. As a result, trade in intermediate goods has flourished, leading to a trade framework rooted in vertical specialization. Additionally, starting in the 2000s, there has been a surge in trade at the process and task levels, making substantial contributions to both the quantitative and qualitative expansion of international trade. This expansion was made possible by the development of information and communication technology and a trade-friendly environment that facilitated long-distance supply chains while reducing trade barriers. This environment allowed companies to identify distant suppliers, subcontract processes and tasks, and establish a detailed international division of labor based on economic efficiency and comparative advantage. For example, in the case of memory semiconductors, a complex global supply chain involving over 70 border crossings has emerged, taking into account equipment, materials, and tasks (Khan et al., 2021). Research on the role and utilization of GVCs in international trade has gained momentum since 2010. The concept of GVCs became more defined as international organizations such as the OECD and WTO developed the `World Input-Output Database (WIOD), which interconnected each country's industrial relationship tables. This development has opened up diverse research possibilities (Trimmer et al., 2013; Trimmer et al., 2014; Los et al., 2015). Previously, the emphasis was primarily on the positive impact of participation itself on economic growth rates, with limited consideration for the nature of international trade (Dollar and Kraay, 2001). With the emergence of GVC research, discussions on how to engage with GVCs expanded beyond simple trade growth.

The degree to which a country engages with GVCs in trade can be evaluated by considering both forward and backward participation. Forward participation involves the production of intermediate goods such as parts and materials, which are then exported to assembly countries. In contrast, backward participation involves the importation of intermediate goods from abroad, followed by processing and assembly to create final goods. Figure 6 provides a comparison of GVC participation levels among EU member states and major countries, distinguishing between forward and backward participation. In general, Central and Eastern European countries exhibit higher levels of GVC participation compared to their Western European counterparts. While Western European nations like the UK, Germany, and France have relatively high proportions of forward participation, Central and Eastern European countries predominantly demonstrate a strong inclination towards backward participation. Notably, Slovakia, Hungary, and the Czech Republic lead in backward participation across Europe, serving as key production hubs on the continent. This pattern of GVC participation is reminiscent of the role played by Vietnam in East Asia. Backward participation typically characterizes emerging economies with a robust manufacturing base, while developed nations tend to exhibit higher forward participation due to their competitive advantage in parts and materials. Variations in the degree of forward and backward participation among EU member states can be attributed to differences in income levels, industrial development, and specialization. This disparity is a prominent feature of the EU economy. Major Western European nations such as Germany, France, and the United Kingdom maintain core competitiveness across both manufacturing and service industries. In contrast, Central and Eastern European countries established their industrial foundations through significant foreign direct investment (FDI) during the transitional phase and EU accession. As a result, their trade structure features modest exports of parts and materials, with a strong emphasis on exporting final products.

〈Figure 6〉 GVC Participation of EU Member Countries vs. Other Countries

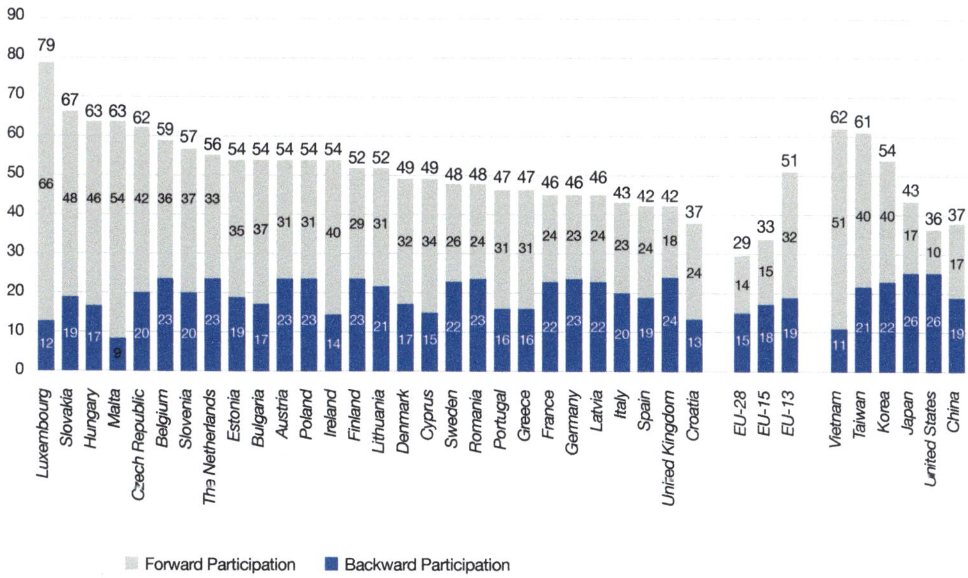

Source: Author's elaboration using the OECD TiVA data.

Trade Relations Reflecting GVCs

Traditional trade statistics are built upon customs-based transactions that occur across national borders. When applied to Korea's exports to the EU, this framework is depicted in Figure 7. Under this framework, export statistics do not differentiate between domestic and overseas value-added, nor do they distinguish between final and intermediate goods within exported items. As a result, the importing country cannot discern whether the imported goods are intended for final domestic consumption (final goods), utilized as intermediate goods in other industries, or re-exported to meet overseas demand. For countries with established processing or intermediate trade, it may appear that both exports (final goods) and imports (intermediate goods) are significantly inflated compared to the nation's actual industrial production capacity. The growth in exports based on domestic value-added may seem much smaller than the export growth reflected in these statistics. For instance, in 2018, the domestic value-added in Hong Kong's manufacturing sector exports accounted for only 28.1%, while Vietnam's reached 44.1%. In contrast, among OECD member countries, the average domestic value-added in manufacturing exports amounted to 88.4%.

〈Figure 7〉 Exports reported according to customs clearance data

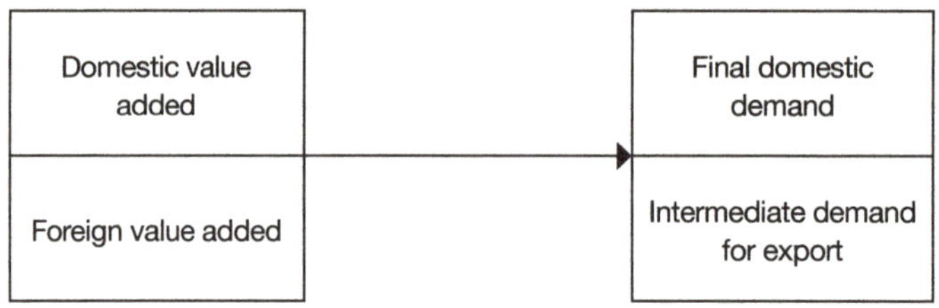

Source: Author's elaboration.

To address these limitations, it becomes essential to examine exports based on domestic value-added. This study, in particular, aims to investigate the extent to which Korea's exports, including domestically value-added production, contribute to the final demand of EU member states, as depicted in Figure 8. This contribution may occur through direct exports, such as [Korea → EU member state], or indirectly via [Korea → third country → EU member state], where a third country utilizes Korean intermediate goods. This study seeks to compare 'total exports' and 'value-added' exports, with both metrics signifying the share of a specific country in the total imports of the export destination country. 'Value-added' exports, however, provide insights into the degree of industrial networking and facilitate the identification of bilateral trade relationships within the supply chain perspective.

〈Figure 8〉 Exports calculated based on value added

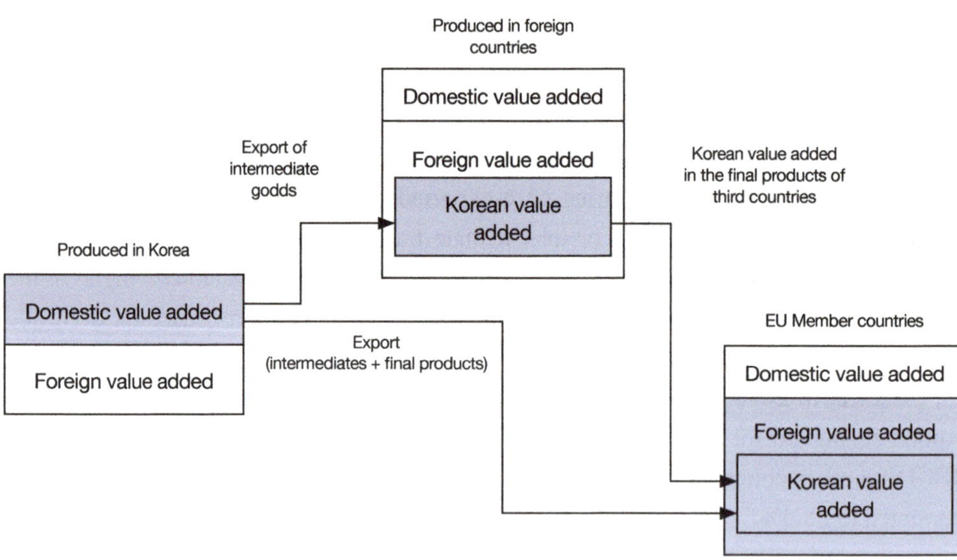

Source: Author's elaboration.

Changes in Korea-EU Trade Relations from a GVC Perspective

Overview of the Entire Manufacturing Industry

This study aims to assess the contribution of Korea's exports to the final demand in EU member countries. It does this by considering both direct exports (where Korean goods are sent directly to EU member states) and indirect exports (where Korean intermediate goods are used in other countries and eventually find their way to EU member states). This approach provides a more comprehensive understanding of how Korea's exports impact the economies of EU member countries and how they are integrated into global supply chains.

Initially, Korea's exports to the EU were categorized into two groups: total exports (based on customs clearance) and exports based on value added. These categories were then compared. As depicted in Figure 9, from 1995 to 2012, the proportions of total exports and exports based on value added remained nearly identical. However, starting in 2013, exports based on value added consistently exceeded total exports, with the gap widening to 0.9 percentage points by 2017. In other words, exports based on value added consistently held a larger market share than exports based on customs clearance.

The analysis further differentiates between Western European nations (Germany, France, the UK, and Italy) and Central and Eastern European countries (the Czech Republic, Poland, Hungary, and Slovakia). It observes that in Western European countries, the share of exports based on value added is higher than total exports. In Western European countries, the share of exports based on value added is higher than total exports. For example, while total exports to Germany ranged from 1.1% to 3.0% during the 2010–2018 period, exports based on value added consistently exceeded this range, with a gap of 0.8 to 1.1 percentage points, reaching 2.1% to 3.8%. This same trend was evident in France, the UK, and Italy, with the gap widening between 2015 and 2018. This suggests that Korea is exporting more added value to these four Western European countries than exports based on customs clearance standards. Regarding the four Central and Eastern European countries, total exports to the Czech Republic and Poland showed a slightly higher share than exports based on value added, although the gap was not significant compared to the Western European countries. However, this trend was inconsistent in Hungary and Slovakia. Notably, exports to Hungary exhibited a significantly higher share of exports based on customs clearance than exports based on value added during the 2008–2012 period, and this phenomenon has been noted in exports to Slovakia since 2007. A higher share of exports based on customs clearance signifies that the criteria for including foreign added value in Korea's exports are stringent or that the proportion of indirect exports through third countries is low. Korea's market share in Central and Eastern European countries was higher than in Western Europe, both in terms of customs clearance standards and value-added standards. In terms of added value, the market share in four Western European countries hovered around 2.0% in 2018, while it was around 3.0% in the Czech Republic, Poland, and Hungary. Slovakia stood out with a market share exceeding 7% and reaching 12% in 2012.

In summary, Korea's exports to EU member states demonstrate a dual pattern between Western Europe and Central and Eastern Europe. The higher share of exports based on added value than on customs clearance in Western Europe is attributed to the extensive use of third countries as processing and assembly bases for indirect exports. These third countries are likely emerging economies, such as Central and Eastern Europe, where Korean companies have made substantial investments, along with Southeast Asia, which has emerged as a production hub for Korean firms over the past decade.

〈Figure 9〉 Changes in Korea's exports to the EU by product: total exports and exports based on added value

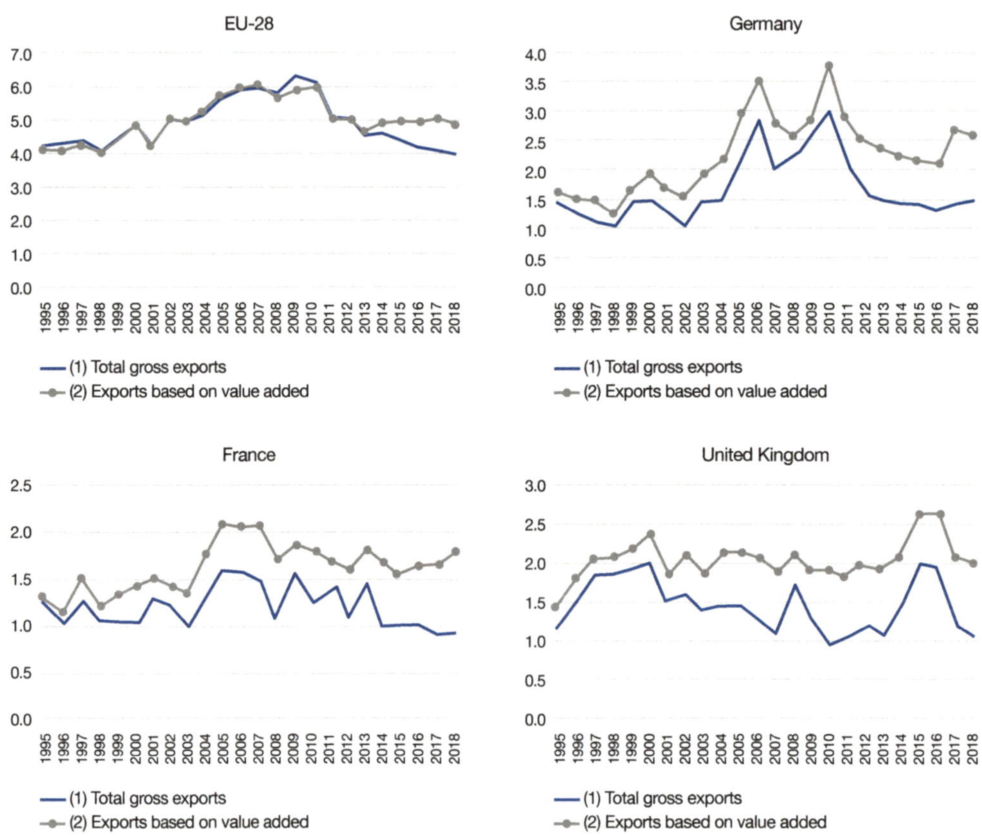

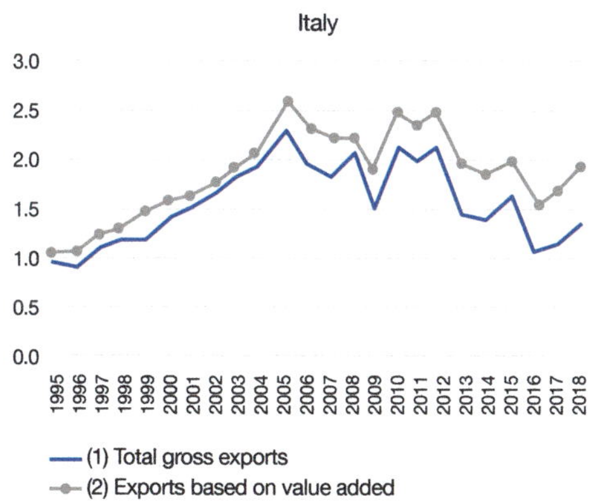

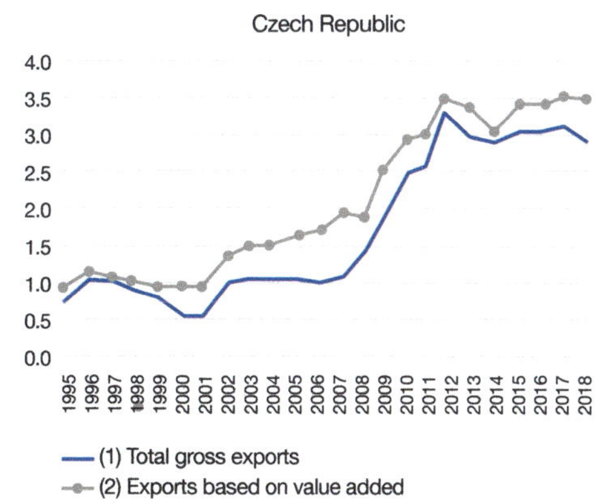

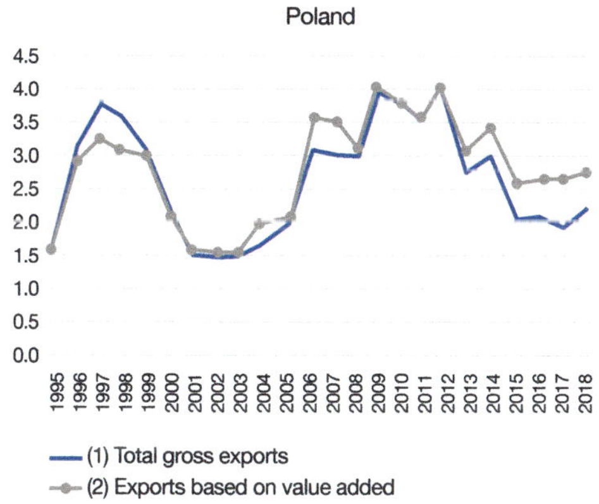

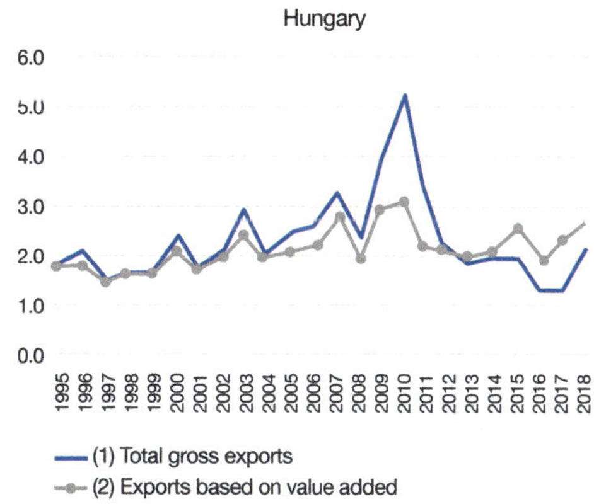

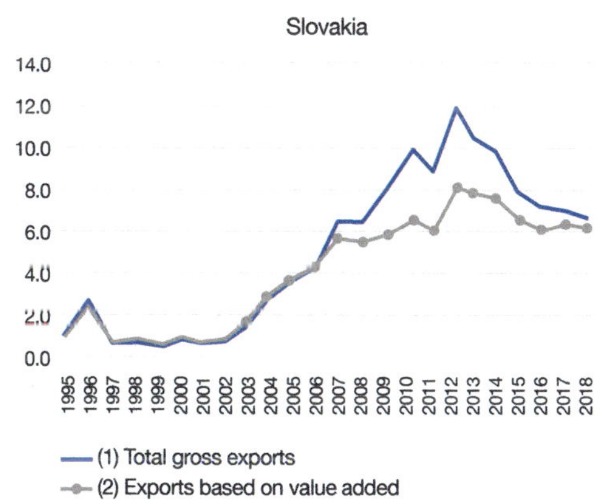

Source: Author's elaboration using the OECD TiVA data.

Review of the main items

Following the examination of exports based on added value across all manufacturing industries, this analysis extends to Korea's major export sectors. The industrial classification is based on the 2-digit International Standard Industrial Classification (ISIC Rev. 4) used by OECD TiVA data, encompassing (1) automobiles (D29), (2) computers, electronics, and optical products (D26), (3) electrical equipment (D27), (4) other transportation equipment (D30, primarily ships), and (5) machinery and equipment (D28).

Figure 10 illustrates Korea's export market share to the EU, considering both total exports and added value from 1995 to 2018. Several key patterns emerge: The export market share is significantly higher in Central and Eastern Europe compared to Western Europe across all sectors. For instance, in 2018, the export market share for the four Western European countries ranged from 1.5% to 2.0%, whereas the four Central and Eastern European countries exhibited much higher rates, ranging from 1.4% to 8.4%. This difference in market share can be attributed to the fact that the five items under consideration represent Korea's primary export items and major overseas investment industries (excluding ships). Given the smaller market size of Central and Eastern Europe, this disparity in market share is not surprising.

Changes in export market share exhibit distinct patterns over time. Between 2000 and 2010, there was a general increase in market share for the four Western European countries. Conversely, for the four Central and Eastern European countries, growth commenced around 2004–05, reaching its peak in 2013–14 before showing signs of decline, although some countries continued to experience growth. In Western European countries, the peak occurred around 2010 and was followed by fluctuations (in sectors such as automobiles, electronics, electricity, and machinery) or declines (especially in the shipbuilding sector). These fluctuations highlight that Western Europe and Central and Eastern Europe follow different timelines, with a lag of 3 to 4 years in terms of growth, peak, and decline. Among Western European countries, Germany stands out with a high export market share. In contrast, among the Central and Eastern European countries, Slovakia takes the lead. This suggests the existence of a more closely integrated industrial network between Korea and these specific countries.

〈Figure 10〉 Comparison of Korea's export market share to EU member states:
(1) Based on total exports vs. (2) Value-added criteria

1) Motor vehicles (D29)

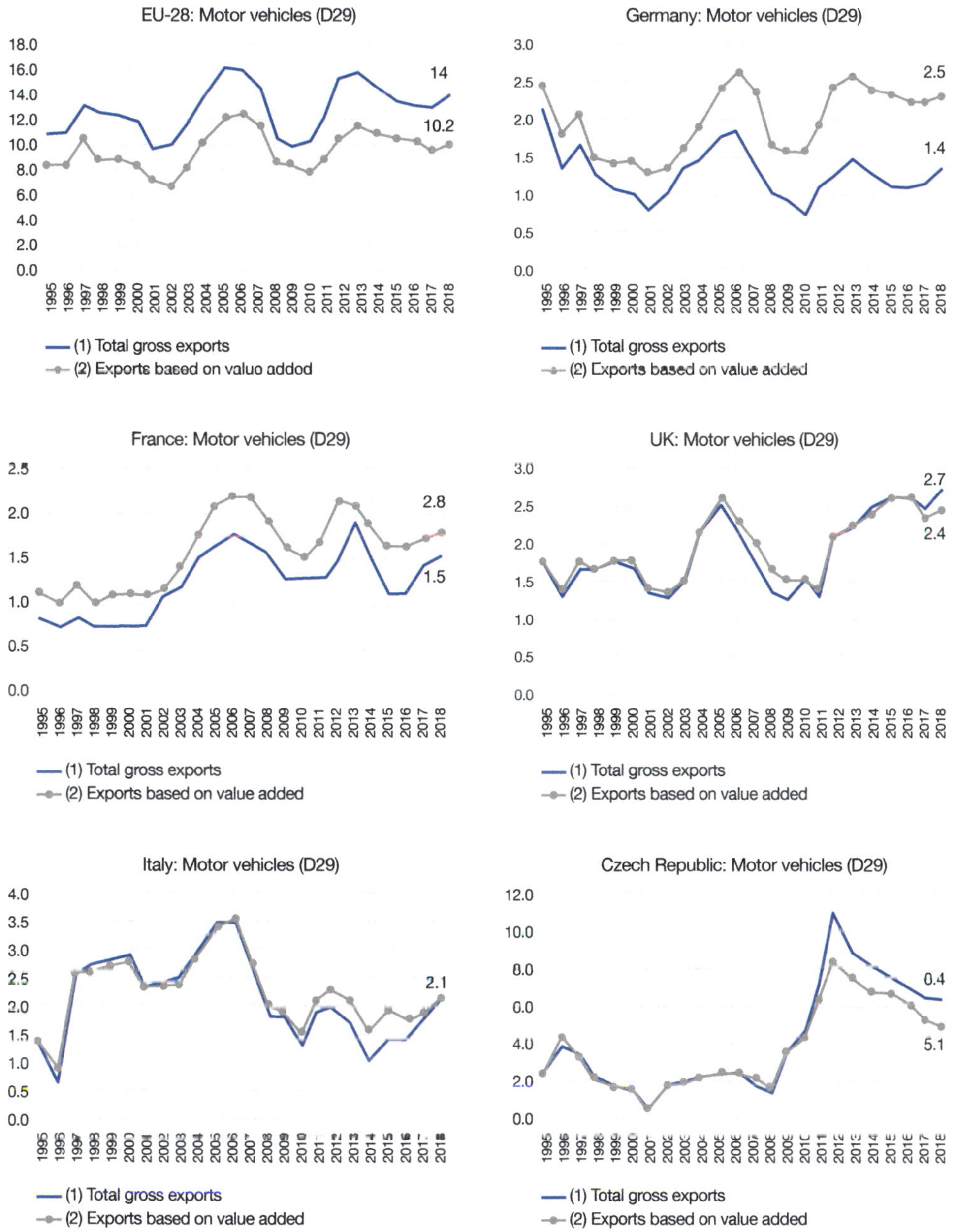

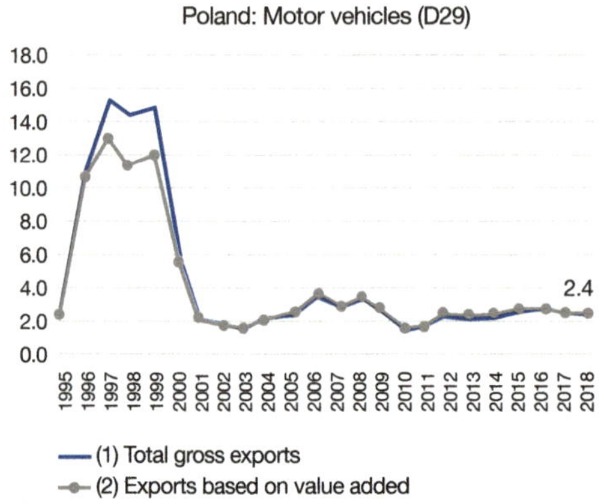

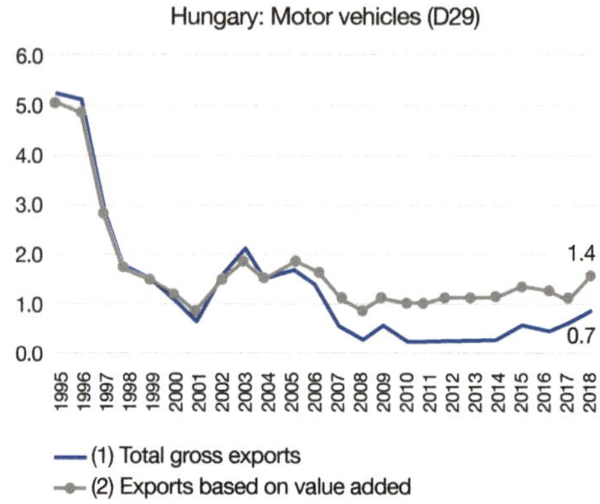

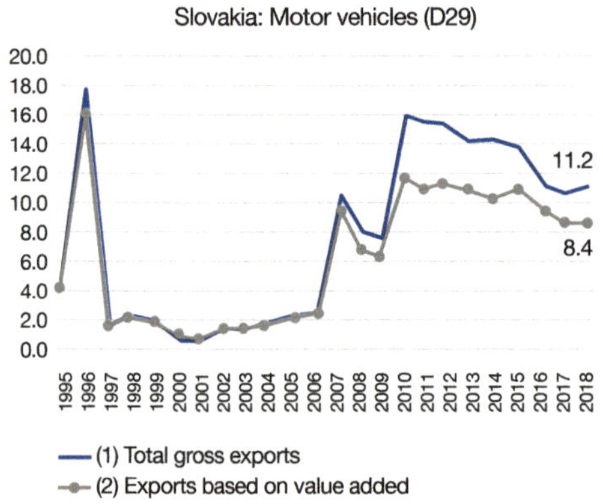

2) Computers, Electronics, and Optics (D26)

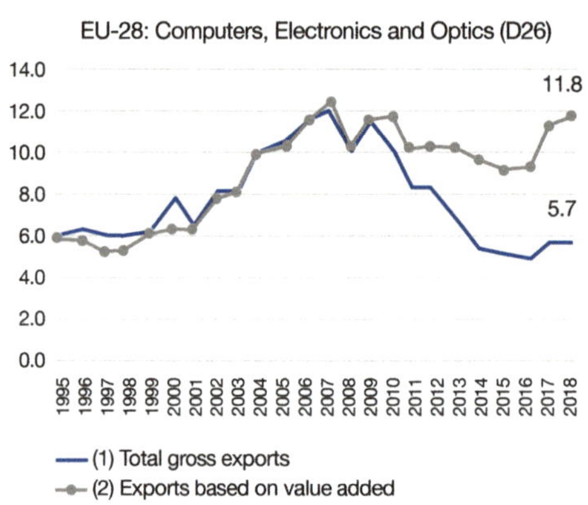

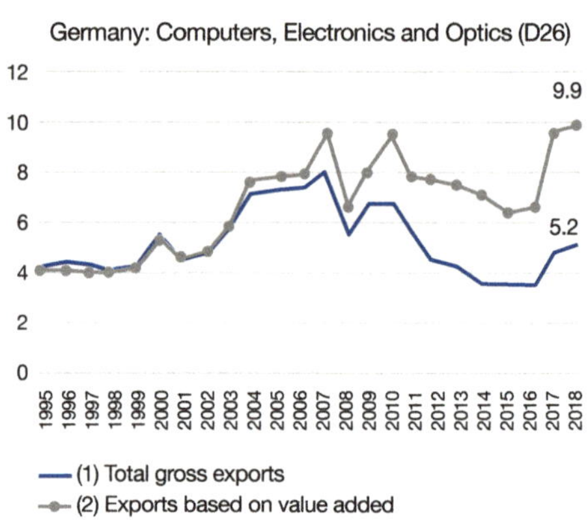

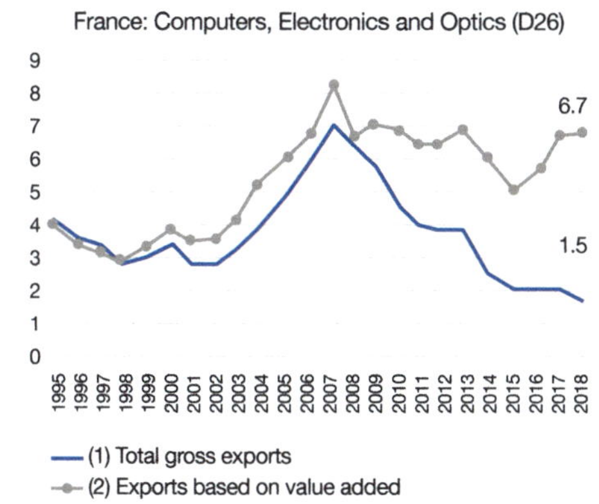
France: Computers, Electronics and Optics (D26)
6.7
1.5
(1) Total gross exports
(2) Exports based on value added

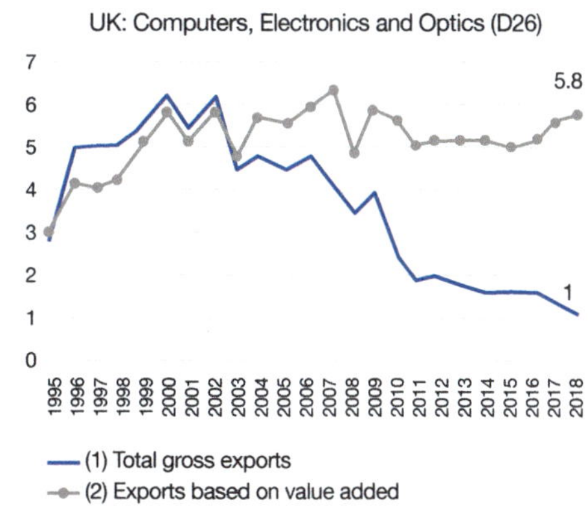
UK: Computers, Electronics and Optics (D26)
5.8
1
(1) Total gross exports
(2) Exports based on value added

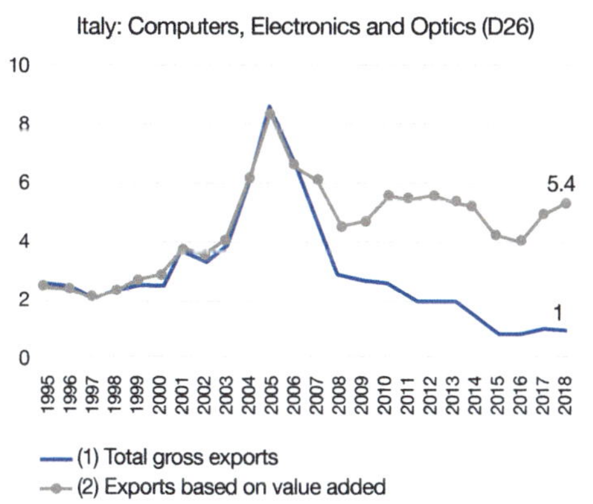
Italy: Computers, Electronics and Optics (D26)
5.4
1
(1) Total gross exports
(2) Exports based on value added

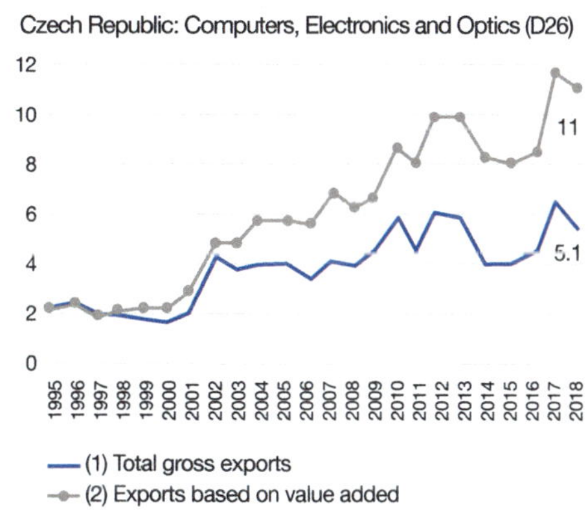
Czech Republic: Computers, Electronics and Optics (D26)
11
5.1
(1) Total gross exports
(2) Exports based on value added

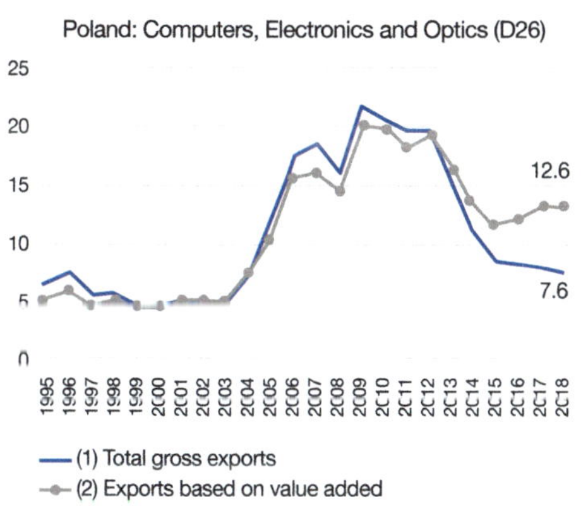
Poland: Computers, Electronics and Optics (D26)
12.6
7.6
(1) Total gross exports
(2) Exports based on value added

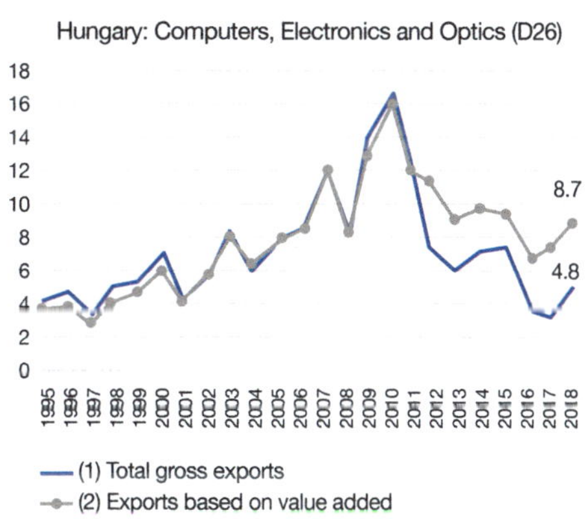
Hungary: Computers, Electronics and Optics (D26)
8.7
4.8
(1) Total gross exports
(2) Exports based on value added

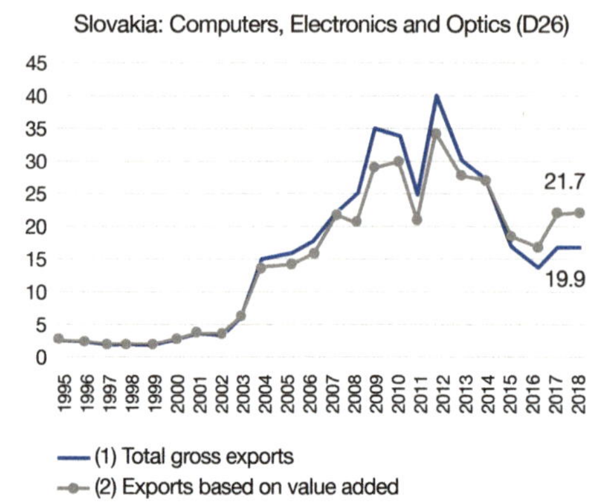

3) Electrical equipment (D27)

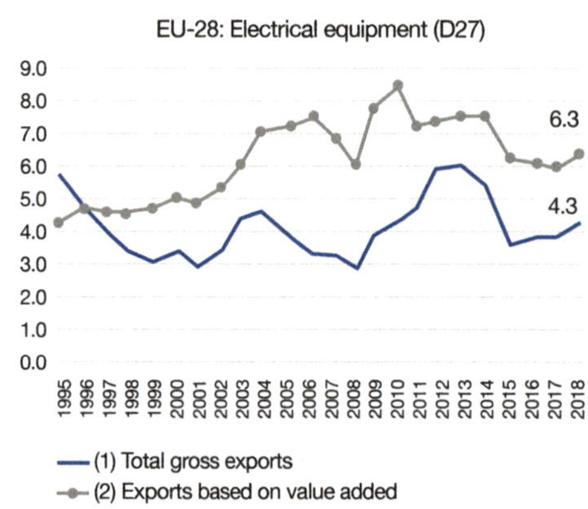

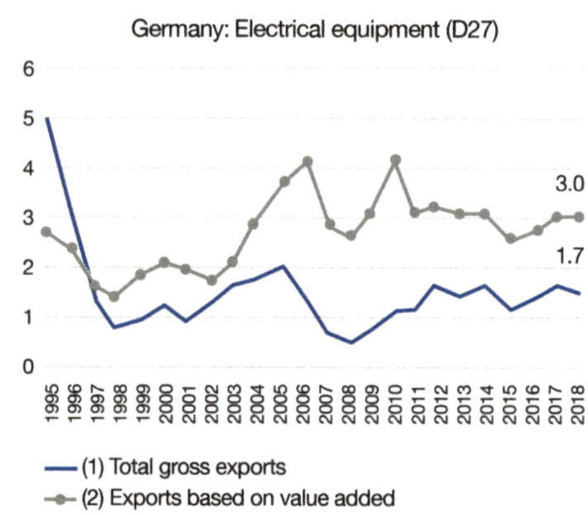

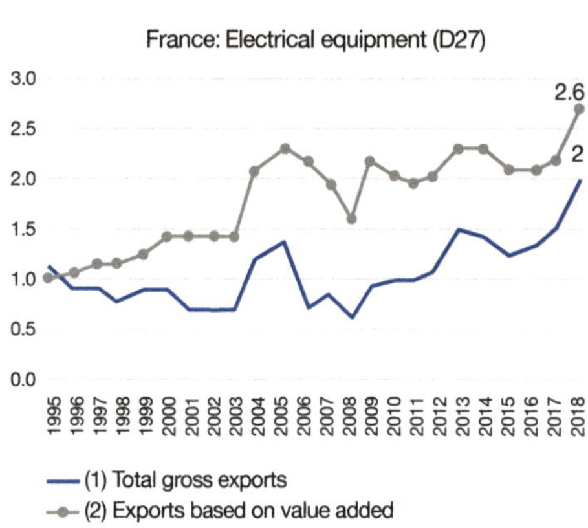

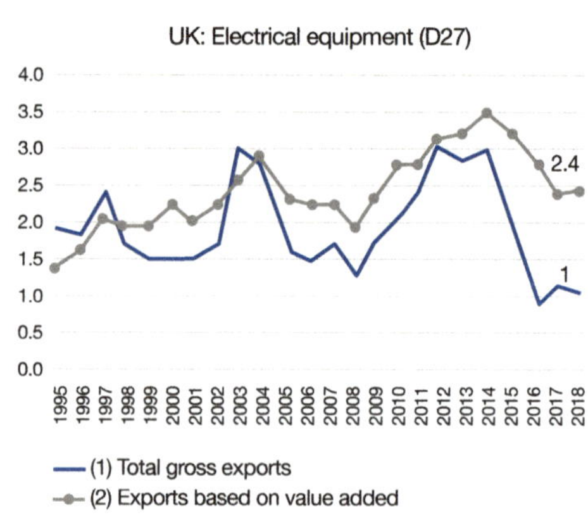

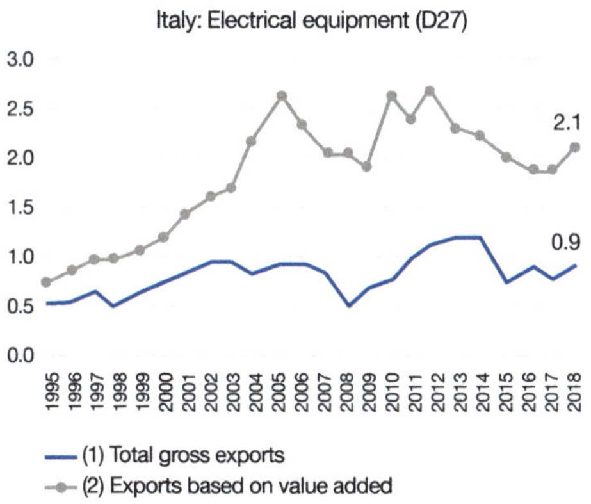
Italy: Electrical equipment (D27)
2.1
0.9
(1) Total gross exports
(2) Exports based on value added

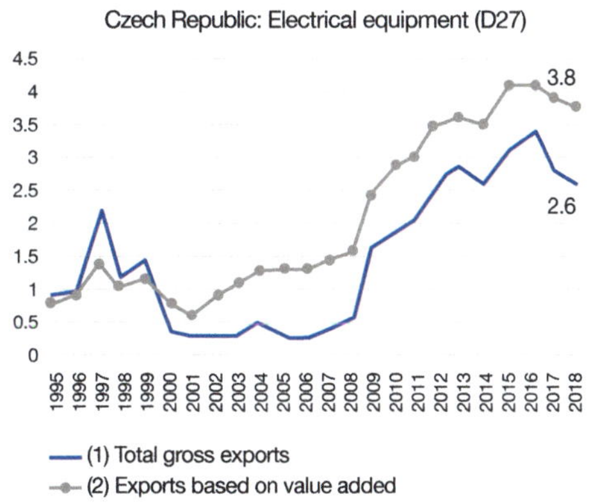
Czech Republic: Electrical equipment (D27)
3.8
2.6
(1) Total gross exports
(2) Exports based on value added

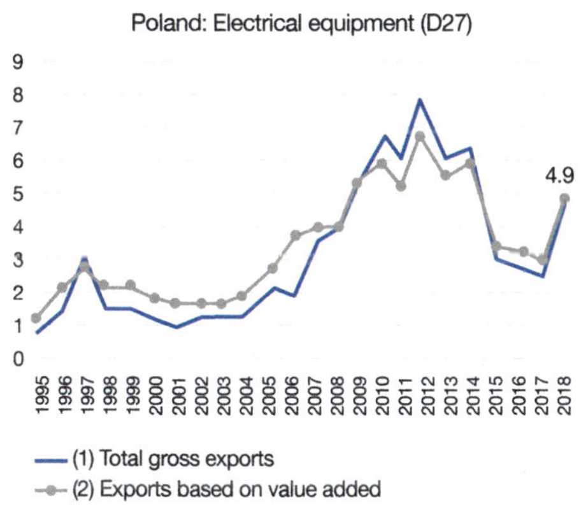
Poland: Electrical equipment (D27)
4.9
(1) Total gross exports
(2) Exports based on value added

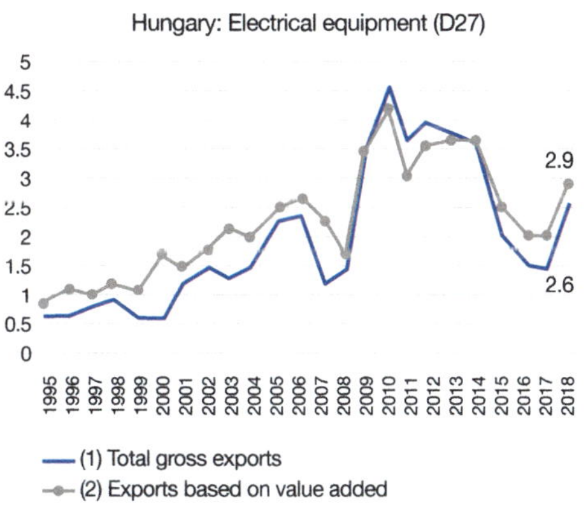
Hungary: Electrical equipment (D27)
2.9
2.6
(1) Total gross exports
(2) Exports based on value added

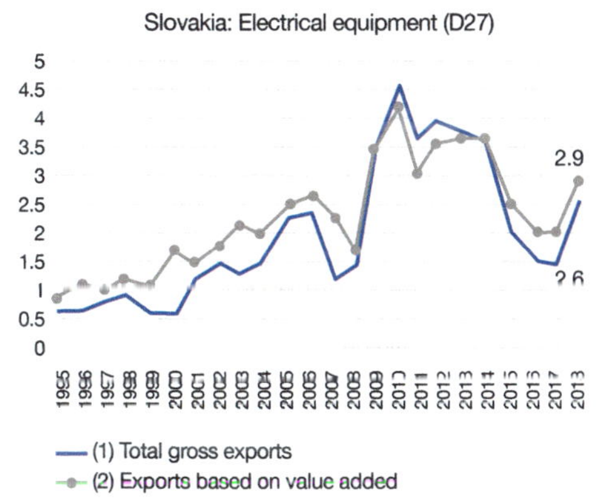
Slovakia: Electrical equipment (D27)
2.9
(1) Total gross exports
(2) Exports based on value added

4) Other transportation equipment (D30)

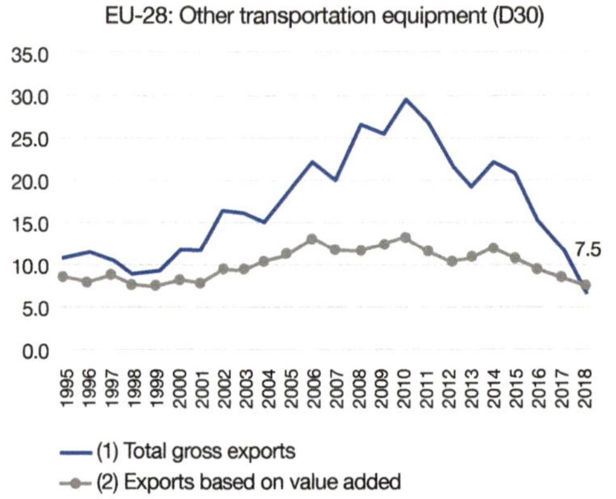

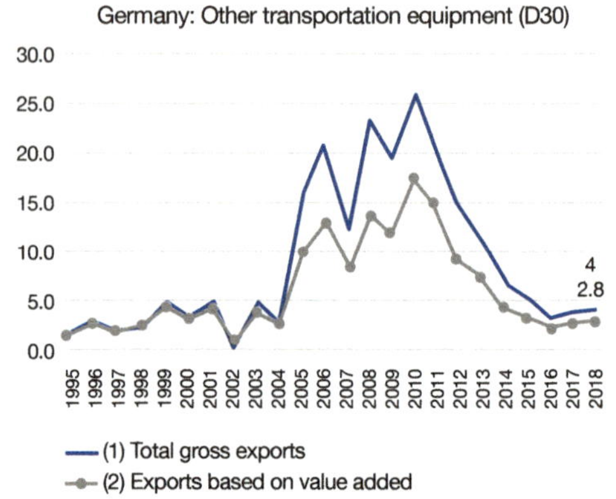

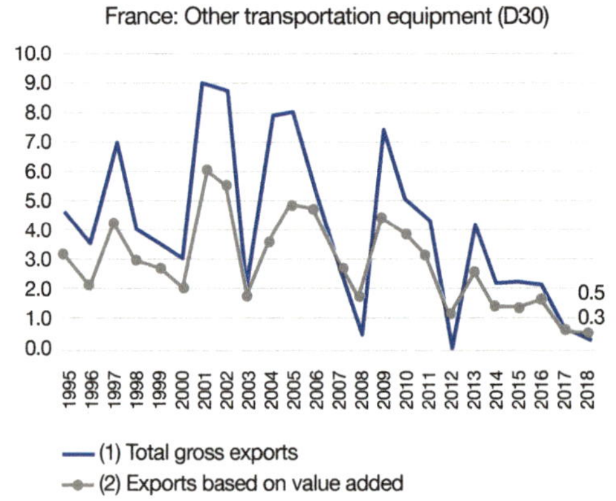

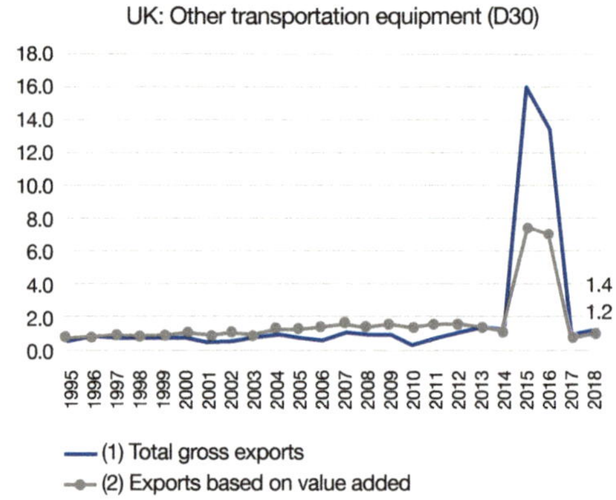

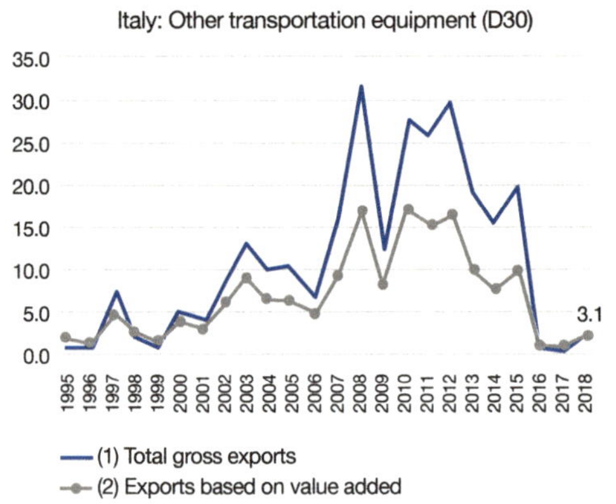

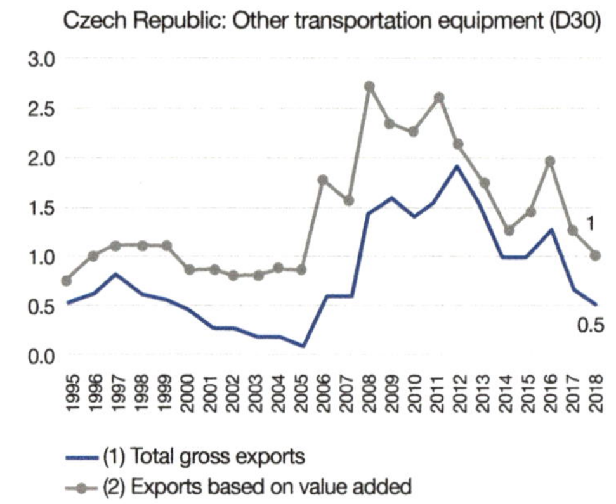

Poland: Other transportation equipment (D30)

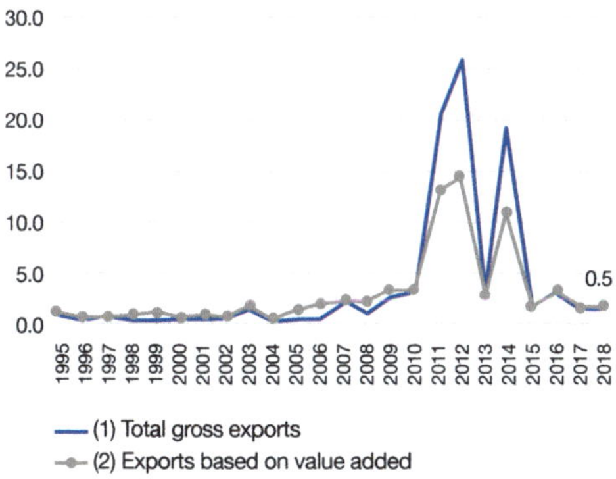

Hungary: Other transportation equipment (D30)

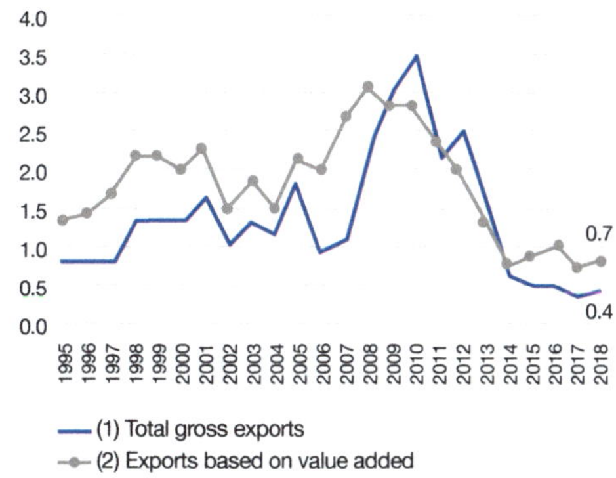

Slovakia: Other transportation equipment (D30)

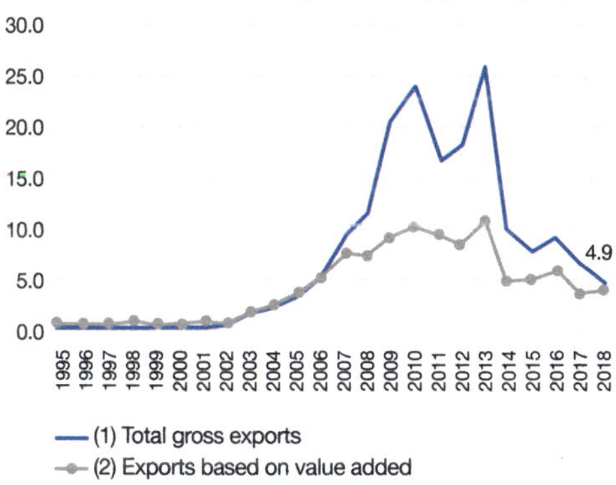

5) Machinery and equipment (D28)

EU-28: Machinery and eqipment equipment (D28)

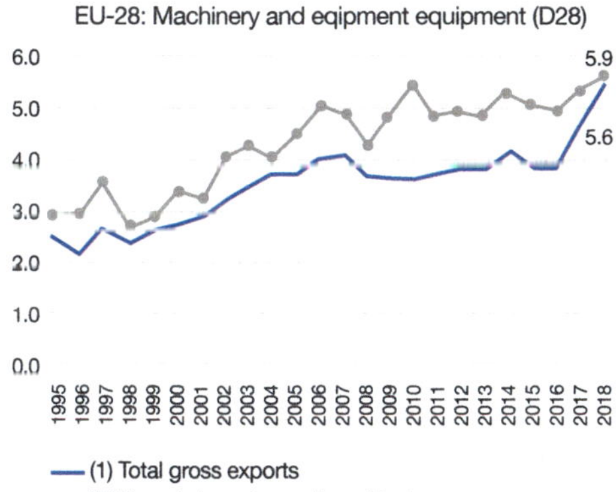

Germany: Machinery and eqipment equipment (D28)

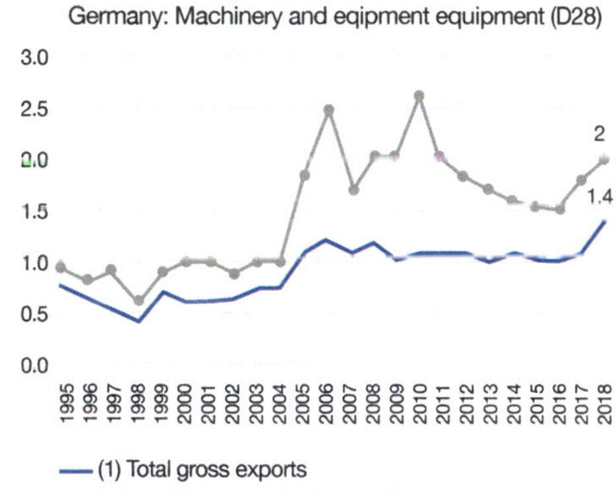

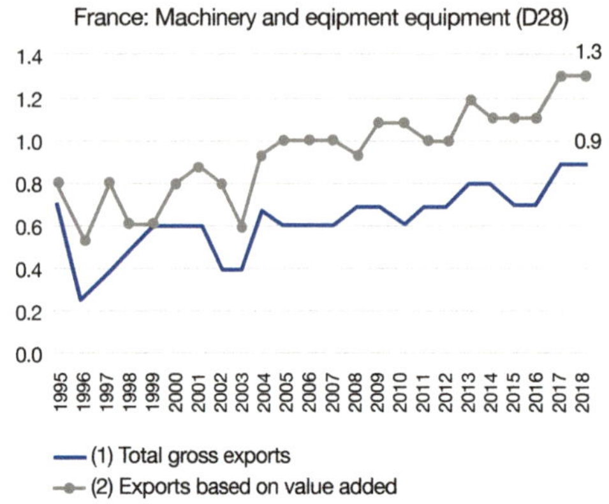
France: Machinery and eqipment equipment (D28)
1.3
0.9
(1) Total gross exports
(2) Exports based on value added

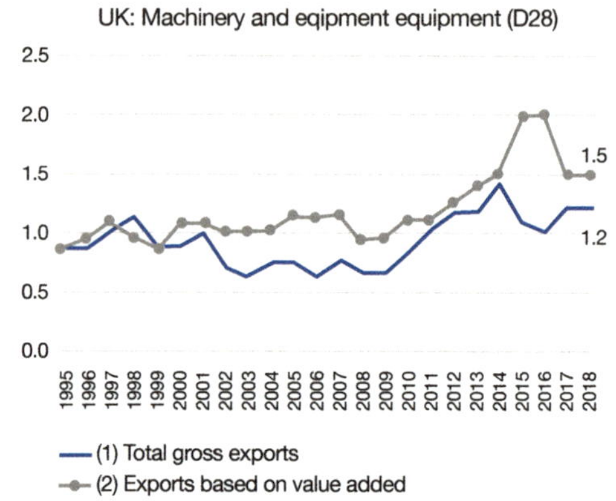
UK: Machinery and eqipment equipment (D28)
1.5
1.2
(1) Total gross exports
(2) Exports based on value added

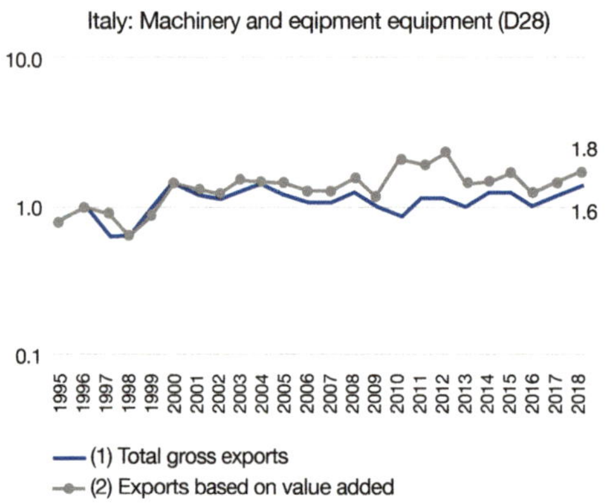
Italy: Machinery and eqipment equipment (D28)
1.8
1.6
(1) Total gross exports
(2) Exports based on value added

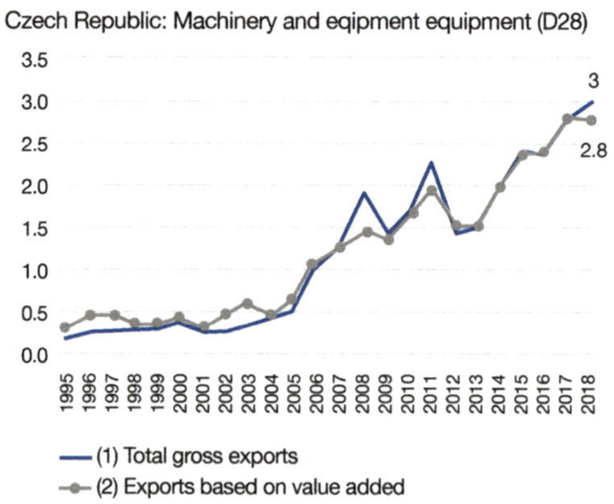
Czech Republic: Machinery and eqipment equipment (D28)
3
2.8
(1) Total gross exports
(2) Exports based on value added

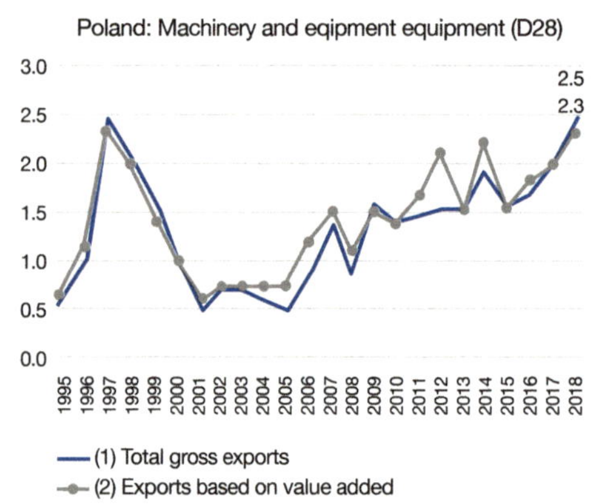
Poland: Machinery and eqipment equipment (D28)
2.5
2.3
(1) Total gross exports
(2) Exports based on value added

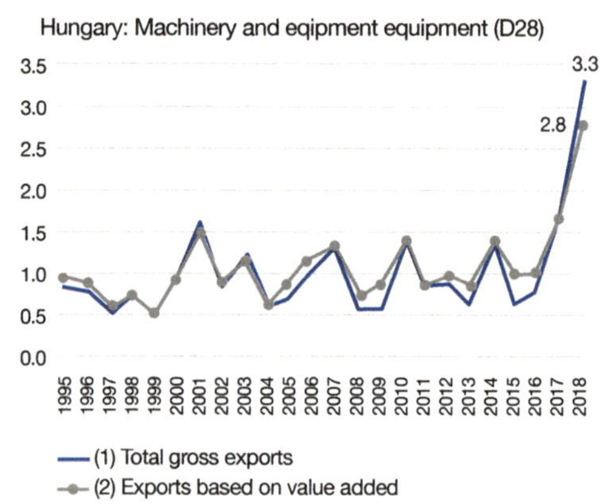
Hungary: Machinery and eqipment equipment (D28)
3.3
2.8
(1) Total gross exports
(2) Exports based on value added

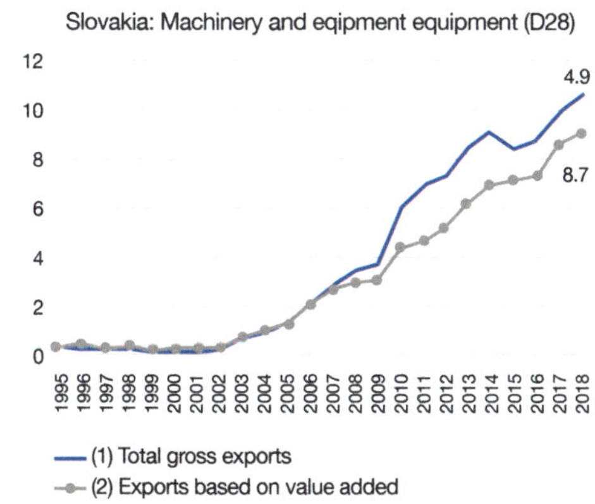

Source: Author's elaboration using the OECD TiVA data.

Summary of Review Results

There is a robust correlation between the proportion of export market share by period and industry and the investments made by Korean companies, especially in Central and Eastern Europe. Our findings can be summarized as follows:

First, the trade deficit appears to be smaller than what is indicated by the customs data, if we take GVCs into account. This discrepancy is particularly notable in the context of trade with Western European countries, with Germany being a prominent example. While the trade deficit, as reported in customs clearance data, surpasses $10 billion annually when dealing with Germany, this figure does not consider indirect exports. These indirect exports involve the shipment of intermediate goods to third countries before ultimately reaching Germany. Furthermore, Korea's reliance on importing intermediate goods, particularly due to its relatively weaker position in material component equipment industries, suggests that the actual imports from Germany for final consumption are likely lower than what the customs clearance figures suggest. This highlights the importance of considering the intricate web of global supply chains and value-added processes when assessing trade balances between countries.

Second, the role of supply chains is more important than ever in explaining bilateral trade relations. In the field of computer, electronic, and optical products, there is a noticeable trend where the share of exports based on total exports is decreasing, while the share based on value-added continues to expand. This trend is particularly pronounced in Western European countries. It reflects a significant increase in indirect exports to Western Europe, highlighting the active utilization of global supply chains that involve third countries. For instance, Korea's export market share to countries like France, Great Britain, and Italy, as measured by customs clearance, is relatively low, ranging from 1.0%

to 1.9%. However, in terms of value-added, these shares increase substantially to 5.4%, 5.8%, and 6.7%, respectively. This implies that several times more exports are achieved through indirect trade routes, underlining the importance of these indirect supply chains. However, it also presents risks, as problems in third countries where Korea exports intermediate goods for assembly and processing can potentially disrupt this indirect trade between Korea and the EU.

Third, there is a dual pattern in trade relations between Korea and European countries. Korea's trade patterns with Western Europe and Central and Eastern Europe exhibit distinct characteristics, a finding consistent with prior studies and reports on the topic. Exports to Central and Eastern European countries have notably increased as Korean companies expanded their investments in the region. Total exports, as reported through customs clearance, are comparable to exports based on value-added in this region, or in some cases, customs clearance figures even exceed value-added exports. Nevertheless, except for machinery and equipment among the items analyzed, the export market share in Central and Eastern European countries seems to be gradually decreasing. This phenomenon is also apparent in export statistics based on value added. It is linked to the gradual diminishing of the initial boost in exports generated through the investment-trade network. Consequently, unless additional investments are made, the trade surplus achieved through exports of intermediate goods to Central and Eastern Europe is likely to decline. Conversely, as income levels in Central and Eastern Europe improve, exports of final goods are expected to increase further.

In conclusion, these findings underscore the evolving nature of Korea's trade relations with the EU within the context of GVCs. Recognizing these shifts and patterns is vital for effective policymaking and trade strategies. The utilization of supply chain-based data and a deeper understanding of the role of global supply chains in international trade can enhance the formulation of policies that foster mutually beneficial trade relations and economic growth between Korea and the EU.

Conclusion and Implications

International trade, which has seen both quantitative and qualitative growth in the era of globalization, is currently confronted with multiple challenges. Long before the intensified rivalry between the US and China, there were clear indications of a global economic transformation. The COVID-19 pandemic has further emphasized the vulnerabilities associated with the international division of labor based on GVCs. This contemporary trade landscape stands in stark contrast to the 2000s, when Korea actively pursued FTAs with major economies such as the US, EU, ASEAN, and India. The completion of an FTA no longer guarantees the same rapid expansion of trade that was witnessed in the past.

While it may appear that Korea's trade performance with the EU has not surpassed that with the United States, which also signed an FTA during the same period, a deeper examination from a GVC perspective paints a more intricate picture. Korea has made significant advancements at the supply chain level in its trade with the EU. Exports now increasingly rely on added value that exceeds traditional customs clearance standards. For instance, in 2015, despite Korea recording a trade deficit of $9.1 billion with the EU, it also marked the year when Korea's overall trade balance reached a surplus of $90.2 billion, the highest ever recorded. This intriguing phenomenon can be elucidated by the GVC puzzle. Additionally, in Korea's current account balance, the primary income balance transitioned from a deficit to a surplus in 2011 and, despite annual fluctuations, maintains an overall upward trajectory. A significant portion of the primary income balance results from Korean companies repatriating overseas investment profits. When overseas investments effectively replace exports, there's a trade-off between a trade balance deficit and a primary income balance surplus. Even if exports decline, an increasing primary income balance reflects a typical path of industrial development rather than a weakening of export competitiveness.

The implications drawn from this study are as follows. First, understanding Korea-EU trade relations requires moving beyond a narrow focus on direct trade between Korea and EU member countries. It is essential to consider the broader GVC network within the EU region, including the triangular structure of trade involving Korea, third countries, and the EU. Moreover, it's important to acknowledge the EU's pursuit of FTAs with numerous countries, some of which have simultaneous agreements with Korea. These countries, including Vietnam, Singapore, Turkey, EFTA, and Canada, play significant roles in Korea-EU trade relations. Second, policymakers should integrate GVC considerations into the formulation of bilateral trade policies. Relying solely on bilateral exports, imports, and trade balance figures is no longer sufficient. A comprehensive approach that considers the supply chains of companies is necessary. The EU's supply chain due diligence system underscores the need to expand the focus of bilateral trade relations to include GVCs, as even subcontractors of Korean companies located overseas are subject to supply chain due diligence. Third, GVC-related data should be actively utilized in evaluating the implementation of FTAs. While current FTA implementation evaluations primarily focus on bilateral trade indicators, the development of GVC-related data allows for a more comprehensive evaluation that considers the global supply chain. This approach aligns with the changing dynamics of international trade. In summary, this study underscores the evolving nature of trade relations in a globalized world and emphasizes the importance of considering GVCs when understanding, formulating, and evaluating trade policies in the Korea-EU context.

References

Dollar, David and Aart Kraay. 2001. "Trade, Growth, and Poverty." *World Bank Paper Series* 2615.

Je, Hyun Jung. 2015. "The Trade Deficit with the EU Widens due to a Surge in Imports and Stagnation in Exports. *Korea International Trade Association Trade Brief.* 11.

Kang, Yoo-Duk. 2016. "The Impact of the European Economic Downturn on Exports to the EU after the Korea-EU FTA: Factor Analysis Using Vector Error Correction Model (VECM)". *Trade Research.* 12(6): 187-206.

Kang, Yoo-Duk and Jun Yup Kim. 2013. "Analysis of Korea's Trade and Investment Trends with the EU after the Korea-EU FTA Took Effect and Future Tasks." *KIEP Today's World Economy.* 13-18.

Khan, Saif M., Alexander Mann and Dahlia Peterson. 2021. "The Semiconductor Supply Chain: Assessing National Competitiveness." *CSET Issue Brief.* Center for Security and Emerging Technology.

Los, Bart, Marcel P. Timmer and Gaaitzen J. de Vries. 2015. "How Global are Global Value Chains? A New Approach to Measure International Fragmentation. *Journal of Regional Science.* 55(1): 66-92.

OECD. *OECD Statistics.* https://stats.oecd.org. (Retrieved August 27, 2023)

OECD. *Trade in Value Added (TiVA)* 2021. https://stats.oecd.org. (Retrieved August 27, 2023)

Porto, Massimiliano. 2018. "EU Trade with Korea: From Deficit to Surplus A Gravity Approach to Assess the Impact of the EU-Korea FTA on Bilateral Trade. *Asia-Pacific Journal of EU Studies.* 16(2): 71-105.

Timmer, Marcel P., Bart Los, Robert Stehrer and Gaaitzen J. de Vries. 2013. "Fragmentation, Incomes and Jobs. An Analysis of European Competitiveness." *Economic Policy.* 28(76): 613–661.

Timmer, Marcel P., Abdul Azeez Erumban, Bart Los, Robert Stehrer, and Gaaitzen J. de Vries. 2014. "Slicing Up Global Value Chains." *Journal of Economic Perspectives.* 28(2): 99-118.

Endnote

1. In this paper, the United Kingdom is considered part of the EU for the sake of data coherence, even though it exited the EU on January 31, 2020.
2. World Bank, Open Data (retrieved September 10, 2022).

Transforming Global Supply Chain and Korea-EU Cooperation in the Fields of Battery Industry

AHN SANGWUK

During 60 years of diplomatic relations, Korea and the EU have strengthened their cooperation in all areas. These developments led the EU and South Korea to upgrade their ties to a strategic partnership in 2010. The Korea-EU FTA was signed on October 15, 2009. The agreement was provisionally applied from July 1, 2011, and entered into force on December 13, 2015, after having been ratified by all signatories.

According to the Korea International Trade Association, Korea has risen to become the European Union's seventh-largest source of imports in the first four months of 2023, after China, the United States, the United Kingdom, Switzerland, Turkey, and Norway. Korea's exports to the EU have eclipsed those of Japan and Russia for the first time.

Korea's main export items to the EU are automobiles, semiconductors, batteries cathode aaterials, automobile parts, and batteries. Korean battery manufacturers have established plants in the European Union. Samsung SDI and SK On are producing their batteries in Hungary, while LG Energy Solution is producing its batteries in Poland.

With the support of the European Union and its member countries, European automobile manufacturers are leading the global EV market with American Tesla. Korean battery manufacturers are the most important battery suppliers for the EVs manufactured by European automakers.

This chapter is focused on the growth of the EU's EV and EV battery markets as well as Korea-EU cooperation in the fields of the EU battery. This chapter is also focused on the issues of the global supply chain of batteries and the responses of the EU and the member countries regarding Chinese dominance in the extraction and the processing of battery raw materials.

〈Figure 1〉 Greenhouse gas emissions trends: emissions, projections, and targets for the EU (million tonnes of CO2 equivalents, the United Kingdom excluding)

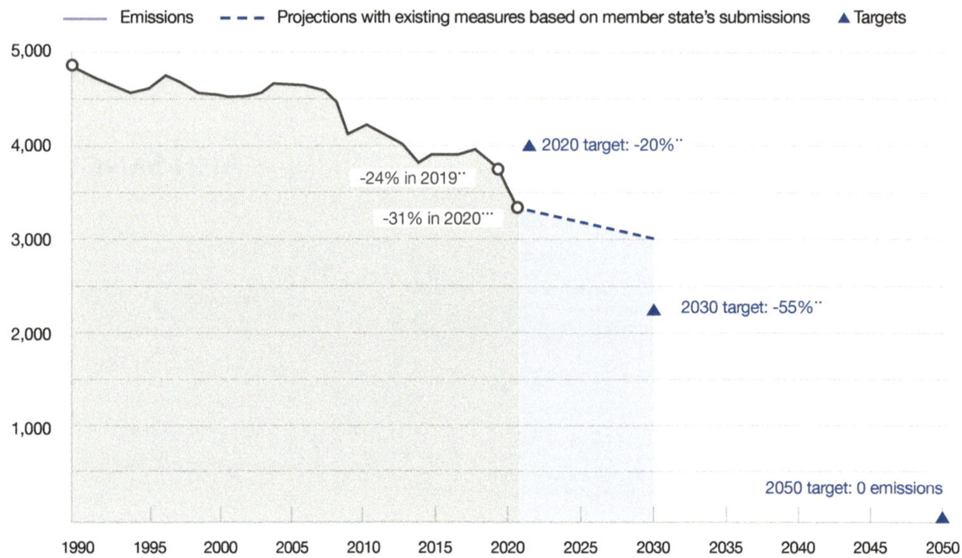

Source: European Commission
http://www.europarl.europa.eu/news/en/headlines/society/20180706STO07407/eu-progress-towards-2020-climate-change-goals-infographic

In order to fight against climate change, the European Union has been leading the reduction of CO2 emissions in the World. In 2008, the EU set a target to cut emissions by 20% compared to 1990 levels by 2020. In 2014, the EU achieved this goal.

In 2019, EU emissions decreased by 24% compared to 1990. In 2020, the EU's net emissions were 34% below 1990 levels. The implementation of EU and national policies and measures contributed to this achievement. The EU and member countries' policies focused on an increase in the use of renewables, a switch from coal to gas for power generation, improvements in energy efficiency, and structural changes in the EU economies.

The European Green Deal is a strategic priority first outlined in 2019 in communication. It sets out a detailed vision to make Europe the first climate-neutral continent by 2050. In September 2020, President von der Leyen announced the new 55% EU emission reduction target for 2030 anda revision of the EU's climate and energy legislation by June 2021.

The Commission announced its proposal for a European Climate Law on March 4, 2020. The European Climate Law has a set target for 2030 of a 55% net reduction in greenhouse gas emissions. Emissions have decreased in almost all sectors, particularly in energy supply, industry and the residential sector. However, emissions from transport have not fallen rapidly enough, despite climate policies and efforts to improve vehicle efficiency. Since 1990, transport emissions in the EU have grown by 33%, even as other sectors have reduced emissions by 32%. Transport currently accounts for a quarter of Europe's greenhouse gas (GHG) emissions. Cars, vans, trucks, and buses emit more than 70% of the overall greenhouse gas emissions from transport. The European Green Deal aims for a 90% reduction in transport emissions.

In 2019, the CO2 emissions in Road Transportation sector were higher than those in Public Electricity and Heat Production sector which was usually the largest CO2 emissions sectors. The reduction of road transport CO2 emissions become one of the most important issues for the EU's fight against climate change.

〈Figure 2〉 Greenhouse gas emissions by IPCC sectors in EU-27 (1990–2021)

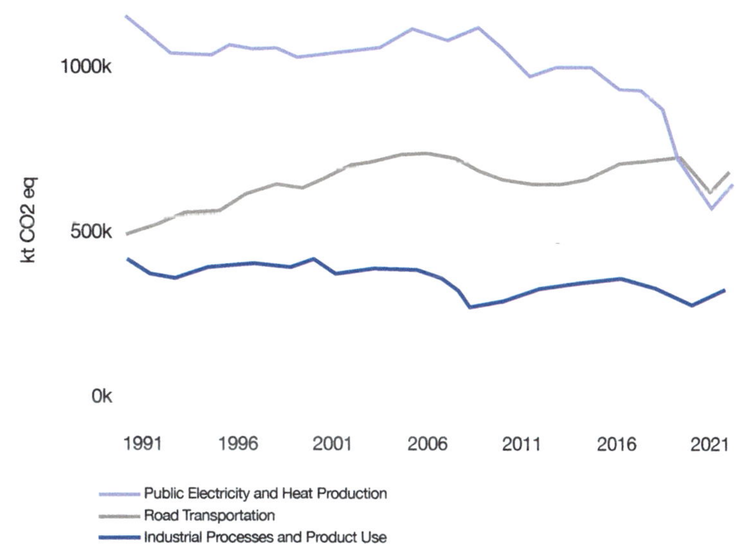

Source: European Environment Agency / https://www.eea.europa.eu/data-and-maps/data/data-viewers/greenhouse-gases-viewer

〈Figure 3〉 Electric car registrations and sales share in selected countries and regions, 2018–2022

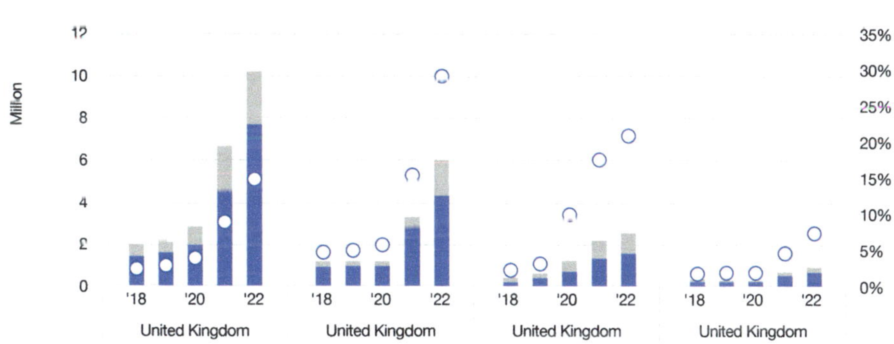

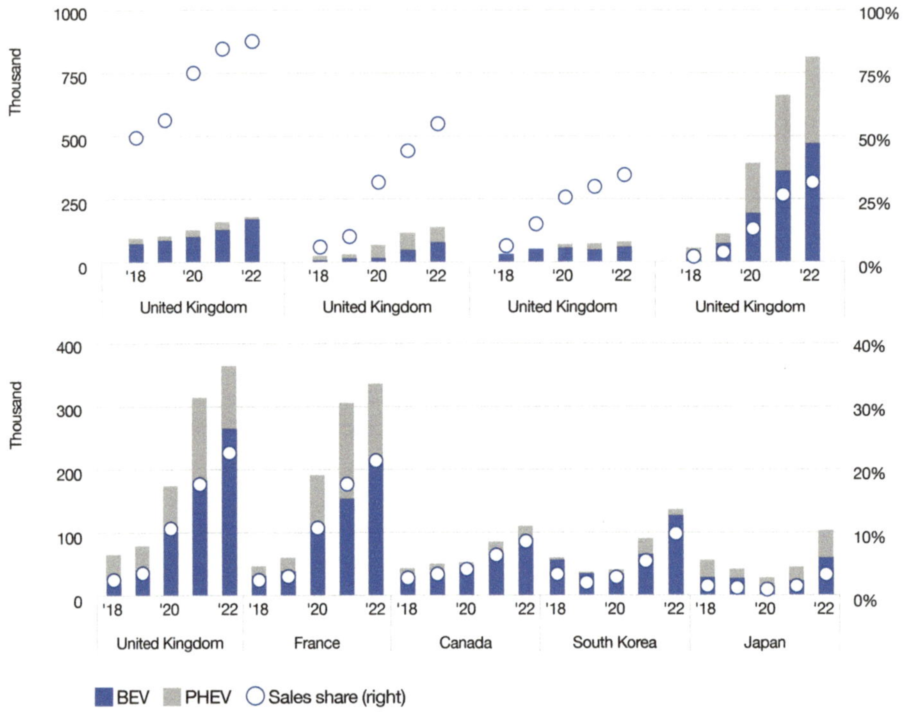

Notes: BEV = battery electric vehicle; PHEV = plug-in hybrid electric vehicle. Passenger light-duty vehicles only. Major markets at the top. Other countries (middle, bottom) ordered by the share of electric car sales in total car sales. Y-axes do not have the same scale to improve readability.
Source: International Energy Agency (IEA) / IEA, Global EV Outlook, 2023, p.19.

The EU and its member states have developed policies to reduce greenhouse gas emissions from transport. The EU has also adopted legislations to reduce greenhouse gas emissions from transport. In order to achieve the goals of the EU's "2020 Climate and Energy Package" and "A Roadmap for Moving to a Competitive Low Carbon Economy in 2050", the promotion of the use of low-carbon vehicles is required. In addition, the EU Commission's white paper, "Roadmap to a Single European Transport Area," published in 2011, laid out the goal to reduce greenhouse gas emissions from transport by at least 60 percent by 2050. A strategy was also proposed to reduce internal-combustion-engine vehicles in urban areas to 50% by 2030 and phase them out by 2050. Transport is the largest source of air pollution in major EU cities. The EU has strengthened its exhaust emission regulations. It encouraged automobile manufacturers to develop eco-friendly mobility, like electric vehicles. With the support of the EU's policies to reduce CO2 emissions and exhaust gas emissions, the EU's electric vehicle market has been expanded.

Europe is currently the world's second-largest market for electric cars after China in 2022, accounting for 25% of all electric car sales and 30% of the global stock. The sales share of electric cars reached 21%, up from 18% in 2021, 10% in 2020, and under 3% prior to 2019. In the first two months of 2023, battery electric car sales were already up by over 30% year-on-year, while overall car sales increased by just over 10% year-on-year.

EU member countries' incentives also contribute to the development of the electric vehicle market in Europe. Table 1 shows examples of the EU member countries' tax benefits and purchase incentives for electric vehicles.

〈Table 1〉 Examples of the EU member countries' tax benefits and purchase incentives: Electric passenger cars (2023)

BEV: Battery electric vehicle / PHEV: Plug-in hybrid electric vehicle / HEV: Hybrid electric vehicle / M1: Passenger car
FCEV: Fuel cell electric vehicle (hydrogen) / EREV: Extended-range electric vehicle / X: No benefit or incentive available

Tax Benefits			Incentives	
Acquisition	**Ownership**	**Company cars**	**Purchase**	**Infrastructure**
		Austria		
VAT deduction and exemption from tax for zero-emission cars used for business purposes (e.g., BEVs and FCEVs). Vehicle gross purchase value (including 20% VAT and pollution tax): • ≤ €40,000: full VAT deduction • €40,000-80,000: VAT deduction for the first €40,000 • > €80,000: no VAT deduction	Exemption from ownership tax for all zero-emission cars. Exemption from pollution tax for all zero-emission cars.	Exemption from ownership tax for all zero-emission cars. A tax investment incentive for the purchase of a zero-emission car amounting to 10% and a special depreciation applies. Exemption from pollution tax for all zero-emission cars. For employees, the private use of a zero-emission company car, and the electricity to charge it are exempt from taxation as a benefit in kind.	Bonus until the end of 2023 for the purchase (private use) of new cars with a fully electric range of ≥ 60km and gross list price of ≤ €60,000: • €3,000 for BEVs and FCEVs • €1,250 for PHEVs and EREVs Additional incentives are granted by provinces and communities.	Bonus until the end of 2023 for the purchase (private use) of the following loading infrastructure: • €600 for an intelligent loading cable • €600 for a wallbox (in a single/double house) • €900 for a wallbox (in a housing complex as single equipment) • €1,800 for a wallbox (in a housing complex as integrated equipment with load management) Additional incentives are granted by provinces and communities. For more details:
		Czech Republic		
BEVs and FCEVs emitting ≤ 50g CO_2/km exempt from registration charges (with a special number plate).	• BEVs and HEVs exempt from road tax. • Vehicles emitting ≤ 50g CO_2/km exempt from road toll. • Reduction of the depreciation period for charging stations for electric vehicles from 10 to five years (wall boxes and standalone charging stations). • Accelerated depreciation for BEVs and PHEVs below 50g CO_2/km.	• Road tax exemption for alternatively powered vehicles (i.e., BEVs, HEVs, FCEVs, CNG, LPG, and E85). • Tax reduction from 0.5-1% for BEVs and PHEVs used for private purposes.	Purchase incentive for low- and zero-emission vehicles by state and local government bodies.	Support from the Ministry of Transport for the development of charging infrastructure.

Tax Benefits			Incentives	
Acquisition	Ownership	Company cars	Purchase	Infrastructure
France				
• Regions provide an exemption (either total or 50%) for alternatively powered vehicles (ie electric, HEVs, CNG, LPG, and E85). • BEVs, FCEVs, and PHEVs (with a range of > 50km) are exempt from the mass-based malus.		Exemption from CO2-based tax component ('TVS') for vehicles emitting < 60g CO2/km (apart from diesel vehicles).	Bonus for a new BEV or FCEV: • €5,000 for households if vehicle ≤ €47,000 • €3,000 for legal persons if vehicle ≤ €47,000 Scrappage scheme for a second-hand or new BEV or FCEV of ≤ €47,000: up to €6,000, based on income.	
Germany				
	• 10-year exemption for BEVs and FCEVs registered until December 31, 2025. Exemption granted until December 31, 2030 • Exemption from the annual circulation tax for vehicles emitting ≤ 95g CO2/km.	• Reduction of the taxable amount for BEVs and PHEVs (from 0.5–1% of the gross catalog price per month). PHEVs must meet further requirements, which become more stringent over time. • Additional reduction of taxable amount for BEVs with a gross list price up to €60,000 (0.25–1% of the gross catalogue price per month).	As of January 1, 2023, funding is only available for new and used BEVs and FCEVs. One-third of the funding is provided by the industry and two-thirds by the government. • Bonus for new cars with a net list price ≤ €40,000: €6,750 • Bonus for new cars with a net list price > €40,000 and ≤ €65,000: €4,500 • From September 1, 2023, only private individuals will be able to apply for funding. • From January 1, 2024, reduction in funding and stricter requirements.	
Hungary				
Tax exemption for BEVs and PHEVs.	Tax exemption for BEVs and PHEVs.	Tax exemption for BEVs and PHEVs.	From June 15, 2020, purchase incentives for electric cars: • €7,350 for a gross price of up to €32,000 • €1,500 if the price is between €32,000-44,000	

Tax Benefits			Incentives	
Acquisition	Ownership	Company cars	Purchase	Infrastructure
Italy				
	• BEVs: five-year exemption from the date of first registration. After this period, 75% reduction of the tax rate applied to equivalent petrol vehicles. • HEVs: Application of a minimum flat rate (€2.58/kW). Some regions apply discounts on the tax ownership.		• €3,000 (€5,000 with scrappage) for a BEV/PHEV emitting ≤ 20g CO2/km and with a selling price of ≤ €35,000 + VAT. • €2,000 (€4,000 with scrappage) for a BEV/PHEV emitting 21-60g CO2/km and with a selling price of ≤ €45,000 + VAT.	For domestic users, a contribution of 80% of the purchase and installation price of standard power infrastructures for recharging electric vehicles, within the maximum limit of €1,500 per applicant.
Netherlands				
Exemption for zero-emission cars.	Exemption for zero-emission cars. 50% tariff for PHEVs	Minimum rate (16%) for zero-emission cars. Cap at €30,000 for BEVs. No cap for hydrogen cars	• Subsidy scheme (SEPP) for individuals to buy/lease a small or compact BEV car, new or used. • Arbitrary depreciation of environmental investments scheme (Vamil) for FCEV cars or taxis and BEV cars equipped with solar panels.	
Poland				
• Exemption for BEVs. • Exemption for PHEVs up to 2,000cc until end 2029.	Depreciation: • up to PLN 225,000 for BEVs and FCEVs • up to PLN 150,000 for vehicles emitting 0-50g CO2/km • up to PLN 100,000 for vehicles emitting > 50g CO2/km		Purchase incentives for individuals and legal persons (purchase, leasing): from PLN 18,750 to PLN 27,000 for BEVs and FCEVs of a max price of PLN 225,000	Up to 50% of the eligible costs for hydrogen stations.

Tax Benefits			Incentives	
Acquisition	Ownership	Company cars	Purchase	Infrastructure
		Spain		
• Exemption from 'special tax' for vehicles emitting ≤ 120g CO2/km • Canary Islands: VAT exemption for alternatively powered vehicles (eg BEVs, FCEVs, PHEVs, EREVs, and HEVs) emitting ≤ 110g CO2/km.	75% reduction for BEVs in main cities (eg Barcelona, Madrid, Valencia, Zaragoza, etc).	The use of a company car for private purposes is regarded as a payment in kind and included in the calculation of personal income tax: • 30% reduction for BEVs and PHEVs ≤ €40,000 • 20% reduction for HEVs ≤ €35,000	Incentive scheme (MOVES III) in 2021-2023: • Cars (M1): €4,500-7,000 for BEVs and FCEVs, and €2,500-5,000 for PHEVs, for private individuals, depending on whether a vehicle is being scrapped • Different incentives for SMEs and large companies (+ MOVES FLOTAS)	Incentive scheme (MOVES III) in 2021-2023: • Self-employed, individuals, neighbouring communities, and administration: 70% of the eligible cost • Companies and public - charging points (power ≤ 50 kW): 35% of the eligible cost for a large, 45% for a medium, and 55% for a small company • Companies and public - charging points (power > 50 kW): 30% of the eligible costs These amounts are increased if the location is in municipalities with less than 5,000 inhabitants.
		Sweden		
	Low annual road tax (SEK 360) for zero-emission vehicles and PHEVs.	The private use of a company car is taxed on benefits. For some cars, there is a permanent tax reduction of the benefit value. The reduction is a fixed amount based on the environmental technology: • BEVs and FCEVs: SEK 350,000 • PHEVs: SEK 140,000 The taxable benefit value is based on the new car price and reduced by the relevant amount. The discount may not exceed 50% of the car price.		• 50% tax deduction (max SEK 15,000) for households installing a charging box at home for an electric car. • Ladda bilen grant for the installation of AC charging for residents in apartment buildings.

Source: European Automobile Manufacturers' Association (ACEA)

Most of the EU member countries offer tax benefits and incentives for the purchase of electric vehicles. However, the EU member countries' tax benefits and incentives do not require that the qualifying vehicles be finally assembled in the specific EU member countries or in the EU. It is different from the requirement of the US's IRA tax credits for electric vehicles. The IRA's content requirements mandate that EVs have a minimum percentage of critical minerals by value from North America or other free trade agreement partners to access the tax credit. The IRA's content requirements also mandate that final assembly of electric vehicle models must occur in North America.

With these incentives for the use of electric vehicles, the EU member countries and the EU use the regulation to restrict the use of internal combustion engines. For example, "Fit for 55." The Fit for 55 package is a set of proposals to revise and update EU legislation and to put in place new initiatives with the aim of ensuring that EU policies are in line with the climate goals. The Fit for 55 package includes progressive EU-wide emissions reduction targets for cars and vans for 2030 and beyond, including a 100% reduction target for 2035 for new cars and vans.

With the incentive for electric vehicles and the restriction on the use of internal combustion engines, the European automobile manufacturers are developing their strategies for the transition from internal combustion engines to electric vehicles. The European automobile manufacturer which took the initiative for the transition to electric vehicle was Groupe Renault. Until 2005, compared to other automobile manufacturers like Toyota, Ford, PSA, etc., the Groupe Renault was late for the transition into alternative vehicles. In May 2005, Carlos Ghosn was named president and chief executive officer of Renault. He believed that the transition to the electric vehicles was important for the future of Groupe Renault.

Since June 2005, the Groupe Renault and the SVE(Société de véhicules électriques, a joint subsidiary of Dassault and the bodybuilder Heuliez) have begun to develop a collaboration for the development of electric vehicles. A Japanese manufacturer of lithium-ion batteries for electric vehicles ASEC(Automotive Energy Supply Corporation) was established in 2007 as a joint venture between Nissan, NEC, and Tokin Corporation. Nissan is a part of the Renault-Nissan Alliance.

However, despite Nissan, a part of the Renault-Nissan Alliance, controlling AESC, the Groupe Renault has chosen LG Chemical (the current LG Energy Solutions) as a supplier of lithium-ion batteries for Renaults electric vehicles. In 2010, LG Chem signed a massive lithium-ion battery supply agreement with Renault.

The Groupe Renault's electric vehicle strategy was supported by the French government.

Due to the high dependence of French electricity generation on nuclear power, which does not create CO2 emissions, the transportation sector is always the sector with the highest CO2 emissions in France. In order to reduce CO2 emissions in France, the policy needs to be focused on the road transportation sector.

The French government held a "Grenelle de l'environment" in 2007 with representatives from the central government, local governments, and private sectors to discuss the introduction of a Bonus-Malnus system in order to reduce greenhouse gas emissions in the transport sector by 20 percent and oil dependence by 2020. The Renault's first passenger electric vehicle, "ZOE," was introduced in 2012. Renault Zoe was a long-running best-selling EV car in Europe.

When the Groupe Renault began to develop its strategy of electric vehicles, German automakers focused on "Clean Diesel" strategy. For about 10 years before Volkswagen's Diesel gate broke out, there was a German automakers' growing belief that so-called clean diesel could solve the noise and vibration problems that were disadvantages of diesel engines and finally minimize exhaust gas and nitrogen oxides emissions in terms of environmental standards.

〈Figure 4〉 Sales of top 20 Top 20 electric cars in Europe in 2020.

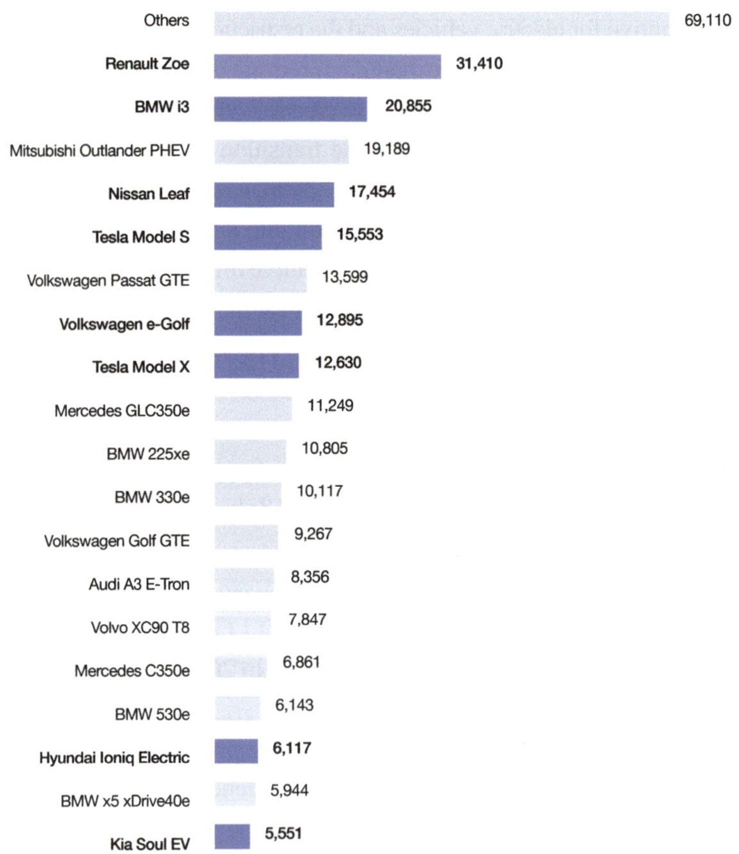

Source: Clean Technica / https://cleantechnica.com/2018/01/27/tesla-surges-renault-zoe-coasts-1-2017-europe-electric-car-sales/

In 2014, the US's ICCT(International Council on Clean Transportation) in Washington DC contracted scientists from the Center for Alternative Fuels Engines and Emissions at West Virginia University in Morgantown to test emissions from three light-duty diesel vehicles under more realistic conditions than are possible in the lab. For the test in a more realistic environment, a portable emissions measurement system was used to gather a continuous stream of data over a variety of US road types.

The tests found that the levels of NOx emitted by a Volkswagen Jetta were 15–35 times greater than dictated by the US standard (31 milligrams per kilometer), depending on the road and driving conditions. With these findings, the US Environmental Protection Agency (EPA) launched investigations into Volkswagen tests in the United States. The EPA threatened to withdraw its approval for all Volkswagen diesel vehicles approved for sale in the USA.

〈Figure 5〉 Global EV sales by OEM / OEM group for 2022

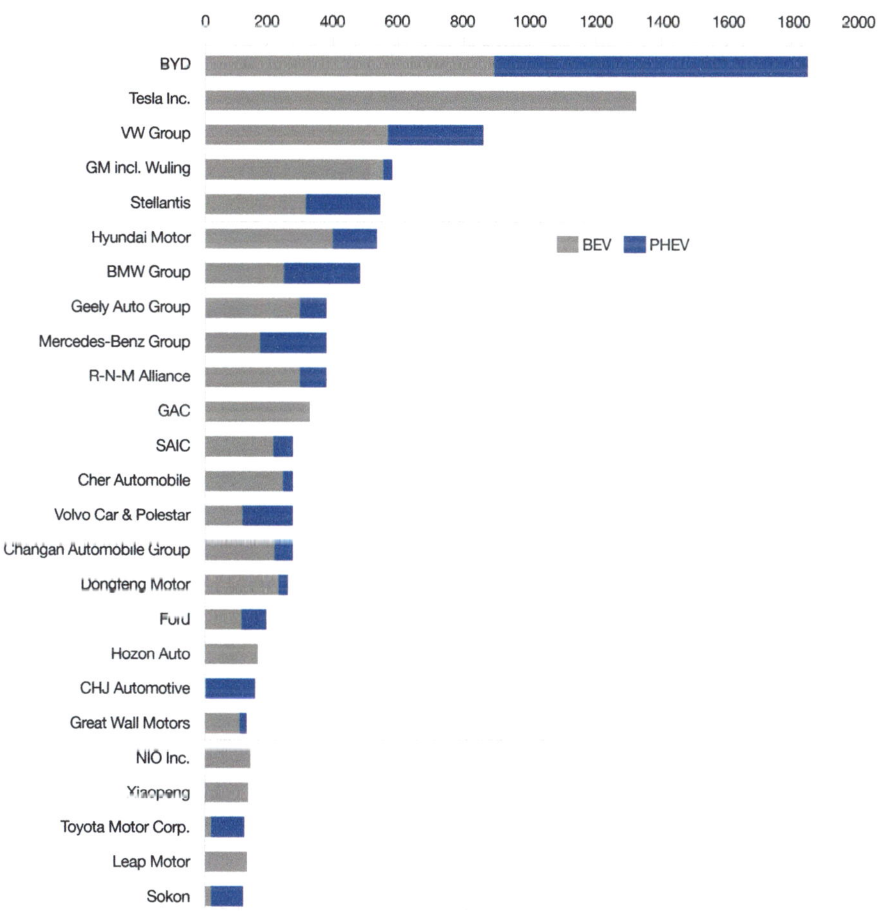

Souce: ev-volumes.com / https://www.ev-volumes.com/news/global-ev-sales-for-2022/

Volkswagen admitted that it had tricked emissions tests by using software that senses when the car is being tested, and switches on full emissions control. On September 18, 2015, the US's EPA accused VW of installing 'defeat device' software that reduces nitrogen oxide emissions while a car is undergoing official tests. Volkswagen paid huge government penalties (242 million USD) in the U.S.

After Dieselgate, Volkswagen completely transformed the company's structure with an aggressive electric vehicle development policy. In 2016, the year after Dieselgate, Volkswagen announced its electric vehicle strategy. After Dieselgate, Volkswagen recognized that the automobile industry was facing the greatest change in history and is rapidly deploying Volkswagen's electric vehicle strategy, "E-Offensive." And in September 2018, Volkswagen announced the "Electric Vehicles for All (Das e-Auto für alle)" strategy to lead the popularization of electric vehicles. The other German automakers also adopted aggressive electric vehicle development strategies.

Figure 5 shows global automobile manufacturers' share of EV sales in 2022. Among the global top 10 EV manufacturers, the following European automobile manufacturers are included: Volks Wagen group, Stellantis, BMW group, Mercedes-Benz group, Renault-Nissan-Mitsubishi alliance.

〈Figure 6〉 Global Lithium-ion Battery Production Capacity Distribution Spilt by Region (2013-2018)

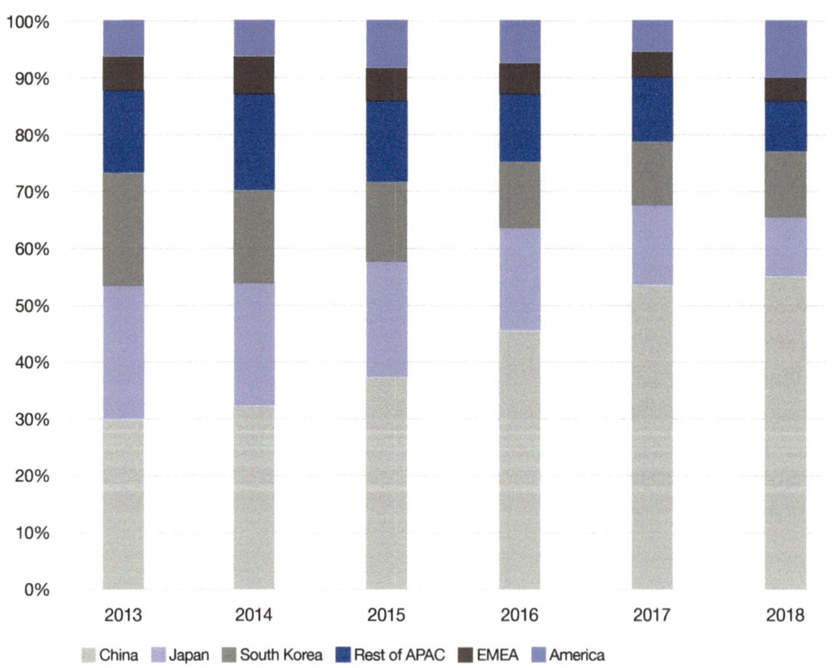

APAC: Asia-Pacific / EMEA: Europe, Middle East, and Africa
Source: Interact Analysis[1]

Despite the fact that battery is the most important part of electric vehicles, the role of the European Union in the global production of Lithium-ion battery was marginal until 2020. In the European Commission's report[2] under the title "the Implementation of the Strategic Action Plan on Batteries: Building a Strategic Battery Value Chain in Europe," the European commission mentioned that the European share of global cell manufacturing is just 3 percent, while Asia has an 85 percent share.

Figure 6 shows that, compared to China, Japan, Korea, and the USA, the European capacity of production of Lithium-ion battery was low. Until 2018, the battery industry was previously considered a contributor to pollution due to the pollution of mineral extraction and processing activities. In the past, battery production was transferred to developing countries, usually China.

However, with the growth of the EV market, the supply of batteries is becoming more important. Europe became the second-largest EV market after China.

With the development of EV markets in Europe, Europe is the second-largest market for batteries.

The EU starts to recognize the importance of fostering the battery industry. In 2017, the European Battery Alliance (EBA) was launched by the European Commission, member countries, industry, and the scientific community. With this alliance, the Commission aims to make Europe a global leader in sustainable battery production and usage, establishing a complete domestic battery value chain. The European Battery Alliance aims to develop an innovative, competitive, and sustainable battery value chain[3] in Europe. Subsidiaries of global leading battery companies, such as CATL, LG Chem, and Samsung SDI, are members of the European Battery Alliance.

In 2018, the Commission adopted a strategic action plan for batteries.[4] It sets out a comprehensive framework of regulatory and non-regulatory measures to support all segments of the battery value chain and includes the 6 priority areas following: "Securing access to raw materials for batteries," "Supporting European battery cell manufacturing and other investments," "Strengthening industrial leadership through accelerated research and innovation programmes," "Securing a highly skilled workforce along the whole value chain," "Supporting a sustainable EU battery cell manufacturing industry," and "Ensuring consistency with broader frameworks."

Battery production is increasing rapidly within the EU, thanks to policies to foster the battery industry in the EU and its member states.

〈Figure 7〉 Global electric car stock in selected regions, 2016-2022, million

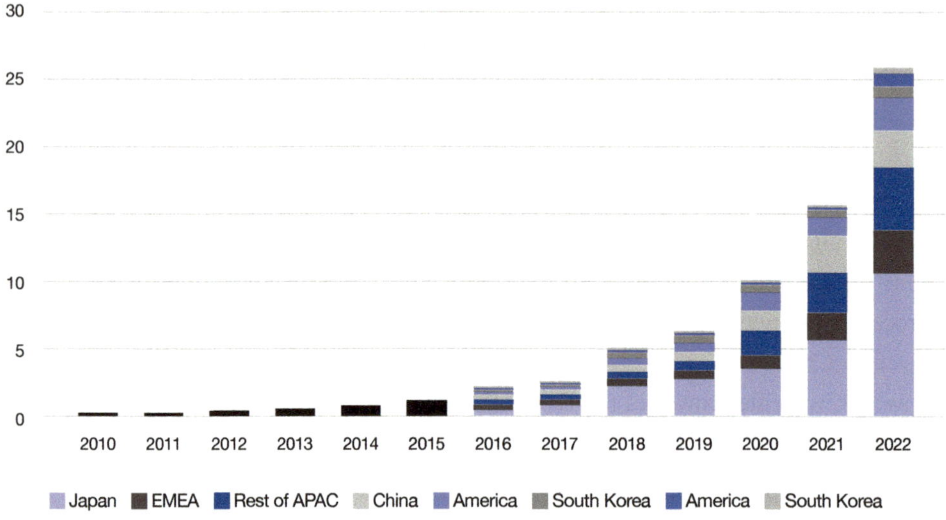

Source: International Energy Agency (IEA)
IEA, Global EV Outlook, 2023, p.15.

〈Figure 8〉 Battery demand by region, 2016-2022, GWh per year

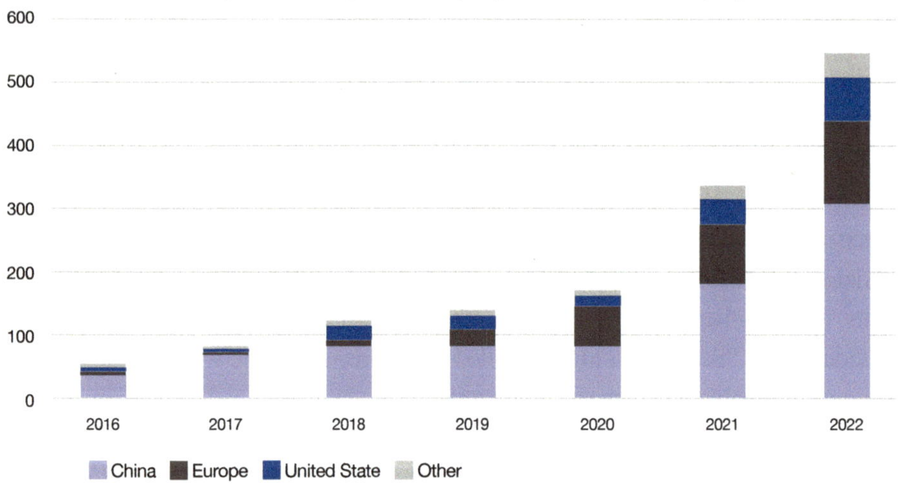

Source: International Energy Agency (IEA)
IEA, Global EV Outlook, 2023, p.56.

〈Table 2〉 Battery Manufacturing Capacity by Country in 2022

Rank	Country	2022 Battery Cell Manufacturing Capacity, GWh	% of total
1	China	893	77
2	Poland	73	6
3	United States	70	6
4	Hungary	38	3
5	Germany	31	3
6	Sweden	16	1
7	Korea	15	1
8	Japan	12	1
9	France	6	1
10	India	3	0.2
Other		7	1
Total		1,163	100

Source: Visual Capitalist[5]

China, Poland, the United States, Hungary, Germany, Sweden, South Korea, Japan, France, and India were among the top countries in terms of battery cell production capacity in 2022, according to the data analysis from Visual Capitalist. Online publishers focused on topics including markets, technology, energy, and the global economy. This is a very important change from the situation in which most of the world's battery cell production capacity was concentrated in China, Korea, and Japan in 2019.

According to this data analysis, with nearly 900 gigawatt-hours of manufacturing capacity, or 77% of the global total, China is home to six of the world's 10 biggest battery makers. European countries (including non-EU members) made up just 14% of global battery manufacturing capacity in 2022. Poland ranks second, with less than one-tenth of China's capacity. In addition, it hosts LG Energy Solution's Wroclaw gigafactory, the largest of its kind in Europe and one of the largest in the world.

ICCT's 2020 report predicted a situation in which the role of Europe and the United States in global battery production led by China, Korea, and Japan is gradually expanding.

In 2019, the European Commission published a document on "Implementation of the Strategic Action Plan on Batteries: Building a Strategic Battery Value Chain in Europe."

〈Figure 9〉 Estimated announced battery production capacity for 2019–2025, by region (Unit: GWh)

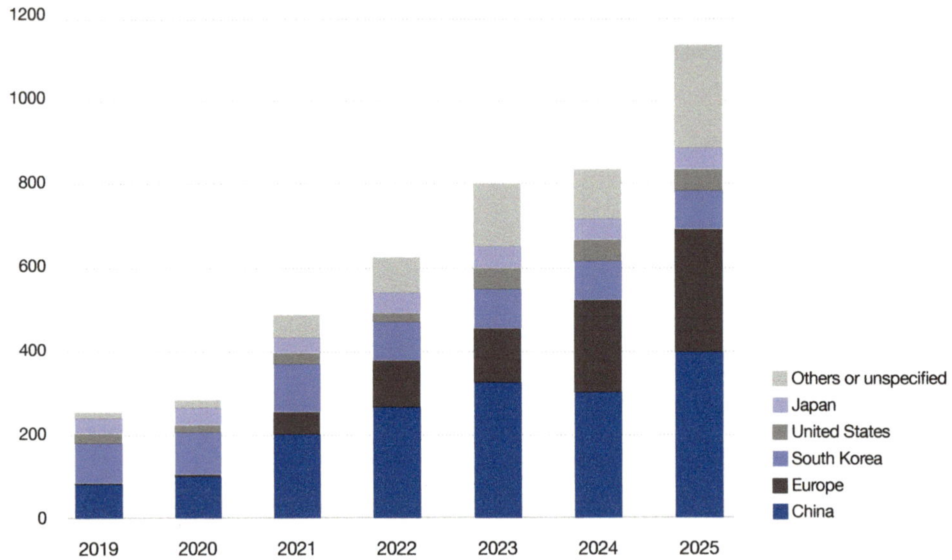

Source: ICCT (International Council on Clean Transportation)[6]

This report emphasized "strategic FTAs with raw material possession countries to secure stable core raw materials (lithium, cobalt, etc.) required for battery manufacturing." In order to secure the battery raw materials supply chain, it also emphasized "the Establishment of The European Innovation Partnership on Raw Materials" and "the research development on supply chain strategies regarding these issues."

According to the IEA report "the Role of Critical Minerals in Clean Energy Transitions"[7], mineral demand for use in EVs and battery storage is a major force, growing at least thirty times to 2040. Lithium sees the fastest growth, with demand growing by over 40 times by 2040, followed by graphite, cobalt, and nickel (around 20–25 times).

Until the EU began to acknowledge the significant importance of the supply chain of critical materials for battery production, battery production was transferred to China from the USA and Europe due to the pollution created by the extraction and processing of critical minerals for the battery. In 2010, the Chinese share from global production of rare earth elements reached 97%.

Compared to 2020, battery demand increased by 140% in China, doubled in the United States, and increased by 70% in Europe in 2021. However, the world currently relies on China for more than 50% of global battery production. In addition, global battery raw material extraction and processing are highly dependent on China.

The development of mineral resources such as rare earths, a key raw material for batteries and semiconductors, was also classified as a pollution industry and transferred to China, and in the mid-2010s, China's global share of rare earth production rose to 80%. Compared to 2020, battery demand increased by 140% in China, doubled in the United States, and increased by 70% in Europe in 2021. However, it currently relies on China for more than 50% of global battery production. In addition, China is highly dependent on battery raw materials and processing.

As IEA data shows, China accounts for 60% of the global mineral resource production of graphite and rare earths. In addition, in the case of mineral resource processing, China occupies an incomparably important proportion of the global processing of copper, lithium, nickel, cobalt, and rare earth elements.

China's share of refining is around 35% for nickel, 50-70% for lithium and cobalt, and as high as 90% for REE processing. Therefore, the United States and the EU have recognized the need to secure stability by transforming the market structure of mineral production and processing, which is dominated by China.

In the context of the US-China trade dispute, which is a hegemony competition between the US and China, the US plans to reduce its dependence on China. The EU also plans to de-risk its dependence on China.

〈Figure 10〉 Share of the top three producing countries in total production for selected minerals and fossil fuels, 2019

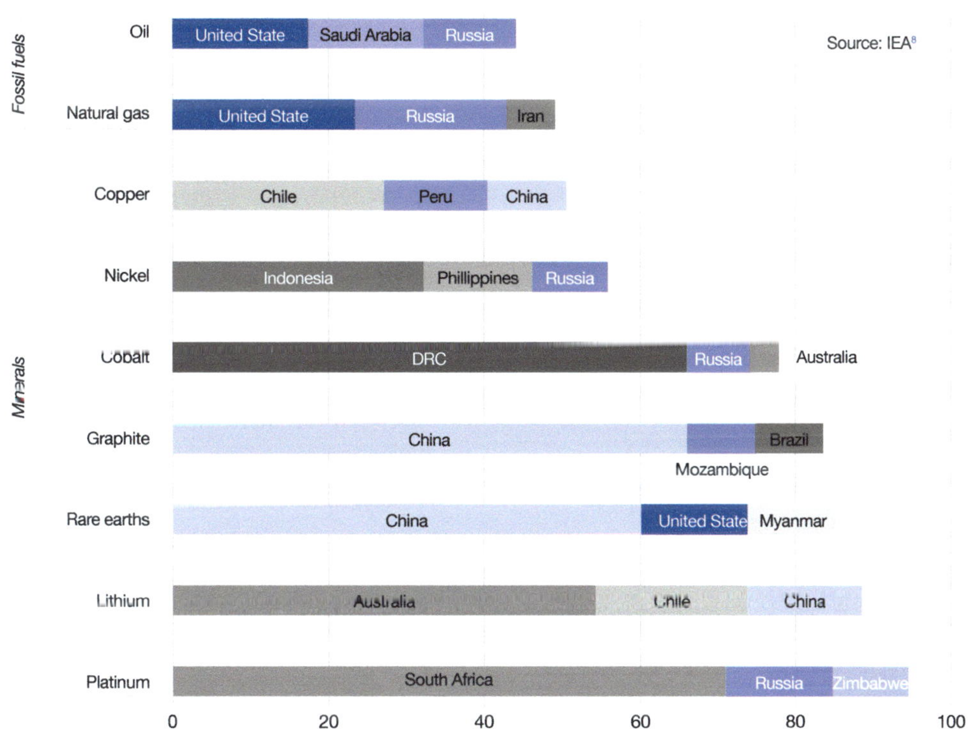

Since 2008, the EU has been paying attention to the supply chain stability of critical minerals. In 2008, the European Commission published its new Communication, "The raw materials initiative — meeting our critical needs for growth and jobs in Europe." The Raw Materials Initiative aims to establish an integrated strategy to face the challenges related to access to critical minerals and facilitate the sustainable supply of these resources. Since 2011, the European Commission has assessed every 3 years a list of Critical Raw Materials for the EU economy within its Raw Materials Initiative.

〈Figure 11〉 Share of processing volume by country for selected minerals, 2019

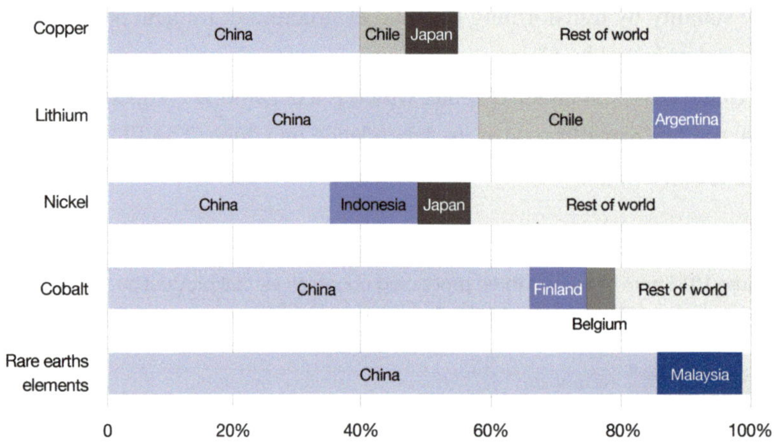

Source: IEA[9]

〈Table 3〉 Fifth list 2023 of critical raw materials for the EU

Bauxite	Coking Coal	Lithium	Phosphorus
Antimony	Feldspar	Light rare earth elements	Scandium
Arsenic	Fluorspar	Magnesium	Silicon metal
Baryte	Gallium	Manganese	Strontium
Beryllium	Germanium	Natural Graphite	Tantalum
Bismuth	Hafnium	Niobium	Titanium metal
Boron/Borate	Helium	Platinum group metals	Tungsten
Cobalt	Heavy rare earth elements	Phosphate Rock	Vanadium
		Copper	Nickel

Source: European Commission[10]

Since 2008, the European Union has developed policies for the stability of critical raw material supply based on a three-pillar-based approach: "International (Ensure a level playing field in access to resources in third countries)"; "Domestic (Foster sustainable supply of raw materials from European sources)"; "Recycling (Boost resource efficiency and promote recycling)". However, in the EU, the supply of many critical raw materials is highly concentrated. For example, China provides 100% of the EU's supply of heavy rare earth elements (REE), Turkey provides 99% of the EU's supply of boron, and South Africa provides 71% of the EU's needs for platinum and an even higher share of the platinum group metals iridium, rhodium, and ruthenium. In particular, battery-grade refining and processing facilities for almost all these materials are currently concentrated in China. China is also the world's largest producer and exporter of rare earth permanent magnets. As of today, China provides 92% of global rare earth magnet production. 16,000 tons of rare earth permanent magnets are exported from China to Europe each year, representing approximately 98% of the EU market.

The European Commission calls for the EU to diversify its sources of battery raw materials, including the promotion of the use of these materials produced in the EU, to utilize the EU's trade policy to ensure a sustainable and safe supply of battery raw materials, and to promote battery recovery, reuse, and recycling. It means that, in order to reduce the EU's dependence on imports of battery raw materials, the extraction and processing of battery raw materials within the EU need to be facilitated. It also means that, with reliable trade partners, the supply of battery raw materials needs to be ensured.

In other words, in order to reduce the EU's dependence on imports of battery raw materials, access to battery raw material sources within the EU must be easy, and at the same time, in order to smoothly supply battery raw materials from outside the EU, safe and sustainable supply from battery raw material supply countries outside the EU must be provided. It is recognized that a possible supply must be guaranteed.

By incorporating these policy considerations into trade policy, the EU included provisions related to raw materials when concluding free trade agreements (FTAs) with trading partners such as Canada and Mexico. In addition, the EU presented provisions on "sustainable sourcing of raw materials" in FTA negotiations with major battery raw material supply countries such as Chile and Australia.

In March 2020, the European Commission announced the "New Industrial Strategy for Europe" and, in September 2020, the "Critical Raw Materials Resilience: Charting a Pathways Greater Security and Sustainability," which contains implementation measures to secure major raw materials stably. The EU's "Critical Raw Materials Resilience" aims to "establish value chains for the EU industrial ecosystem", "reduce dependence on raw materials through recycling, sustainable products and innovation", "strengthen the supply of major raw materials in the EU", and "diversify suppliers to strengthen rule-based free trade of major raw materials and prevent trade distortion". And on September 29, 2020, with the aim of developing raw materials and expanding raw material processing facilities in the region, the European Raw Materials Alliance was established.

In her State of the Union address on September 14, 2022, the European Commission President von der Leyen announced that she plans to introduce the Critical Raw Material Act to build an EU-centered supply chain for such minerals as lithium and rare earth elements that are highly dependent on China.

In March 2023, the draft of the European Critical Raw Materials Act was adopted. The Act sets these benchmarks along the strategic raw materials value chain and for the diversification of the EU supplies at least 10% of the EU's annual consumption for extraction, at least 40% of the EU's annual consumption for processing, at least 15% of the EU's annual consumption for recycling and no more than 65% of the EU's annual consumption from a single third country. In addition, the EU is trying to diversify imports so that key minerals can be introduced from trusted partner countries such as Canada. In European core raw material law, China was indirectly targeted by linking "labor rights, human rights, and environmental protection" issues with the supply chain. In this way, the EU level is trying to reduce its dependence on China for critical material supplies.

〈Figure 12〉 Biggest supplier countries of CRMs to the EU

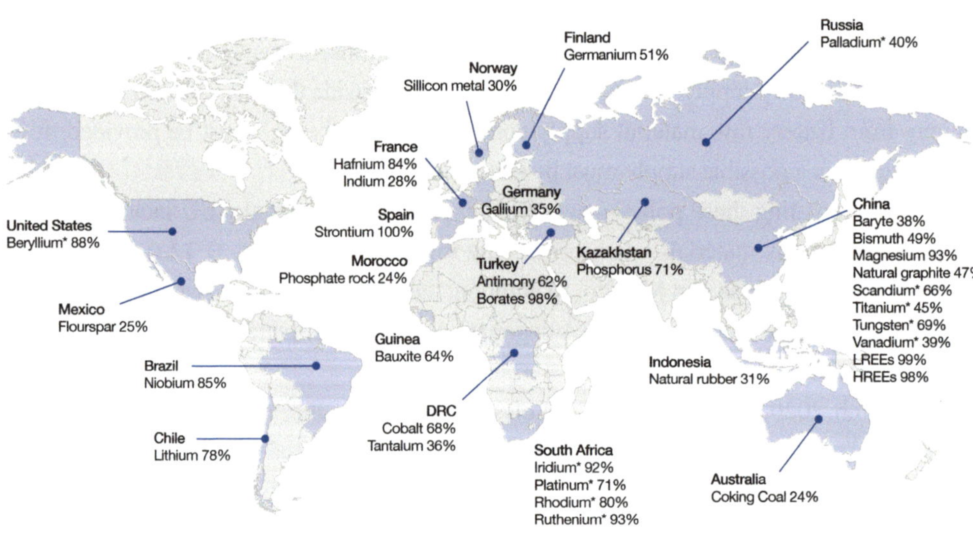

Source: European Commission[11]

The *circumstances of EU-China* relations have undergone many changes *over the past decade.* Until the US-China tensions rise and intensify, the EU has developed relations with China. The EU established the EU-China Comprehensive Strategic Partnership with China in 2003, and the EU-China 2020 Strategic Agenda for Cooperation was adopted in 2013. In the EU-China 2020 Strategic Agenda for Cooperation, EU-China expressed strengthening cooperation in security, trade and investment, industry and IT, agriculture, transportation and infrastructure, aerospace, energy, urbanization, climate change and environmental protection, ocean, and cultural-educational cooperation.

However, when the Trump administration strengthened the protectionist barrier, China tried to respond jointly with the EU. But the EU refused to stand up to the US in solidarity with China. Rather, on December 20, 2018, the EU filed a complaint with the WTO for forcing the Chinese government to transfer technology to EU companies that entered China, and the EU raised the issue of the Chinese government's investment approval in the Chinese electric vehicle and bio industry.

Ahead of Chinese President Xi's visit to Europe in 2019, the European Commission reviewed its relations with China. The European Commission stated in a press release on March 12, 2019, that *"China is simultaneously a cooperation partner with whom the EU has closely aligned objectives, a negotiating partner, with whom the EU needs to find a balance of interests, an economic competitor in pursuit of technological leadership, and a systemic rival promoting alternative models of governance."*

However, after seven years of negotiations, on December 30, 2020, the EU and China concluded, in principle, the negotiations on the Comprehensive Agreement on Investment (CAI). China promised an unprecedented level of market access for the EU investors. However, when the EU sanctioned four Chinese officials and one organization for human rights issues in Xinjiang in March 2021, China responded to the European Parliament and the EU Council with retaliatory sanctions on the same day. On May 20, 2021, the European Parliament *passed a resolution to freeze ratification of the EU-China* Comprehensive Agreement on Investment (CAI).

The energy and environmental sectors are under the field of shared competence between the EU and its member states, as specified in Article 4 of the Treaty on the Functioning of the European Union (TFEU). The EU plans to de-risk the dependency of the supply chain on critical raw. However, EU member states such as France and Germany are strengthening cooperation in the supply chain with China, unlike the EU's policy to reduce their dependence on China.

In 2022, the German government issued a production permit for batteries to a Chinese battery manufacturer, CATL. CATL started series production of battery cells in Germany in December 2022.

In 2019, Chinese battery manufacturer, Farasis also planned to produce batteries in Bitterfeld-Wolfen (Saxony-Anhalt), Germany. However, Farasis has finally chosen Turkey.

〈Figure 13〉 Battery cell production in Europe

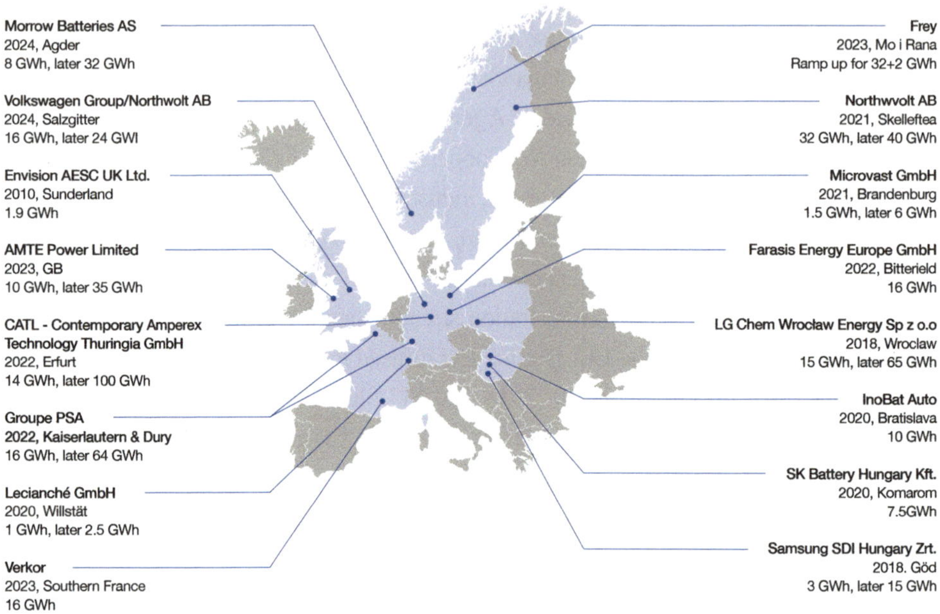

Source: ees-Europe[12]

Siro, a joint venture between Farasis Energy and Turkish global mobility technology brand Togg, has started production at the new Gemlik site in Turkey on March 31st.

In May 2023, the EU prepared sanctions against countries that help Russia evade penalties, potentially hitting China. China warns of a 'Strong' reaction if the EU sanctions Chinese companies However, the German government warns the EU against hitting China with Russian sanctions.

During his state visit to China in April 2023, at the event of the French Community in China, French President Macron said that Europe must not be separated from China. During the meeting with Chinese Premier Li Qiang, Macron mentioned that France is ready to strengthen cooperation in economy and trade, agriculture, aviation, finance, nuclear energy, innovation, tourism, and people-to-people and cultural exchanges with an open attitude, and deepen communication and coordination on major issues concerning international peace and stability.

German and French automobile manufacturers are also strengthening their cooperation in the supply chain with Chinese manufacturers. In 2021, German Automaker Volkswagen announced that it will manufacture batteries for electric vehicles in Germany with a leading Chinese manufacturer, starting in 2025. In 2021, German Automaker Daimler completed a new battery production line as part of its Chinese joint venture Beijing Benz with BAIC. In 2021, French Automaker Renault has chosen China's Envision AESC to produce batteries in the future Douai plant in northern France. This battery plant will supply Renault in early 2025. In August

2022, Chinese battery manufacturer EVE Energy Co. Ltd. signed a contract to be BMW's primary supplier of battery cells in Europe for its new series of electric vehicles from 2025.

In order to expand their cooperation with European Automakers, Chinese battery manufacturers are increasing their investment in Europe.

Chinese battery suppliers like CATL, SVOLT, Envision, and EVE Energy are increasing their investments in the global battery supply chain. In 2022, it reached 14.2 billion euros. According to Reuters, CATL's $7.6 billion Hungarian facility, scheduled to start mass production in 2025, will be Europe's biggest ever, with an annual capacity of 100 gigawatt hours. Likewise, Putailai's $1.3 billion Swedish plant will be Europe's largest anode factory.

〈Figure 14〉 Chinese investments into the global EV battery supply chain

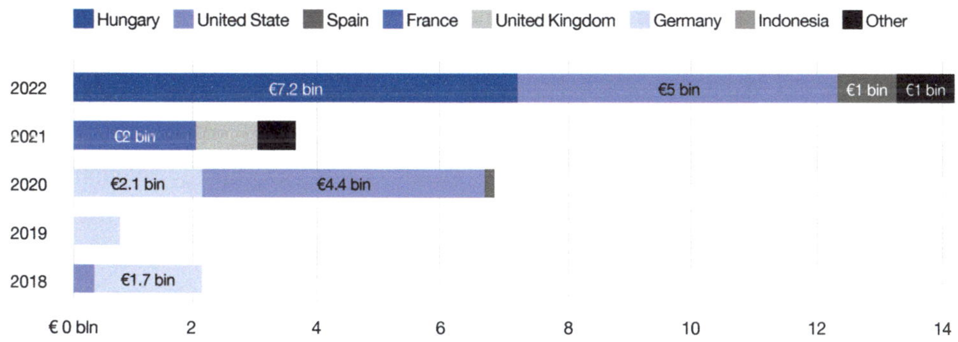

Source: Reuters[13]

〈Figure 13〉 Share of the EU battery market (Unit: %)

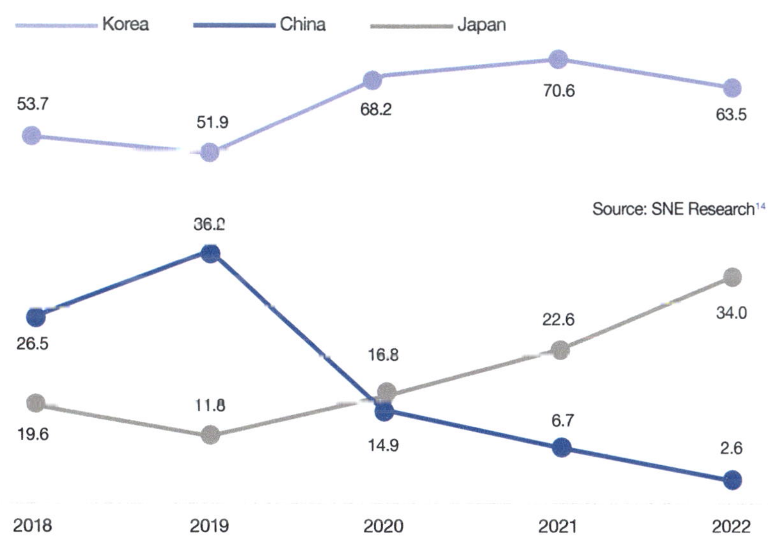

Source: SNE Research[14]

Accordingly, Korean companies that are highly dependent on sales in the EU battery market face challenges from Chinese companies in the EU market. According to the statistics of KITA (Korea International Trade Association), EV and Battery are among Korea's top 10 export items (MTI4) to the EU(EU27) in 2022.[15] Korea's total export volume to the EU in 2022 was 68,072,166,000 USD. Korea's battery export volume to the EU in 2022 was 2,488,133,000 USD. Korea's electric vehicle export volume to the EU in 2022 was 2,566,445,000 USD.

For decades, Korean and European industrial manufacturers have strengthened their co-operation in the battery supply chain.

Among European automakers, French automaker Renault took the initiative for the transition to electric vehicles. In 2009, the former chairman and chief executive officer of the Renault-Nissan Alliance, Carlos Ghosn, announced a new strategy. "Groupe Renault would be offering a full range of affordable all-electric vehicles by 2012." In 2011, Carlos Ghosn predicted that by 2020, electric cars would make up 10% of the global market. In 2010, LG-Chemical (Current LG-Energy Solution) signed an agreement with Renault to supply lithium batteries for the French auto manufacturer's upcoming electric vehicle. Since 2010, LG-Energy Solution and Renault have continuously developed their partnership.

As of today, the top 10 global Korean battery manufacturers—LG Energy Solution, Samsung SDI, and SK Innovation—are producing the batteries in the European Union. In Poland, LG Energy Solution started mass production in the first quarter of 2018. In Hungary, Samsung SDI started production in May 2018 and SK On also started production in October 2019.

Currently, compared to Chinese and Japanese battery manufacturers, Korean battery manufacturers' global sales have a high dependency on the European market.

〈Figure 14〉 Global battery deployment by manufacturers (Unit: GWh)

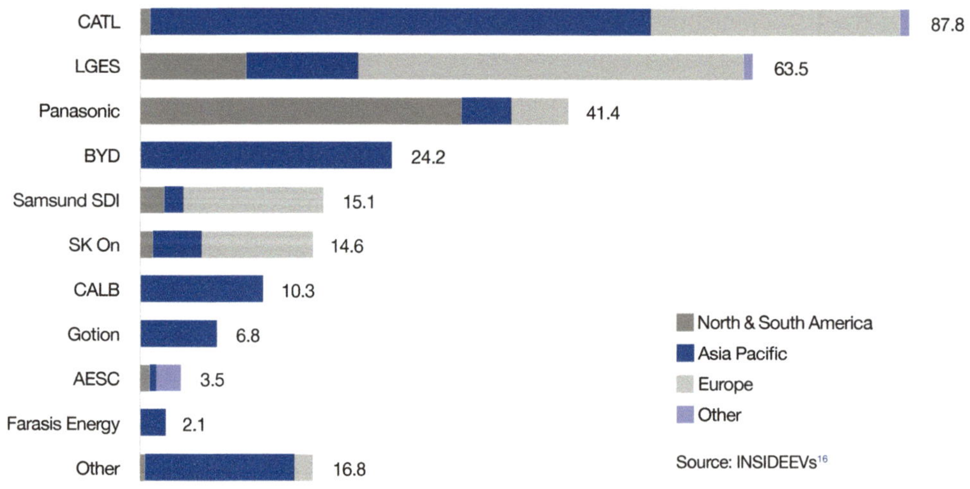

Source: INSIDEEVs[16]

The European Union plans to de-risk the supply chain of critical raw materials from China. For example, the Critical Raw Materials Act, Battery Regulation, etc., while member countries like Germany, France, Spain, and Italy, plan to develop industrial cooperation with China. However, in a democratic society, decisions are not made only "on the governmental level." The industry is also an active player in policy-making. For the EU, member countries and industry are important players in policy-making. In the USA, the implementation of the IRA aims to decouple the supply chain from China. However, under the pressure of the automaker, Ford, the White House authorized a Ford battery plant, licensing technology from CATL.

Korean battery manufacturers have a strong dependency on China for critical minerals. Korean manufacturers' change in the supply chain of critical raw minerals creates the cost. However, if the EU's member countries develop industrial cooperation with China and the EU enforces Korean manufacturers to de-risk the supply chain from China, Korean manufacturers will prepare responses in consideration of the circumstances.

The year 2023 is the 60th anniversary of diplomatic relations between Korea and the EU. Korea and the EU have developed cooperation in all areas. Under the EU's strong responses to climate change, the EU's CO2 emissions from electricity generation have significantly reduced. The emissions from road transport became the EU's largest CO2 emission sector, according to IPCC.

The EU and its member countries have encouraged the use of electric vehicles in order to replace internal combustion engines. Europe became the second-largest EV market after China. European electric vehicles are leading the global EV market with American Tesla. The growth of EV sales resulted in an increasing demand for EV battery. However, the global EV battery production is led by Asian manufacturers such as CATL, LG Energy Solution, Panasonic, Samsung SDI, and SK On. The EU and the member countries implemented policies to promote battery production in the EU, such as the European Commission's strategic action plan for batteries in 2018.

The increasing demand for battery requires the stability of the supply chain of the critical raw materials for EV battery. However, the global extraction and processing of battery raw materials are dominated by China. European countries have experienced the weaponization of energy resources by Russia during the Russian invasion of Ukraine. In 2010, China already weaponized its rare earth elements against Japan regarding the territorial dispute.

The European Union tried to de-risk the supply chain of the critical raw materials for EV battery. However, some EU member countries and some European automobile manufacturers are strengthening cooperation with Chinese battery manufacturers.

The European battery market is the most important market for Korean battery manufacturers. Under the EU's policy to de-risk Chinese supply chain, Korean battery manufacturers are required to replace Chinese suppliers of battery-critical raw materials. In the European market, Korean battery manufacturers are facing a challenge from Chinese battery manufacturers, which have increased their investment in Europe.

Endnote

1. Interact Analysis, "Global Lithium-ion Battery Production Capacity Distribution Spilt by Region (2013-2018)," https://www.interactanalysis.com/wp-content/uploads/2019/07/Lithium-Ion-Battery-market-poised-for-strong-growth-in-Europe-Asian-players-expected-to-open-European-Factories.p
2. European Commission, Report from the Commission to the European Parliament, the Council, the European Economic and Social Committee, the Committee of the Regions and the European Investment Bank on the Implementation of the Strategic Action Plan on Batteries: Building a Strategic Battery Value Chain in Europe (COM(2019) 176 final), 2019.
3. European Commission, the Implementation of the Strategic Action Plan on Batteries: Building a Strategic Battery Value Chain in Europe (COM(2019) 176 final), 2019.
4. European Commission, Communication from Commission to the European Parliament, the Council, the European Economic and Social Committee, the Committee of the Regions Europe on the Move: Sustainable Mobility for Europe: safe, connected and clean (COM(2018) 293 final), 2018.
5. Visual Capitalist, "Visualizing China's Dominance in Battery Manufacturing (2022-2027P)," https://www.visualcapitalist.com/chinas-dominance-in-battery-manufacturing/
6. ICCT, Driving a green future: A Retrospective review of China's electric vehicle development and outlook for the future (2020), p.19.
7. IEA, "The Role of Critical Minerals in Clean Energy Transitions," https://www.iea.org/reports/the-role-of-critical-minerals-in-clean-energy-transitions/executive-summary
8. IEA, The Role of Critical Minerals in Clean Energy Transitions, 2022, p.30.
9. IEA, The Role of Critical Minerals in Clean Energy Transitions, 2022, p.31.
10. European Commission, "Fifth list 2023 of critical raw materials for the EU," https://single-market-economy.ec.europa.eu/sectors/raw-materials/areas-specific-interest/critical-raw-materials_en
11. European Commission, Communication from the Commission to the European Parliament, the Council, the European Economic and Social Committee and the Committee of the Region: Critical Raw Materials, Resilience: Charting a Path towards greater Security and Sustainability, 2020. https://eur-lex.europa.eu/legal-content/EN/TXT/?uri=CELEX:52020DC0474
12. ees-Europe, "Battery cell production in Europe," https://www.ees-europe.com/market-trends/battery-cell-production-jobs-in-europe
13. Reuters, "Chinese battery cash will fuel Europe's EV drive", (31 May 2023) https://www.reuters.com/breakingviews/chinese-battery-cash-will-fuel-europes-ev-drive-2023-05-31/
14. Korea JoongAng Daily, "[News Analysis] Chinese battery makers threaten Korean lead in EU", (May 29, 2023) https://koreajoongangdaily.joins.com/2023/05/29/business/industry/korea-battery-catl/20230529163121175.html
15. KITA's trade statistics, https://stat.kita.net/newMain.screen
16. INSIDEEVs, "Global Passenger xEV Battery Market Doubled In 2021: 286 GWh" https://insideevs.com/news/566626/global-xev-battery-market-2021/

EU-Korea Digital Partnership
A New Era for Bilateral Partnership?

CHUNG SAEWON

Introduction

The European Union and Korea have formed a digital partnership to boost trade, investment, and sustainable economic development. The partnership focuses on 11 core areas: joint research, semiconductors, next-generation mobile networks, quantum computing, cybersecurity, artificial intelligence, platforms, data, and technology. The first digital partnership council was held in Seoul in June 2023, focusing on six prioritized areas. In order to enhance cooperation, the two countries should recognize the importance of new global partnerships, focus on technological innovation, tackle common challenges, involve relevant businesses, governments, and interest groups, and establish a global impact.

On May 22, 2023, the European Union (hereafter the EU) and the Republic of Korea (hereafter Korea) held a summit to commemorate the 60 years of their bilateral ties. Within their strategic partnerships, the central topics were peace (stability), economy (trade), and sustainable development. For the future agenda, they promised to strengthen digital (data) security and industrial competitiveness and to suggest the EU-Korea Green Partnership (Korea-EU Research Centre 2023). In an era marked by unprecedented technological advancements and globalization, the EU and Korea have recently embarked on a new and future-oriented partnership. The EU and Korea established an EU-Korea digital partnership on November 28, 2022. This partnership will strengthen EU-Korea bilateral trade and investment cooperation and sustainable economic development. This partnership will facilitate collaboration on semiconductors, next-generation mobile networks, Quantum and high-performance computing, cybersecurity, artificial intelligence, platforms, data, and technology

(Korean Ministry of Science and ICT 2022a).

In their partnership, there are 11 core task areas for further cooperation. They are: 1. Joint research, 2. Semiconductors, 3. Ultra High-Performance computing and quantum technologies, 4. Cybersecurity and trust, 5. Next generation 5G and 6G, 6. Human competency, human resource exchange and digital inclusion, 7. Artificial intelligence, 8. Online and digital platform cooperation, 9. Data-related laws and systems, 10. Digital identity and trust services, and 11. Digital trade. These tasks show that the two parties attempt to deal with new challenges and search for further beneficial opportunities. In these tasks, three emphases were found. First, the two want to draw win-win strategies for their future. Second, they seek closer economic connectivity by strengthening digital partnerships. Third, they wish to deal with further upcoming challenges.

Arguably, several key factors formed the partnerships. The first factor is their shared vision. This vision has been established through 60 years of bilateral cooperation. Their strategic partnership reflects similar objectives in global society. The two have strengthened their cooperation for an inclusive and resilient digital transformation. They share the same vision for "a fair and secure online environment" (European Commission 2023). The second factor is their interconnected digital economy. The outcome of this partnership is related to the economic benefits, such as developing a platform economy, advanced digital infrastructure and strengthening economic resilience. Their leading semiconductor capabilities would have driven further development (Innovation News Network 2023). The third factor is the fast-changing digital environment. To tackle the challenges caused by such an environment, like-minded partners should intensify their cooperation in handling further challenges. When someone fails to address the challenges, they might face a decrease in their economic growth rates (Qureshi 2022). The fourth factor is that EU-Korea cooperation has been significantly expanded. Since the EU-Korea FTA, their economic ties have become stronger and closer (European Union External Action, 2020). The last factor is their necessity in establishing future-oriented partnerships. They aspire to strengthen their trusted and advanced partnership for future sustainability (European Commission 2022).

This chapter focuses on digital partnerships as a step toward the next level of their bilateral relationships. The rest of this chapter will further introduce the background and context of EU-Korea bilateral digital partnerships. Subsequently, it will introduce several key issues of bilateral digital partnerships. After the presentation, it will argue the meaning and consequences of this partnership. Finally, the conclusion will point out some further implications.

Background and Contextual Development

The EU's dgital partnerships have proven to be essential in establishing unity and connectivity throughout the EU and the rest of the world. The EU aspires to cooperate with like-minded states, and it can address the digital divide and strengthen its ties with global partners. This partnership follows the Digital Compass Strategy, which seeks to make Europe a digitally connected continent by 2030. Based on this strategy, the EU has committed to establishing solid partnerships using the four pillars of the Digital Compass—skills, infrastructure, business transformation, and public service transformation (European Commission 2023a).

Korea has recently shown a strong commitment to leading global innovation. In September 2022, Korean President Yoon Suk-yeol announced the New York Initiative, which proposed a new digital order for the future of digital innovation in Korea. Subsequently, the Ministry of Science and ICT (MSIT) announced 'the Digital Strategy of Korea' to implement the New York Initiative. It consists of five strategies (elements): 1. The World's Best Digital Capability, 2. Burgeoning Digital Economy, 3. Digitally Inclusive Society, 4. Open Digital Platform Government, 5. Innovating Digital Culture (Korean Ministry of Science and ICT 2022b). After that, the Korean Ministry of Science and ICT had a series of talks with major partners in Europe (the EU, Germany, and the UK) (Korean Ministry of Science and ICT 2022a). In November 2022, at the B20 Summit in Bali, President Yoon emphasized that the Korean government will focus on digital transformation and lead discussions at the G20 level to establish a new global digital order (KITA 2022a).

After signing the EU-Korea digital partnership in November 2022, they held the first digital partnership council in Seoul on June 30, 2023. It is a ministerial-level consultative body established by the Korean Minister of Science and ICT and the EU Commissioner for the domestic market, who were the chief representatives to implement the digital partnership. This Council will be held on an annual basis on both sides, alternatively for discussion of plans of bilateral digital cooperation. This Council was held due to one of the achievements of the EU-Korea Summit in May 2023 to mark the 60th anniversary of their diplomatic ties. Both parties discussed six prioritized areas in this council meeting: 1. Semiconductors, 2. HPC and Quantum technology, 3. Cybersecurity and trust, 4. Beyond 5G and 6G, 5. Artificial Intelligence, and 6. Online and Digital Platform (Korean Ministry of Science and ICT 2023a).

The EU-Korea digital partnership is a new development in EU-Korea relations. It has several implications for strengthening economic, political and R & D (Research and Development) cooperation ties. In the next section, we will look more in detail at the six key agendas of bilateral digital partnership.

Key Issues in Bilateral Digital Partnerships

This part addresses the six prioritized tasks (1. Semiconductors, 2. HPC and Quantum technology, 3. Cybersecurity and trust, 4. Beyond 5G and 6G, 5. Artificial Intelligence and 6. Online and Digital Platforms) after the first Korea-EU Digital Partnership Council, held on June 30, 2023.

Semiconductors

After the Council meeting, both sides announced the establishment of an ROK-EU Forum for Semiconductor Researchers to discuss the most up-to-date technologies and trends. In this forum, the two sides will find ways to contribute to global supply chain stability through cooperation in the semiconductor industry and establish an early warning system. They strengthen cooperation in international standardization related to semiconductor security, which will be promoted by the Korean Ministry of Trade, Industry, and Energy (KITA 2022b). Regarding practicality, both sides attempt to promote research in the complementary fields of semiconductors. Such research collaboration may be explored under the Chips Joint Undertaking on the EU side (European Commission 2023c). This forum will be held alternatively once a year (MK 2023).

HPC and Quantum Technology

In the field of High-Performance Computing (HPC) and quantum technology, the researchers will first increase access to mutual infrastructure by signing a memorandum of understanding (MoU). This MoU will increase the accessibility of researchers to mutual infrastructure and promote and implement applied research fields. Additionally, through the working group of quantum technology experts, the Council decided to discover joint research fields such as quantum computing, quantum sensors, and quantum communication and to discuss ways to build supply chains and ecosystems such as standardization and revitalization of the industry (Economic Diplomacy Utilization Portal 2023).

Cybersecurity and Trust

In the field of cybersecurity, it was decided to continue to expand cybersecurity policy sharing through the Korea-EU Cybersecurity Conference 2023. This conference was held on the same date as the EU-Korea Digital Council meeting. In this conference, both sides discussed the possibility of joint research on cybersecurity and ways to share information on cyber threats. They also proposed to sign an MoU between the Ministry of Science and ICT for Korea and the European Cyber Security Agency (ENISA) to establish a cybersecurity cooperation system between the two sides (Economic Diplomacy Utilization Portal 2023).

Among these six areas, cybersecurity is worth further attention. The EU has checked over the expansion of online market influence led by giant global firms through digital policy. The EU seeks to restore its technological sovereignty and secure its leadership. In this vein, the EU has recognized the threats in cyberspace and emphasized the importance of improving cybersecurity (European Commission 2020). It is because of the expansion of the coverage of cyberattacks and their subsequent threats. Consequently, improving cybersecurity can help build trust and usage of digital innovation, connectivity, and automation and be essential to protecting personal information and freedom of expression (KISA 2023). Due to this importance, the two will intensify their cooperation in boosting cybersecurity capability.

Beyond 5G and 6G

In the area beyond 5G/6G, they checked the current status of international joint research between Korea and the EU, including upcoming joint research in 2024. Korea and the EU decided to continue their cooperation throughout the entire process of 6G standardization by 2030, sharing that the draft of the 6G vision recommendation had been prepared (Economic Diplomacy Utilization Portal 2023). The Council envisions that their research cooperation should focus on Radio Access Networks (RAN) and integrated device-network approaches demonstrating 6G Functional properties and their impact on standardization. The two sides will accelerate collaborative R&D activities, led by industrial needs for topical cooperation with selected partners (European Commission 2023).

Artificial intelligence

In artificial intelligence, the EU and Korea established a regular communication channel to define high-risk artificial intelligence and share the current status of law and policy instruments for reliable artificial intelligence. Also, they committed to strengthening cooperation in various ways, such as international cooperation in the Global Partnership on Artificial Intelligence (GPAI), which promotes human-centerd and reliable artificial intelligence and maximizes the benefits of artificial intelligence (Economic Diplomacy Utilization Portal 2023).

Online and Digital Platforms

For online/digital platforms, the two sides shared the importance of creating a platform ecosystem based on a harmonious balance of innovation, safety, and processes. They shared the current status of platform policies such as Korea's 'Platform Self-Regulation', the EU's Digital Market Act, and the Digital Service Act. Subsequently, they emphasized the importance of further cooperation (Economic Diplomacy Utilization Portal 2023).

Indeed, this partnership will contribute to developing connectivity between these two remote partners. There are potential benefits to the partnerships. First, the two sides will create innovation by strengthening their cooperation. In semiconductors, we could expect technological innovation, which might lead to the supply chain of semiconductors and their relevant products. In the areas of HPC and quantum technology, these advanced technologies will undoubtedly bring some innovative solutions for the global economy (such as industrial simulation and prototyping) and scientific research (application and HPC supply chain) (KISTI 2023). In the area of cybersecurity and trust, the two sides can guarantee competitiveness on the global stage. Also, they can keep the transition leadership on the security paradigm. The two are expected to strengthen their entry into emerging markets by creating a foundation for collaboration. They will eventually secure next-generation information protection technology's competitiveness. In the areas beyond 5G and 6G, they will lead in building inclusive and innovative digital technology. In the areas of online and digital platforms, businesses, including start-ups, can provide innovative services (National Strategy Information Portal 2022).

Second, their cooperation might contribute to strengthening digital security. Semiconductors have been reorganized into a globalized supply chain based on technology and business efficiency, not security. However, there is a necessity for building a self-centered supply chain through the COVID-19 outbreak. A recent US-China competition intensified this trend. Therefore, a more secure supply chain of semiconductors seemed to be more important for protecting the survival, prosperity, and democratic values of the country (INSS 2021). HPC and Quantum technology, advanced internet data provision (beyond 5G and 6G), AI, and online and digital platforms might become valuable tools for intensifying digital security. Cybersecurity cooperation is likely to help create beneficial strategies.

Third, their cooperation could provide economic benefits for both. The South Korean economy is more vulnerable to the decline in the semiconductor economy since it is focused on highly volatile-memory semiconductors (KDI 2023). Especially for key manufacturing industries like the motor vehicle industry, chip shortages greatly influence production (European Central Bank 2021). Some member states like Germany or France might be affected significantly by such shortages. By cooperating, they might reduce uncertainty about the related industries, making a significant economic contribution for both. HPC and quantum technology can make tremendous progress and changes, which might trigger industry and technology. In other words, these technologies might have huge potential. However, this potential can only be guaranteed by a constant commitment to research and development (KISTI 2022). Cybersecurity is an essential factor in virtual convergence economic development.

Virtual convergence technology is an interface which connects the real world with the virtual world, and such connectivity is rapidly spreading to the core industries. Indeed, virtual convergence technology can provide both opportunities and challenges. The challenges can be caused by security vulnerabilities in the metaverse and firmware. The attackers can steal vital information and authority, further threatening the convergent economy (NCSC 2023). 5G technology enables a broad application of the Internet of Things (IoT). 6G technology organically connects people to things, spaces, data, and processes. Subsequently, it is expected to open an era of 'AIoE' (Ambient Internet of Everything), in which the environment becomes the IoT (KOTRA 2018). When 6G is enabled in the future, enormous economic value might be created in the process of further connection. AI decreases labor hours and reduces tasks due to automation. It has huge potential for those who are using such AI as a tool. In other words, such AI will change the work structure by automating some tasks to strengthen individual capabilities (MK 2023). Online and digital platforms have led to the growth of e-commerce. Mainly, since COVID-19, the expansion of telework and online shopping has led to the exponential growth of the digital economy. Online and digital platforms began with search portals, which have expanded to social media, e-commerce, and financial technology. Additionally, new platform-based service markets continue to be created with the emergence of new technologies such as metaverse blockchain (NCSC 2022).

Finally, their cooperation might increase global influence by securing a more intensified digital structure. These areas have tremendous potential to increase connectivity, strengthen digital security, and create economic benefits between the EU and Korea. For such reasons, their partnership would be built up and consolidated further. However, the digital partnership might have some side effects which need further attention. First, it might create an infringement om privacy and data protection. Second, it could create economic disparity, creating an enormous gap between the rich and the poor. Third, it could put some populations at risk of job security (e.g., losing jobs due to AI). Therefore, the government, businesses, and interest groups should focus more on achieving sustainable development.

Conclusion

Reconsidering EU-Korea bilateral relations over the last 60 years, they have established a strong partnership due to a series of agreements (Framework Agreement, Free Trade Agreement and Crisis Management Agreement), which led to considering future-oriented agendas for further development. In this regard, they have formed a digital partnership to enhance trade, investment, and sustainable economic development. The partnership focuses on 11 core areas: joint research, semiconductors, next-generation mobile networks, Quantum and high-performance computing, cybersecurity, artificial intelligence, platforms, data, and technology. The partnership is based on the EU's Digital Compass Strategy, which aims to make Europe a digitally connected continent by 2030. Korea has shown a strong commitment to global innovation, with President Yoon Suk-yeol introducing the New York Initiative in September 2022. The first digital partnership council was held in Seoul in June 2023, focusing on six prioritized areas: semiconductors, HPC and quantum technology, cybersecurity and trust beyond 5G and 6G, artificial intelligence, and online and digital platforms. The partnership aims to develop connectivity, strengthen digital security, and create economic benefits. However, it may also create privacy and data protection issues, economic disparity, and job security threats.

To enhance further productive cooperation, we suggest some points to consider. First, they should recognize the importance of new global partnerships to support digital cooperation/partnership. Second, they put more effort into creating technological innovations. Third, they need to tackle common challenges caused by the new digital environment actively. Fourth, they should make more effort in the role-making of relevant businesses, governments, and interest groups. Finally, they need to seek to establish a global impact by inviting more like-minded partners other than them. Hopefully, this partnership will undoubtedly be a win-win opportunity for all sides.

Reference

Economic Diplomacy Utilization Portal, Seeking to lead Global Digital Technology with the Ministry of Science and ICT and the EU, https://president.globalwindow.org/kz.info.SupprtSysDetail.do;jsessionid=wz3BOwyBJBLZ-Pn-0FL13Jf-hgMx6zjDO3tS0V79o.PD?supprt_sys_seq=1596 (Accessed October 26 2023).

European Central Bank, 2021, the Semiconductor shortage and its implications for Euro area trade, production and prices, https://www.ecb.europa.eu/pub/economic-bulletin/focus/2021/html/ecb.ebbox202104_06~780de2a8fb.en.html (Accessed October 26 2023).

European Commission, "JOINT COMMUNICATION TO THE EUROPEAN PARLIAMENT AND THE COUNCIL, The EU's Cybersecurity Strategy for the Digital Decade", JOIN(2020) 18 final, 2020.12. https://eur-lex.europa.eu/legal-content/EN/TXT/?uri=CELEX:52020JC0018 (Accessed 26 October 2023).

European Commission, Republic of Korea – European Union Digital Partnership, November 28, 2022, https://digital-strategy.ec.europa.eu/en/library/republic-korea-european-union-digital-partnership (Accessed October 24 2023).

European Commission, 2023a, Digital Partnerships, https://digital-strategy.ec.europa.eu/en/policies/partnerships , updated on February 1 2023, (Accessed October 24 2023).

European Commission, 2023b, Press Corner, EU and Republic of Korea Digital Partnership: Strengthening our Economic Resilience June 30, 2023, https://ec.europa.eu/commission/presscorner/detail/en/ip_23_3607 (Accessed October 24 2023).

European Commission, 2023c, Republic of Korea – EU Joint Statement, https://digital-strategy.ec.europa.eu/en/news/republic-korea-eu-joint-statement (Accessed October 25 2023).

European Union External Action, EU-Republic of Korea Strategic Partnership June 30, 2020, https://www.eeas.europa.eu/eeas/eu-republic-korea-strategic-partnership_en (Accessed October 24 2023).

Innovation News Network, First Digital Partnership Council held by the EU and the Republic of Korea, July 4, 2023, https://www.innovationnewsnetwork.com/first-digital-partnership-council-held-by-eu-republic-of-korea/34467/ (Accessed October 24 2023).

INSS, 2022, Semiconductor Supply Chain and Digital Cold War (In Korean) https://inss.re.kr/publication/bbs/ib_view.do?nttId=410200&bbsId=ib&page=1&searchCnd=0&searchWrd= (Accessed October 26 2023).

KDI. 2023, Recent Semiconductor Business Trends and Macroeconomic Impact (In Korean) https://www.kdi.re.kr/research/analysisView?art_no=3480 (Accessed October 26 2023).

KISA, 2023, KISA Insight Digital and Security Policy, directions for Cybersecurity and Implications for Building the Digital Future of the EU (In Korean) https://www.kisa.or.kr/20301/form?postSeq=19&page=1 (Accessed October 26 2023).

KISTI, 2022, Game Changer in Future Industries, Quantum Information Science and Technology (QIST): The Age of Quantum 2.0, https://repository.kisti.re.kr/handle/10580/17724 (Accessed October 26 2023).

KISTI, 2023, KISTI Issue Brief, New Supercomputing Era Opens: Exaflops, AI and Quantum Computer (In Korean), https://doi.org/10.22810/2023KIB055 (Accessed October 26 2023).

KITA, 2022a, [Ministry of Trade, Industry and Energy] Holding the B20 Summit in the Wake of the G20 Bali Summit, https://www.kita.net/cmmrcInfo/cmmrcNews/relateInsttNews/relateInsttNewsDetail.do?pageIndex=1&nIndex=30377 (Accessed October 24 2023).

KITA, 2022b, Comprehensive Trade News, Korea-EU, Intensifying Semiconductors, Digital Trade cooperation… established Digital Partnerships, (In Korean) https://www.kita.net/cmmrcInfo/cmmrcNews/cmmrcNews/cmmrcNewsDetail.do?searchOpenYn=&pageIndex=1&nIndex=71830&logGb=A9400_20221130 (Accessed October 24

2023).

Korea-EU Research Centre, 2023, Korea-EU Summit, to be held on 22 May 2023 (In Korean) https://k-erc.eu/%ED%95%9C-eu-%EC%A0%95%EC%83%81%ED%9A%8C%EB%8B%B4-%EC%98%A4%EB%8A%94-5%EC%9B%94-22%EC%9D%BC-%ED%95%9C%EA%B5%AD%EC%97%90%EC%84%9C-%EA%B0%9C%EC%B5%9C/ (Accessed November 10 2023).

Korean Ministry of Science and ICT, 2022a, Korea-EU Digital Partnership entered into force, https://www.msit.go.kr/bbs/view.do?sCode=user&mId=113&mPid=112&pageIndex=&bbsSeqNo=94&nttSeqNo=3182412&searchOpt=ALL&searchTxt= (in Korean) (Accessed October 23 2023).

Korean Ministry of Science and ICT, 2022b, Korea to Come up with the Roadmap of Digital ROK, Realising the New York Initiative, https://www.msit.go.kr/eng/bbs/view.do?sCode=eng&mId=4&mPid=2&bbsSeqNo=42&nttSeqNo=742 (Accessed October 23 2023).

Korean Ministry of Science and ICT, 2023a, The First ROK-EU Digital Partnership Council was held, https://www.msit.go.kr/bbs/view.do;jsessionid=-ZafKnIe6dHWS4cOKf1C8w26H9TG5E7IBjHWqsa0.AP_msit_1?sCode=user&mPid=238&mId=113&bbsSeqNo=94&nttSeqNo=3183244 (Accessed 24 October 2023).

Korean Ministry of Science and ICT, 2023b, By strengthening the competitiveness of our information protection industry Realising 'Strong Cyber Security' (In Korean) https://www.msit.go.kr/bbs/view.do?sCode=user&mId=113&mPid=238&pageIndex=&bbsSeqNo=94&nttSeqNo=3183454&searchOpt=ALL&searchTxt= (Accessed October 26 2023).

KOTRA, 2018, International Market News, China, Surpassing 5G and Looking at 6G, (in Korean) https://dream.kotra.or.kr/kotranews/cms/news/actionKotraBoardDetail.do?SITE_NO=3&MENU_ID=180&CONTENTS_NO=1&bbsGbn=243&bbsSn=243&pNttSn=171198 (Accessed October 30 2023).

MK, Korea-EU to conduct a joint research on semiconductors…'Semiconductor Researchers' Forum' newly established, https://stock.mk.co.kr/news/view/162466 (Accessed October 24 2023).

MK, 2023, Potential of 'Generative AI'…"Creating KRW 5,600 trillion a year in the global economy" (In Korean) https://stock.mk.co.kr/news/view/148358 (Accessed October 30 2023).

National Strategy Information Portal, Plan for Digital Platform Development, https://nsp.nanet.go.kr/plan/subject/detail.do?newReportChk=list&nationalPlanControlNo=PLAN0000034719 (Accessed October 26 2023).

NCSC, 2023, Virtual Convergence Economy and Cyber Threats (In Korean) https://www.ncsc.go.kr:4018/main/cop/bbs/selectBoardArticle.do?bbsId=EducationData_main&nttId=69749&menuNo=070000&subMenuNo=070600&thirdMenuNo=070400 (Accessed October 26 2023).

Qureshi, Zia, How Digital Transformation is Driving Economic Change, https://www.brookings.edu/articles/how-digital-transformation-is-driving-economic-change/ January 18, 2022 (Accessed October 24 2023).

EU-Korea Education Cooperation

KIM BONGCHUL

Introduction

As globalization has stimulated interaction and integration around the world, international mobility is the most active phenomenon of various forms of flows, including goods, services, capital, labor forces, refugees, and others. Also, while exchanges between higher education institutions have been expanded around the world, the importance of mobility among international students is also growing rapidly. Furthermore, after COVID-19, mobility among existing direct exchange programmes among international students decreased, but new forms of exchange began to appear, such as an increase in new academic and research exchange activities centered on online platforms.

'International education cooperation' is generally defined as promoting the internationalization of higher education that includes the policies and practices undertaken by academic systems and institutions and even individuals to cope with the global academic environment.[1] Through international education cooperation, participating actors can establish and develop partnerships and international cooperation networks between universities, companies, governments, and other organizations. These types of mobility support students to gain cross-cultural awareness, develop adaptability and tolerance, open-mindedness, an understanding of complex global issues, and learn global citizenship.[2] Furthermore, it highlights the academic benefits of participation in mobility, improved career outcomes of students who participate in mobility, and increased civic engagement and public diplomacy.

In this regard, the European Union (EU) is a leading actor in promoting international mobility inside and outside Europe in the fields of education and research. Representatively, the Erasmus programme is for cultivating international mobility, promoting educational cooperation among countries, and the EU aims to spread its norms and values to the international community in network formation with other countries based on this type of cooperation. As part of these activities, it supports educational cooperation through Erasmus programme, activities by the European External Action Service (EEAS) and the Education, Audio-visual, and Culture Executive Agency (EACEA).

In particular, the EU's interest in promoting international mobility and educational cooperation with East Asian countries is evident as the international status and influence of the region have increased worldwide. They show significant outward and inward student mobility. The number of international students from the countries in the European area has increased over the past 10 years to achieve a better quality of education, but in the other direction, East Asian countries such as Korea are major destinations for foreign students keen to study abroad.[3]

In 2023, Korea and the EU celebrated the 60th anniversary of diplomatic relations. Both sides have collaborated on various economic and political issues in the international community over the years, and recently, they have been strengthening their cooperation in relatively new areas such as public diplomacy, digital, culture, and more. In particular, both sides have a keen interest in human exchanges in the field of education as a preparatory step for cooperation among future generations. Considering the successful outcomes of the human exchange programs the EU has undertaken in the past, the EU-Korea cooperation in the field of education holds significant implications for the East Asian region. The diverse and active educational cooperation between the EU and Korea provides a reference for closer educational cooperation in the East Asian area.

In this context, this paper will examine the EU higher education system of Erasmus Programme and Bologna process in order to look at the EU's experience with higher education cooperation, and analyze the educational cooperation between Korea and the EU focusing on the case of Hankuk University of Foreign Studies (HUFS) in Korea. After evaluating the EU-Korea educational cooperation, it will examine the Campus Asia Plus project conducted by countries in East Asia and the Trilateral Cooperation Secretariat (TCS) programmes among the three Northeast Asian countries and draw implications and future directions by comparing the contents of educational cooperation between the EU and Korea.

The EU Mobility and Higher Education Cooperation System

Erasmus Programme and Bologna Process

At the EU level, the higher education policy was launched in earnest in the Erasmus programme (European Community Action Scheme for the Mobility of University Students), set up by the Council Decision in 1987 (87/327/EEC). The fundamental goal of the programme is to contribute to the revitalization of the European economy by improving the quality of education based on human exchanges between higher education institutions and improving the skills and employment capabilities of students in higher education institutions.[4] The Erasmus programme specifically set three major goals, as follows:

1) the establishment of a university network
2) financial support for students
3) recognition of degrees and research periods at the EU level

Since 1987, the European programme, which was introduced in earnest as part of a programme for cooperation between universities in the region, developed in a way that provided scholarships to participating university students, later contributed greatly to the establishment of the Bologna Process for the integration of European higher education system and expanded its field and application coverage over time.

In 1997, the EU signed the Lisbon Recreation Convention under the leadership of the Council of Europe, which included mutual recognition of university degrees and related certificates between European countries. After that, in 1999, the ministers of education of 29 member countries of the Council of Europe adopted the Bologna Declaration and the EU supported the Bologna process for promoting internationalization of higher education and established various cooperative systems between the Erasmus programme and the Bologna process.[5] The main objective of the Bologna process is to remove barriers to higher education among EU member states and European countries and to establish a European Higher Education Area (EHEA)[6] which has three categories of EU member states, consultative members, and partners, with 49 countries participating in the process as of 2023.

In March 2000, the Lisbon European Council decided to link higher education, represented by the Erasmus programme, to the Bologna process, with EU member states sharing the EHEA objectives set by the Bologna process and various projects and institutions between the two sides.[7] Also, the EU operates the European Credit Transfer System (ECTS) and the European Qualifications Framework (EQF) to provide comparative information on the degree system and academic level of the EU member states as a framework for promoting student exchange between higher education institutions in Europe. Meanwhile, the process added the Framework for Qualifications, more widely known as the Bologna cycle, and established the European Association for Quality Assessment (ENQA) for higher education institutions.[8]

In 2004, the EU launched the Erasmus Mundus programme with the aim of cooperating with external countries by promoting a modern education and training system in line with the academic traditions, culture, and information age of European higher education institutions.[9] Erasmus Mundus was a higher education cooperation with all regions of the world, including the Third World. However, cooperation with advanced industrial countries in North America and East Asia has been criticized as very insufficient. In reality, EU higher education institutions require strategic cooperation in advanced industrial countries in North America and East Asia, but joint degree operation is restricted due to the different academic and academic systems from higher education institutions in this region.[10]

Since 2014, theexisting EU programme has been upgraded to Erasmus+ (Erasmus Plus). Erasmus+ is the EU mobility programme for education, training, youth, and sport. It combines previous funding programmes in the sector, including the Lifelong Learning Programme (Comenius, Leonardo, Erasmus, Grundtvig and Transversal Programmes), Youth in Action, Jean Monnet, Tempus and Erasmus Mundus. It provides the participant with a a great opportunity to travel to another country to upskill and train in their sector while improving their linguistic ability in the language of the host country. From 2021 on, Erasmus+ has set new targets for cooperating with other mobility programme of the EU and its budget has also been set at around €26.2 billion from 2021 to 2027, which is double the budget for 2014–2020.[11]

International Cooperation Partnerships

The EU mobility and higher education system does not limit participants to Europe, and there are various European educational cooperation partnerships targeting the world. The main objectives of the cooperation partnership are to increase the quality and relevance of activities, develop and strengthen partner networks, improve the ability to jointly operate at a transnational level, promote internationalization of activities, exchange or develop new practices and methods, share ideas and confrontations.

Through a system called International Credit Mobility (ICM), the EU supports research or classes in designated partner countries. In addition, not only students but also those belonging to companies, public institutions, and research institutes belonging to higher education institutions get an opportunity to receive training in partner countries through a system called High Education Instructions (HEIs). Although the application requirements are stricter than those of the Erasmus program in Europe because it meets the requirements of the partner country's institutions, it is a system that can accumulate experience outside of Europe and develop global civic capabilities as it supports the cost of movement and education.[12]

As of 2023, in addition to 27 EU member states, Erasmus+ has designated countries, including members of the European Free Trade Association (EFTA) and the EU acceding, candidate, and potential candidate countries, as programme participants based on Article 16 of the Erasmus+ Regulation. Also, based on Article 17 of the Erasmus+ Regulation, the EU stipulates that third countries not associated with the programme that meet the EU's human dignity and values can participate in Erasmus+ as partners. The range of partner countries is almost all over the world, and due to the institutional development of Erasmus+, the number of age groups supported is expanding, as well as the choice of higher education, vocational education, and training. For example, Korea is one of the 25 countries in Region 5 and is included in 7 high-income countries. Furthermore, Korea and the EU have operated various educational cooperation partnerships through ICI-ECP, Erasmus Mundus, Jean Monnet activities, Horizon Europe, and others.[13]

Korea-EU Educational Cooperation and East Asian Cooperation Cases

Korea-EU Cooperation Programmes: Three Examples of ICI-ECP, Erasmus Mundus and Jean Monnet Activities

After Korea achieved rapid economic growth in the 1980s, it introduced the institutional development process of its higher education evaluation. At this time, capabilities and autonomy were comparatively weak because they were in their early stages, so until the 1990s, the capabilities and autonomy of Korean higher education institutions were highly vulnerable. However, since 1995, as the opening of higher education services began in earnest, the government has promoted the internationalization of higher education in the country. Since the 2000s, over the past 20 years, higher education institutions across Korea have developed internationalization policies to meet the needs of globalization in the 21st century. Korean universities have implemented internationalization policies through the provision of international graduate schools and enhanced student and professor exchange programmes.[14]

Along with this policy stance, EU-Korea educational cooperation has increased, with a special push since 2011 after the ratification of the Korea-EU Free Trade Agreement (FTA). The EU's international political capabilities under the Lisbon Treaty, which aimed to transform the EU into a major global actor wielding significant influence in a wide range of world affairs, raised interest in the EU. In turn, the EU has focused on the Asia-Pacific region and especially Korea. The EU-Korea relationship gained traction given Korea's high economic profile and the strategic importance of Northeast Asia. Thus, there was increased interest in closer cooperation between the two partners, both in the realms of economics and socio-politics.[15]

Based on this, Korea and the EU agreed at the 7th Korea-EU summit in 2013 on a new era of cooperation in the field of education and strengthening higher education partnerships.[16] As a result of the joint declaration, the educational cooperation between the two sides has become closer and Korea and the EU share and implement educational cooperation programmes, like the ICI-ECP, Erasmus Mundus, and Jean Monnet Activities.

First, the EU started its higher education cooperation projects with Japan and Australia as a pilot programme in 2002, and officially launched the Industrialized Countries Instrument-Education Cooperation Programme (ICI-ECP) with major countries in the Asia-Pacific region as a special project within the Erasmus Mundus program in 2008. The governments of Australia, Japan, New Zealand, and the Republic of Korea were major participating countries, and a total of 19 Korean universities had joined the programme.[17] However, the ICI-ECP between Korea and the EU suffered from the lack of institutional framework to efficiently convert ECTS, which hindered practical cooperation between Korea and the EU in various academic fields. For this reason, since 2014, the ICI-ECP has been integrated and operated under the Erasmus+.[18]

Second, Erasmus Mundus I began with a master course in 2004, and the doctoral course was added in 2009 through Erasmus Mundus II. Thanks to the master's course, about 2,000 students have been able to annually complete degree courses at higher education institutions in Europe since 2010. But competition has been very fierce, as the door to Erasmus is open to all countries around the world as well as the EU.[19] In the case of Korea, higher education through this programme has not been successful due to the difficulty of forming a well-matched consortium and the high level of competition with higher education institutions in other countries. After 2014, the Erasmus Mundus was integrated with the launch of the Erasmus+ system into the Erasmus Mundus Joint Degrees (EMJMD). Under the EMJMD, participating institutions should form a consortium between at least three higher educational institutions. All EU universities participating in the consortium must have different nationalities, and at least one non-EU country must participate.[20]

Third, Jean Monnet activities aim to promote European studies and studies in the field of higher education. Specifically, they support education and research through Jean Monnet Modules, Jean Monnet Chairs, and Jean Monnet Center of Excellence.[21] This Jean Monnet activity provides policy discussions through Jean Monnet Networks and Jean Monnet Projects, related research institutes, and academic support. Currently, Jean Monnet Centres of Excellence are operated by only four universities in Korea, including HUFS.[22]

The Case of Hankuk University of Foreign Studies (HUFS)

Since its inception in 1954, in the aftermath of the Korean War, the role of the Hankuk University of Foreign Studies (HUFS) has been providing foreign language education with international studies for upbringing qualified diplomats, public officials, and international business people. Also, HUFS has been playing a leading role in the development of European Studies in Korea, combining different academic disciplines ranging from languages and cultures to social sciences and policy-oriented studies.[23] The university has cultivated European Studies in its diverse programmes: EU Studies Major as undergraduate courses, EU Studies Department at the Graduate School of International and Area Studies (GSIAS).

At the undergraduate and graduate level, the university also runs the largest and most comprehensive programmes for International Relations (IR) and EU studies in Korea. The university established its GSIAS in 1997 with the founding of EU Studies Department, which offers MA and PhD courses with interdisciplinary perspectives. While having an independent Faculty of International Studies, the university began to offer a joint BA degree programme in EU studies in 2005, enabling students to obtain two bachelor's degrees upon successful completion of the degree requirements. This programme has been continuously strengthened by adding a few new programmes and reforms. For instance, a BA/MA joint degree programme was introduced, allowing students to pursue the two degrees within five years, one year less than the standard case. Up to 100 undergraduates are studying at European universities each year via various exchange programmes.[24]

At the research level, IR and EU-related research have also been very active. HUFS has operated the Institute of EU Studies and other Europe-related institutes since 1993, and has initiated numerous joint research projects with internationally recognized universities, research institutions, and scholars/experts all around the world. In addition to organizing high-impact policy workshops and international conferences with them, they have conducted a lot of joint research projects. Also, the University has established a world-wide web of networks with top-class universities, think tanks, and research institutes of highest academic reputation. The university has established a solid foundation for research and education cooperation with a wide range of universities and institutions all around the world. HUFS carries out annual student and researcher exchanges and organizes annual international seminars and conferences with these institutions.[25]

Based on these academic and research capabilities, HUFS had operated diverse joint programme with the EU in the fields of mobility and education cooperation, such as ICI-ECP, Jean Monnet Lifelong Learning Programme, HUFS-HRI EU Centre, HUFS Jean Monnet Centre of Excellence. In this regard, HUFS has attracted the Korean branch of EU-RAXESS, an educational and research cooperation organization that is networking platform and information tool for talented researchers on the move to explore and develop careers in Europe under the EU. It continues to strengthen its educational and research cooperation capabilities with Europe.

First, HUFS ICI-ECP was a joint mobility project implementing a Korea-EU student exchange project to institutionalize a Korea-EU partnership for three years. Participating universities were four in Europe, the Institut d'Etudes Politiques de Bordeaux (France), Universitat Autonoma de Barcelona (Spain), Vrije Universiteit Brussel (Belgium) and Ca' Foscari University of Venice (Italy). HUFS had selected 4-5 outstanding graduate students in the GSIAS each semester to give them the opportunity to study abroad and to become regional experts with expertise and practical skills to play a key role in many areas covered by the Korea-EU partnership, such as economy, trade, diplomacy, and culture.[26]

Secondly, HUFS Jean Monnet Lifelong Learning Programme, a part of the EU Jean Monnet Programme, was to inspire awareness of the EU under the theme of 'EU Learning in Korea'. HUFS Jean Monnet Lifelong Learning Programme hosted events for Korean middle and high school students to raise awareness of the EU and expand cultural exchanges. The selection of the programme can be seen as the result of the EU's recognition of the capabilities and achievements of the University performing EU studies—significantly, HUFS was the only one selected in Asia.[27]

Third, HUFS operated HUFS-HRI EU Centre from 2011 to 2015. The EU Centre was established in 2011 by HUFS cooperating with Hyundai Research Institute (HRI). This Centre performed a wide range of activities related to EU policy, as well as programmes to educate students about studying European integration. The EU Centre was an educational, research and external activity organization established by the European Commission in the Asia-Pacific region to raise awareness of the EU and promote education and research related to the EU. HUFS-HRI EU Centre was pursuing four main goals, which were as follows:[28]

- Conducting educational programmes on various topics on European integration and research activities
- Integrated European education and research by establishing a network between domestic and foreign EU centres
- Improving the understanding of EU and community policy in Korea through various external activities

Based on the above, the HUFS-HRI EU Centre has held international and domestic conferences, collaborated with research institutes from both home and abroad, and promoted EU studies at HUFS by opening an innovative curriculum and hosting the Model European Union (MEU) multiple times. In particular, the Centre co-hosted with the EU Delegation to Korea a series of events to celebrate milestones in the relationship, such as the strategic partnership and the FTA. In doing so, the Centre has become a locus for the EU's successful public diplomacy in Korea. The EU model of 27 members that demonstrate harmony and cooperation towards a common goal has also allowed us to help widen the horizons of Korean diplomacy as a middle power in the global arena.[29]

Fourth, HUFS Jean Monnet Centre of Excellence was established to promote excellence in teaching and research in the field of EU studies in Korea since 2016. The actions taken by the Centre focused on fostering dialogue between the academic world and policymakers, with the aim of raising awareness about EU policies and governance.

〈Table 2〉 Main Programmes of HUFS-HRI EU Centre

No.	Category	Activities
1	Academic Research	EU Young Challenge Publications of Reports and Books National/International Conference Curriculum Development for EU Major
2	Education	Meet the EU Lecture Future Expert Training Programme. Experts and Entrepreneurs Forum EU Certificate Course
3	Cooperation and Promotion	Broadcasting and Video Programme EU Barometer Survey EU Centres Networking Digital Service (Homepage, Applications, and etc.)

Source: Kim Bong Chul (2023) p. 162.

〈Table 3〉 Academic and Research Goals of HUFS Jean Monnet Centre of Excellence

State	Subject	Contents
1st Stage (2016-19)	EU-related interdisciplinary Research	New EU Global Strategy and East Asia Critical Engagement Policy of the EU Emerging Areas of Policy Cooperation between the EU and Korea
2nd Stage (2019-22)	Korea-EU Connectivity Research	Security Connectivity between Europe and Asia Economic and Trade Connectivity between Europe and Asia Connecting Europe to Asia in Mobility
3rd Stage (2022-25)	New Paradigm for EU-Korea Relations	From Connectivity to Global Gateway Securing Resilience of Global Supply Chain between Europe and East Asia EU-Korea@60: Consolidating EU-Korea Cooperation

Source: Author Writing based on HUFS Jean Monnet Centre of Excellence (2021) pp. 27-33.

As mentioned above, the subject and contents of Jean Monnet Centre of Excellence are divided into three stages. In terms of academic endeavours, the HUFS Jean Monnet Centre formed a Centre of academic excellence in EU studies by strengthening the EU knowledge base among students, teaching staff, and researchers, and the project also introduced new EU-related courses at the undergraduate and graduate levels in order to promote educational cooperation between Korea and the EU.[30]

CAMPUS Asia Projects and Trilateral Cooperation Secretariat (TCS) Programmes

As previously discussed, European higher education cooperation, related programmes, and mobility and education cooperation between Korea and the EU are actively taking place, while mobility and education cooperation in East Asia are also expanding faster than in the past. And among the major educational cooperation programmes in Asia centerd on East Asia, the most representative program is the educational cooperation program of CAMPUS Asia and the Trilateral Cooperation Secretariat (TCS) programmes.

The CAMPUS Asia is a cross-border student mobility programme among Korea, Japan, and China, initiated by the agreement of the Summit Meeting of Korea, Japan, and China, which stands for 'Collective Action for Mobility Programme of University Students in Asia. The CAMPUS Asia aims to strengthen networks among academic institutions of higher education in Asia and promote student exchanges at the undergraduate and graduate level through joint and double degree programmes and exchange programmes.[31]

In 2010, it was adopted as a pilot programme for a new cooperative project in the field of higher education at the 3rd Korea-Japan-China Summit in Korea. During 2011–2015, there was the implementation of the Korea–Japan–China CAMPUS Asia project with 10 consortia. In January 2016, the 1st Korea–Japan–China Education Minister Meeting agreed to expand the pilot programme to the full-fledged programme. The CAMPUS Asia full-fledged programme was officially launched in October 2016 with 17 consortia among the three Northeast Asia. In particular, the 2021–2026 Campus Asia Project was renamed Campus Asia Plus, literally expanding its cooperative region to ASEAN countries beyond the existing trilateral higher education cooperation.[32] This CAMPUS Asia Plus project is significant in that it has a framework for multilateral cooperation, including Southeast Asian countries beyond East Asia, by establishing an educational cooperation system to promote mutual understanding and improve international capabilities among college students from three countries, Korea, China, and ASEAN countries.

Selected universities will be provided with programme management costs, including the development of online and offline joint curriculums for a total of 5 years, with an average of about 100,000 dollars per year, and in this project, settlement subsidies and emergency subsidies as well as stay expenses for dispatched students.

〈Table 4〉 Development of CAMPUS Asia Project (2011-2026)

State	Title
1st Stage (2011-2015)	CAMPUS Asia Pilot Programme (10 consortia)
2nd Stage (2016-2021)	CAMPUS ASIA Project (17 consortia)
3rd Stage (2021-2026)	CAMPUS ASIA Plus (20 consortia)

Source: Author Writing based on CAMPUS Asia Homepage.

Representatively, HUFS was also selected as the CAMPUS Asia Plus project among 20 consortia, and the consortia is composed of Hankuk University of Foreign Studies (Korea), Beijing Normal University, Changchun University (China), Hiroshima University (Japan), Indonesia University of Education (Indonesia), and Kasetsart University (Thailand). Under the project title of 'International Collaborative Human Resources Development Program in Asia to Foster Inclusive Minds', HUFS and the consortia is going to cooperate together through Collaborative Education Program, Short-term Study Abroad Program, Summer School "Inclusive Asia", and Semester Exchange Program.[33]

There are diverse programmes of TCS, a major organization promoting various kinds of cooperation, including education and research cooperation, in East Asia. TCS was officially launched in Seoul in September 2011 under an agreement signed and ratified by the governments of the three countries, respectively. The establishment of the TCS marked an important milestone and achievement in terms of institutionalizing trilateral cooperation, which began in 1999.[34] The TCS is an international organization established with a vision to promote lasting peace, common prosperity, and shared culture among Korea, Japan, and China. In this regard, TCS has operated diverse Youth Platform and related educational programmes among the three and also cooperated with CAMPUS Asia project. TCS operates diverse programmes such as Trilateral Youth Exchange Network, CAMPUS Asia Alumni Network and Exchange, Youth Ambassador Program, Trilateral Youth Summit, Trilateral Youth Speech Contest, and Children's Story Exchange Alumni Exchange.[35]

For instance, from August 13 to 22, 2023, the 2023 Trilateral Youth Summit (TYS) was held in Beijing and Chengdu, China. This programme has been designed to promote friendship and mutual understanding among young people from Korea, Japan, and China since 2014. Under the theme of "Embrace Shared-Future", 2023 TYS featured a variety of activities, including lectures and cultural events on various topics, including youth mock summits and committees from the three Northeast Asian countries. A total of 100 undergraduate and graduate students from three countries participated in the event.[36] During the programme, delegates from each country published a 'joint declaration' for cooperation among the countries in culture, tourism, education, sports, and health, and especially in the field of education, they covered CAMPUS Asia, youth exchanges, and future-oriented cooperation in depth.

Until now, the method of educational cooperation between European and Asian countries has mainly adopted a bilateral-centerd method. However, with the expansion and development of mobility and educational cooperation in Asia through the Campus Asia Project and TCS education cooperation programmes, there was the potential to lead to multilateral forms of educational cooperation between Europe and East Asia in the future.

Conclusion

The EU is strengthening its standing as a distinct entity in the international community. Drawing from its experience of fostering internal human exchanges with the goal of integration, the EU is currently enhancing its external human exchange programmes. Korea has rapidly developed in the trend of globalization, and has become a middle-power country capable of creating values and norms in the international community, and is emerging as a leading country in public diplomacy in the international community based on cultural and digital diplomacy. Until 2023, the EU and Korea have maintained diplomatic relations for 60 years and have cooperated on significant economic and political issues in the international community.

Now, both sides are making efforts to foster cooperation in even newer and more diverse areas. Recently, they have expanded the scope of their cooperation, engaging in diverse collaborations in areas such as culture, research, and education. Education is an area that should be further activated for the benefit of both sides' future generations. Considering the advancement of digital technology and the COVID-19 pandemic situation, exchanges and cooperation in the field can utilize new methods, such as online platforms.[37] In this respect, Korea has carried out several higher education projects with the EU for the globalization of higher education.

Some Korean universities are actively participating in the Erasmus programme, a student exchange programme for external partners by the EU. And this educational cooperation with Europe had a great impact on educational cooperation in Asia, including East Asia. Through mobility and educational cooperation with the EU and European countries, the need for regionalism and the importance of regional cooperation based on it were emphasized in Asia. As a result, efforts to cooperate in the field of education, which can be the cornerstone of regional cooperation, are continuously being made, and CAMPUS Asia project and TCS educational programmes are representative examples.

In the midst of this cooperation process, HUFS has been actively participating in educational cooperation programmes with the EU based on the Erasmus programmes as well as educational cooperation programs in East Asia. As a leading university in European studies in Korea, HUFS operates Jean Monnet Centre of Excellence under the theme of 'The New Paradigm for EU-Korea Relations', provides academic research and exchanges by the Institute of EU Studies, and actively participates in exchange programmes with European universities. Also, HUFS is participating in consortia with other Asian universities to promote cooperation under the CAMPUS Asia Plus project, and encourages undergraduate and graduate students to participate in diverse TCS education programmes.

Despite such active educational cooperation, limitations for Korea-EU and Asian educational cooperation still remain. In the case of Korea, the limitations remain that it is still focusing on attracting Asian students, including China, and does not have a concrete and compatible system for exchanges with higher education institutions around the world, such as the ECTS, such as credit certification, degree, and qualitative certification throughout EHEA.

However, in an era where connectivity continues to be strengthened, the EU's educational cooperation programs, cooperation with Korean higher education institutions, and examples of educational cooperation in East Asia can be understood in a more multi-layered framework. In this regard, Korea can use the experience created by carrying out projects such as educational cooperation and student mobility with Europe to develop and implement new projects in East Asia, and it will be important to find ways to expand cooperation through institutional improvement.

Bibliography

Åse Gornitzka (2006). "The Open Method of Coordination as Practice - A Watershed in European Education Policy?" *Advanced Research on the Europeanisation of the Nation-State.* Working Papers 06/16.

Barragán Codina, José Nicolás & Leal López, and Rubén Hernán (2013). "The Importance of Student Mobility, Academic Exchange and Internationalization of Higher Education for College Students in a Globalized World: The Mexican and Latin American Case." *International Journal of Good Conscience.* Vol. 8 No. 2. http://www.spentamexico.org/v8-n2/A3.8(2)48-63.pdf

CAMPUS Asia. About CAMPUS Asia. http://www.campusasiaprogram.kr/com/cmm/EgovContentView.do?menuNo=1110000001

Council of the European Union (1987). 87/327/EEC: Council Decision of 15 June 1987 adopting the European Community Action Scheme for the Mobility of University Students (Erasmus)

ENQA (2016). European Association for Quality Assurance in Higher Education, History. https://www.enqa.eu/

European Commission. Cooperation partnerships, https://erasmus-plus.ec.europa.eu/programme-guide/part-b/key-action-2/cooperation-partnerships

__________________. Erasmus+ EU programme for education, training, youth and sport, https://erasmus-plus.ec.europa.eu/opportunities

__________________ (2013). Higher Education: EU and Korea agree new era of cooperation. https://ec.europa.eu/commission/presscorner/detail/en/IP_13_1061

__________________ (2014). Erasmus+ The EU programme for Education, Training, Youth and Sport 2014-2020. https://erasmus-plus.ec.europa.eu/

__________________ (2016). Erasmus Mundus joint master degrees The story so far. https://op.europa.eu/en/publication-detail/-/publication/6f52e9bb-31f2-11e6-b497-01aa75ed71a1

__________________ (2017). From Erasmus to Erasmus+: a story of 30 years, https://ec.europa.eu/commission/presscorner/detail/en/MEMO_17_83

__________________ (2021). Erasmus+ Programme Guide, Eligible countries.

https://erasmus-plus.ec.europa.eu/programme-guide/erasmusplus-programme-guide

__________________. (2021). Jean Monnet Actions: stimulating teaching and research on the European Union, https://erasmus-plus.ec.europa.eu/opportunities/organisations/jean-monnet-actions-stimulating-teaching-and-research-on-the-european-union

HUFS CAMPUS Asia Plus. https://campusasia.hufs.ac.kr/campusasia/6457/subview.do

HUFS GSIAS, http://gsias.hufs.ac.kr/

HUFS-HRI EU Centre, https://www.hufs.ac.kr/user/hrieng/

HUFS Jean Monnet Centre of Excellence (2021). "10 years of EU Centre at Hankuk University of Foreign Studies 2011-2021."

International Organization for Migration(IOM) (2019). WORLD MIGRATION REPORT 2020 https://publications.iom.int/system/files/pdf/wmr_2020.pdf

John D. Palmer, Cho Young Ha (2012). "South Korean higher education internationalization policies: perceptions and experiences." *Asia Pacific Education Review.* Vol. 13.

John McCormick (2011). Understanding the European Union, 5th. ed., Palgrave Macmillan.

Christine Loyd (2013). "The Erasmus Mundus programme: providing opportunities to develop a better understanding about inclusion and inclusive practice through an international collaborative programme of study." *International Journal of Inclusive Education.* Vol. 17 No. 4.

Kim Bong Chul, Shin Eui Chan (2021). "Institutions and Activities of Research and Education of European Studies in Korean Universities." *The Journal of Contemporary European Studies.* Vol. 39 No. 4.

Kim Bong Chul (2023). "Mobility and Educational Cooperation between Korea and the EU", in Kim Sihong and Michael Reiterer (Eds.). *Connecting Europe and Asia: Security, Economy and Mobility.*

Kim Ho, Kim Yong Hee (2021). "Non-contact Education in ASEAN and the Proposal of ASEAN Educational Development Cooperation after COVID-19." *Southeast Asia Journal.* Vol. 31.

Kim Si Hong (2018). "Forty Years of European Studies at HUFS: Looking back, looking forward." *Journal of European Union Studies,* Vol. 49.

Maria da Conceição Pereira Ramos (2014). "Mobility, Internationalisation, Higher Education: European Challenges." Alina Mihaela Dima et al. (eds.). *Handbook of Research on Trends in European Higher Education Convergence.* IGI Global.

The Korea Heralrd Economy (2012). "Institute of EU Studies-EU Centre at Hankuk University of Foreign Studies (HUFS) is selected for the first time in Asia for 'EU Jean Monnet Programme." http://news.heraldcorp.com/view.php?ud=20120723001130

Trilateral Cooperation Secretariat, https://www.tcs-asia.org/en/about/overview.php

Yang Su Young, Kim Su Jin (2022). "The EU Erasmus Programme and Educational Cooperation among European universities: Focusing on the case of Spain." *Journal of European Union Studies,* Vol. 61.

Endnote

1. Maria da Conceição Pereira Ramos (2014), "Mobility, Internationalisation, Higher Education: *European Challenges,*" Alina Mihaela Dima et al. (eds.), *Handbook of Research on Trends in European Higher Education Convergence,* IGI Global.
2. Barragán Codina, José Nicolás & Leal López, and Rubén Hernán (2013), "The Importance of Student Mobility, Academic Exchange and Internationalization of Higher Education for College Students in a Globalized World: The Mexican and Latin American Case," *International Journal of Good Conscience,* Vol. 8, No. 2, http://www.spentamexico.org/v8-n2/A3.8(2)48-63.pdf
3. International Organization for Migration(IOM) (2019), WORLD MIGRATION REPORT 2020, https://publications.iom.int/system/files/pdf/wmr_2020.pdf
4. Council of the European Union (1987), 87/327/EEC: Council Decision of 15 June 1987 adopting the European Community Action Scheme for the Mobility of University Students (Erasmus)
5. European Commission (2014), Erasmus+ The EU programme for Education, Training, Youth and Sport 2014-2020, https://erasmus-plus.ec.europa.eu/
6. John McCormick (2011), Understanding the European Union, 5th. ed., Palgrave Macmillan, p. 389.
7. Åse Gornitzka (2006), "The Open Method of Coordination as Practice - A Watershed in European Education Policy?" Advanced Research on the Europeanisation of the Nation-State, Working Papers 06/16, p. 15.
8. ENQA (2016), European Association for Quality Assurance in Higher Education, History. https://www.enqa.eu/
9. loyd, Christine (2013), "The Erasmus Mundus programme: providing opportunities to develop a better understanding about inclusion and inclusive practice through an international collaborative programme of study," *International Journal of Inclusive Education.* Vol. 17, No. 4 pp. 329–335.
10. Kim Bong Chul (2023), "Mobility and Educational Cooperation between Korea and the EU", in Kim Sihong and Michael Reiterer (Eds.), *Connecting Europe and Asia: Security, Economy and Mobility,* p.155
11. Yang Su Young, Kim Su Jin (2022), "The EU Erasmus Programme and Educational Cooperation among European universities: Focusing on the case of Spain," *Journal of European Union Studies,* Vol. 61, p. 122.
12. European Commission, Erasmus+ EU programme for education, training, youth and sport, https://erasmus-plus.ec.europa.eu/opportunities
13. European Commission, Cooperation partnerships, https://erasmus- plus.ec.europa.eu/programme-guide/part-b/key-action-2/cooperation-partnerships
14. John D. Palmer, Young Ha Cho (2012), "South Korean higher education internationalization policies: perceptions and experiences," *Asia Pacific Education Review,* Vol. 13, pp. 387–401
15. Kim Bong Chul (2023), op. cit., p. 157.
16. European Commission (2013), Higher Education: EU and Korea agree new era of cooperation, https://ec.europa.eu/commission/presscorner/detail/en/IP_13_1061
17. loyd, Christine (2013), op. cit., p. 339.
18. Kim Bong Chul (2023), op. cit., p. 158.
19. European Commission (2016), Erasmus Mundus joint master's degrees: the story so far, p. 7. https://op.europa.eu/en/publication-detail/-/publication/6f52e9bb-31f2-11e6-b497-01aa75ed71a1
20. Sue Hubble, Alex Bellis, Paul Bolton (2021), "The Erasmus Programme", p. 4. https://researchbriefings.files.parliament.uk/documents/CBP-8326/CBP-8326.pdf.
21. European Commission, Jean Monnet Actions: stimulating teaching and research on the European Union, https://

erasmus-plus.ec.europa.eu/opportunities/organisations/jean-monnet-actions-stimulating-teaching-and-research-on-the-european-union

22. Kim Bong Chul (2023), op. cit., p. 159.
23. Kim Si Hong (2018), "Forty Years of European Studies at HUFS: Looking back, looking forward," Journal of European Union Studies, Vol. 49, p. 121.
24. Ibid, p. 159.
25. Ibid, p. 161.
26. Ibid, p. 161.
27. The Korea Heralrd Economy (2012), "Institute of EU Studies-EU Centre at Hankuk University of Foreign Studies (HUFS) is selected for the first time in Asia for 'EU Jean Monnet Programme," http://news.heraldcorp.com/view.php?ud=20120723001130
28. HUFS-HRI EU Centre, https://www.hufs.ac.kr/user/hrieng/
29. HUFS Jean Monnet Centre of Excellence (2021), "10 years of EU Centre at Hankuk University of Foreign Studies 2011-2021," pp. 24-25.
30. Kim Bong Chul (2023), op. cit., p. 163.
31. CAMPUS Asia, About CAMPUS Asia, http://www.campusasiaprogram.kr/com/cmm/EgovContentView.do?menuNo=1110000001
32. Ibid.
33. HUFS CAMPUS Asia Plus, https://campusasia.hufs.ac.kr/campusasia/6457/subview.do
34. Trilateral Cooperation Secretariat, https://www.tcs-asia.org/en/about/overview.php
35. Ibid.
36. Ibid, TCS News. "2023 trilateral youth mock summit to be held in Beijing"
37. Kim Ho, Kim Yong Hee (2021), "Non-contact Education in ASEAN and the Proposal of ASEAN Educational Development Cooperation after COVID-19," *Southeast Asia Journal,* Vol. 31, pp. 300-301.

EU-Korea Cultural Cooperation

Current Issues and Challenges[1]

YOON SUNGWON

Introduction

Sixty years have passed since the official signing of the EU-Korea relations. Due to the geographical distance, the bilateral relationship in earlier days was not regarded as much salient as those with the US, China, and Japan. South Korea established its embassy in Brussels in 1963, but it was only in 1990 that the EU established its delegation to Seoul. However, the bilateral relationship has evolved gradually and constantly since then without experiencing any fluctuation or turmoil. Both parties have already signed three major agreements, such as the "Framework Agreement for Trade and Cooperation" (1996), the Free Trade Agreement (2010), and the Crisis Management Agreement[2] (2014), while enjoying 'Strategic Partnership' with each other. Against this backdrop, this chapter explores cultural cooperation between the EU and Korea over the past decades. Typically, the EU has been perceived as an exotic tourist destination by many Koreans.[3] As the Protocol on Cultural Cooperation was adopted with the free trade agreement between the EU and Korea, not little attention was paid to the future prospects of EU-Korea cultural exchanges and cooperation. In the 2007 communication entitled "European Agenda for Culture in a Globalizing World", the European Commission emphasized that it is essential to utilize culture in its external relations.[4] Furthermore, in the 2016 joint communication under the title "Towards an EU strategy for international cultural relations", the EU officialized the term 'International Cultural Relations(ICR)' and suggested a policy guideline with which the EU implements in its external relations to its partner countries around the world.[5] As the Protocol on Cultural Cooperation was adopted upon the EU's suggestion, the Protocol can be understood as the EU's ICR strategy targeted for South Korea. Following the provisions of the protocol, the EU and South Korea hold the Committee on Cultural Cooperation on an annual basis to monitor and discuss cultural exchanges and cooperation.

It has been almost a decade since the Protocol came into effect, and the EU and Korea celebrate their 60th anniversary of their diplomatic ties. At this point, it is significant to look back on the progress of bilateral cultural relations. There have been not a few cases where the so-called ‘Brussels effect’ took place. The Brussels effect, which means any regulations or policies the EU implements will eventually affect those of other countries is applied to the field of culture as well. This chapter is composed of six parts. After the introduction, the second part explores the EU’s framework of cultural exchanges and cooperation. Subsequently, the third part discusses the main issues of the EU-Korea Protocol on Cultural Cooperation and the Committee on Cultural Cooperation. The fourth and fifth parts deal with the general overview of EU-Korea cultural exchanges, audio-visual exchanges, and cooperation respectively, and then the conclusion follows.

EU Cultural Policy: Strategic Orientation

EU Cultural Policy, which has evolved for the past 30 years since its initiation in the 1992 Maastricht Treaty, can be classified into five different stages depending on the main features and target recipients.[6]

〈Table 1〉 Classification of EU Cultural Policy by Stage

<table>
<tr><th>Stage</th><th>Title</th><th>Target Recipients</th></tr>
<tr><td rowspan="3">Stage 1
(1992~1999)</td><td>Kaleidoscope</td><td>Performing arts, visual arts, and applied arts</td></tr>
<tr><td>Raphael</td><td>Cultural heritage preservation</td></tr>
<tr><td>Ariane</td><td>Book publishing & distribution, literary translation</td></tr>
<tr><td>Stage 2
(2000~2006)</td><td>Culture 2000</td><td>Innovative & experimental cultural activities
Multi-annual cultural activities
European or international cultural events</td></tr>
<tr><td>Stage 3
(2007~2013)</td><td>Culture 2007-2013</td><td>Trans-cultural mobility & exchange activities
Trans-national distribution of cultural artworks
Inter-cultural dialogue</td></tr>
<tr><td>Stage 4
(2014~2020)</td><td>Creative Europe</td><td rowspan="2">Preservation, development & dissemination of European cultural & linguistic diversity
Reinforcement of competence in culture & creative sector (ex. audio-visual)
Transnational policy cooperation & content creation in cultural & creative sectors
Development of innovative solutions in challenging issues</td></tr>
<tr><td>Stage 5
(2021~2027)</td><td>New Creative Europe</td></tr>
</table>

Source: Yoon(2023b: 322)

One of the most striking changes can be found in Stage 4. Up to Stage 3, the official title of the cultural programme was 'Culture'. However, the title was changed to 'Creative Europe' in 2014. This implies that the EU puts more emphasis on the creative feature of culture than culture per se in implementing its cultural programme. In fact, the main type of target recipients of the programme has changed from cultural artworks to transnational cooperation activities. Another striking feature is that Creative Europe incorporated the audiovisual policy which existed separately from cultural policy. In other words, the existing cultural policy was incorporated into 'Culture Strand' and the audiovisual policy into 'MEDIA Strand'. Also, transnational cooperative activities both from Culture Strand and MEDIA Strand comprise 'Cross-Sectoral Strand'. The structure of Creative Europe programme is as in the following table.

〈Table 2〉 Structure of Creative Europe Programme

<table>
<tr><th colspan="2">Creative Europe</th></tr>
<tr><th>Culture Strand</th><th>Media Strand</th></tr>
<tr><td>Objective: Support & encourage European cultural sector
Target recipients:
Artistic creation & innovation
Dissemination of European contents to Europe & the world
Transnational opportunity of artistic creation and performance
Digital transformation in European cultural & creative sector</td><td>Objective: Support & encourage European film & audiovisual sector
Target recipients:
Value chain cooperation in audiovisual industry for widening enterprise & contents worldwide
Discovery of talented artists & knowledge-sharing
Innovative solutions to fit the market needs & trends
Widening of consumer group to all ages including teenagers</td></tr>
<tr><th colspan="2">Cross-Sectoral Strand</th></tr>
<tr><td colspan="2">Objective: Address challenging issues in cultural & creative sectors; support cooperation activities for innovative solutions
Target recipients:
Promotion & dissemination of programme visibility through cross-sectoral policy cooperation
Innovative solution of content creation, access, dissemination & promotion in cultural & creative sectors
Adjustment of structural & technological changes by means of news media
Establishment of Creative Europe Desk & support of the activities</td></tr>
</table>

Source: Yoon(2023a: 281)

In short, it can be said that the EU's cultural policy is oriented to generating economic effects from cultural and creative sectors[7] and establishing a value-added business model by using creative competences in those sectors.[8] In the digital era, in particular, it is one of the EU's crucial ICR strategies to create digital contents and disseminate them on online platform. The fact that the EU took an initiative in adopting the Protocol on Cultural Cooperation in the free trade deal can be understood in this regard.

EU-Korea Protocol on Cultural Cooperation and the Main Issues

In adopting the Protocol, the EU suggested that the Korean government should ratify the UNESCO Cultural Diversity Convention[9] as the condition of putting the protocol into effect.[10] The 2005 UNESCO Convention is an agreement made by European countries such as France that wish to protect their 'cultural sovereignty' against the United States' 'cultural imperialism' based on their massive resources.[11] The structure of the Protocol is as follows:

〈Table 3〉 **Structure of the EU-Korea Protocol on Cultural Cooperation**

Category	Provisions	Remarks
Introduction	Article 1: Scope, objectives & definitions	
Horizontal Provisions	Article 2: Cultural exchanges & dialogue	
	Article 3: Committee on Cultural Cooperation; Dispute settlement	
	Article 4: Artists & other cultural professionals & practitioners	
Sectoral Provisions	Article 5: Audio-visual co-productions	Audio-visual sector
	Article 6: Other audio-visual cooperation	
	Article 7: Temporary importation of material and equipment for the purpose of shooting audio-visual works	
	Article 8: Performing arts	Other sectors
	Article 9: Publications	
	Article 10: Protection of cultural heritage sites and historic monuments	

Source: The EU-Korea Protocol on Cultural Cooperation[12]

The protocol is composed of three parts. The first part identifies the scope, objectives, and definitions of the terms used in the Protocol (Article 1). The following parts comprise 'horizontal provisions' (Articles 2~4) and 'sectoral provisions' (Articles 5~10). These provisions focus on two issues: (1) short-term exchanges of cultural professionals, and (2) audio-visual co-production. Especially, as the latter takes up a substantial part of the entire Protocol, both the EU and South Korea emphasized encouraging the audio-visual co-production in this protocol.[13] It should be noted as well that the overall content of the Protocol is quite similar to that of the Creative Europe programme (i.e., audio-visual co-production and facilitation of cultural practitioners' exchanges).[14]

As stipulated in the Protocol, the Committee on Cultural Cooperation takes place every year to discuss the bilateral cooperation issues. The main agendas of the past committee meetings are as follows:

〈Table 4〉 Main Agendas of EU-Korea Committee on Cultural Cooperation

Sequence	Date	Venue	Agenda
1st meeting	05/Dec/2013	Brussels	Adopt the Rule of Procedure of the Committee Explain the policies on culture & art, cultural industry & copyright Share the experience of cultural exchanges & difficulties Discuss the recognition condition of audio-visual products
2nd meeting	10/Oct/2014	Seoul	Approve the list of arbitration panel Share information on the policies of culture & cultural industry, cultural heritage, film, artistic mobility Discuss the difficulties in co-producing audio-visual products (i.e. animation)
3rd meeting	05/Feb/2016	Brussels	Share information on culture & creative sectors, artistic residency & mobility, audio-visual co-production Support for cultural technical convergence between artistic enterprises A new funding model for enhancing financial access (i.e. crowd funding) Incubating financial support for creative SMEs Benefit for international co-production and promotion campaign
4th meeting	06/Mar/2017	Seoul	Share information on the Performing Arts Market in Seoul(PAMS) Exchange statistical information on EU content industry Facilitating ACC-R(Asia Culture Center-Residency) & other creative talents' exchange programmes Reviewing the establishment of audio-visual co-production funding Facilitating pilot co-productions of audio-visual products on the theme of EU-Korea cultural exchanges
5th meeting	09/Apr/2018	Brussels	Culture & City(policies of European Capital of Culture & Culture City of Korea) Developing new growth area in cultural & creative industry(i.e. content industry) Participating in PAMS as a guest-country of honour Information-sharing on European Year of Cultural Heritage 2018 Korean Week in 2018 Heidelberg Festival & 2019 Korea-Denmark Cultural Year
6th meeting	13/May/2019	Seoul	Co-producing performing arts, architecture, audio-visual products City-to-city cooperation Connecting art, technology & science Introducing Korean history & culture

Sequence	Date	Venue	Agenda
7th meeting	09/Dec/2020	Online	Knowledge-sharing of cooperation cases between EU-Korea cultural cities Comparing art-technology convergence of both sides & developing joint research on EU-Korea co-production Exchange of human resources(i.e. young & talented architects) Facilitating audio-visual co-production(i.e. film, animation)
8th meeting	16/Dec/2021	Online	Countermeasure against the COVID-19 in cultural sector Information-sharing on international cultural exchanges Cultural cooperation between cities(cultural city both in Korea and the EU) Enhancing exchanges in architecture & theatre, audio-visual sector

Sources: Reconstructed from Kim(2016: 116); MCTS press releases[15]; European Commission[16], quoted from Yoon(2023b: 325-326)

While audio-visual co-production was one of the most dominant agendas of the Committee, the issues of cultural practitioners' exchanges and cultural cities were also quite often discussed. In this context, the following part explores the current situation of EU-Korea cultural exchanges.

EU-Korea Cultural Exchanges: General Overview

Not a few institutions are running cultural exchange programmes. The Korea Foundation (under the supervision of the Ministry of Foreign Affairs) is actively operating the related programmes. Also, institutions like the Arts Council Korea and the Korea Arts Management Service (under the supervision of MCST) also take initiative in this field. As one of the most representative institutions regarding cultural exchanges, the Korea Foundation has been implementing 'Korea Festival', an annual event to promote Korea outside the world. Besides, the Foundation selects a strategic region and hosts a cultural event customized to that region. The past events for the period 2018–2022 are tabulated as follows:

〈Table 5〉 Europe-Korea Cultural Exchanges (2018~2022)

Year	Country	Event	Remarks
2018	Denmark	VOID International Animation Festival	Cultural Event in Strategic Region
	Finland	Korean Film Academic Conference	
	Netherlands, Portugal	WoongSan Band Jazz Concert	
	Czech, Slovakia	KBS Symphony Orchestra Performance	

Year	Country	Event	Remarks
2019	Germany, Czech	Fusion MC & DongRak Performance Group: B-Boy & Korean Traditional Music Concert	Korea Festival
	Sweden	Nanta & Coreyah: Percussion & Fusion Korean Traditional Music Concert	Cultural Event in Strategic Region
	Serbia	U-Angel Voice Classic Concert	
	UK	8th Korean Visual Culture Academic Conference	
	Germany, Netherlands, Denmark	Korean Cultural Events in European Universities	
	Denmark	Korean Cultural Event	
	Russia, Germany	Traditional Percussion Performance	
	Spain	Las Palmas & Dom Art Performance: Fusion Concert	
2020	Online Korea Festival	"Shaping the Future Together" Creative Traditional Music, B-Boying, Retro Music Contents Creation under the Theme of Public Diplomacy(Peace, Hope, Courage, etc.)	Korea Festival
	Online Celadon Special Exhibition	"Essence of Korean Aesthetics – Celedon" Exhibition of Celadons through Virtual Reality	
	Netherlands	Kim Ja-Kyeong Opera Gala Concert	Cultural Event in Strategic Region
	France	Korean Cultural Festival in European Universities	
2021	Denmark	8th Kimchi Festival in Copenhagen	Comprehensive Korean Cultural Festival
	Korea, UK	UK-Korea 'Gathering Moss' Project for Climate Change	
	Portugal	Portugal-Korea 60th Celebration Concert	
	Germany	Kim Sun-Wook Piano Recital	
	Finland	Ceramic Exhibition 'On the Edge'	
	Czech	Traditional Korean Doll Exhibition in Praha	
2022	Latvia	Korean Traditional Music & B-Boy Concert	
	Korea, UK	UK-Korea Creative Project for Climate Change	

Sources: Reconstructed from Korea Foundation(2018: 39; 2019: 39; 2020: 43; 2021: 47; 2022: 45), quoted from Yoon(2020b: 327-328)

According to Table 5, a total of 24 Europe-Korea cultural events were held for the period of 2018–2022. Despite some annual fluctuation, 4.8 events were held annually. Denmark was the most favorite partner country with a total of 4 events during the period, followed by the Netherlands, the UK, and Germany (3 times each). Regional deviation was perceived as well. While Northern European countries (i.e., Denmark, Finland, Latvia) hosted 7 times and Western countries (i.e., UK, Germany, France, and the Netherlands) did 10 times, Southern countries (i.e., Spain and Portugal) hosted only 3 times.[17] As Western and Northern European countries participated more frequently than Southern countries, it seems necessary to develop new partner countries as well as new items.

EU-Korea Audio-visual Exchanges & Cooperation

Broadcast Content

Broadcast content refers to a wide range of contents, such as drama, entertainment, documentary, animation, cartoon, and sports. The largest proportion of them is taken by drama in terms of export volume(Terrestrial broadcaster: 85.1%, Programme provider: 88.4% as of 2021).[18] In order to compare any changes before and after the implementation of the EU-Korea Protocol on Cultural Cooperation, the statistical data on exporting and importing broadcast content by region is indicated in the following table.

〈Table 6〉 Export & Import of Broadcast Content by Region (2011 vs. 2021)

Region	Type of Business	Export				Import			
		2011		2021		2011		2021	
		Number	Amount (Thousand USD)	Number	Amount (Thousand USD)	Number	Amount (Thousand USD)	Number	Amount (Thousand USD)
Asia	Terrestrial Broadcaster	51,703	153,884.4	50,758	98,710.6	160	322.8	150	244
	Programme Provider	3,632	9,272.1	17,839	104,682.4	5,410	7,816.7	7,983	16,169
America	Terrestrial Broadcaster	1,525	2,722.2	3,282	10,920.2	520	1,910.4	156	276
	Programme Provider	1,575	967	3,722	18,798.3	15,052	112,302	10,782	37,057.1
Europe	Terrestrial Broadcaster	1,771	1,412.1	1,900	728	1,166	2,005.9	464	2,743.5
	Programme Provider	9	67.4	1,121	610.4	2,423	2,827.4	3,072	2,686.1

Region	Type of Business	Export				Import			
		2011		2021		2011		2021	
		Number	Amount (Thousand USD)	Number	Amount (Thousand USD)	Number	Amount (Thousand USD)	Number	Amount (Thousand USD)
Oceania	Terrestrial Broadcaster	0	0	44	80.2	3	10	17	287
	Programme Provider	196	20	196	6.5	123	237.3	18	13
Africa	Terrestrial Broadcaster	404	45.3	248	253.8	0	0	6	134
	Programme Provider	0	0	571	132	258	484	0	0
Other	Terrestrial Broadcaster	33	6	2,819	32,171.7	0	0	0	0
	Programme Provider	28	544.2	7,475	69,750	0	0	0	0
Total		60,876	168,941	89,975	336,844	25,115	127,917	22,648	59,610

Sources: Reconstructed from Korea Communications Commission(2012: 151-158; 2022: 147-153), quoted from Yoon(2023b: 329-330)

Most of all, the changes in export and import volumes should be noted. While the export volume was $169 million in 2011, the volume increased by 99% to $337 million in 2021. Over the same period, the import volume has decreased by 53%, from $128 million to $60 million. In short, the export volume was quite similar to that of import in 2011, but the export volume is 5.6 times higher than that of import in 2021. Such change reflects the remarkable leap of the Korean content in the global market. The statistics in Table 6 are projected in Figure 1, with a focus on regional comparison.

〈Figure 1〉 Comparison of Broadcasting Contents Export & Import (2011 vs. 2021)

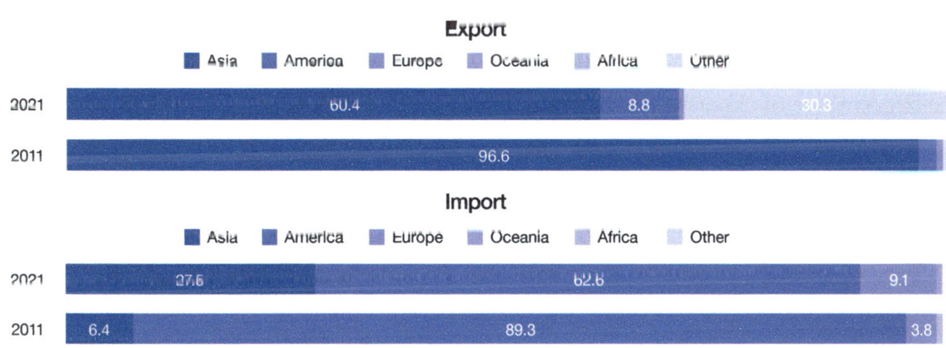

Sources: Reconstructed from Korea Communications Commission(2012: 151-158; 2022: 147-153), quoted from Yoon(2023b: 330)

As for export, Asia has been the most dominant export market. Asia took up 96.6% of the total exports in 2011, for instance. Such dominant volume was reduced to 60.4% in 2012, but still, Asia remains the most important export market of Korean broadcast content. Europe, in comparison, occupies only a marginal volume in the Korean export market. Its share was as much as 0.9% in 2011, and the proportion even decreased to 0.4% in 2021. However, the portion of 'other' has notably increased over the same period—from 0.3% in 2011 to 30.3% in 2021. It implies that as global OTT(Over-The-Top) services became actively used across the world and this service was classified in the 'other' category, the share of 'other' became substantial in the recent statistics.

Regarding import, the import from North America constitutes the largest proportion both in 2011 and 2021. However, the absolute share has decreased from 89.3% to 62.6%. The import from Asia increased instead(6.4%→27.5%). The proportion Europe occupies is very marginal, although it has slightly increased(3.8% in 2011 and 9.1% in 2021). It means that the visibility and perception of the European broadcast content quite are weak in South Korea.

Animation

According to the EU-Korea Protocol on Cultural Cooperation, animation is the sector most highly expected for the bilateral co-production. In fact, as was discussed in Table 4, both sides have constantly paid attention to enhancing the possibility of co-producing animation works. The reason why animation was given high attention for co-production is not only because Europe has a strong competence in this sector, but also because South Korea has established a solid foothold in the world market in recent years thanks to its high-quality products. South Korea has held 'Cartoon Connection' for the period of 2010 –2020 thanks to the initiative of CARTOON, EU animation association.

Table 7 tabulates the export and import data of South Korea's animation industry by region. From 2008 to 2018, the export volume has increased by 117% ($81 million to $175 million). The import volume has risen only by 28% ($6 million to $7.9 million) for the same period. It means that Korean practitioners' competitiveness has been recognized . While the largest share of export is directed to North America (53%), that of Europe is quite small (19%). The actual figure in 2018 is slightly higher than that of Japan, but notably, the annual growth rate Europe recorded is as high as 9.3%. In this respect, European market seems to be more rapidly growing than Japan in terms of export. Import has a totally different story. As of 2018, 98% of the entire import was made from Japan. In other words, there is almost no room for other countries to penetrate the Korean market, including Europe.

With the constant growth of export, co-production has been constant between Europe and South Korea. Table 8 listed the number of works Korean animation companies co-produced with European counterparts for the period of 2013 to 2021. A total of 105 animation works have been co-produced over the years. Out of them, 81.4% (or 85.5 works) were carried out with Asian companies. Co-works with China were the most frequent, and those with Japan were also active. Co-production with European companies was active, especially in 2013 and 2014, after which the co-production was only sporadic. Unfortunaely, there was no co-production at all in 2020 and 2021. This reflects the fact that the expectations represented in the Protocol have not yet been met.

〈Table 7〉 Export & Import of South Korea's Animation Industry by Region

(Unit: Thousand USD)

	Amount of Export											Share (%)	CARG* (%)
	2008	2009	2010	2011	2012	2013	2014	2015	2016	2017	2018		
China	1,136	1,356	1,577	1,659	1,712	1,603	1,848	2,162	1,825	2,188	7,629**	4	18.9
Japan	16,851	17,369	18,810	21,688	21,421	19,909	20,109	23,529	26,254	26,461	32,681	19	6.2
South-east Asia	469	967	1,151	1,239	1,260	1,208	125	336	635	810	3,650	2	20.5
North America	47,568	50,358	52,463	59,397	59,167	60,355	62,490	66,621	69,654	75,286	91,784	53	6.2
Europe	12,387	16,496	19,527	28,598	25,433	25,180	26,541	27,841	28,842	31,132	33,031	19	9.3
Other	2,172	3,105	3,299	3,477	3,587	1,658	4,479	6,081	8,412	8,993	5,743	3	9.2
Total	80,583	89,651	96,827	116,058	112,580	109,973	115,652	126,570	135,622	144,870	174,517	100	7.3

* CAGR: Compound Annual Growth Rate

** This figure includes Taiwan and Hong Kong as well as the mainland China.

	Amount of Import											Share (%)	CARG* (%)
	2008	2009	2010	2011	2012	2013	2014	2015	2016	2017	2018		
China	16	10	11	11	11	11	11	12	10	11	75	1	15.1
Japan	6,088	7,365	6,905	12,228	6,219	12,440	6,782	6,965	7,274	7,553	7,678	98	2.1
South-east Asia	-	-	-	-	-	-	-	-	-	-	27	-	-
North America	28	22	35	512	2,963	3,066	32	34	40	40	88	1	11.0

Amount of Import												Share (%)	CARG* (%)
Europe	-	-	-	625	1,002	971	-	-	-	-	-	-	-
Other	-	-	-	516	52	-	-	-	-	-	11	-	-
Total	6,132	7,397	6,951	13,892	10,260	16,488	6,825	7,011	7,324	7,604	7,878	100	2.3

Sources: Reconstructed from KOCCA(2015: 49-50; 2018: 32-33; 2019: 128-129; 2020a: 169-170), quoted from Yoon(2023b: 332-333)

⟨Table 8⟩ Number of Co-produced Animation Works by Region

		2013	2014	2015	2016	2017	2018	2019	2020	2021	Total
Asia	Malaysia	3	1	2	1	0	0	0	1.5*	0.5*	9
	Japan	5	3	4	2	1	1	2	1	4	23
	China	5	3	5	5	7	6.5*	6	7	6	50.5
	Singapore	0	0	0	0	0	0	0	1.5*	1.5*	3
Sub-total		**13** (72.2%)	**7** (63.6%)	**11** (84.6%)	**8** (88.9%)	**8** (80%)	**7.5** (75%)	**8** (88.9%)	**11** (91.7%)	**12** (92.3%)	85.5
Europe	Netherlands	1	1	1	0	0	0	0	0	0	3
	UK	1	1	1	1	0	0	0	0	0	4
	France	3	0	0	0	0	0	0	0	0	3
	Italy	0	0	0	0	0.5*	1	1	0	0	2.5
Sub-total		**5** (27.8%)	**2** (18.2%)	**2** (15.4%)	**1** (11.1%)	**0.5** (5%)	**1** (10%)	**1** (11.1%)	**0**	**0**	**12.5**
America	USA	0	1	0	0	0	1	0	1	1	4
	Argentina	0	1	0	0	1	0	0	0	0	2
Sub-total		**0**	**2** (18.2%)	**0**	**0**	**1** (10%)	**1** (10%)	**0**	**1** (8.3%)	**1** (7.7%)	**6**
Oceania	New Zealand	0	0	0	0	0.5*	0.5*	0	0	0	1
Sub-total		0	0	0	0	0.5 (5%)	0.5 (5%)	0	0	0	1
Total		**18** (100%)	**11** (100%)	**13** (100%)	9 (100%)	**10** (100%)	**10** (100%)	9 (100%)	**12** (100%)	**13** (100%)	105

* In case of three-country partnership, the overseas partner country is counted as 0.5 each.
Sources: Reconstructed from KOCCA(2018: 71; 2019: 162; 2020b: 274; 2022: 247-248), quoted from Yoon(2023b: 333)

〈Table 9〉 Europe-Korea Co-production of Animation Works (2013~2019)

Year	Title	Korean Company	Partner Country
2013	<Me & My Robot1>	Synergy Media	France
	<Me & My Robot2>	Synergy Media	France
	<Papier Friend2>	Characterplan	France
	<Tickety Toc>	FunnyFlux	UK
	<Balloopo>	Fov Studio	Netherlands
2014	<Zack & Quack>	High1 Entertainment	UK, Israel
	<Balloopo>	Fov Studio	Netherlands
2015	<Zack & Quack>	High1 Entertainment	UK, Israel
	<Balloopo>	Fov Studio	Netherlands
2016	<Tickety Toc 2>	FunnyFlux	UK
2017	<Cubyzoo>	Aurora World	China, Italy
2018	<Robot Train S2>	CJ E&M	Italy
2019	<YooHoo to the Rescue>	Aurora World	Italy

Sources: Reconstructed from KOCCA(2015: 81; 2016: 115; 117; 2018: 70; 2019: 162; 2020b: 274), quoted from Yoon(2023b: 334)

Table 9 lists the animation works Europe and South Korea produced together. The European countries involved in the co-production were France, the United Kingdom, the Netherlands, and Italy.

Film

Film is another representative audio visual product. Table 10 comparatively indicates the development of audience share in South Korean cinemas between 2012 and 2022.

〈Table 10〉 Audience Share in Domestic Cinemas (2012 vs. 2022)

Region	2012	2022
South Korea	59.0%	57.4%
USA*	34.1%	37.7%

Region	2012	2022
Chinese Region	0.3%	0.2%
Europe	4.9%	0.7%
Japan	1.4%	3.9%
Other	0.3%	0.2%
Total	100%	100%

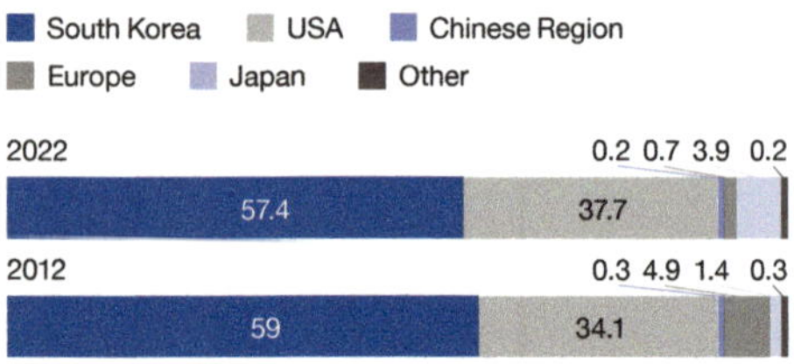

* It includes both imported and directly distributed films.

** It includes China, Taiwan, and Hong Kong.

Sources: Reconstructed from Korean Film Council(2013: 14; 2023: 51), quoted from Yoon(2023b: 335)

The largest share is taken by South Korean films, although the actual figure is slightly reduced (59.0%→57.4%). Next to the South Korean films, it was the United States' films that occupied the second largest proportion(34.1% in 2012 and 37.7% in 2022). European films took up a very marginal proportion. It was 4.9% in 2012, and the figure even decreased to 0.7% in 2022. The decrease seems to be offset by the increase in the shares of the United States and Japan.

Table 11 demonstrates the export volume of Korean films by region. It identifies every 5 years' statistics from 2007 to 2022 and puts them into Figure 2 for visual interpretation.

〈Table 11〉 Export Volume of Korean Film by Region

Region	Export Volume (USD)			
	2007 (%)	2012 (%)	2017 (%)	2022 (%)
Asia	6,943,118 (56.5)	14,439,757 (71.6)	21,684,201 (53.2)	34,408,677 (48.2)
North America	307,260 (2.5)	2,872,752 (14.2)	4,933,250 (12.1)	9,507,462 (13.3)
Europe	4,553,625 (37.1)	2,455,745 (12.2)	3,801,695 (9.3)	5,818,835 (8.1)
Central & South America	199,100 (1.6)	233,500 (1.2)	1,540,452 (3.8)	1,270,546 (1.8)
Oceania	111,571 (0.9)	134,196 (0.7)	411,274 (1.0)	295,888 (0.4)
Middle East/Africa	17,465 (0.1)	39,000 (0.2)	158,500 (0.4)	163,210 (0.2)
Other	151,200 (1.2)	-	8,196,785 (20.1)	19,975,762 (28.0)
Total	12,283,339 (100)	20,174,950 (100)	40,726,157 (100)	71,440,380 (100)

Sources: Reconstructed from Korean Film Council(2008: 17; 2013: 45; 2018: 61; 2023: 73), quoted from Yoon(2023b: 335-336)

First of all, the export volume in 2022 has risen by 580% from that in 2007. Such a sharp rise in export results from the great success of 〈Minari〉, 〈Parasite〉, 〈Squid Game〉, as well as the nominations of Yoon Yeo-Jung, Bong Joon-Ho, and Lee Jung-Jae for globally renowned film awards. Figure 2 comparatively demonstrates the share of Korean film export by region.

Asia has remained the biggest export market throughout the period. Interestingly, Europe was the second-largest export market (37.1%) next to Asia in 2007, but its share has substantially shrunk to 8.1% in 2022. However, it should be noted that while the share of 'other' was only as low as 1.2% in 2007, its percentage has increased to 20.1% in 2017 and again to 28% in 2022. Since global OTT channels emerged and are widely spread among the public, they have became the main consumption channel for audio-visual products. As such OTT channels are categorized as 'other' in the statistical data, the 'other' keeps on becoming more and more visible. Therefore, it seems necessary to come up with a more reasonable aggregating system which reflects the changes of audio-visual consumption environment. The following table lists the Top 10 countries to which Korean films are exported.

According to Table 12, the major export destinations are the Chinese region as well as Asian countries. Germany (2020; 2021) and France (2022) are the only European countries on the list, and their shares are absolutely marginal. As was in the case of animation, Chinese presence is quite visible in the film export as well. The current estranged relationship with China affected China's ranking on the list, but any recovery in the relationship would positively influence the export market. The data on film co-production with European countries is demonstrated in the following table.

〈Figure 2〉 Share of Korean Film Export by Region

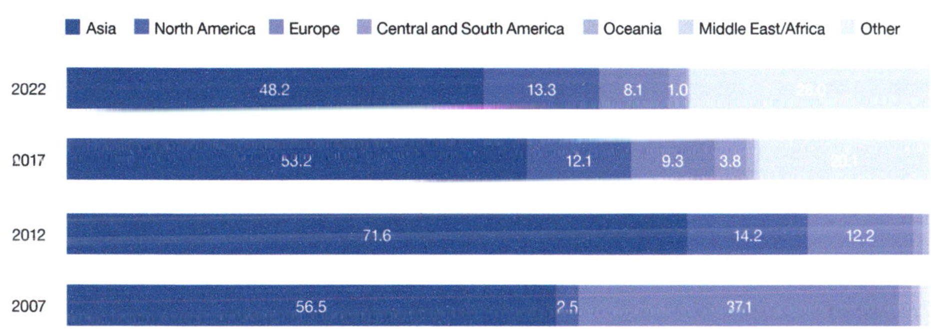

Sources. Reconstructed from Korean Film Council(2008: 17; 2013: 45; 2018: 61; 2023: 73), quoted from Yoon(2023b. 336)

〈Table 12〉 Export Volume of Korean Films by Country (2020~2022)

(Unit: USD)

Rank	2020			2021			2022		
	Country	Amount	Share	Country	Amount	Share	Country	Amount	Share
1	Taiwan	7,924,412	14.6%	China	8,396,220	19.5%	Taiwan	9,779,476	13.7%
2	Japan	5,110,593	9.4%	Japan	6,963,322	16.2%	Japan	9,212,205	12.9%
3	Singapore	3,798,225	7.0%	Taiwan	6,690,404	15.5%	USA	5,814,455	8.1%
4	Hong Kong	2,467,961	4.6%	Singapore	4,295,609	10.0%	Singapore	5,869,534	8.2%
5	China	2,448,126	4.5%	USA	4,452,554	10.3%	Hong Kong	4,418,580	6.2%
6	USA	1,525,595	2.8%	Hong Kong	1,414,200	3.3%	France	3,104,006	4.3%
7	Vietnam	1,242,103	2.3%	Germany	762,728	1.8%	China	1,961,100	2.7%
8	Germany	824,857	1.5%	Malaysia	625,500	1.5%	Russia	992,156	1.4%
9	Malaysia	799,000	1.5%	Thailand	490,584	1.1%	Uruguay	701,408	1.0%

Source: Korean Film Council(2023: 74), quoted from Yoon(2023b: 337)

〈Table 13〉 Europe-Korea Film Co-production (2013~2019)

	2013	2014	2015	2016	2017	2018	2019	Total
Total	12	2	5	8	7	3	2	39
Co-produced with Europe	1		2			1		4
Titles of the Films (Director, Country)	• Snowpiercer (Director Bong Joon-ho, Czech)		• Twenty Again (Director Park Heung-sik, Italy) • Black Stone (Director Roh Kyeong-tae, France)			• Beautiful Days (Director Yoon Jae-ho, France)		

Source: Reconstructed from Korean Film Council, quoted from Yoon(2023b: 338)

Out of 39 films co-produced for the period of 2013–2019, four were produced with European countries. One of the most representative films is 〈Snowpiercer〉 directed by Bong Joon-ho and co-produced with Stillking Films, a Czech production company. By recording more than 9 million views, this film is regarded as a successful case of co-production.[20] Also, 〈Twenty Again〉 by Park Heing-sik, 〈Black Stone〉 by Roh Kyeong-tae, and 〈Beautiful Days〉 by Yoon Jae-ho are another co-production cases. However, given the total co-production cases with other countries or regions, those with European countries are quite few. It is thus necessary to come up with any practical institutional solution to facilitate co-production with Europe.

The EU is now making an effort to create 'networks' in order to execute its ICR strategies. As a way to establish networks between cultural institutes and Ministries of the Member States, the EU created the 'European Union National Institute for Culture' (EUNIC). Currently, 139 Clusters are organized in 107 countries worldwide. By hosting European cultural events customized to each country or region, EUNIC aims at creating 'European Spaces of Culture' around the world.[21] In Korea, the EUNIC Korea Film Festival has been held annually since 2016. The European films played at the festivals are listed in Table 14.

〈Table 14〉 List of European Films Played in EUNIC Korea Film Festivals

Year	Theme	Films (Year of Production, Country)	
2016	Migrants in European Cities	• Fire at Sea (2016, Italy) • Journey to Portugal (2011, Portugal) • Cozy Dens (1999, Czech Republic) • Almanya (2011, Germany) • All Thing Fair (1995, Spain)	• La cour de Bebel (2013, France) • A Man Named Ove (2015, Sweden) • Four Lions (2010, UK) • Kim Ki Dok (2006, Poland)
2017	Preserving Our Heritage for Future Generations	• TheCityofTomorrow—ExperimentalGroundAsia (2014, Germany) • Tomorrow (2015, France) • Work in Progress (2001, Spain) • The Plan (2014, Czech Republic) • Good Things Await (2014, Denmark)	• God Save the Green (2012) / The Flying Gardeners (2015, Italy) • A Moving Image (2016, UK) • The Glass Painter – The Art of Miksa Róth (2015, Hungary)
2018	1968: A Year of Change	• The Chinoise (1967, France) • Made in Hungaria (2009, Hungary) • The Legend of Paul and Paula (1972) / I'm an Elephant, Madame (1969, Germany)	• Raise Raven (1976, Spain) • Storming Heaven (2010, Italy) • Persona (1966, Sweden) • 2001: A Space Odyssey (1968, UK) • Those Wonderful Years That Sucked (1997, Czech Republic)
2019	Wind of Change	• Berlin is in Germany (2001, Germany) • Anthropoid (2016, Czech Republic) • Warsaw 44 (2014, Poland) • The Swedes in the Korean War (2019, Sweden)	• Kincsem - Bet on Revenge (2017, Hungary) • A Prominent Patient (2016, Slovakia) • Farewell, My Queen (2012, France) • We Believed (2010, Italy)

Year	Theme	Films (Year of Production, Country)	
2020	An Imaginary Journey to European Cities	• Utopia Revisited (2018, Austria) • French Tour (2016, France) • Noma, My perfect Storm (2016, Denmark) • Darkness (2019, Italy) • Fever at Dawn (2015, Hungary)	• Solidarity According to Women (2014, Poland) • From Slovakia with Love (2015, Slovakia) • Afternoon (2007, Germany) • Goat Story: The Old Prague Legends (2008, Czech Republic)
2021	Family Matters	• Those Who Remained (2019, Hungary) • Italo (2014, Italy) • Cleo: If I Could Turn Back Time (2019, Germany) • Summer Rebels (2020, Slovakia)	• Empties (2007, Czech Republic) • Becoming Astrid (2018, Sweden) • Letters to Santa 4 (2020, Poland) • A Gift from Bob (2020, UK) • Christmas & Co (2017, France)
2022	New Beginnings	• Skies of Lebanon (2020, France) • Another Round (2020, Denmark) • Dark Blue Almost Black (2006, Spain) • Even Mice Belong in Heaven (2021, Czech) • Sonata (2021, Poland) • Letters from Antarctica (2019, Bulgaria)	• A Steady Job (Il Posto) (2022, Italy) • Tigers (2021, Sweden) • 1945 (2017, Hungary) • 107 Mothers (2017, Slovakia) • Phoenix (2014, Germany) • Love Sarah (2021, UK)

Sources: Reconstructed from Yoon(2023b: 350)

Conclusion: Some Challenges & Policy Suggestion

In this chapter, EU-Korea cultural relations were explored by referring to various cases. Certainly, the adoption and implementation of the Protocol on Cultural Cooperation officialized the bilateral cultural relations. But at the same time, the enhanced soft power of South Korea caused by the 'Korean Wave' or 'Hallyu' enabled the acceleration of bilateral cultural exchanges and cooperation between the EU and Korea. As was discussed earlier, there have been a substantial number of cultural exchanges and cooperations at the governmental level, and this is expected to continue. On the contrary, unlike the initial expectations of both parties, the audio-visual co-production has not been satisfactory. It is because there are some policy issues that hinder from accrediting EU or Korean products as both sides have different policy standards. Also, their cultural differences make it all the more difficult to make co-production plausible.

However, the content of cultural exchanges is constantly evolving. The EU has established EUNIC in most countries, through which cultural institutes and cultural ministries are linked and collaborate. South Korea also has the EUNIC Korea Cluster and the latter signed the memorandum of understanding with the Arts Council Korea(ARKO) in 2022.[22] This will be a meaningful occasion to foster the bilateral cultural relations in many diversified ways. As the EU has gradually developed and implemented its ICR strategies, South Korea also needs to set up a long-term plan to promote its enhanced soft power as well as develop its soft power more sustainably. For the past 60 years, the EU and South Korea have focused on 'widening' the relationship in diverse fields. Both sides now face the task of 'deepening' the relationship for the next 60 years. As it is important to attract the public's attention and interest in order to make the relationship sustainable, the role of culture will be crucial in developing the EU-Korea relationship further.

References

Arts Council Korea, Press release, 4 May 2022, https://www.arko.or.kr/board/view/4057?cid=1804523 (accessed 09/Sep/2023) [in Korean]

Chaban, Natalia, and Sae Won Chung, "Public Perceptions of the EU in South Korea: Longitudinal Study (2004-2006)", Asia-Pacific Journal of EU Studies, Vol. 7, No. 1/2 (2009), pp. 19-39.

Commission of the European Communities, "Communication on 'European Agenda for Culture in a globalising world'", COM(2007) 242 final.

European Commission, "Towards an EU strategy for international cultural relations", Joint Communication to the European Parliament and the Council, JOIN(2016) 29 final.

Kim, Kyu-Chan, "Issues and Agendas om EU-Korea Cultural Cooperation Committee," Research Series 2016-11, (2016), Korea Culture & Tourism Institute. [in Korean]

Korea Communications Commission, "Report on Broadcasting Industry 2012," 2012. [in Korean]

Korea Communications Commission, "Report on Broadcasting Industry 2022," 2022. [in Korean]

Korea Creative Content Agency(KOCCA), "2014 Animation Industry White Paper," 2015. [in Korean]

Korea Creative Content Agency(KOCCA), "2017 Animation Industry White Paper," 2018. [in Korean]

Korea Creative Content Agency(KOCCA), "2018 Animation Industry White Paper," 2019. [in Korean]

Korea Creative Content Agency(KOCCA), "2019 Animation Industry White Paper," 2020a. [in Korean]

Korea Creative Content Agency(KOCCA), "2020 Animation Industry White Paper," 2020b. [in Korean]

Korea Creative Content Agency(KOCCA), "2021 Animation Industry White Paper," 2022. [in Korean]

Korean Film Council(KOFIC), "2007 Report on Korean Film Industry," 2008. [in Korean]

Korean Film Council(KOFIC), "2012 Report on Korean Film Industry," 2013. [in Korean]

Korean Film Council(KOFIC), "2017 Report on Korean Film Industry," 2018. [in Korean]

Korean Film Council(KOFIC), "2022 Report on Korean Film Industry," 2023. [in Korean]

Korean Film Council, "KoBiz," https://www.kobiz.or.kr/new/kor/02_overseas/production/productionCaseList.jsp# (accessed 03/Sep/2023) [in Korean]

Korea Foundation, "Annual Report 2018," 2018. [in Korean]

Korea Foundation, "Annual Report 2019," 2019. [in Korean]

Korea Foundation, "Annual Report 2020," 2020. [in Korean]

Korea Foundation, "Annual Report 2021," 2021. [in Korean]

Korea Foundation, "Annual Report 2022," 2022. [in Korean]

Littoz-Monnet, Annabelle, "Encapsulating EU Cultural Policy into the EU's Growth and Competitive Agenda: Explaining the Success of a Paradigmatic Shift in Brussels," Evangelia Psychogiopoulou (ed.), Cultural Governance and the European Union: Protecting and Promoting Cultural Diversity in Europe (Palgrave Macmillan, 2015), pp. 25-36.

Ministry of Culture, Sports and Tourism(MCST), Press release, 6 March 2017.

Ministry of Culture, Sports and Tourism(MCST), Press release, 9 April 2018.

Ministry of Culture, Sports and Tourism(MCST), Press release, 9 December 2020.

Ministry of Culture, Sports and Tourism(MCST), Press release, 16 December 2021.

Yoo, Su-kyeong, "Snowpiercer, Coming Back Again on Netflix," 11 May 2020, Hankook Ilbo, https://www.hankookilbo.com/News/Read/202005111582725293 (Accessed 21/Sep/2023) [in Korean]

Yoon, Sung-Won, "Some Considerations of the EU's International Cultural Strategy," Korean Journal of European Integration, Vol.14, No.2 (2023a), pp.275-306, DOI: https://doi.org/10.32625/KJEI.2023.30.275 [in Korean]

Yoon, Sung-Won, "EU-Korea at 60 and Their Cultural Relations," Journal of European Union Studies, No.67 (2023b), pp.317-350, DOI: http://dx.doi.org/10.18109/jeus.2023.67.1 [in Korean]

Yoon, Sung-Won, and Sung-Hoon Park, "EU-Korea Cultural Cooperation in Audio-visual Industry: Current Situation and the Role of 'Protocol on Cultural Cooperation' in Future Cooperation," Korean Journal of EU Studies, Vol.18, No.1 (2013), pp.81-110. [in Korean]

Endnote

1. This chapter is mainly based on the following journal article: Sung-Won Yoon, "EU-Korea at 60 and Their Cultural Relations," *Journal of European Union Studies,* No.67 (2023b), pp.317-350, DOI: http://dx.doi.org/10.18109/jeus.2023.67.1 [in Korean]
2. The official title of the Agreement is the "Agreement between the Republic of Korea and the European Union Establishing a Framework for the Participation of the Republic of Korea in European Union Crisis Management Operations."
3. Natalia Chaban and Sae Won Chung, "Public Perceptions of the EU in South Korea: Longitudinal Study (2004-2006)", *Asia-Pacific Journal of EU Studies,* Vol. 7, No. 1/2 (2009), p. 28.
4. Commission of the European Communities, "Communication on 'European Agenda for Culture in a globalising world'", COM(2007) 242 final.
5. European Commission, "Towards an EU strategy for international cultural relations", JOINT COMMUNICATION TO THE EUROPEAN PARLIAMENT AND THE COUNCIL, JOIN(2016) 29 final.
6. Sung-Won Yoon, "Some Considerations of the EU's International Cultural Strategy," *Korean Journal of European Integration,* Vol.14, No.2 (2023a), pp.275-306, DOI: https://doi.org/10.32625/KJEI.2023.30.275 [in Korean]
7. Annabelle Littoz-Monnet, "Encapsulating EU Cultural Policy into the EU's Growth and Competitive Agenda: Explaining the Success of a Paradigmatic Shift in Brussels," Evangelia Psychogiopoulou (ed.), *Cultural Governance and the European Union: Protecting and Promoting Cultural Diversity in Europe* (Palgrave Macmillan, 2015), pp. 25-36.
8. Yoon, *op. cit.,* p.282.
9. Its full name is "UNESCO Convention on the Protection and Promotion of the Diversity of Cultural Expression."
10. The Korean government officially signed the UNESCO Cultural Diversity Convention on 1 April 2010.
11. Yoon, *op. cit.,* p.293.
12. FTA website of the Korean government, https://www.fta.go.kr/webmodule/_PSD_FTA/eu/doc/eng/k_eu_ccp.pdf (accessed 29/Sep/2023)
13. Sung-Won Yoon and Sung-Hoon Park, "EU-Korea Cultural Cooperation in Audio-visual Industry: Current Situation and the Role of 'Protocol on Cultural Cooperation' in Future Cooperation," Korean Journal of EU Studies, Vol.18, No.1 (2013), pp.99-100. [in Korean]
14. Yoon, *op. cit.,* p.293.
15. Ministry of Culture, Sports and Tourism(MCST), Press releases, 6 March 2017; 9 April 2018; 9 December 2020; 16 December 2021.
16. European Commission, "Cultural cooperation between the EU and the Republic of Korea discussed in Seoul", 3 June 2019, https://culture.ec.europa.eu/news/cultural-cooperation-between-the-eu-and-the-republic-of-korea-discussed-in-seoul (accessed 11/Sep/2023)
17. In case more than two countries participated together in one event, each country is individually counted.
18. Korea Communications Commission, "Report on Broadcasting Industry 2022," 2022, p.146. [in Korean]
19. Korean Film Council, "KoBiz," https://www.kobiz.or.kr/new/kor/02_overseas/production/productionCaseList.jsp# (accessed 03/Sep/2023) [in Korean]
20. Su-kyeong Yoo, "Snowpiercer, Coming Back Again on Netflix," 11 May 2020, *Hankook Ilbo,* https://www.hankookilbo.com/News/Read/202005111582725293 (Accessed 21/Sep/2023) [in Korean]
21. For the detailed discussion on EUNIC, see Yoon(2023a).

22. Arts Council Korea, Press release, 4 May 2022, https://www.arko.or.kr/board/view/4057?cid=1804523 (accessed 09/Sep/2023)

Reciprocal Perceptions on Korea and the EU

HAN JEONGHUN

Introduction

The modern European encounter with South Korea (herein Korea) dates back to 1948, when Korea established a diplomatic relationship with France, Germany, and Italy. Although the first historical encounter was made earlier when the Korean Empire opened its border to foreign countries through the Treaty of Ganghwa (1876) and the Treaty of Jemulpo (1882), the interactions between Korea and Europe have been strongly limited as Korea became a colony of Japan in 1905. It is thus only after Korea was liberated from the Japanese colony in 1945 and established a modern republic political system that Korea actively sought diplomatic relations with European countries.

Specifically, for the European Union (herein EU), Korea set up a diplomatic relationship in 1963 and reached a 'Framework Agreement for Trade and Cooperation between Korea, on the one hand, and the European Community and its member states, on the other hand, in 1996. In addition, the relationship has been strengthened with the revision of the Framework and the signing of the Korea-EU FTA in 2010. As of 2023, with the launch of the Korea-EU digital partnership in 2022, the interactions between two political systems encompass a wide range of areas, including trade, diplomacy, culture, education, etc. Considering the long history of encounters, it is natural to assume that the two political systems have fostered mutual understanding, cooperation, and friendship. However, unlike active studies covering the macro-level trends of deepening cooperation in the fields of economy and security (Dent 1998, Kim 2008; Jun. 2013; Marx et al. 2014; Ramon and Klingler-Vidra 2019), there has been little systematic analysis of individual perceptions on how the public on both continents understands each other.

The aim of this chapter is to lay the empirical groundwork for studying public perceptions in both the EU and Korea toward the partner system by exploring at the individual level certain distinct features of mutual comprehension between the EU and Korea. In so doing, it relies on data from two pieces of a recent public survey carried out in 2022 by the Jean Monnet EU Centre at Seoul National University, with sponsorship from the Embassy of the Republic of Korea to the Kingdom of Belgium and the EU and a permanent mission to the North Atlantic Treaty Organization. The surveys were designed to gauge contemporary public perceptions of counterparts in both political systems, namely the EU and Korea, after 60 years of diplomatic relations. Specifically, concerning the EU, one survey focuses on the public in fourmember states: France, Germany, Italy, and Belgium. The selection of these countries stems from budgetary constraints for the public survey, but it can offer valuable insights into how public perceptions in long-standing EU member states have evolved with regard to Korea, as these four countries have been EU member states since its inception. The other survey targets the Koreans' perceptions on the EU and the relations between the EU and Korea.

Methodologically, with varying techniques of measuring attitudes across history and professions, scholars have believed that there is not necessarily one optimal way to achieve the goal of accuracy. This chapter is not an exception. Recognizing the constraints of using survey data to assess individual attitudes, I acknowledge that this data-driven exploration of individual attitudes towards the partner system will have significant limitations when it comes to drawing conclusions and making broad generalizations. With only the small number of items in the survey questions, this study may only partially describe the current understanding of the partner system between the EU and Korea. Nonetheless, given the lack of studies on how the public in both systems understands each other after long periods of cooperation, this research may provide an empirical foundation for following research on the topic.

This chapter is organized as follows. I will begin by addressing the theoretical concern regarding how to characterize individual attitudes toward the partner system. Subsequently, I will delve into the functional theory of attitude formation, empirically examining the four aspects of attitudes. This will involve an exploration of four dimensions of attitude formation: adjustment, ego-defense, value expression, and knowledge. Lastly, a conclusion will follow.

Functional Theory of Attitude Formation

Egaly and Chaiken (1993, 1) define attitudes as a psychological tendency that is expressed by evaluating a particular entity with some degree of favor or disfavor. While attitudes are not a simple production that is ripe for measurement, they, as complex cognitive processes (Krosnick et al. 2018, 63), manifest themselves in many different shapes. Accordingly, a variety of models for dealing with attitude formation and change have been developed since the early 1920s. According to McGuire (1969), there are four basic theoretical approaches: informational process, consistency, social judgement, and function. While they are considered to be more complementary than competitive (Locander and Spivey 1978, 576), the functional approach to understanding attitudes has come to be a dominant tool by furnishing a more comprehensive framework for taking into account the complexities of attitude formation (Katz 1966, 159). It differs from the others in its emphasis on understanding the motivational underpinnings of the attitude itself, as the other approaches put heavy emphasis on individuals' belief structures and see how they craft attitude change. In this regard, it helps us to provide a consistent description of individuals' attitude formation toward an object to the extent that we can validly measure the motivational underpinnings.

This chapter, focusing on the functional theory of attitude formation, examines four motivational underpinnings suggested by Katz (1960, 1966): adjustment, ego-defense, value expression, and knowledge. First, the adjustment function of attitudes arises through the activation of needs and changes through the maximization of external rewards and the minimization of punishment. Attitudes serving this function can be seen as either positive toward the means of reaching a desired goal, or negative toward objects or behaviors that are unpleasant. The survey question concerning this motivation is "As an overall point of view, please tell me how positive or negative you feel about the following countries (EU for Koreans and South Korea for EU citizens)?"

Second, the origin and dynamics of the ego-defensive function is to protect against internal conflicts and external dangers. If a threat is posed, an attitude serving the ego-defense function can arise. I use, to measure this motivation, two survey questions, "From the EU(Korea)'s perspective, how important is it in your opinion that the EU establishes a close partnership for international affairs with South Korea(EU)?" and "From the EU(Korea)'s perspective, how much cooperation, do you think, has been advanced between the EU and South Korea in the following policy areas?"

Third, attitude serving value expression function underlies the dynamics of maintaining self-identity or enhancing favorable self-image. It can be built on the salience of cues associated with values. To measure this attitude, I provide respondents with ten candidate cues, including modern, peaceful, efficient, strong, united, trustworthy, multicultural, aggressive, hypocritical, and arrogant, and ask them to choose three cues among them.

Lastly, attitude serving knowledge function originates from the need for understanding or for meaningful cognitive organization for consistency and clarity. This attitude may arise when individuals can reinstate the old problem itself or the cues associated with it. For the development of general knowledge toward the partner system, I use the question, "Please tell me, from a general point of view, how much do you think you know about South Korea (EU)?", for both the EU and Korean citizens. In addition, to examine the robustness of this knowledge, I use three specific questions concerning South Korea for EU citizens and the EU for Korean citizens and develop a new measure of individual knowledge of the counterpart by summing the answers. Next, by empirically examining the four motivational underpinnings for the attitude formation, I will show which motivations in the relations between the EU and South Korea have relatively developed stronger than the others.

Empirical Evaluation of Motivational Underpinnings

Adjustment Function

According to Katz (1960), attitudes that serve an adjustment function can be cultivated through the use of rewards and punishments, particularly as they pertain to an individual's attitudes and goals. When it comes to the attitude formation toward a political system, numerous factors within the system may operate to influence individuals' attitude formation. While we do not enumerate these factors here, we posit that both positive and negative attitudes toward a political system stem from the accumulation of distinct individual experience on those factors. Thus, if an individual has encountered or observed more rewards stemming from the political system, he/she is more likely to harbor a positive evaluation of it, and vice versa.

〈Figure 1〉 Adjustment Function (positive vs. negative)

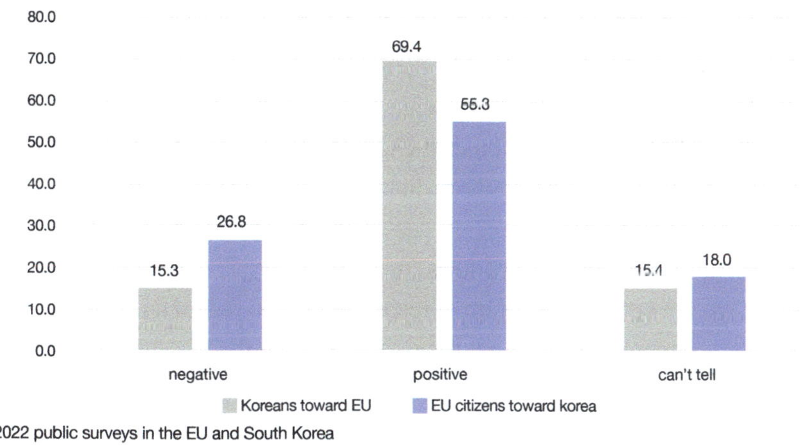

Source: 2022 public surveys in the EU and South Korea

Figure 1 illustrates that both EU citizens and Koreans have developed positive attitudes toward the partner system. A significant majority of individuals in both systems express positive evaluations of the partner system. Notably, Koreans exhibit notably stronger positive attitudes toward the EU in comparison to EU citizens. Specifically, 69.4% of Koreans hold a positive view of the EU, while 55.3% of EU citizens share the same perspective. Meanwhile, the proportion of EU citizens who hold a negative evaluation of Korea exceeds that of Koreans by 10%. This suggests that while both EU citizens and Koreans have experienced more rewards than punishments from the partner system during their long periods of cooperation, Koreans have garnered greater benefits from their interactions with the EU than EU citizens. In this context, we can posit that the enduring relationship between these two systems has played a significant role in fostering positive adjustments in the attitudes of citizens toward the partner system.

Ego-defense Function

Katz (1960, 172) claims that ego defense mechanisms are known to be the mechanisms by which an individual protects his/her ego from his/her own unacceptable impulses. In the context of attitudes towards the partner system, the origin and nature of the ego defense mechanisms encompass the strategies employed by individuals to avoid confronting the external realities and perils that the world presents. In this regard, two types of defense mechanisms are evident: one involving denial and complete avoidance, and the other encompassing rationalization, projection, and displacement (Miller and Swanson 1960).

To explore the attitude formation through the lens of the ego-defense function in the context of individuals' understanding of the partner system, we posit that individuals' attitudes may vary depending on whether they deny or embrace a partnership with the other system. Specifically, an individual may choose to avoid a partnership if he/she perceives that there will be a potential threat or danger from it. This, in turn, makes him/her deny the importance of the partnership.

However, it is important to note that a political system itself may not directly trigger the ego-defense mechanism because the influence of a political system on individuals is not intrinsically interconnected. In this context, ego-defense mechanisms are more inclined to affect individuals' attitudes toward the political system through the projection or rationalization of their attitudes based on the views of other members of their community. Therefore, even though it is less plausible to assume a direct link between individuals' attitudes toward the partner system and ego defense function, we can still assess the influence of the ego defense mechanism by evaluating whether individuals consider the partnership to be important or not.

In Figure 2, we present the proportion of respondents who regard a partnership with the other system as either 'important' or 'not important'. In both the EU and Korea, a substantial majority of respondents concur that the partnership between the EU and Korea holds importance. While a slightly larger percentage of EU citizens than Koreans indicate that the

〈Figure 2〉 Ego-defense Function (not important vs. important)

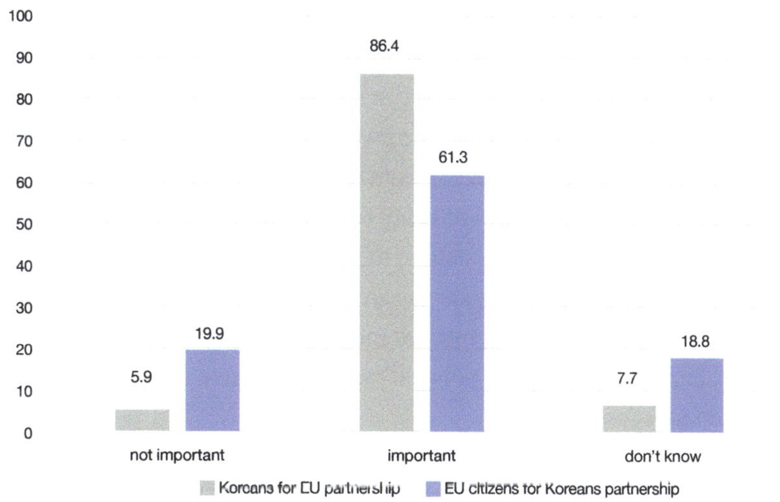

Source: 2022 public surveys in the EU and South Korea

partnership is not important, the influence of attitude formation based on negating the partnership appears to be less pronounced. This suggests that the attitudes of both EU citizens and Koreans are not strongly influenced by the avoidance type of ego-defense mechanism, but are instead shaped by the rationalization type of ego-defense mechanism. Furthermore, as a considerable number of citizens in both the EU and Korea consider the partnership to be important, either the rationalization or the projection mechanism tends to guide the formation of attitudes toward the partner system in that direction.

Value-expression Function

In contrast to the functions of adjustment and ego defense, which serve to prevent individuals from revealing their true nature, the value expression function is a motivation for giving positive expression to individuals' central values (Katz 1960). In certain contexts, the value expression function can lead individuals to maintain their self-identity or enhance their favorable self-image by either embracing a sense of group identity or freeing themselves from some degree of suppression of their expressive behavior. An example of this value-expressive attitude is found in political behavior, such as voting (Katz 1960, 188).

To measure the attitudes that serve the value expression function, we propose that choosing a particular image of a political system from a set of potential candidate images is a symbolic expression of an individual's values. Individuals may select an image of a political system that aligns with their own values. For instance, a EU citizen may choose the image of 'peaceful' for Korea as a means of expressing their value for peace when confronted with the task of selecting an image of a divided Korea. This understanding of the value expression function is also reasonable, as value expressive attitudes may shift when an individual's central belief system is disrupted by some degree of dissatisfaction with their self-concept (Katz 1960). In other words, the choice of a political system's image can vary depending on changes in an individual's value orientation. In the given example, the EU citizen may opt for an alternative image of Korea when his/her orientation towards pacifism undergoes a change.

With this understanding in mind, we believe that if the images chosen by each individual converge into a dominant representation, the value expression function may contribute to the formation of a consistent attitude towards the political system among individuals. Conversely, if the images recognized by each individual vary widely and are dispersed into several images, attitudes towards the political system may have a weaker connection to the value-expression function.

In Figure 3, we analyze the distribution of individuals who associate the partner system with the top six images out of the candidate images provided by the survey. To begin with, in the case of Koreans, depicted by a solid line, approximately 34.4% of respondents identify the EU image as 'united'. While this falls short of a majority, the other five images are only chosen by less than 10% of respondents each. From this perspective, it can be asserted that there exists a relatively strong link among Koreans between the EU image as 'united' and their understanding of the EU. Consequently, it can be inferred that a significant proportion of Koreans channel their value expression into the 'united' EU image when they are faced with the task of selecting an image representing the EU.

〈Figure 3〉 Value-expression Function (top 6 images)

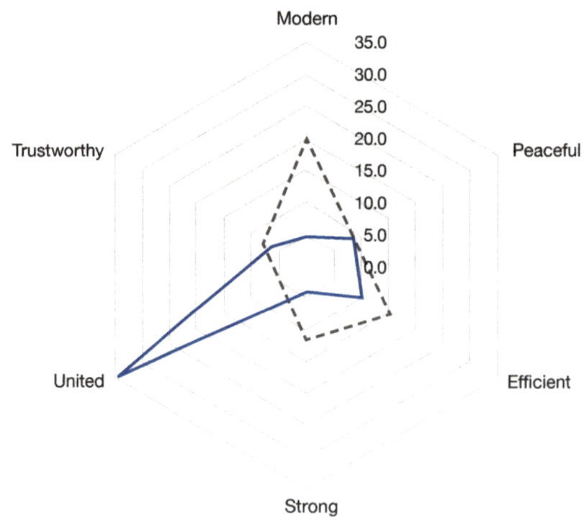

Source: 2022 public surveys in the EU and South Korea

Moving on, for the EU citizens, represented by a dotted line, discerning a dominant image proves to be challenging. The foremost image associated with Korea is 'modern', selected by 19.7% of respondents. Simultaneously, 'efficient' and 'strong', are chosen by 15.1% and 11.5% of respondents, respectively. This suggests that there is no strong link between the Korean image and their understanding of Korea. Consequently, it appears that the value expression serves as a weak motivational function in shaping EU citizens' attitudes toward Korea.

Knowledge Function

Attitudes serving knowledge function become evident when an individual seeks knowledge to imbue meaning into an otherwise disordered and chaotic universe (Katz 1960). The role of knowledge acquisition appears particularly crucial in shaping attitudes towards two political systems: the EU and Korea. Referred to as a multi-level governance (Marks 1993), understaninding the EU itself is often shrouded as it is derived from the understanding of the member states or regional communities. If a Korean's attitudes towards the EU are primarily influenced by their knowledge of the lower levels of governance, his/her attitudes towards the EU may lack a solid foundation. Likewise, when an EU citizen forms attitudes towards Korea, he/she may frequently grapple with the complexities arising from the South-North division of Korea. Despite South Korea's increased presence in the international arena following its accession to the UN in 1991, and the OECD in 1993, attitudes towards South Korea may remain flawed if they are not based on accurate information about the country but are instead shaped by the knowledge of North Korea.

To examine the attitudes serving knowledge function, this chapter undertakes an analysis of two facets of individuals' knowledge concerning the partner system: one from a general perspective and the other from a compositive perspective. Knowledge from a general perspective is measured by the question, 'Please tell me, from a general point of view, how much do you think you know about South Korea (EU)?'. Knowledge from the composite perspective is gauged by employing three specific questions related to the respective political system. In the case of Korea, we assess the extent of EU citizens' knowledge by tallying the number of accurate responses to the following three statements: 'In 2020, the South Korean share of trade in goods with the EU was greater than that of India', 'The South-North Korean division was terminated by the 2020 summit meeting', and 'Both South Korean and China use the same language'. For Korean's depth of knowledge regarding the EU, we reuse the first question and introduce two additional statements: 'Greece exited from the EU membership after the Brexit', and 'The official language of the EU is English'.

Figure 4 first presents the distribution of the general knowledge level regarding the partner system, with EU citizens' knowledge of Korea represented by diagonal lines. On one hand, the majority of the population in both the EU and Korea expressed their limitations

〈Figure 4〉 Knowledge Function (general knowledge)

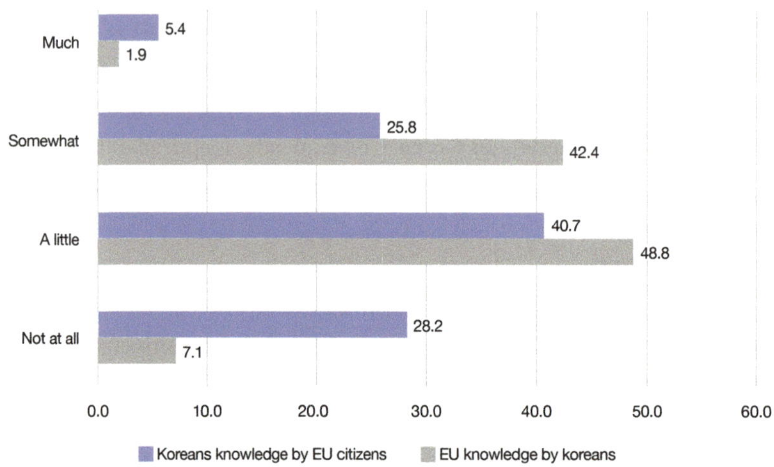

Source: 2022 public surveys in the EU and South Korea

〈Figure 5〉 Knowledge Function (composite knowledge)

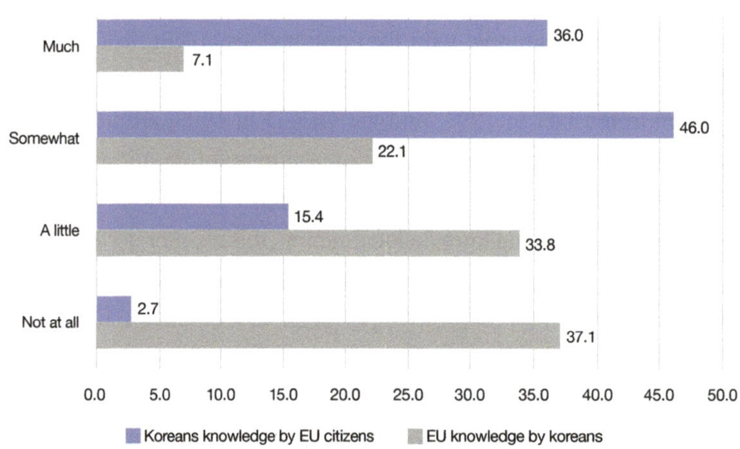

Source: 2022 public surveys in the EU and South Korea

in possessing sufficient information about the partner system. Specifically, 68.9% of the EU citizens categorized themselves as having 'a little' or 'no' knowledge of Korea. Similarly, 55.9% of Koreans admitted to having 'a little' or 'no' knowledge of the EU. On the other hand, Koeans exhibit comparatively stonger knowledge of the partner system than EU citizens. About 44% of Koreans claim to possess 'some' or 'much' knowledge of the EU, whereas only 31% of EU citizens report a similar level of knowledge regarding Korea. In this regard, it can be argued that while Koreans are more inclined to base their attitudes towards the EU on their knowledge of the EU, the influence of knowledge on attitude formation for both political systems appears to be relatively weak.

Figure 5 once again underscores the limited influence of knowledge on attitude formation within both political systems. When we assess the degree of knowledge regarding the partner system by tallying the correct responses to specific items for each system, a striking reversal occurs between EU citizens and Koreans. Among EU citizens, when confronted with three questions gauging their knowledge of Korea, 82% of respondents provide correct answers to at least two questions. In contrast, among Koreans, fewer than 30% provide correct answers to more than two questions on the EU-specific items. We acknowledge that this significant difference in the degree of knowledge between respondents' self-reported knowledge and their accuracy in responding to specific items for each system may be attributed to variations in the difficulty levels of the items used. Nonetheless, the inconsistent findings regarding the knowledge function imply that individual attitudes towards the partner system are not strongly linked with their knowledge of the partner system in both societies.

Conclusion

This chapter examines the current state of public perceptions in both the EU and Korea regarding the partner system. It accomplishes this by delving into specific facets of mutual comprehension at the individual level. In particular, this analysis applies the functional theory of attitude formation, encompassing four motivational dimensions: adjustment, ego-defense, value-expression, and knowledge. The basis for this exploration is recent public surveys conducted in four member states of the EU and Korea.

Some intriguing findings emerge with respect to these four dimensions. Firstly, over the course of their longstanding cooperation, individuals in both systems appear to experience more rewards than punishment, leading to the development of positive attitudes toward the partner system. Secondly, both the EU citizens and Koreans demonstrate a proclivity toward a positive projection of the partner system, with a significant majority considering the partnership important. However, thirdly, a convegence in the internalized values and their expression through the selection of a specific image of the partner system is not apparent. While Koreans exhibit a certain degree of value expression by choosing the 'united' image of the EU, EU citizens' value expressions do not coalesce into a specific image of Korea. Fourthly, the majority of individuals in both the EU and Korea struggle to establish their attitudes toward the partner system based on their knowledge of it. Koreans are more likely to claim a decent knowledge of the EU for attitude formation, but their actual knowledge, as measured by specific issues concerning the EU, remains weak. In contrast, EU citizens tend to underestimate their knowledge of Korea while providing more accurate answers to specific issues concerning Korea.

As of 2023, it is undeniable that the relationships between the EU and Korea in many areas have advanced significantly in numerous areas over the past six decades through the attainment of crucial formal agreements. In addition, these two regions are furthering their collaborative efforts to extend their amicable relationship to emerging global issues, including those related to the environment and digital technology. However, this optimistic assessment wasn't apparent just a decade ago, when Spanish young students ranked Korea lower in importance to Spain compared to China, Japan, India, Taiwan, and even ASEAN (Insua 2014). Prolonged cooperation at the systemic level did not automatically translate into enhanced mutual understanding.

Nontheless, the findings presented in this chapter confirm that rapid changes are occurring in both regions as they celebrate the 60th anniversary of their diplomatic relationship. While the internal mechanisms responsible for attitude formation may require more time, external factors seem to positively influence individuals' attitudes in each system, prompting adjustments and ego-defense mechanisms. We expect that this change may advance further and eventually make both the value expressive function and the knowledge function significantly contribute to the formation of clear attitudes toward the partner system. To realize this expectation, it is imperative to place greater emphasis on enhancing the internalization of positive attitudes toward the partner system in future relations between the EU and Korea.

Bibliography

Allport, Gordon. 193. The Handbook of Social Psychology.

Dent, Christopher M. 1998. "Economic Exchange and Diplomacy in Korea-EU Relations" Korea Observer 29(2):401-425.

Eagly, A. H., and S. Chaiken. 1993. The Psychology of Attitudes. Harcourt Brace Jovanovich College Publishers.

Herek, Gergory M. 1987. "Can functions be measured? A new perspective on the functional approach to attitudes" Social Psychology Quaterly 50(4):285-303.

Locander, W. B., and W. A. Spivey. 1978. "A Functional Approach to Attitude Measurement" Journal of Marketing Research 15(4):576-587.

McGuire, W. J. 1969. "The nature of attitudes and attitude change," In G. Lindsay and G. Aronson (eds.) The Handbook of Social Psychology. Vol 3. Addison-Wesley publishing company, pp. 136-314

Katz, Daniel. 1960. "The Functional Approach to the Study of Attitudes" The Public Opinion Quarterly 24(2):163-204.

Katz, Daniel. 1966. "Attitude formation and Public Opinion" The ANNALS of the American Academy of Political and Social Science 36791):150-162.

Kim, Heung Chong. 2008. "An Evaluation of the Ongoing Negotiation of the Korea-EU FTA: A Comparison with the Korea-US FTA" Korean Journal of EU Studies 1391):1-32

Krosnick, Jon A., Charles M. Judd, and Bernd Wittenbrink. 2018. "The Measurement of Attitudes" In Dolores Albarracin and Blair T. Johnson (eds.) The Handbook of Attitudes, VOL 1. Basic Principles. Routledge. Pp.21-76.

Jun, Hae-Won. 2013. Cooperation in the Field of International Peace and Security: A Newcomer to the Legal Framework for EU-Korea Relations.Edinbrugh University Press.

Marks, G. 1993. "Structural Policy and Multilevel Governance in the EC" In A. Cafruny and G. Rosenthal (eds.) The State of the European Community (volume 2). Harlow: Longman.

Marx, Axel, Jan Wouters, Woosik Moon, Yeongseop Rhee, and Sunhee Park. 2014. "EU-Korea Relations in a Changing World Project: Main Results and Recommendations" Asia Europe Journal 12(3):231-250.

Miller, Daniel R., and Guy E. Swanson. 1960. Inner Conflict and Defense. New York: Holt. pp.194-288.

Ramon, Pacheco Pardo, Robyn Klingler-Vidra. 2019. "The Entrepreneural Developmental State: What is the Perceived Impact of South Korea's Creative Economy Action Plan on Entrepreneurial Activity?" Asian Studies Review 43(2):313-331.

Strengthening Mutual Alliances

Science Research and Innovation Cooperation between the European Union and the Republic of Korea

TOMASZ WIERZBOWSKI

Advancing Science Research and Innovation (SR&I) Collaboration Between the European Union and the Republic of Korea

Korea[1] stands as a prominent member among the European Union's eleven strategically aligned partners, with these connections forged through a series of accords that encompass economic, political, and security collaboration, alongside their joint engagement in the domains of science, technology, and innovation. The foundation of the EU-Korea Strategic Partnership is fortified by three distinct pillars, namely an augmented Partnership and Cooperation Agreement, a comprehensive Free Trade Agreement, and a Framework Participation Agreement pertaining to EU crisis management operations. This institutional framework is also augmented by the Digital Partnership launched in November 2022[2] and Green Partnership established and announced in May 2023[3] during the last top summit between the leaders.

Recognizing the pivotal role of Science, Technology, and Innovation (STI) in shaping the global economic and political landscape, the EU and Korea entered into the Agreement on Scientific and Technological Cooperation in 2007. Preceding this accord was the Agreement for Cooperation between Euratom and Korea in the field of fusion energy research, which had been operational since 2006. The institutional platform for their collaborative STI efforts is embodied in the EU-Korea Joint Science & Technology Cooperation Committee (JSTCC), which convenes biennially.

The scheduled 7th JSTCC meeting for spring 2020 was regrettably postponed due to the outbreak of the COVID-19 pandemic and was eventually held in Seoul on February 14,

2022. The event was co-chaired by Mr. Jean-Eric Paquet, Director-General of the Directorate General for Research and Innovation of the European Commission, and Mr. Yong Hongtaek, Vice Minister of Science and ICT of Korea. This meeting, conducted in a hybrid format, attracted high-ranking Korean officials from the Ministry of Science and ICT (MSIT), representatives from Korean Research Centers, Science Counsellors from EU Member States, and EU officials. Consequently, as an outcome of the 7th JSTCC, both the European Union and Korea delineated five paramount areas for their collaborative focus: Information and Communication Technology (ICT), Health/Biotechnology, Climate Change, Emerging Future Technology, Research Hub, and Human Capital Development. These strategic domains underscore the commitment of both parties to harnessing the potential of STI to address contemporary global challenges.

To bolster collaborative efforts, the EURAXESS - Researchers in Motion initiative was inaugurated in May 2018. EURAXESS, a pan-European initiative backed by the EU Commission, is dedicated to providing information and assistance to professional researchers. With the endorsement of the EU, Member States, and associated countries, this program facilitates the mobility and professional advancement of researchers while simultaneously fostering scientific cooperation between Europe and Korea.

EU Policies in Science and Research

Despite comprising a mere 7% of the global population, Europe allocates 20% of the worldwide resources towards research and development (R&D), generates a third of the world's top-tier scientific publications, and maintains a preeminent standing in industrial domains, notably pharmaceuticals, chemicals, mechanical engineering, and fashion. Additionally, research and innovation have played pivotal roles in the efforts to combat the COVID-19 pandemic.

Starting in 1984, the EU has structured and executed its research and technological development endeavors through a sequence of Framework Programmes for Research and Technological Development, commonly referred to as Framework Programmes, FP, or FP1 through FP9.

The Framework Programmes have served as the primary financial mechanisms for the EU's backing of research and development across a wide spectrum of scientific domains. These FPs are initially presented by the European Commission and subsequently approved by the member states within the Council and the European Parliament. The funding allocation for the FPs commenced at 3.8 billion Euros during FP1 and has witnessed consistent growth, culminating at 95.5 billion Euros for Horizon Europe (FP9), the most recent iteration.[4]

Horizon Europe

Horizon Europe, also known as FP9, endeavors to enhance the goals set forth in the preceding framework, Horizon 2020, by providing extensive support for scientific and research initiatives across EU member states, Associated Countries and, in a different scope to non-associated Third Countries. Although thc implementation was hindered by the COVID-19 pandemic, a political consensus was achieved in November 2020 among the European Parliament, EU Member States within the Council, and the Commission, concerning the future long-term budget of the European Union, including the NextGenerationEU initiative. A total of 95.5 billion Euros were allocated to Horizon Europe, encompassing 5.4 billion Euros from NextGenerationEU, aimed at promoting recovery from the pandemic's impact, and an additional infusion of 4.5 billion Euros to further bolster the program.

Horizon Europe Structure

The intricate funding framework of Horizon Europe adheres to the established structure of previous Framework Programs and is based on three fundamental pillars: Excellent Science; Global Challenges and European Industrial Competitiveness; and Innovative Europe.

〈Figure 1〉 Structure of Horizon Europe

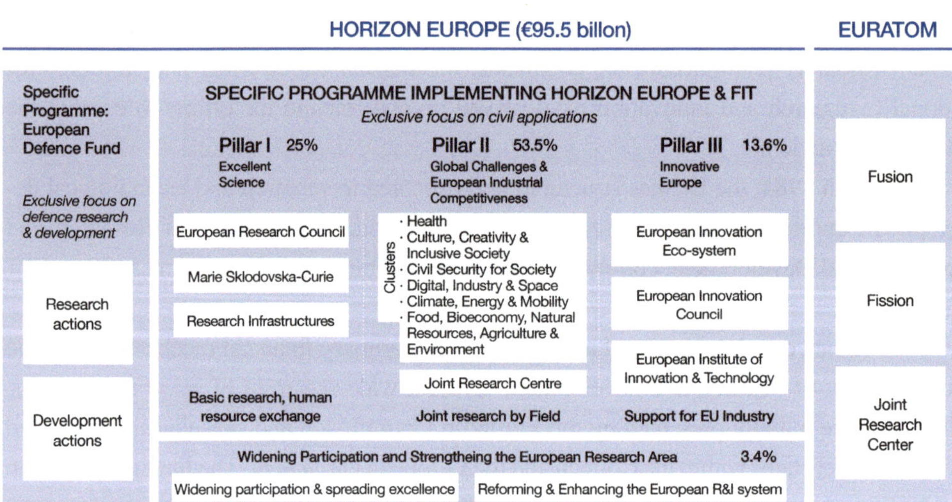

· The European Institute of Innovation & Technology (EIT) is not part of the Specific Programme

Pillar I

The Excellent Science pillar is tailored to individual researchers through provisions such as fellowships, knowledge exchanges, and research initiatives devised and spearheaded by researchers themselves (bottom-up approach to research activities). This pillar encompasses the European Research Council, the Marie-Skłodowska-Curie Actions, and Research Infrastructures programs.

The European Research Council (ERC) is specifically designed to lend support to the most outstanding and inventive researchers, empowering them to explore new frontiers and avenues within any scientific discipline, whether it pertains to the physical sciences, engineering, life sciences, social sciences, or humanities. Importantly, the ERC adopts an investigator-driven approach, eschewing any prioritization of specific research domains. Researchers themselves proffer project proposals, which often span interdisciplinary boundaries, engage with nascent fields, and employ novel and unconventional approaches to invigorate scientific excellence across Europe. The ERC dispenses long-term grants to individual researchers, regardless of nationality or age, provided they intend to execute their research undertakings within a European host organization (within the European Research Area). The singular assessment criterion is excellence. Under the aegis of Horizon Europe, the ERC boasts a substantial budget exceeding 16 billion Euros for the period extending from 2021 to 2027.[5]

Marie Skłodowska-Curie Actions (MSCA) represents a research fellowship initiative that provides support to researchers from Ph.D. programs for graduate students to postdoctoral fellowships for Ph.D., irrespective of their age or geographic origin. The important change under Horizon Europe in comparison to previous FPs is that currently a Ph.D. holder can apply for MSCA within 8 years of obtaining ones doctoral degree. This program is inclusive of researchers spanning the entire spectrum of scientific domains, encompassing engineering, mathematics, life sciences, social sciences, and humanities. Moreover, MSCA not only extends its support to individual researchers, who can submit their own original proposals using a bottom-up approach, but it also promotes collaboration between academia and industry. It offers innovative training opportunities for academic staff, with the goal of enhancing their employability and career advancement (MSCA Staff Exchanges). The MSCA program is open to all areas of research and innovation, spanning from fundamental research to the application of research outcomes in the market and innovation services. It endeavors to address the challenges encountered by researchers by providing them with attractive working conditions and facilitating transitions between academic and alternative professional environments. Under Horizon 2020, the MSCA was allocated a budget of 6.2 billion Euros, representing 8% of the overall budget. For Horizon Europe, the budget will experience a 6.4% increase, resulting in a funding allocation of 6.6 billion Euros.[6]

The domain of Research Infrastructures (RI) pertains to how research communities will actively participate in advancing the objectives of the five mission areas outlined in the context of Horizon Europe. The collaborative efforts of the European Strategy Forum on Research Infrastructures (ESFRI) have yielded comprehensive plans for 55 European RIs, with 37 of these initiatives having already been established, spanning the entire spectrum of scientific disciplines. The collective investments mobilized for these endeavors have approached nearly 20 million Euros.[7]

During the period between 2014 and 2020, the allocation for funding new, world-class research infrastructures amounted to 2.48 billion Euros. As Horizon Europe unfolds, an estimated budget of 2.4 billion Euros is expected to be designated for this purpose, underscoring the continued commitment to enhancing research infrastructure within the European scientific landscape.[8]

Pillar II

The second Pillar within the Horizon Europe framework, known as "Global Challenges & Industrial Competitiveness," serves as a facilitator and advocate for research endeavors that specifically target the most urgent societal concerns, which are organized into six thematic areas through a top-down approach:

1. Health: the objective is to enhance our comprehension and control of health and diseases, encompassing cross-border health threats and infections. This aims to provide inclusive, patient-centric healthcare and equal access throughout Europe. Additionally, it seeks to promote a sustainable digital transformation of healthcare systems in Europe, emphasizing secure and ethical cross-border data management;

2. Culture: anticipated to elevate research in the realms of democratic governance and citizen engagement, as well as the preservation of cultural heritage and the promotion of creativity;

3. Civil Security for Society: Aiming to advance research pertaining to the safeguarding of citizens through police, civil protection, customs, law enforcement agencies, and the regulations governing them, while also directing research efforts toward cybersecurity and data protection:

4. Digital, Industry, and Space: Geared towards facilitating the shift to a climate-neutral, circular, and ecologically sustainable industrial sector, and supporting research in clean, secure, and accessible transportation and mobility;

5. Climate, Energy, and Mobility: Intended to foster research in the areas of clean energy production and storage, intelligent, clean, and secure transportation, strategies for reducing greenhouse gas emissions, and alignment with the European Green Deal to attain climate neutrality by 2050;

6. Food, Bioeconomy, Natural Resources, Agriculture, and the Environment aim to sup-

port research that reduces the negative environmental impact of food production and agriculture, addresses biodiversity preservation and ecosystem restoration, and focuses on resource management and the safety of food and water.[9]

The multifaceted societal challenges addressed by the six thematic areas often exhibit intricacy, necessitating the application of interdisciplinary methodologies. In this context, the involvement of social sciences and humanities is of paramount significance and should be integrated into the research framework. Furthermore, the second pillar of Horizon Europe seeks to enhance Europe's competitiveness in technologies encompassed by these six thematic areas. The issuance of calls for proposals is a systematic and ongoing process throughout the duration of the Horizon Europe program.

As a component of this pillar, the Joint Research Centre fulfills a vital role by providing European Union policymakers with impartial scientific evidence and technical assistance. Additionally, through the research and training program of the European Atomic Energy Community, the Joint Research Center extends support to the European Union's endeavors aimed at reinforcing nuclear safety, ensuring the safety of its citizens, and safeguarding against radiation hazards.

Approximately 48 billion Euros, constituting 52.7% of the total Horizon Europe budget, have been earmarked to finance research initiatives falling within the purview of the second pillar. Notably, Cluster 4 (Digital, Industry, and Space) and Cluster 5 (Climate, Energy, and Mobility) have secured the lion's share of this budget, amounting to 13.4 billion Euros.

Pillar III

The restructuring of the Horizon framework saw a consolidation of programs previously falling under the purview of the third pillar of Horizon 2020, known as "Societal Challenges," into the second pillar of Horizon Europe. Simultaneously, a novel pillar named "Innovative Europe" was conceived with the primary objective of positioning Europe as a front-runner in fostering innovative solutions that generate new markets. To support this ambition, the European Innovation Council (EIC) was established to provide backing to audacious, high risk, and high impact concepts aimed at translating scientific accomplishments into new enterprises and amplifying the presence of transformative innovators, often referred to as "game-changers."

The creation of the European Innovation Council was spurred by the observation that Europe, despite being a leading contributor to research in artificial intelligence, significantly lags behind other regions in terms of effectively commercializing these advancements. Notably, Europe claims a mere 8% of the world's billion-dollar start-ups, colloquially known as "unicorns," with the United States hosting nearly half of this elite category, and Asia commanding a substantial share as well. The principal aspiration of the European Innovation Council (EIC) is to position Europe at the forefront of the forthcoming wave of pioneering and disruptive innovations that engender new markets, particularly by amalgamating physical and digital products and services grounded in novel technological business models. This endeavor aims to elevate Europe's appeal on the global stage for the development, investment, and expansion of exceptionally innovative technologies and enterprises. It is worth noting that the EIC is open to a broad spectrum of innovative concepts across various domains. Applications are welcome at any time, and the EIC caters to two distinct categories of innovators: (i) Pathfinders, which encompass researchers with groundbreaking ideas for the next generation of technological advancements, and (ii) Accelerators, encompassing start-ups, small and medium-sized enterprises (SMEs), or entrepreneurs equipped with a business plan for nurturing and expanding a high-risk yet high-potential enterprise.[10]

Within this pillar, one can also find the initiatives of the European Innovation Ecosystems (EIE) and the European Institute of Innovation and Technology (EIT). The European Innovation Ecosystems (EIE) is geared toward fostering the interconnection of innovation ecosystems throughout Europe, facilitating access to complementary expertise, infrastructure, and market opportunities. These ecosystems can collaborate, forming coalitions aimed at addressing and surmounting various societal challenges. The primary focus of EIE lies in the cultivation and fortification of innovation ecosystems, alongside the facilitation of collaboration among diverse ecosystems.[11]

The European Institute of Innovation and Technology (EIT), an autonomous entity within the European Union, situated in Budapest, Hungary, is dedicated to enhancing Europe's capacity for innovation. EIT actively encourages and reinforces synergistic relationships and cooperation among businesses, educational institutions, and research entities, fostering dynamic cross-border partnerships. EIT empowers innovators and entrepreneurs to translate their most promising concepts into tangible products, services, employment opportunities, and economic expansion.[12]

The Innovative Europe pillar has been allocated a total budget of 11.8 billion Euros.

The de facto Pillar IV

The inherent fourth element within the framework of Horizon Europe, which pertains to "Widening Participation and Reinforcing the European Research Area (ERA)," serves as a mechanism for extending assistance to European Union Member States with the aim of enhancing their domestic research and innovation capabilities. Notably, there is a distinct emphasis on incentivizing and supporting nations that exhibit comparatively lower levels of performance in the realms of research and innovation.

Launched in 2020 as part of the Lisbon Strategy, the ERA was conceived to address the fragmentation of the European Union's research and innovation landscape, which then featured the coexistence of national research and innovation systems alongside EU-level funding initiatives. The ERA's core objective is to establish a unified scientific and technological domain within the EU, facilitating the creation of a single market for research and innovation that promotes the unhindered mobility of researchers, the dissemination of scientific knowledge, innovation, and the bolstering of European industrial competitiveness. This endeavor entails reshaping the European research landscape to foster increased cross-border collaboration, continent-wide competition, the development of critical mass and coordination, and the enhancement of national research policies and systems.

During the past two decades, considerable advancements have been achieved in eliminating geographical impediments to the mobility of researchers and mitigating the disunity in research careers across Europe. These developments have been propelled by the implementation of the European Charter for Researchers and a Code of Conduct[13] for the Recruitment of Researchers, which have already been embraced by 1,242 institutions. Furthermore, the EURAXESS[14] initiative plays a pivotal role in facilitating the mobility and career progression of researchers by furnishing them with comprehensive information and support services.

The ERA has improved accessibility to open, freely available, and reusable scientific data through the Open Science initiative,[15] as well as the recently inaugurated European Open Science Cloud (EOSC). The EOSC has established a dedicated cloud environment for research data in Europe, facilitating enhanced scientific endeavors by fostering open and collaborative knowledge dissemination.

The Strategy of Horizon Europe

The European Commission underscores the significance of strategic planning that retains adaptability, enabling rapid responses to unforeseen crises, such as the emergence of the COVID-19 pandemic. The implementation strategy of Horizon Europe prioritizes the optimization of outcomes, the enhancement of transparency, streamlining processes, promoting harmonization with other EU financial initiatives, and facilitating accessibility through digital modernization and outreach efforts.

The strategic planning process primarily centers on Horizon Europe's second pillar, "Global Challenges and European Industrial Competitiveness," while also encompassing pertinent activities in the first pillar, "Excellent Science," the third pillar, "Innovative Europe," and the "Widening Participation and Strengthening the European Research Area" component. This inaugural strategic plan for Horizon Europe establishes the guiding principles for research and innovation investments from 2021 to 2024, aligning with the Commission's political priorities, particularly focusing on achieving a climate-neutral, digitally advanced Europe that benefits its citizens. The aim is to facilitate a harmonious interconnection between EU policy priorities, program initiatives, and the research and innovation projects funded through Horizon Europe, thereby catalyzing investments where they are most impactful. Horizon Europe has been robustly supporting the dual transitions toward a sustainable, environmentally friendly, and digitally transformative recovery. In response to the imperatives arising from the COVID-19 pandemic, the level of investment has significantly risen compared to the previous programming period, commensurate with the Commission's ambitious objectives in these domains. The formulation of this plan involved the collaborative contributions of EU Member States, European Economic Area (EEA) countries, the European Parliament, as well as engaged stakeholders and concerned citizens.[16]

Missions under Horizon Europe

A novel facet within this Framework Programme is termed "Missions." A Mission area is delineated as an amalgamation of initiatives aimed at attaining an ambitious, motivating, and quantifiable objective within a predefined timeframe, one that will leave a lasting imprint on science, technology, society, and the general populace, transcending isolated endeavors.[17] Missions that bear relevance to a diverse array of stakeholders and the public should be executed employing a bottom-up approach.

Five mission areas have been established with the objective of tackling some of the most formidable global challenges. Each mission is facilitated by a dedicated mission board and assembly, entrusted with the task of delineating, structuring, and executing the particular missions scheduled for launch under Horizon Europe in 2021. These five missions are designed to confront five distinct societal challenges, as elaborated below.

〈Figure 2〉 Horizon Europe Missions

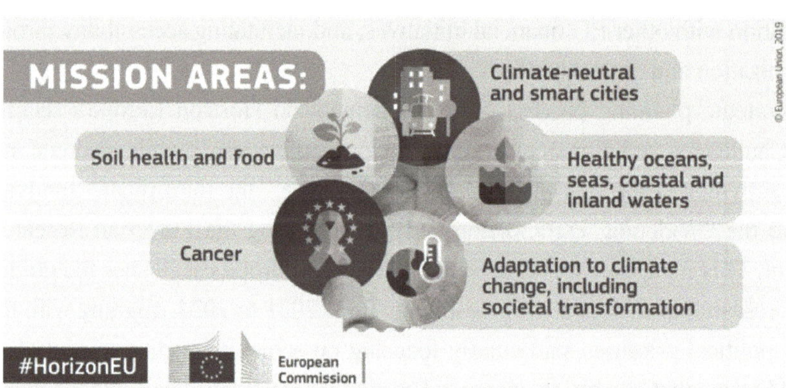

Source: EU Commission

Adaptation to climate change, including societal transformation

This mission is primarily dedicated to addressing the rapidly escalating global warming phenomenon. The profound implications of the COVID-19 crisis underscore the critical need for readiness in facing unforeseen circumstances. The mission's core focus lies in the formulation of strategies and readiness measures to mitigate the repercussions of climate change, with a paramount objective of safeguarding both human lives and valuable assets. Moreover, it encompasses the dimensions of behavioral modifications and social dynamics, extending its reach to communities not typically regarded as stakeholders, thus fostering a process of societal transformation. The mission seizes the challenge posed by climate change as an avenue to enhance social resilience and elevate living standards.

By the year 2030, the mission is tasked with several overarching objectives: firstly, to prepare Europe to effectively confront climate-induced disruptions and facilitate the understanding, preparation, and management of climate-related risks among all citizens, communities, and regions. Secondly, it endeavors to expedite the transition towards a climate-resilient future by actively supporting 200 European communities and regions in the co-creation of a comprehensive vision, innovative pathways, and the development of solutions that adhere to sustainable planetary boundaries. Thirdly, the mission aims to instill profound resilience by scaling up practical solutions that stimulate societal transformations through the implementation of 100 deep-seated resilience demonstrations across various European communities and regions, with a pronounced emphasis on cross-border collaboration and cohesion.[18]

Cancer

The Cancer Mission is designed to comprehensively address the entire spectrum of cancer control, spanning from risk factor prevention to support for survivors and end-of-life care, encompassing all age groups and cancer types. This includes rare and less-understood cancers, those affecting children, adolescents, young adults, and the elderly, as well as cancers afflicting socially or economically disadvantaged families and individuals residing in remote areas across all Member States. While the Mission lays out research and innovation directions and objectives, it will also generate empirical evidence to identify constraints on effective policy and support actions in the battle against cancer. In this context, the actions of this Mission will significantly contribute to the realization of Europe's Beating Cancer Plan, with reciprocal opportunities for complementarity between the Cancer Plan and the Cancer

Mission.

By the year 2030, this Mission is projected to not only save in excess of 3 million lives but also extend the lifespan and enhance the quality of life for patients. Its objectives encompass the attainment of a comprehensive comprehension of cancer, the prevention of avoidable cases, the optimization of diagnostic and treatment procedures, the enhancement of the quality of life for all individuals affected by cancer, and the assurance of equitable access to these advancements throughout Europe.[19]

Soil health and food

The mission's objective is to achieve a 75% improvement in soil health by the year 2030, enabling soils to fulfill crucial ecosystem functions such as food and biomass production, biodiversity support, water storage and regulation, and climate change mitigation. This target represents a doubling of the current baseline for healthy soils. This interim report outlines the strategic vision and plan for attaining this goal, which involves a combination of research and innovation, training, advisory services, as well as the practical demonstration of effective soil management techniques through the use of "Living labs" (on-ground experimental and innovative sites) and "Lighthouses" (showcase locations for best practices).

Living Labs can be comprehensively defined as dynamic, user-centered, open innovation ecosystems that are founded on a structured approach to co-creating solutions with end-users, thereby seamlessly integrating research and innovation activities within real-life communities and settings. The core principle driving Living Labs is the prioritization of citizens, who are placed at the epicenter of the innovation process. In effect, Living Labs serve as catalysts for innovation by enhancing the adaptability and appropriateness of emerging information and communication technology (ICT) concepts and solutions. This adaptability stems from their unique capability to align novel ICT advancements with the specific requirements, aspirations, and cultural nuances of local contexts, ensuring the harnessing of the full creative potential inherent within these communities. By positioning the citizen as a central contributor and influencer in the innovation journey, Living Labs not only foster a participatory approach but also stimulate context-driven advancements, leading to more relevant and effective solutions for diverse locales and cultures. Consequently, Living Labs facilitate a symbiotic relationship between technological innovation and local ingenuity, resulting in a more refined and contextually fitting landscape for the development and deployment of ICT solutions.

The Helsinki Manifesto, which emerged during the Finnish EU Presidency[20] in November 2006, initially brought to attention the concept of Living Labs as an initial stride toward ushering in "a transformative European Research and Development (R&D) and Innovation System, signifying a substantial shift in the fundamental approach to innovation processes as a whole."

"Lighthouses" refer to individual locations, such as farms or parks, specifically designated for the exhibition of exemplary practices. These sites serve as platforms for the presentation and mutual knowledge exchange among practitioners. At lighthouse sites, best practices are not only implemented but also actively assessed, with the aim of offering inspiration to fellow practitioners seeking to transition towards sustainable land management strategies. Furthermore, these sites foster collaboration between researchers and land managers, facilitating a responsive research approach that aligns with the practical requirements and challenges encountered in the field.[21]

For the mission to attain its objectives, it will necessitate enhancements in the surveillance of soil health and the factors impacting it, the mobilization of financial investments, and the advocacy for policy reforms. This mission represents a collective enterprise involving a spectrum of stakeholders, encompassing researchers, policymakers, and engaged citizens. Its overarching purpose is to propel Europe towards the attainment of sustainable land and soil management, thereby contributing substantively to the broader societal transition towards environmental sustainability.[22]

Climate-neutral and smart cities

The Mission stands as a proactive advocate, supporter, and a dynamic showcase for the advancement of 100 European cities in their comprehensive transition towards achieving climate neutrality by the pivotal year 2030. This ambitious undertaking aspires to evolve these cities into focal points of experimentation and innovation, effectively serving as pioneers in the ongoing drive for sustainability that will reverberate across urban landscapes far and wide.

Cities represent a crucible where multifaceted decarbonization strategies for energy, transportation, architectural structures, and even the realms of industry and agriculture converge and interconnect. The exigency of addressing the climate crisis compels us to confront this challenge at the urban epicenter, engaging not only with the inhabitants as political actors within the governance structure but also as integral stakeholders who wield multiple roles—ranging from users and producers to consumers and property owners.

Guided by a multi-tiered, co-creative process encapsulated within a tailor-made Climate City Contract adapted to the distinctive realities of each urban locale, the Mission stands firmly grounded in the overarching strategic vision of the European Green Deal. This vision is emblematic of the continent's collective resolve to attain climate neutrality by the seminal year 2050, signifying a unified commitment to a sustainable, greener future for Europe and the world at large.[23]

Healthy oceans, seas, coastal, and inland waters

The overarching objective of this Mission is to effectuate a comprehensive rejuvenation of the European ocean and freshwater bodies, with a target set for the year 2030. This endeavor is underpinned by a multifaceted approach aimed at diminishing the manifold anthropogenic pressures exerted on marine and freshwater environments, rehabilitating ecosystems that have been adversely impacted, and instituting sustainable methodologies for harnessing the vital resources and services that these environments proffer.

The safeguarding and revitalization of our oceanic and freshwater domains stand as quintessential challenges of our era, given that the very existence of humanity, along with the broader spectrum of life on our planet, is fundamentally intertwined with the health and sustainability of these aquatic systems. These aquatic realms, comprising both the ocean and freshwater bodies, harbor pivotal solutions that can address our imperatives for nourishment, energy generation, and medical advancements, thereby underpinning the well-being of our citizenry.

Nevertheless, for a protracted duration, societies have regrettably underestimated the existential and environmental significance of these domains, often neglecting to accord them the requisite attention. Such neglect carries the potential to transform the ocean and freshwater environments from fountains of life into existential threats to our way of life. The imperative at hand is to redress this oversight, recognizing that the ocean and waters are not merely resources but indispensable cornerstones of our sustainable future, warranting our immediate focus and concerted efforts to ensure their enduring vitality.[24]

Korea and Framework Programmes

The Korean participation across Framework Programs increased from 2 in FP4, 8 in FP5, and 67 in FP7 to 128 in H2020, while the EU contribution across programs significantly rose from 1,94 million under FP 7 to 2,44 million euros under the Horizon 2020.

Key Figures for Horizon 2020 (FP9)[25]

A total of 496 applications originating from Korea were tendered within the Horizon 2020 program, constituting approximately 0.05% of the global proposal submissions received. Among these applications, 391 met the eligibility criteria[26], representing about 0.14% of the overall proposal count. Consequently, this led to the successful participation of 128 distinct organizations in Horizon 2020 projects, constituting a modest 0.28% of the total number of project participants. These organizations were signatories to 130 grant agreements[27], which collectively garnered a net EU contribution of 2.44 million Euros. This monetary figure corresponds to approximately 1.17% of the total net EU contributions[28] directed to other countries.

In Korea, 61.9 % of all applications were submitted by research-performing organizations, 20.2% by higher or secondary education institutions, 15% by public bodies (excl. research and education), 0.8% came from the private sector. The top organization was the International Vaccine Institute with a 1.42 million-euro net EU contribution, followed by Seoul National University (492,550 euros), and the Korea Technology Finance Corporation (208,130 euros). Regarding participation[29], the Electronics and Telecommunications Research Institute (20) was at the top of the list, followed by the Seoul National University (17) and Korea Advanced Institute of Science and Technology (13).

A total of 26 Korean entities or individuals actively are engaged in projects funded through the Marie Skłodowska-Curie Actions within the Horizon 2020 framework, accounting for 0.08% of the cumulative participation from other countries. Among these 26 entities, 22 were unique participants in the Marie Skłodowska-Curie Actions, representing 0.26% of the total participation from other nations.

Within the context of the European Innovation Council (EIC) scheme, 3 Korean legal entities secured funding, constituting 0.07% share of the overall participation from other countries. Additionally, it's noteworthy that 15 experts from Korea were instrumental in the evaluation process of Horizon 2020 projects. The proportion of Korean proposals evaluated per expert stood at 37.67%, which exactly met the average evaluation load for experts from other countries.

Collaboration with other countries

Korea's principal European collaborative partners within the Horizon 2020 program include France with 20 149 collaborative links, Spain with 17 834 collaborative links, and Germany with 17 142 collaborative links. Korean institutions actively engaged in several substantial Horizon 2020 initiatives, which encompassed projects such as "Internet of Food and Farm 2020,"[30] characterized by a net EU contribution of 29.999 million euros, "5G Co-operative & Connected Automated Mobility on X-border Corridors,"[31] which secured a net EU contribution of 21.410 million euros, and "Automated Driving Progressed by Internet Of Things,"[32] attaining a net EU contribution of 19.924 million euros. Notably, these three projects were funded under Horizon 2020's Industrial Leadership pillar II, with a thematic focus on Information and Communication Technologies.

In the realm of Societal Challenges, Korea also made significant contributions to projects like "Advancing Novel and Promising TB Vaccine Candidates for Discovery to Preclinical and Early Clinical Development,"[33] with a net EU contribution of 18.200 million euros, and "Integrated Arctic Observation System,"[34] which garnered a net EU contribution of 15.490 million euros. These endeavors reflect Korea's active involvement and commitment to addressing critical societal challenges within the framework of Horizon 2020.

A total of 45 SMEs were involved under Horizon 2020 with 42 of them as unique participants. 10 SMEs from Korea submitted their applications,[35] representing approximately 2.04% of the overall participation from the country. Among these, 7 Korean SMEs actively participated in Horizon 2020 projects, which accounted for a notable 6.09% of Korea's total involvement in the program. Furthermore, it's worth highlighting that 2 Korean SMEs were recipients of funding under the EIC.

Outside Framework Programmes

An additional initiative established to advance and foster collaboration in the domain of science and technology between the EU and non-EU countries, including Korea, is the European Union Partnership Instrument (PI). As a direct consequence of the cooperation between the EU Delegation to Korea and diverse stakeholders such as governmental bodies, enterprises, civil society entities, educational institutions, and individuals, a multitude of PI projects have materialized within the Korean context.

These key PI projects encompass a wide array of subject matter, encompassing areas such as environmental sustainability and the green economy (e.g., The EU Gateway Program), climate change mitigation (e.g., Implementation of an Emissions Trading System in Korea), as well as trade facilitation (e.g., Implementation of ILO Fundamental Convention 111 in Korea and the EU Member States). Moreover, an ongoing PI initiative, known as the EU-ROK Policy Dialogue Support Facility, has been designed with the specific purpose of bolstering the strategic partnership between the EU and Korea. This is achieved through the provision of pertinent information and expertise from a cadre of experts spanning various domains, thereby assisting decision-makers in their policy endeavors. Another PI, EU-Korea Green Partnership Action aimed at facilitating the implementation of the Paris Agreement and several multilateral environmental agreements is going to be launched at the beginning of 2024.

Korean entities actively participating in international R&D initiatives have the opportunity to access funding through a range of distinct programs, including EUREKA Network projects, Globalstars, Eurostars, and Clusters programs. EUREKA, which was initially instituted in 1985 through an agreement involving 18 countries and the European Commission, was primarily conceived to stimulate competitiveness and enhance market integration. A fundamental objective of this collaborative effort was to promote cross-border R&D cooperation.

Over the years, EUREKA has undergone substantial expansion, evolving into a cooperative consortium that now encompasses 48 countries, transcending geographical boundaries both within Europe and extending beyond its borders. These nations, united by shared aspirations and common objectives, facilitate the provision of national funding to organizations that choose to engage in R&D projects by participating in the various programs that EUREKA offers. This collective endeavor not only nurtures innovation but also promotes cross-border collaboration, thereby contributing to the broader advancement of research and development on a global scale.

Over time, initiatives such as EUREKA have been refined and customized to effectively bolster cross-border, industry-driven research and development endeavors. These programs have been meticulously structured to provide adaptability and responsiveness to international collaborators, as evidenced by the Network projects and Globalstars initiatives. Furthermore, they actively promote diverse consortia formation, which includes prominent corporations, as exemplified by the Clusters program.

EUREKA also facilitates the ascension of SMEs, enabling them to reach loftier objectives in R&D pursuits, as is the case with the Eurostars program. Additionally, these initiatives serve as catalysts for research and business ventures to explore new, uncharted markets, as underscored by the Innowwide program. Moreover, they play a pivotal role in steering companies toward embracing private investments, further reinforcing their readiness for such capital infusion. These concerted efforts collectively contribute to fostering innovation and augmenting the engagement of businesses in research and development activities on a global scale.[36]

What is ahead?

Beginning in 2018, the concept of connectivity has evolved into a fundamental pillar of the EU's Indo-Pacific Strategy. The concept of connectivity is intricate and multifaceted, encompassing various dimensions. However, from the EU's perspective, 'connectivity' predominantly revolves around the intricate networks that facilitate the convergence of individuals, regions, and prospects, with specific emphasis placed on enhancing connectivity in the realms of transportation, energy, digital infrastructure, and fostering people-to-people connections.[37]

In the Joint Communication titled "Connecting Europe and Asia – Building Blocks for an EU Strategy," the European Commission has made a dedicated commitment to further advancing initiatives like Erasmus+ and the Marie Skłodowska-Curie actions, along with associated reciprocal agreements. The primary objective of this commitment is to augment opportunities for educational and professional exchange and mobility within the Asian context.

The EU recognizes the increasingly significant economic, demographic, and political influence wielded by the Indo-Pacific region. This ascendancy positions the region as a pivotal actor in shaping the international order based on established rules and regulations and addressing global predicaments. Through the implementation of this novel strategy and the Global Gateway initiative, the EU seeks to make substantive contributions to the region's stability, security, affluence, and sustainable development. These efforts are consistently aligned with the fundamental principles of democracy, the rule of law, human rights, and adherence to international legal standards.

The EU's Strategy for Cooperation in the Indo-Pacific will pave the way for augmented collaboration in a spectrum of priority domains. These encompass initiatives aimed at promoting sustainable and inclusive prosperity, facilitating digital connectivity, supporting the transition to environmentally friendly practices, enhancing security and defense measures, addressing ocean governance issues, bolstering human security considerations, overseeing digital governance, and fostering strategic partnerships. Korea, being a like-minded strategic partner, is poised to play a pivotal role in co-executing this strategy, further amplifying bilateral collaboration with the EU.

During the 7th convened assembly of the EU-Korea Joint Science & Technology Cooperation Committee on February 14, 2022, Korean authorities formally presented a letter of intent, expressing Korea's earnest desire to initiate discussions regarding its prospective membership in the Horizon Europe program as an associated country. The process of negotiations to associate Korea was officially announced during the top-summit on May 22, 2023. Korea holds a position among the five third countries under consideration for associated status within the Horizon Europe program, alongside Australia, Canada, Japan, and Singapore with New Zealandalready associated. Such an association would entail a fundamental transformation in the manner in which Korean participants engage with Horizon Europe projects. Association with EU R&D initiatives extends nearly equivalent access and privileges to non-member nations, contingent upon a specified financial contribution.

By March 2022, several countries, including Albania, Georgia, Iceland, Israel, Moldova, Montenegro, North Macedonia, Norway, Serbia, and Turkey, had formalized their association with Horizon Europe. In September 2023, the UK joined the association, while Bosnia and Herzegovina, Kosovo, and Ukraine had signed agreements signaling their intention to do so. The extent to which Korea will attain association across all the various pillars of Horizon Europe remains uncertain. Nevertheless, most probably Korean academic and corporate entities stand to reap substantial benefits from this association, notably through the capacity to directly seek funding without the requirement to participate in consortiums led by entities from EU Member States under Pillar II of Horizon Europe.

Regardless of its association or non-association with Horizon Europe, Korea stands as a like-minded partner of the European Union, characterized by a shared set of values and aligned policy objectives. Among the most pivotal policy objectives that the EU and Korea mutually espouse is the ambition to achieve net-zero greenhouse gas emissions by 2050. This objective dovetails seamlessly with the EU's unwavering dedication to global climate action, in consonance with the stipulations of the Paris Agreement.

The blueprint for a climate-neutral EU was outlined by the European Commission in November 2018. This comprehensive vision encompasses nearly all facets of EU policies and aligns harmoniously with the Paris Agreement's overarching aim to cap the global temperature increase at levels substantially below 2°C, with a concerted pursuit to restrict it to a mere 1.5°C. As an integral component of the European Green Deal, the European Commission introduced the inaugural European Climate Law on March 4, 2020, which currently finds itself in the conclusive stages of negotiation among EU institutions.

This European Climate Law was officially published in the Official Journal on July 9, 2021, subsequently taking effect on July 29, 2021. This legislation not only transformed a political commitment into a binding legal obligation but also signifies an embodiment of the resolute dedication shared by the EU and like-minded partners such as Korea in the pursuit of sustainable and climate-conscious objectives.

In parallel fashion, the Korean government has officially introduced the 2050 Carbon Neutral Strategy, which entails a commitment to achieving a net-zero level of greenhouse gas (GHG) emissions by the year 2050. The administration under President Moon Jae-in has undertaken a resolute commitment to implement a robust national energy strategy designed to significantly curtail the reliance on fossil fuels and nuclear energy while concurrently promoting the widespread adoption of renewable energy sources.

This strategic plan is multifaceted in its goals, encompassing objectives such as employment generation, economic recuperation from the impacts of the COVID-19 pandemic, and a comprehensive agenda involving the renovation of public infrastructure, the establishment of urban green spaces, the enhancement of recycling practices, the creation of a foundation for emerging renewable energy technologies, and the formation of low-carbon energy industrial zones, all with the overarching objective of diminishing the nation's dependence on fossil fuels.[38]

Conclusions

Korea's engagement in the European Union's Framework Programmes, aimed at bolstering research and innovation, has historically been largely symbolic. However, this level of participation has incrementally increased with each successive edition of the EU's Framework Programme. The nature of this involvement is expected to undergo a significant transformation when Korea attains the status of an associated country within Horizon Europe. Such an association would enable Korean entities to directly access European funding opportunities, eliminating the requirement to participate in consortia led by European counterparts. In this arrangement, the Korean government would contribute to European funds in accordance with Korea's degree of involvement.

Both the EU and Korea have concurred on the prioritization of collaboration within five key thematic areas: Information and Communication Technology (ICT), Health and Biotechnology (Health/BIO), Climate Change, Emerging Future Technologies, Research Hub, and the development of human capital.

Within the domain of ICT, there have been two notable instances of collaboration through Joint Call projects in the years 2016 and 2018. These initiatives serve as illustrative examples of the evolving partnership between Korea and the EU in the realm of ICT.

Furthermore, Korea has introduced a pioneering endeavor known as the Digital New Deal Initiative, which represents an upgraded and comprehensive approach to integrate and enhance the nation's ICT policy. This initiative has gained prominence by proposing promising areas of focus for the third EU-Korea ICT Joint Calls scheduled for 2023. These fields include Beyond-5G/6G, Cloud-Edge/AI, Cybersecurity, and Quantum technologies, all of which reflect the dynamism and innovation inherent in contemporary ICT landscapes.

On the EU side, there is a reciprocal inclination towards strengthening the ICT collaboration with Korea. The EU has suggested that the EU-Korea consultation can be conducted within the overarching framework of the Digital Partnership. This underlines the EU's commitment to fostering closer ties in the realm of digital innovation and technology with

Korea, underscoring the potential for deeper cooperation and shared advancements in the ICT sector.

In the forthcoming domains of collaboration within the Health/Bio sector, a significant development occurred in February 2022, when Korea put forth a proposal for the development and dissemination of animal models relevant to COVID-19 infection. Simultaneously, the suggestion was made to engage in a cooperative effort involving the joint analysis and sharing of preclinical data pertinent to the COVID-19 infection.

From the European Union's perspective, there is a strong emphasis on the importance of international cooperation, particularly in the realm of research related to antibiotic resistance. The EU provided insights into the European One Health Antimicrobial (OH AMR) Partnership, underscoring its commitment to tackling antibiotic resistance comprehensively. Additionally, the EU expressed its optimism and desire for Korea to participate as a partner country within the OH AMR, highlighting the significance of Korea's potential contribution to this global effort.

Regarding matters related to climate change and emerging future technologies, the EU acknowledges and endorses the synergistic potential between Korea's legislative framework, the Carbon Neutrality and Green Growth Act for Climate Change (CNGGA), and the EU's own initiatives aimed at advancing the decarbonization of urban centers. These EU initiatives encompass the Horizon Europe Climate Neutral and Smart Cities Mission and the Urban Transitions Mission, which have been developed in collaboration with Mission Innovation.

Moreover, the prospect of synergies extends to Korea's CNGGA and two specific missions within the Mission Innovation framework, namely the Net-zero industries mission and the Integrated Biorefineries mission. This alignment is strengthened by recent pronouncements such as the "Carbon Neutrality Vision and Strategy for Industry and Energy," which outline ambitious objectives for attaining carbon neutrality in the industrial and energy sectors. It is within this context of shared objectives and ambitions that the potential for fruitful collaboration and mutual reinforcement between Korea and the EU becomes apparent.

The potential for collaboration with Korea in the realm of human capital development has been on the rise and is anticipated to continue expanding. This growth is notably attributed to initiatives such as the MSCA, which are designed to support the training, mobility, and career progression of researchers, as well as the establishment of high-quality doctoral programs. Within this context, the EU envisions substantial room for enhancing cooperation, with positive outcomes anticipated for both European and Korean institutions and researchers.

During the JSTCC meeting, the EU expressed its eagerness to facilitate follow-up activities through working-level videoconference meetings. These follow-up discussions would serve as a means to exchange information, strengthen collaborative ties, and further advance joint efforts. This proposal was warmly received and embraced by the Korean Ministry of Science and ICT, underscoring the shared commitment to fostering continued cooperation.

The EU and Korea have the potential to combine their efforts and shape a framework for collaborative research and innovation within the context of multilateral arrangements, notably within the G20, ASEM, and the UN Framework Convention on Climate Change. Both entities can be characterized as middle powers and are tasked with the challenge of navigating and proactively addressing pressing global issues within the contemporary international system, which is marked by a power struggle between the G2 nations and has experienced destabilization due to the recent Russian invasion of Ukraine and warfare in the Middle East. In this context, they are compelled to explore avenues for development and collectively seek resolutions to the most urgent global challenges.

Endnote

1. The Republic of Korea or South Korea.
2. Republic of Korea - European Union Digital Partnership | Shaping Europe's digital future (europa.eu) (accessed 04 May 20223)
3. EU and Republic of Korea - Green Partnership (europa.eu) (accessed 20 June 2023)
4. "Research Projects under Framework Programmes," accessed 7 February 2023, https://ec.europa.eu/eurostat/cros/content/research-projects-under-framework-programmes-0_en.
5. "European Research Council," accessed 12 March 2023, https://erc.europa.eu/.
6. "Science Business, HORIZON BLOG," accessed 13 March 2023, https://marie-sklodowska-curie-actions.ec.europa.eu/news/msca-announces-eu822-million-for-researchers-and-organisations-in-2021.; "European Commission, MSCA," accessed 13 March 2023, https://ec.europa.eu/research/mariecurieactions/msca-actions_en.
7. "European Strategy Forum on Research Infrastructures," accessed 13 March 2023, http://roadmap2018.esfri.eu/.
8. "Excellence Science Budget," accessed 20 March 2023, https://www.catalyze-group.com/fund/horizon-europe/budget/.
9. "Global challenges and European industrial competitiveness,", accessed 22 March 2023, https://www.vinnova.se/en/m/horisont-europa/industrial-competitiveness/.; "Horizon Europe – Global Challenges & European Industrial Competitiveness pillar," accessed 22 March 2022, https://www.catalyze-group.com/fund/horizon-europe/global-challenges-european-industrial-competitiveness/.
10. "The European Innovation Council," accessed 21 July 2023, https://eic.ec.europa.eu/about-european-innovation-council_en
11. "European Regions Research and Innovation," accessed 2 April 2023, https://errin.eu/RI-Policy/european-innovation-ecosystems-horizon-europe-pillar-iii.
12. "The European Institute of Innovation & Technology," accessed 2 April 2021, https://eit.europa.eu/.
13. "Researchers and a Code of Conduct," accessed 20 October 2023, https://ec.europa.eu/info/funding-tenders/opportunities/docs/2021-2027/horizon/guidance/european-code-of-conduct-for-research-integrity_horizon_en.pdf.
14. "EURAXESS," accessed February 6, 2021, https://euraxess.ec.europa.eu/.
15. "EU support for open access," accessed 20 October 2023 https://research-and-innovation.ec.europa.eu/strategy/strategy-2020-2024/our-digital-future/open-science_en.
16. "Horizon Europe Strategic Plan 2021-2024," accessed 20 October 2023, https://www.eeas.europa.eu/sites/default/files/horizon_europe_strategic_plan_2021-2024.pdf
17. "EU Missions in Horizon Europe," accessed 20 October 2023, https://research-and-innovation.ec.europa.eu/funding/funding-opportunities/funding-programmes-and-open-calls/horizon-europe/eu-missions-horizon-europe_en
18. Horizon Europe Mission "Adaptation to Climate Change" https://research-and-innovation.ec.europa.eu/funding/funding-opportunities/funding-programmes-and-open-calls/horizon-europe/eu-missions-horizon-europe/adaptation-climate-change_en accessed 20 October 2023
19. Horizon Europe Mission "Adaptation to Climate Change" https://research-and-innovation.ec.europa.eu/funding/funding-opportunities/funding-programmes-and-open-calls/horizon-europe/eu-missions-horizon-europe/eu-mission-cancer_en accessed 20 October 2023
20. "Heslinki Manifesto," accessed April 24, 2022, https://www.scribd.com/document/290101063/Helsinki-Manifesto-201106.
21. "EU Mission: A Soil Deal for Europe," accessed 24 April 2022, https://ec.europa.eu/info/research-and-inno-

vation/funding/funding-opportunities/funding-programmes-and-open-calls/horizon-europe/eu-missions-horizon-europe/soil-health-and-food_en.

22. "Caring for soil is caring for life, " accessed 7 February 7 2022, https://op.europa.eu/en/publication-detail/-/publication/32d5d312-b689-11ea-bb7a-01aa75ed71a1/language-en/format-PDF/source-150223991.
23. "100 climate-neutral cities by 2030 - by and for the citizens, " accessed February 7, 2021, https://op.europa.eu/en/publication-detail/-/publication/82f1df57-b68b-11ea-bb7a-01aa75ed71a1/language-en/format-PDF/source-150223552.
24. "European Commission, Directorate-General for Research and Innovation, *Regenerating our ocean and waters by 2030 : interim report of the mission board healthy oceans, seas, coastal and inland waters,* Publications Office, 2020," accessed 24 April 2022, https://op.europa.eu/en/publication-detail/-/publication/d0246783-b68a-11ea-bb7a-01aa75ed71a1/language-en/format-PDF/source-150222923.
25. "All data derived from Horizon 2020 Dashboard," accessed 05 November 2023, https://webgate.ec.europa.eu/dashboard/sense/app/a976d168-2023-41d8-acec-e77640154726/sheet/d23bba31-e385-4cc0-975e-a67059972142/state/analysis.
26. Proposals that have not failed at the eligibility admissibility step of the evaluation, that have not been withdrawn, that are not duplicates nor not fully evaluated yet.
27. Agreements signed, including suspended, terminated, and closed grant agreements.
28. Funding received by the project's participants after deduction of their linked third parties' funding.
29. The act of involvement of a legal entity in a grant agreement. A single participant can be involved in N grant agreements and therefore being counted as N participants.
30. "CORDIS," accessed 25 April 2022, https://cordis.europa.eu/project/id/731884.
31. "CORDIS," accessed 25 April 25 2022, https://cordis.europa.eu/project/id/825496.
32. "CORDIS," accessed 30 November 2023 https://cordis.europa.eu/project/id/731993.
33. Ibid.
34. Ibid.
35. Number of SMEs applying for H2020 grants through calls of proposals. One SME applying in N proposals in counted N times.
36. "EUREKA Network," accessed 6 March 2022, https://www.eurekanetwork.org/.
37. "Joint Communication: Connecting Europe and Asia – Building Blocks for an EU Strategy," accessed 24 April 2022, https://www.eeas.europa.eu/sites/default/files/joint_communication_-_connecting_europe_and_asia_-_building_blocks_for_an_eu_strategy_2018-09-19.pdf.
38. "South Korea's Moon targets carbon neutrality by 2050," accessed 6 March 2022, https://www.reuters.com/article/us-southkora-environment-greenewdeal-idUSKBN27D1DU.

Looking at 2083

Perspectives for EU-Korea Relations

MICHAEL REITERER

In 2023, the EU and the Republic of Korea celebrate the 60th anniversary of bilateral diplomatic relations. Three years earlier, it was the tenth anniversary of the Strategic Partnership in 2020,[1] and in 2021, the tenth anniversary of the EU-ROK Free Trade Agreement (FTA). Although all jubilees have delivered for both sides, we need a forward-looking agenda, drawing on the trust created by these successful agreements. Recent EU-policy papers, especially the EU's Indo-Pacific Strategy,[2] the Global Gateway,[3] the Strategic Compass,[4] and the proposed European Economic Security Strategy,[5] once adopted, provide a new framework for policy action in times of mounting geopolitical tensions.

Global Gateway is the new flagship of the EU's connectivity policy. This reflects the ever-increasing importance of infrastructure investment as a tool of global foreign and security policy. Importantly, Global Gateway also provides the funding for projects outlined in the Indo-Pacific Strategy thereby also replying to the Chinese Belt and Road Initiative (BRI).

The COVID-19 crisis did not hamper expanding and intensifying bilateral relations between the EU and South Korea, a good sign of maturity. The lesson to be learned is that "after" the pandemic is "before" the pandemic; thus, cooperation on health care issues and improving global health governance structures should remain high on the agenda of two partners who managed the COVID-19 pandemic relatively well.

There are mutual benefits to deepening cooperation on climate action and research to support the green and digital transition. The former still needs more engagement; the latter is a strength of Korea, one of the most connected societies globally.

Therefore, cooperation in cybersecurity is important in all its aspects. Cyber defense, protection of critical infrastructure, multilateral rule-making, and eventually a multilateral and more effective sanction regime to deter or stop identified aggressorsand hackers should be on the drawing board.

In sum, sustainable connectivity is vital for the green and digital transitions. This is also an important feature where the EU approach and China's Belt and Road project differ substantially. Thus, work on shared norms and standards has to go hand in hand with support for physical infrastructure. This will also help attract much-needed private capital to these projects. This is an area where both partners, the EU and South Korea, have much to offer; this opens the door for third country cooperation. ASEAN is the prime candidate as both are interested in fostering 'ASEAN centrality' and strengthening its resilience.

Future cooperation in implementing and intensifying the strategic partnership is best explored by taking challenges and policy designs, as evidenced in policy papers or declarations as a basis.

Therefore, this chapter focuses first on the commonalities of the respective Indo-Pacific strategies. It then examines the impact of geo-economics from the angle of security (re-, near-, and friend-shoring). Finally, South Korea's plan to become a global pivotal state provides the geo-political angle for this analysis.[6]

Common ground between the EU and South Korea in their respective Indo-Pacific strategies

Basic principles

Through its Indo-Pacific Strategy, the EU aims, in terms of politics, to promote, firstly,rules-based international order and, secondly, access to open markets and ensure a stable trading environment. The latter will entail further deepening and diversification of trade and investment ties. Collaboration is necessary and aims to accelerate the green and digital transitions and spur innovation and connectivity.

The EU seeks to promote an open and rules-based regional security architecture, including secure sea lanes of communication and Member States' enhanced naval presence in the Indo-Pacific. Capacity building for Indo-Pacific partners to ensure maritime security and tackle cybercrime is part of the program.

Unlike others, but in line with South Korea's ideas, the EU's approach to the region is one of cooperation, not confrontation. In the sense of inclusiveness, all partners wishing to cooperate with the EU are welcome, including China. This will not be a one-size-fits-all approach but will be individualized to meet the interests of partners who share principles, values, or mutual interests. The Global South is not forgotten. Africa is part of the EU's Indo-Pacific concept and the future recipient of €150 bn earmarked under the Global Gateway label.

The Strategies

South Korea's Indo-Pacific Strategy[7] dovetails well with the EU-Strategy allowing for the definition of a commonality of interests: health, physical and digital high-quality and secure connectivity, maritime security, and fostering resilience.[8]

Resilient value chains are essential for highly developed countries in general and necessary to spur the post-Covid recovery. The EU will work with its Indo-Pacific partners to reinforce value chains by strengthening and diversifying trade relations, implementing existing trade agreements, finalizing ongoing trade negotiations, and developing cooperation in strategic sectors, including to address strategic dependencies in supply chains. Concerning semiconductors, the EU will do so with partners such as the Republic of Korea, Taiwan, and Japan.

Trade: South Korea and the EU as major trading entities, depend on a stable, rules-based environment. Therefore, implementing and enforcing the existing comprehensive free trade agreement needs particular attention, including an update after more than a decade to include, for instance, e-commerce. The agreements of the EU with other partners, like Japan, Singapore, Vietnam, and New Zealand, contribute to strengthening stability as well as ongoing negotiations (Malaysia, the Philippines, India, and soon Thailand). Enlarging participation in the Economic Partnership Agreement (EPA) with the Pacific States[9] is another goal. EU investment protection agreements are on the negotiating agenda with Singapore, Vietnam, and India.

Green transition: The fifth meeting of the EU-Republic of Korea Working Group on Energy, Environment, and Climate took place on January 30, 2023, in Brussels, providing for an in-depth exchange of views on respective policies. The prospects for further upgrading bilateral cooperation in the areas covered by the Working Group, including through a potential EU-Republic of Korea Green Partnership[10] were discussed. The changed circumstances because of the energy crisis created by the war in Ukraine impact on finding the "right," e.g., available and doable policy-mix with 'renewable' energy resources like solar, wind, hydro, tidal, geo-thermal, biomass, and 'clean' energy. This caused a discussion as to the nature of nuclear energy, or hydrogen, which comes in different colors. In contrast to the previous administration, nuclear energy has been revived, domestically and as an important technology export industry. This could have a negative impact on advancing other green energy-related research, such as wind and solar.[11]

Fisheries: South Korea and the EU have affirmed their intention to cooperate closely in the 2018 Joint Statement to fight against Illegal, Unreported, and Unregulated (IUU) fishing.[12] This partnership will help implement the goals of the EU's Ocean Governance Strategy. The EU will continue to assist Indo-Pacific partners in achieving reforms in fisheries management and control systems, which Korea will support.

The EU and South Korea concluded a digital partnership agreement in November 2022.[13] This aims at fostering joint work on semiconductors, next-generation mobile networks, quantum and high-performance computing, cybersecurity, artificial intelligence, platforms, data, and skills.

Data protection regimes to ensure safe and free data flows, both within the region and beyond, including with the EU. This includes actively engaging with key partners to reach an "adequacy finding," where the conditions are met. In the region, Korea and Japan have become essential partners for the EU in creating the world's largest area of free and safe data flows between them and other partners. This is very much in the interest of companies and research institutions.

Research and innovation: South Korea has finally taken up the chance to become an associated partner in the Horizon Europe programme, offering more systemic joint Research and Innovation opportunities. Informal discussions have started with Australia, Japan, New Zealand, and Singapore to this end; this offers opportunities for joint regional cooperation.

Connectivity partnerships: The EU's first two "Connectivity Partners," Japan and India, are core Indo-Pacific partners, as is ASEAN, with which the EU agreed a joint Ministerial Declaration on Connectivity in December 2020. The EU will seek to collaborate with these partners on joint projects, while also seeking increased collaboration with other regional partners such as the Republic of Korea[14] and Australia, as well as with international actors such as the United States and Canada, both multilaterally (G7/G20) and bilaterally.

A comprehensive transport dialogue, including maritime security and maritime protection, is necessary. The EU has shown in concluding the world's first interregional comprehensive air transport agreement with ASEAN, that also highly technical issues can be solved. This is also relevant for South Korea, which is separated from the Eurasian landmass by North Korea, and therefore interested in strengthening its function as a regional air traffic hub in Incheon and beyond.

Enhancing Security Cooperation in and with Asia (ESIWA), which covers counterterrorism, cybersecurity, maritime security, and crisis management, aims at translating words into deeds. The pilot partners are India, Indonesia, Japan, the Republic of Korea, Singapore, and Vietnam, with EU military experts already operating in Indonesia and Vietnam. Framework Participation Agreements are in force with Australia, the Republic of Korea, New Zealand, and Vietnam.

According to our analysis, cybersecurity offers a huge potential for increased cooperation.[15] The EU is already implementing sanctions against cyber attackers. Joining a multilateral sanction regime would also increase deterrence for South Korea, which is cautious about acting alone. Having reached agreement on the adequacy of Korean legislation on personal data protection with the EU regulation (GDPR) is a useful base for further cooperation, whether on expanding protection to industrial data, working towards the resilience and security of production and supply chains, or preventing cyber theft. Fighting disinformation and misinformation is a particularly important area for like-minded partners who must defend democracy, elections, and human rights. Improving internet governance and fostering rule-setting in general, as well as fighting cybercrime—South Korea should accelerate adhering to the Convention on Cybercrime of the Council of Europe (Budapest Convention)[16]—are common endeavors.

Geoeconomics

After the heydays of globalization, there was a resurgence of industrial policy with the goal of increasing national security impacts on the economy. Because of emerging industries and technologies, the scope of nationally sensitive industries and technologies has grown in volume and importance. This is reflected in the increase of dual-use goods in exports, the increased use of tariffs, or limiting foreign inward direct investment, especially in what is classified as 'critical infrastructure and technologies'.

The 2023 Economic Security Strategy[17] proposed by the European Commission would enlarge the toolbox significantly. As an example, the Commission issued a Recommendation on critical technology areas for the EU's economic security for further risk assessment with Member States[18] on October 3, 2023, covering four sensitive areas: Advanced Semiconductors technologies, Artificial Intelligence technologies, Quantum technologies, and Biotechnologies. This raises questions about whether, as part of 'friend-shoring', sensitive technology should be controlled either by excluding others from the present state of art of technology or by limiting access to 'friends' only through restrictions on investment or export controls. Disadvantages for research and development and possible substitution effects, including loss of market share and economic costs, in general must be measured against the gains in increased security.

Impact on Global Value Chains: Danger of De-globalisation?

Changing supply chains and production basesalready started a few years ago and was accelerated during the COVID period. Thus, this is not as recent as it might appear. While economic security is important, there is much to lose when the legitimate interest of establishing more resilient supply, production, and global value chains were to endanger achievements gained by globalization in the past.

If global value chains are built on non-economic considerations, such as ideological blocks, on political affiliation (like-minded, antagonistic; democratic, autocratic; US-, China-led), they would become less global, with negative effects on efficiency and welfare. This danger also exists as a side effect of parallel value and production chains as de-risking, does not necessarily mean de-investing.

South Korea might be interested in supporting the EU to "intensify its efforts to reduce vulnerabilities" in technology, maritime and space security, innovation, and fighting disinformation, in particular vis-à-vis China. Furthermore, as neither the EU nor South Korea intend to de-invest in China, part of a policy of de-risking would be to put up in certain sensitive sectors parallel supply chains and production lines, necessitating additional investments in factories and infrastructure. Cooperating to realize such a policy in the most cost-effective and least disturbing manner could become an important part of bilateral cooperation.

De-globalization has its own disadvantages, and in many areas, it is either not possible or would produce high costs. Already, regionalization of global value chains will impact high-tech industry and emerging critical technologies such as high-end semiconductors.

Therefore, concepts like 're-shoring, friend-shoring, near-shoring, autonomy, and economic sovereignty' need to be handled very carefully to achieve the intended legitimate goals of supply and production line security and resilience.

Avoiding discrimination: revitalizing the WTO

These policies, or those aiming at greening economies, can lead to discriminatory measures even among partners, like the effects of Inflation Reduction Act in the US—to the detriment of foreign producers of electric cars and batteries, a measure South Korean and EU companies are affected by. This economic measure clearly reaches into the political sphere, impacting negatively on relationships between allies—this applies to South Korea and the EU.

To achieve the intended purpose, the appropriate tools need to be applied in a manner to avoid negative spillovers or collateral damages. This is of particular importance when economic measures are used for security purposes, which ultimately can lead to the weaponization of policies that leverage influence and advance economic or political interests. Preventing the spiralling out of control of conflicts through action and reaction, sanction, and countersanction is one of the main goals for which the WTO was built, providing a legal mechanism for dispute settlement or reaching a compromise as part of the procedure.

The bottom line for policymakers should remain, that economic autarky is not achievable, trade wars only produce losers, and there is no protection in protectionism. Therefore, the WTO should be revitalized in times of geo-economics where there is an urgent need for rules; otherwise, 'might is right' will creep in again.

These are areas where South Korea and the EU, implementing the strategic partnership, can work together as they share the same interests. Furthermore, South Korea has consistently shown interest in the WTO, filing candidates for the position of Director General twice.

Policy tools

There are, of course, costs associated with increasing the resilience of global value chains. The European Bank for Reconstruction and Development is quite clear in its warning: "Geo-political tensions and disruptions to global value chains have led policymakers to re-evaluate their approach to globalization. Many countries are considering regionalization and friend-shoring—trading primarily with countries sharing similar values—as a way of minimizing exposure to weaponization of trade and securing access to critical inputs. If followed through, this process has the potential to reverse the global economic integration of recent decades." In a working paper, it is concluded that "friend-shoring may lead to real GDP losses of up to 4.6% of global GDP. Thus, although friend-shoring may provide insurance against extreme disruptions and increase the security of the supply of vital inputs, it would come at a significant cost."[19]

Against this backdrop, sharing best practices to find solutions adapted to specific needs is mutually beneficial but not enough to orchestrate change for which joint action is needed.

In the case of the EU, the innovative step of EU-bonds was taken to provide financing to overcome the negative effects of the pandemic and to contribute to the costs of the digital and green transition. The name "Next Generation Europe"[20] stands for the content.

While this operation was successful, there is now the additional challenge of exploding energy and food prices, which contribute to a general rise in the price level and rocketing inflation fuelled by Russia's war of aggression.

While governments and the European Union struggle to take steps to cushion the costs through price caps and collective action as collective buyers, like during the pandemic, private households and companies will have to bear higher costs. The limit of public debt is already an issue as states try to compensate for or cushion the soaring costs of energy, for instance. This adds to inflation in turn, which states would like to reduce to the original 2% target. The risk of stagflation is looming.

Participation in Regional Trade Agreements

South Korea has experienced how FTAs work. As a result of the FTA,the volume of trade between the EU and South Korea increased over the past ten years by 70%.

Therefore, South Korea can play an important stabilizing role through its participation in the growing web of regional trade agreements in which the EU is not participating[21] in watching over the conformity of these regional agreements with multilateral trade rules. South Korea is already participating in the Regional Comprehensive Economic Partnership (RCEP) and is considering joining the Comprehensive and Progressive Agreement for

Trans-Pacific Part (CPTPP).

Thereby, South Korea can take on the important role of ensuring that these agreements are trade-creating, not protectionist, and not turned into instruments of economic statecraft. This also applies to the Indo-Pacific Economic Framework, which is designed to remain below the threshold of a free trade agreement without market access commitments and outside the scope of WTO rules applicable to FTAs.

Emerging critical technologies

Making sure to remain in the lead or to catch up in the race for new emerging technologies, including AI, the Internet of Things, and quantum computing, unites the EU and South Korea. This also contains three important security challenges: securing data; securing the supply of semi-conductors; and securing the supply of critical raw materials.

Data—new lifeline of the economy

Data is becoming the new lifeline of the economy, like oil in the past. South Korea has already joined hands with the EU to secure them through the General Data Protection Regulation (GDPR) for private use. Providing a secure digital environment, cybersecurity, and securing the ever-increasing critical infrastructure are common goals as previously mentioned.

The Importance of semi-conductors

High-end semi-conductors, their use, production, and trade dominate the security discussion—an area in which South Korea and the EU have much to gain or much to lose. A coordinated policy to handle the ever-growing trade of dual-use goods because of digitalization is necessary. They also impact heavily on the security situation as their production is concentrated in Taiwan, South Korea, and Japan. The possible "Taiwan contingency" renders this a major global concern. Diversifying investment is a valuable instrument; thus, South Korean companies are invited to invest not only in the United States but also in Europe, for security and commercial reasons.

Secure supply of rare earth and metals

The mentioned emerging new technologies need different raw materials in large amounts compared to previous technologies. These precious raw materials are—tellingly—called rare earth, rare metals, and rare minerals.

Securing their supply, lessening the dependence on the extraction, processing and recycling of critical raw materials, has emerged as another security problem, requiring anticipatory policymaking.[22] The strategic goal is to avoid slipping from one dependency, namely on producers of fossil oil and gas, to another dependency, on the providers of rare earth and metals. *"China produces 98% of Europe's supplies of rare earth, and Europe needs to de-risk this dependency" (von der Leyen).*

To this end, a Critical Raw Materials Act (CRMA) has been in place since 2022[23]; a Critical Raw Materials Board and a central purchasing agency should ensure that the EU acts collectively and manages to produce by 2030 at least 10% and process at least 40% of strategic materials needed for the green transition and realizing the 2050 goals. No third country should resource more than 60% of the EU's annual consumption of any raw material.[24] The proposal includes the formation of a Critical Raw Materials Club for all like-minded countries willing to strengthen global supply chains.[25]

In contrast, unilateral measures, like "Securing a Made in America Supply Chain for Critical Minerals"[26], should be avoided. Thus, President Biden and President of the European Commission, Ursula von der Leyen, agreed at their summit in Washington to "immediately begin negotiations on a targeted critical minerals agreement".[27]

This issue was also high on the agenda with Canada as part of the critical mineral alliance established in 2021. Canada is of particular interest as a producer of green hydrogen. This policy area, reducing dependencies, should also be on the bilateral agenda of the EU and South Korea as a function of the strategic partnership.

Security

As strategic partners, the EU and South Korea are committed to cooperating beyond the bilateral realm. Because of the all-out attack on the present system by Russia and the grumbling in the Global South about the focus of the Global North on itself and its problems, support for effective multilateralism and the rules-based international order is a necessity and not a nicety for Sunday talks.

It is necessary to clearly defend a rules-based system. Otherwise, 'might becomes right', a position which we thought having overcome after WWII. It is necessary to recognize, that there are problems world-wide, not only in Ukraine but also in Africa, Latin America, and the neighborhood of Korea, often part of the Sino-US tensions.

To a certain degree, the dilemma faced by South Korea is like the one faced by the EU - how to position itself between the US, a like-minded security partner, and its major economic partner China, which is increasingly perceived not only as a challenge but as a systemic rival posing a threat.

Concerning China, the EU and Korea seek a cooperative approach, as expressed in their respective Indo-Pacific strategies. There is a common interest in presenting the exercise of enhanced cooperation between like-minded partners as inclusive and not confrontational with China. The tryptic approach of the EU—partner, competitor, systemic rival—allows a realistic and functional approach with different shades of gray!

In terms of security, closer cooperation with NATO and the participation of the four Asian partners—Korea, Japan, Australia, and New Zealand—in the NATO summits in Madrid (2022) and Vilnius (2023), are clear signals of increased engagement, complementing the bilateral security partnership with the US.

Bilateral security cooperation: South Korea was the first Asian partner to conclude a Framework Participation Agreement facilitating Korea's contributions to EU CSDP missions and operations. While Korea contributes to EUNAVFOR Operation Atalanta, this could be stepped up in frequency, personnel, and beyond, e.g., in scope, through participation in additional military civilian CSDP missions. Preventive diplomacy lends itself to cooperation and is an emulation of a value-driven foreign policy the EU and South Korea want to pursue.[28]

The EU's security strategy is built on an operative approach with concrete timelines and timetables for implementation. It also highlights areas of cooperation with South Korea, referring to constructive security and defense consultations, security cooperation, joint naval exercises, and port calls. At the 19th meeting of the Joint Committee for EU-Korea Cooperation (March 10, 2023), "expanded EU-ROK security cooperation, including in maritime security, cybersecurity, counterterrorism and Foreign Information Manipulation and Interference" was pledged.[29]

The situation in and around North Korea remains not only of concern but mutates to 'high' concern: While for some time attention was concentrated on Taiwan, North Korea profited from this diverted attention to further develop missiles and submarines. An unprecedented series of tests, including ICBMS, demonstrates this leap forward for the international community. It also enshrined its nuclear capability in its constitution to ensure its "rights to existence" and to "deter war"[30]. In addition, the war in Ukraine offers the North Korean regime the chance to demonstrate its utility for its few friends in China and Russia. The latter is interested in buying the much-needed ammunition and might offer in exchange for further cooperation to develop missiles or nuclear warheads[31].

There is also a need to develop a new policy vis-à-vis North Korea in light of the crumbling international order and the fact that the previous policy obviously has not prevented North Korea from going nuclear in the first place and resisting denuclearization in the second place.

The idea that the DPRK would one day agree to give up its nuclear weapons in return for access to the world economy is inconceivable in the context of China and Russia opposing the West. To continue insisting that this must be the policy objective is akin to sticking one's head in the sand.

There is a need for a policy that seeks to slow and freeze the DPRK's nuclear and missile programmes and to build a context through deterrence where Pyongyang will never use or proliferate the weapons. It remains to be seen whether the Audacious Initiative can deliver on this goal, as it remains largely anchored in the traditional approach to North Korea. In support of a diplomatic solution, the EU expressed "support for the objectives set out in the ROK's Audacious Initiative aimed at achieving a denuclearized, peaceful, and prosperous Korean peninsula."[32]

While a nuclear weapon-free world remains the ideal, changing from denuclearization to talks about disarmament could turn out to be inevitable. The EU can be expected to continue its support for a diplomatic solution; a military one would produce only losers. Working on a regional security structure and insisting on the need for a rules-based system is part of this support.

Furthermore, nuclear proliferation—a danger linked to the present situation and facilitated by the loose talk of President Putin about a nuclear option (tactical nuclear weapons)—should be avoided: neither Korea nor Japan should go nuclear, whether directly or indirectly.

South Korea: A global or regional pivotal state?

The development of EU–South Korea relations in the last decade lays proof that South Korea's foreign policy has constantly internationalized. It recognizes that success and economic growth might create the obligation to shoulder more responsibility—a path the EU has also followed. It is, of course, understood that the divided Korean Peninsula, with the secretive and constantly becoming more aggressive Kim dynasty in the North, is the prime concern at the doorstep. However, a "global pivotal state" must look beyond the immediate neighborhood; the same applies to the EU, which is active beyond its immediate eastern and southern neighborhoods.

Maintaining or re-establishing the rule of law, strengthening the UN-based system and shouldering the duties and responsibilities that flow from it, contributing to furthering global governance, implementing the SDGs the prodigious Korean Ban Ki-moon established as the 8th UN-Secretary General, and taking on responsibility for the global commons, including climate change, are just a few illustrations of this responsibility.

The EU appreciated this endeavor in establishing with South Korea one of the only eleven strategic partnerships. In order to qualify, strategic partners should be able and willing to work with the EU beyond a strictly bilateral relationship, striving to achieve some of the goals mentioned above. This applies in particular to strategic partners of 'choice', e.g., those with a commonality of values, as opposed to strategic partners of 'necessity'[33], whom you have to deal with irrespective of fundamental disagreements, like in the case of China.

Already, candidate Yoon Suk-yeol[34] advocated a foreign policy of 'clarity and boldness', values-based with strengthened ties with the US, becoming more assertive and less tolerant vis-à-vis North Korea but also less hostile towards Japan.

The Korean Indo-Pacific Strategy advocated inclusivity, reciprocity, and trust in focusing on nine core areas,[35] to build a "regional order based on norms and rules", and the National Security Strategy circumscribed this policy. This is an approach comparable to the one of the EU with its mentioned package of policy papers, namely the Indo-Pacific Strategy, complemented by the operational Global Gateway. The Strategic Compass provides context based on an in-depth risk evaluation.

While clearly critical of previous liberal administrations, the vision to become a global pivotal state, allows the Yoon Administration to maintain some continuity with the previous administrations.

Given the dependency of South Korea on international exchanges, ranging from the export of goods and services to the import of energy and raw materials, 'global Korea' is a core interest of South Korea. This also includes, importantly, the relations with ASEAN built on the New Southern Policy of the previous Moon Administration. This is an area where the EU and Korea find common ground and have an interest in cooperating. 'ASEAN centrality' to which the EU and South Korea subscribe needs concrete actions to survive as a concept in providing the necessary platform for exchange and cooperation.

South Korea's cooperation with the US has become more pronounced, and the security cooperation has strengthened. The recognition of common threats has also brought an outreach to Japan, culminating in the Camp David meeting, the Spirit of Camp David[36], expressed in the Joint Statement and the Camp David Principles by the US, Japan, and South Korea. Anchoring the relationship with Japan deeper in the minds of the respective citizens to render it sustainable will be the foremost challenge for both governments. The EU has always advocated and supported a closer and frictionless relationship between the two neighboring countries, not least to render the region more secure and cooperation more efficient.

Concerning insecurity, the recent missile testing activism of North Korea, a looming further nuclear test, and the regime's warming up to Russia in supporting the war of aggression in Ukraine, intensify security concerns and demand measures to address them. Thus, the Korean air force and navy participated in international maneuvres, and South Korea got closer to NATO[37], as Asia Pacific Partners in the 'AP4' set-up with NATO.

Whether to deploy tactical US nuclear arms on Korean soil or go nuclear needs careful reflection, not only in terms of regional impact—non-proliferation—but also globally, where a value-based policy advocates a nuclear weapons-free world.

Furthermore, this security policy needs careful management vis-à-vis China. China has not hesitated in the past to make use of its economic statecraft to counter policies it disagreed with, like the positioning of the US-THAAD system on Korean territory. Trilateral meetings with Japan and China, which could lead to another trilateral summit to mirror Camp David, could be an indication that taking risks pays off. While there are efforts to change from a policy of ambiguity to a policy of clarity, there remain strings attached—it is geopolitics at its best!

In terms of global outreach, South Korea's successful economic development model gives it high credibility with developing countries and could be an asset in meeting the demands of the Global South. It claims not only more attention but also better involvement in the international system, in the sense of not being left behind. South Korea will only sustain a global outreach in close cooperation with like-minded partners, like the EU. Exercising leadership with the Global South could bring South Korea big dividends, as there is an urgent need to address this situation.

Participating in meetings of various groupings, like the G20 or often as a guest in the G7, and serving repeatedly as a non-permanent member of the UN Security Council offers a platform but needs action for concretization beyond prestige. Light tower events, like organizing events or hosting international organizations, serve the purpose of raising awareness. They are, however, no panacea for concrete, substantive engagement. Green and digital transitions as well as fighting climate change are not only a necessity but also offer the chance to show leadership as a pivotal state.

Another area where South Korea can play an important role is due to its technological prowess in emerging technologies. Cooperation to assure responsible application and development as well as rule setting should be part of a common EU-South Korea agenda. As demonstrated, cybersecurity and digitization also fall into this category and fall under the digital partnership.

As a country depending on imports and exports, Korea has an interest in a stable, reliable, and predictable system, which so far has been centerd on the WTO. The need for its reform is recognized but it needs a reform agenda beyond the improvement of the status quo: geo-economics puts a new focus on economic security, industrial policies, the role of subsidies, as well as trade and investment defense measures in general. The need for new rules of the road without opening the Pandora's Box of protectionism or isolationism and of further weaponization of policies, including economics and finance, implies trotting a fine line. Therefore, as previously discussed in the context of the Indo-Pacific strategies, the various regional agreements, like RCEP, where Korea is a member, and TPTPP, where Korea is not (yet?) a member, as well as the Indo-Pacific Economic Partnerships, need to be thoroughly examined from this point of view. South Korea should find itself closer to the EU's position to strive for WTO-compatible solutions rather than unilateral actions.

Participation or non-participation in minilateral groupings needs analysis measured against national and global interests, whether they meet the goals they were tasked to fulfill, in the interest of all or a few. Are they detracting from global ambitions or are they supporting them, like effective multilateralism? Also, the added value of various conferences on the same issue needs to be proven; otherwise, they ultimately weaken them through duplication. The activation of existing platforms can contribute to streamlining and avoiding conference fatigue.

Conclusions

Global ambitions are necessary to keep policies aligned with the demands which derive from this goal. However, in order to avoid a perception and credibility gap—very familiar to a former EU diplomat—working on the region in a result-oriented manner, is the stepping-stone to the global arena, where it is presently difficult to make an independent entrance as the Sino-US rivalry is dominating. Looming behind in the minds of policymakers in Korea and the EU is whether the transactional policies of the US under President Trump will return and whether the US will remain a reliable partner. Hence thoughts in Europe and in South Korea on how to prepare to not be surprised again like in 2016. Some degree of 'strategic' or better 'cooperative' autonomy and resilience need to be factored into policy planning in the EU and South Korea.

Such a situation in the US in the face of China's assertiveness will put additional demands on policy designs. This can turn into the litmus test for a 'global pivotal role' in deeds not only for South Korea but also with repercussions for the EU.

South Korea's New Security Strategy and its Indo-Pacific Strategy offer guidance, domestically and internationally, for partners—a necessary ingredient for the government to follow a steady course in foreign policy in order to be able to play a pivotal role, whether regional or global.

Concerning China specifically, its role in the South China Sea and possibly in the Taiwan Straits the Yoon Administration was more forthcoming in its policy statements, but there remains the need to hedge between its number one economic and number one security provider. The after-effects of the results of the Camp David trilateral summit might help, as China is contemplating its own trilateral summit with Japan and South Korea in order not to let the stage uncontested by the US. A chance for smart diplomacy to contribute to the stabilization of a volatile situation.

The Global South, joined and supported by China, Russia, and India, advocates for change through policy declarations and by creating new platforms or institutions. Giving a voice to those who do not profit or are even disadvantaged by the present system should not be left to others: the EU and South Korea have the chance to take the lead. Devising a reform agenda and engaging with partners means taking the initiative, which is always the better tactic instead of reacting. South Korea brings its successful development model to the table, while the EU takes a different approach to international politics based on multilateralism, rule of law, and cooperation. 'Leaving nobody behind' needs to become an action program and not remain just a slogan leading to reform. The 2024 UN Summit of the Future[38] could be the rallying point to move forward, not only as Team Europe but as a Global Team where South Korea could play an important role.

While this Summit is part of UN long-term planning, it has become crucial because of Russia's aggression, which has shaken the international order to its fundamentals. Other crises erupt in its shadow: the war between Armenia and Azerbaijan about Nagorno-Karabakh, new tensions on the Balkans, the terrorist attack by Hamas on Israel provoking a war, most likely with the geopolitical background to prevent a re-ordering of the Middle East to the detriment of Iran. These are signs of instability, which some forces want to profit from to realize their ideas and their order. The dawning of a new era might turn things bad before they (hopefully) get better.

Foreign policy starts at home: national division and disagreement on crucial foreign policy goals weaken any foreign policy, as does a lack of continuity of administrations on the main axes of a foreign policy. Divided societies tend to become the new normal in the US, South Korea, and the EU, weakening not only the appeal of democracy but also negatively impacting the international scene when credibility and reliability are put in question. The US, as the longstanding stand bearer of democracy, is under special scrutiny.

Amongst allies and partners, consultations should take place before policy measures are taken, not only afterwards, like in the case of the US Inflation Reduction Act (IRA) which impacted negatively on the EU and South Korea.

The securitization of trade policy, its weaponization and the re-orientation of supply and value chains necessitate cooperation well beyond trade policy. It has become an integral part of security policy where two close allies share common interests. Such a weaponization of the world economy is not in the interest of the EU and South Korea, neither in relation to China nor the US.

Squaring the circle in pursuing an interest- and values-based policy to serve citizens at home and the citizens of the world in parallel requires strong innovative leadership and international cooperation because of the nature of the challenges to meet. In this quest, the relations with the EU have recently moved to the chorus line, with the US, China, Russia, and Japan taking center stage. From a long-term perspective, a good director brings all actors to the limelight when it is their turn!

Looking at the next 60 years, Envisioning Peace in a Time of War, preserving the Crumbling Edifice of Global Peace[39] would be an excellent work program for South Korea and the EU in 2083. There is room to develop a policy of cooperation with countries which want to pursue their interests with their own policies in cooperation with the United States, which will continue to play a primordial role in the region.

Endnote

1. Michael Reiterer (2020). "The 10th Anniversary of the EU-Korea Strategic Partnership" (extended Korean version). Journal of European Union Studies, Institute for EU Studies Hankuk University of Foreign Studies Vol. 56 October 2020; pp. 3-20. English version: Journal of European Union Studies, pp.3-15.
2. https://www.eeas.europa.eu/eeas/joint-communication-indo-pacific_en
3. https://ec.europa.eu/info/sites/default/files/joint_communication_global_gateway.pdf
4. https://www.eeas.europa.eu/sites/default/files/documents/strategic_compass_en3_web.pdf
5. https://eur-lex.europa.eu/legal-content/EN/TXT/PDF/?uri=CELEX:52023JC0020
6. Some overlaps in the presentation are due to the overlapping content of the Indo-Pacific Strategy and the pivot concept.
7. Government of the Republic of Korea (2022). Strategy for a Free, Peaceful, and Prosperous Indo-Pacific Region, 10 December 2022; at https://www.mofa.go.kr/ . The similarity of the title with the Japanese and US strategies is striking and in itself a program.
8. For an in-depth analysis see Linde Desmaele, Maximilian Ernst, Tongfi Kim, Ramon Pacheco Pardo; Michael Reiterer. The EU's Indo-Pacific Strategy: Prospects for Cooperation with South Korea. KF-VUB Korea Chair Report, September 2021; at https://www.korea-chair.eu/wp-content/uploads/2021/11/KF-VUB-Korea-Chair-The-EUs-Indo-Pacific-Strategy.pdf
9. https://trade.ec.europa.eu/doclib/docs/2020/october/tradoc_158988.pdf
10. Republic of Korea: 5th Working Group on Energy, Environment and Climate takes place with European Union 30 January 2023; at https://www.eeas.europa.eu/eeas/republic-korea-5th-working-group-energy-environment-and-climate-takes-place-european-union_en?s=179 See also Michael Reiterer (2022) "Climate Change and the EU's and South Korea's New Green Deals: Greenwash or Actions?". KIEP (Korea Institute for International Economic Policy). Challenges and Opportunities of Korea's Foreign Policy as a Developed Country. Policy Analysis 22-01; 2022; pp. 53-75; at https://www.nkis.re.kr:4445/subject_view1.do?otpId=OTP_0000000000010358&otpSeq=0&menuNo=203001#none
11. Sun Ryung Park, Charlotte Bull (2023). South Korea's nuclear U-turn threatens its green energy transition. EastAsiaForum, 16 March 2023; at South Korea's nuclear U-turn threatens its green energy transition | East Asia Forum
12. https://ec.europa.eu/commission/presscorner/detail/en/IP_18_6142
13. https://digital-strategy.ec.europa.eu/en/library/republic-korea-european-union-digital-partnership
14. Kim Shihong, Michael Reiterer (eds.) Connecting Europe and Asia: Security, Economy and Mobility. Hankuk University Press, Seoul (2023).
15. See Gertjan Boulet, Michael Reiterer, Ramon Pacheco Pardo (eds.). Cybersecurity Policy in the EU and South Korea from Consultation to Action. Theoretical and Comparative Perspectives. Palgrave, 2022.
16. See Council of Europe, 'Budapest Convention and related standards,' 2001, available at <https://www.coe.int/en/web/cybercrime/the-budapest-convention#: :text=The%20Convention%20on%20Cybercrime%20of,international%20instrument%20on%20this%20issue.&text=The%20Budapest%20Convention%20is%20supplemented,Racism%20committed%20through%20computer%20systems>, (accessed 7 July 2021).
17. https://eur-lex.europa.eu/legal-content/EN/TXT/PDF/?uri=CELEX:52023JC0020
18. https://defence-industry-space.ec.europa.eu/system/files/2023-10/C_2023_6689_1_EN_ACT_part1_v8.pdf
19. Beata S. Javorcik, Lucas Kitzmueller, Helena Schweiger, Muhammed A. Yıldırım Economic (2022). Costs of Friend-Shoring. Working Paper No. 274, December 2022; at https://www.ebrd.com/documents/oce/econom-

ic-costs-of-friendshoring.pdf

20. https://next-generation-eu.europa.eu/index_en (accessed 5 October 2023).
21. Michael Reiterer (2022). "Regional trade agreements in the Indo Pacific does the EU risk losing sight of their importance?" CSDS Policy Brief 1/2022, 28 January 2022; at https://brussels-school.be/sites/default/files/CSDS%20Policy%20brief_2201.pdf
22. European Parliamentary Research Service (2022) Securing the EU's supply of critical raw materials. 8 July 2022; at https://epthinktank.eu/2022/07/08/securing-the-eus-supply-of-critical-raw-materials/
23. Blog of Commissioner Thierry Breton 14 September 2022; at https://ec.europa.eu/commission/presscorner/detail/en/STATEMENT_22_5523 https://www.reuters.com/world/europe/eu-set-up-central-buying-agency-critical-minerals-draft-law-2023-03-07/
24. European Parliament (2023). Critical raw materials: Securing the EU's supply and sovereignty. Press Release 14 September 2023; at https://www.europarl.europa.eu/news/en/press-room/20230911IPR04927/critical-raw-materials-securing-the-eu-s-supply-and-sovereignty
25. European Council. Infographic - An EU critical raw materials act for the future of EU supply chains; at https://www.consilium.europa.eu/en/infographics/critical-raw-materials/ provides also a list of critical and strategic raw materials.
26. https://www.whitehouse.gov/briefing-room/statements-releases/2022/02/22/fact-sheet-securing-a-made-in-america-supply-chain-for-critical-minerals/
27. Joint Statement, 10 March 2023; at https://www.whitehouse.gov/briefing-room/statements-releases/2023/03/10/joint-statement-by-president-biden-and-president-von-der-leyen-2/
28. Hae-won Jun, Michael Reiterer (2021). Preventive diplomacy and crisis management in EU-Korea security relations" in Nicola Casarini (ed.) EU-Korea Security Relations. Routledge Focus, 2021; pp. 98 - 119.
29. Republic of Korea: 19th Joint Committee with the European Union takes place in Brussels | EEAS Website (europa.eu)
30. Reuters (2023). North Korea amends constitution on nuclear policy, cites US provocations 28 September 2023; at https://www.reuters.com/world/asia-pacific/north-korea-parliament-amends-constitution-enshrine-nuclear-policy-kcna-2023-09-27/
31. Frida Lampinen (2023). Russia-DPRK Space Cooperation: It's Politics, Not Science. Institute for Security & Development Policy, Issue Brief, 6 October 2023; at https://isdp.eu/content/uploads/2023/10/Brief-Space-Oct-6-2023-final2.pdf
32. Republic of Korea: 19th Joint Committee with the European Union takes place in Brussels | EEAS Website (europa.eu)
33. Michael Reiterer (2013). "The Role of 'Strategic Partnerships' in the EU's Relations with Asia" in Thomas Christiansen/Emil Kirchner/Philomena Murray (eds.) The Palgrave Handbook of EU-Asia Relations. Palgrave Macmillan, 2013; pp.75-89
34. Yoon Suk-seoul (2022). South Korea Needs to Step Up Foreign Affairs, 8 February 2022; at https://www.mofa.go.kr/eng/brd/m_5676/view.do?seq=322133 https://www.foreignaffairs.com/articles/south-korea/2022-02-08/south-korea-needs-step
35. MOFA (2022). Strategy for a Free, Peaceful, and Prosperous Indo-Pacific Region, 28 December 2022; at https://www.mofa.go.kr/eng/brd/m_5676/view.do?seq=322133
36. https://www.whitehouse.gov/briefing-room/statements-releases/2023/08/18/the-spirit-of-camp-david-joint-statement-of-japan-the-republic-of-korea-and-the-united-states/
37. Ramon Pacheco Pardo (2022). Korea falls in love with NATO. EuroActiv, 22 November 2022; at https://www.euractiv.com/section/defence-and-security/opinion/korea-falls-in-love-with-nato/
38. https://www.un.org/en/common-agenda/summit-of-the-future
39. Reiterer Michael (2022). "The Crumbling Edifice of Global Peace" in Ursula Werther-Pietsch (ed.) Envisioning Peace in a Time of War. facultas, 2022; pp. 19-40.

List of Contributors

AHN SANGWOOK is a Professor of the Division of International and Area Studies of Pukyong National University, Korea. He has studied his B.A at Seoul National University, M.A. at Sorbonne-Nouvelle University and Sciences Po Paris and Ph.D. at Sorbonne-Nouvelle University. He is a vice-president of Korean Society of Contemporary European Studies which is the largest academic association of European Studies in Korea. His main research interests are 'Regional Economic Integration in Europe and Asia', 'Trade policies', and 'Climate Change and Energy transition'.

ERIC J. BALLBACH serves as Korea Foundation Fellow at the German Stiftung Wissenschaft und Politik, SWP in Berlin. He previously served as the director of the Research Unit "North Korea and International Security" at Freie Universität Berlin's Institute of Korean Studies. His research focuses on North and South Korean foreign and security policies, especially North Korea's participation in international organizations, EU-Korea relations and identity politics on the Korean peninsula. Dr. Ballbach advises the German Parliament and various Ministries on Korea-related issues.

NICOLA CASARINI is associate fellow at the Istituto Affari Internazionali (IAI) and Global Fellow at the Wilson Center in Washington DC. He obtained PhD in International Relation at LSE. He has held positions at the Graduate Institute in Geneva, at the EU Institute for Security Studies in Paris, at Bocconi University in Milan, at the European University Institute in Florence. Nicola is the founder and director of Orientedworld.com, a global consultancy platform.

CHUNG SAEWON is an interdisciplinary area studies specialist. He earned his doctorate from the University of Canterbury, New Zealand. His research interests lie in the diverse issues related to Europe and Asia. He is currently an associate professor of international and area studies at Pukyong National University. Prof. Chung also serves as a research director of the Korean Society of Contemporary European Studies.

HAN JEONGHUN is a professor of the Graduate School of International Studies and serves as the chair of the Jean Monnet EU Center of Excellence at Seoul National University. He earned his doctoral degree from the University of Rochester, NY, USA. He is the chief editor of the 'Oxford Handbook of South Korean Politics,' and his recent publications appear in the Journal of European Public Policy, SAGE Open, Korea Observer, etc. Prof. Han's primary research interests lie in the comparative examination of elections and party politics, legislative politics and EU policies.

KANG YOO-DUK is a professor in economics of the Division of Language and Trade at Hankuk University of Foreign Studies (HUFS) and is an editor of the Asia Pacific Journal of EU studies. Prof. Kang received his doctorate from Science Po Paris. He served as Team Leader in Europe at KIEP, Korea. His main research interest is trade policy, economic integration, and comparative studies of economic policies.

KIM BONGCHUL is a professor of the Division of International Studies at the Hankuk University of Foreign Studies (HUFS) and Director of EU Research Institute at HUFS. Prof. Kim received doctorate in law from King's College London and is also a regular contributor to the Korea Legal Research Institute (KLRI) as well as to other newspapers, journals and magazines on Asian and Korean laws on international relations. He also serves as managing director of the HUFS Jean Monnet EU Centre.

KIM SIHONG is Jean Monnet Chair professor of EU Studies Department of the GSIAS at the Hankuk University of Foreign Studies (HUFS), Seoul, Korea. He obtained MA and PhD in sociology from Gregorian University, Rome. Currently he is director-general of the HUFS Jean Monnet EU Centre of Excellence which is supported by the European Commission. He was president of the Korean Society of Contemporary European Studies (KSCES) in 2009. In 2013, Prof. Kim was decorated as a Cavaliere, Order of Merit of the Italian Republic (OMRI).

LEE MOOSUNG is Professor of the department of Political Science and Diplomacy, Myongji university, Seoul, Korea. He has his PhD at the University of Birmingham, UK, and since then has undertaken a variety of academic and public services. Mostly recently, he has served as president of the Korean Society of Contemporary European Studies. His research interests are wide-ranging, from small states and EU enlargement to the EU-Korea relations, and his research outputs have also been widely published both as journal articles and monographs.

MICHAEL REITERER is Distinguished Professor, Centre for Security, Diplomacy & Strategy, Brussels School of Governance. He was Former Ambassador of the European Union to the Republic of Korea, having previously held the position of Principal Advisor at the Asia and Pacific Department, European External Action Service (EEAS), Brussels, in charge of strategic and security matters. He previously served as EU Ambassador to Switzerland and the Principality of Liechtenstein (2007-2011), Minister/Deputy Head of the EU-Delegation to Japan (2002-2006), and ASEM Counselor (1998-2002).

MASON RICHEY is professor of international politics at Hankuk University of Foreign Studies (Seoul, South Korea), senior contributor at Asia Society Korea, president of the Korea International Studies Association (KISA), and editor-in-chief of the Journal of East Asian Affairs. Dr. Richey has also held positions as a POSCO Visiting Research Fellow at the East-West Center (Honolulu, HI) and a DAAD Scholar at the University of Potsdam. His research focuses on European foreign and security policy, as well as US foreign policy in the Indo-Asia-Pacific. He is also a frequent participant in a variety of Track 1.5 meetings on Indo-Asia-Pacific security and foreign policy issues.

BERNHARD SELIGER is resident representative of Hanns Seidel Foundation (HSF) in Korea, based in Seoul. He frequently travels to North Korea, where he implements projects on forestry, environment and renewable energy as well as medical cooperation. He earned a PhD in Economics at Kiel University in Germany and is honorary professor of East Asian Economies at the University of Applied Sciences in Zwickau, Germany. He serves as associate of North Korean Review as well as founding editor of the website "East Asian Integration Studies" (https://www.ostasien-zwickau.de/oaz/asianintegration). He is honorary citizen of Seoul and Gangwon province.

TOMASZ WIERZBOWSKI holds a Ph.D. in International Relations from Hankuk University of Foreign Studies and MA in International Politics obtained at Sungkyunkwan University under Korean Government Scholarship. He is focused on the Northeast Asia region and offers academic courses in International Relations and Comparative Politics. His academic interest lies also in the methodology of the social sciences. Dr. Wierzbowski is currently Head of EURAXESS Korea and also serves as a research associate at the EU Research Institute of HUFS.

Yoon Sungwon is a professor in Global Business Major of the Division of Business Administration, The University of Suwon. She is also the 2024 President of The Korean Society of Contemporary European Studies. Having received her MSc from London School of Economics and Political Science and her Ph.D. from Korea University, she has actively participated in a multi-country research projects funded by European Commission and NATO. Her main research interests include EU cultural policy, EU's perception in South Korea and EU-Korea cultural relations.